SHETLAND DOCUMENTS
1580-1611

SHETLAND DOCUMENTS 1580-1611

Edited by
John H. Ballantyne
and
Brian Smith

Shetland Islands Council & The Shetland Times Ltd.
Lerwick, Shetland
1994

First published 1994

A CIP catalogue record for this book is available from the British Library.

ISBN 0 900662 96 4

Jointly published by
Shetland Islands Council Leisure & Recreation Department
and
The Shetland Times Ltd., Prince Alfred Street, Lerwick, Shetland, ZE1 0EP.

Gordon Donaldson
1913-1993

And gladly wolde he lerne and gladly teche

Contents

Preface

The idea of compiling for publication a collection of early Shetland documents occurred to the editors more than ten years ago. While there has been a small renaissance in research and writing on Shetland history in recent years, very little of the source material itself has got into print. A start has been made with this volume of documents from the era of the Stewart earls.

The history of publication of early Shetland documents goes back to 1840, when Sheriffs Maconochie and Neaves edited, anonymously, a small collection under the title *Deeds relating to Orkney and Shetland 1433-1581.* In 1859 David Balfour published the lengthy report made in 1577 of the royal commission appointed to look at Shetlanders' grievances, in *Oppressions of the Sixteenth Century in the Islands of Orkney and Shetland.* A small collection of Norse deeds, *Diplomatarium Hialtlandense*, appeared in 1886-8, culled by Arthur Laurenson from the great Norwegian record series *Diplomatarium Norvegicum.* The most significant collections of early Shetland documents to have appeared in print are in Gilbert Goudie's *The Celtic and Scandinavian Antiquities of Shetland* (1904), and in *Orkney and Shetland Records*, edited by Alfred W. Johnston and Amy Johnston for the Viking Society between 1907-13. J. Storer Clouston's *Records of the Earldom of Orkney* (1914) also contains several Shetland items, especially from the late medieval period.

Since 1914 scarcely any early Shetland documentary source material has been published, with the notable exceptions of two court books edited by Gordon Donaldson: *Court Book of Shetland 1602-1604* (1954), and *Court Book of Shetland 1615-1629* (1991). During this period there have been some unfortunate losses of documents (see Introduction, *infra*). However, the establishment of the Shetland Archives in 1976 has helped to redress the situation.

At an early date we realized that a major untapped source of Shetland historical material was the extensive records of the Court of Session, preserved in the Scottish Record Office. The most important of these records are the two series of registers known as the Deeds and the Acts and Decreets. For the period before 1661 there are more than 1,200 of these registers: only a handful have been indexed to date. There are also some 300 boxes of court process papers. Grant aid was made available to enable John Ballantyne to undertake the task of searching through these records for Shetland material, and we gratefully acknowledge the generosity of Shetland Folk Society in providing this funding. This work has brought to light a mass of interesting information concerning

Shetland, and much of it appears in the present volume.

We would like to pay tribute to the late Professor Gordon Donaldson for his support for this venture. He also gave much practical help, by directing our attention to records and assisting with especially difficult texts. It is sad that he did not live to see the finished work. Professor Knut Helle of the University of Bergen gave us assistance with translations. Thanks are also due to the following, for help beyond the normal course of their duties: Dr Peter Anderson and Dr Frances Shaw of the Scottish Record Office; Tommy Watt of Shetland Museum; the Riksarkivet in Oslo and the Staatsarchiv, Bremen, for advice concerning translations; Harry Watson of the Dictionary of the Older Scottish Tongue, for his help in elucidating several problematical words; and John and Wendy Scott, for welcoming us on our frequent visits to Gardie House. The staff of various archives centres, particularly the Scottish Record Office, and Alison Fraser of the Orkney Archives, are to be thanked for their forbearance: we made many demands on their time. Finally, Robert Wishart and his staff at Shetland Litho have ensured that the resulting work is attractive and readable; and the Leisure and Recreation Department of Shetland Islands Council initiated the present joint publication with The Shetland Times Ltd.

We are grateful to the following for permission to publish texts and summaries of documents in their possession: John Scott, Gardie House, Bressay; Mr and Mrs G. Mouat, Braefield House, Dunrossness; the earl of Erroll; and Mrs Olive Borland, East Calder. Public and other records held by the Scottish Record Office are quoted with the approval of the Keeper of the Records of Scotland. In addition, the trustees of the National Library of Scotland and the council of the Society of Antiquaries of Scotland are thanked for permission to cite material.

JOHN H. BALLANTYNE
BRIAN SMITH

February 1994

Abbreviations

GENERAL

APS	*Acts of the Parliaments of Scotland*
CB1	G. Donaldson ed., *The Court Book of Shetland 1602-1604*, Edinburgh 1954
CB2	G. Donaldson ed., *Court Book of Shetland 1615-1629*, Lerwick 1991
CSP	*Calendar of State Papers relating to Scotland and Mary, Queen of Scots*
Deeds	[J. Maconochie and C. Neaves eds.,] *Deeds Relating to Orkney and Zetland 1433-1581*, [Edinburgh 1840]
GH	Papers at Gardie House, Bressay
NLS	National Library of Scotland
OA	Orkney Archives
OSD	Francis Grant, 'Old Shetland Documents', *Shetland News*, 1893-4
OSR	A.W. and A. Johnston eds, *Orkney and Shetland Records*, i, London 1907-13
PSAS	*Proceedings of the Society of Antiquaries of Scotland*
REO	J. S. Clouston ed., *Records of the Earldom of Orkney*, Edinburgh 1914
RMS	*Register of the Great Seal of Scotland*
RPC	*Register of the Privy Council of Scotland*
RSS	*Register of the Privy Seal of Scotland*
SA	Shetland Archives
SHR	*Scottish Historical Review*
SN	*Shetland News*
SRO	Scottish Record Office

ORKNEY ARCHIVES

D.2	Balfour Papers
D.8	Miscellaneous Papers
D.23	J.S. Clouston Papers
SC.11/5	Sheriff Court Papers

SHETLAND ARCHIVES

D.6	E.S. Reid Tait Papers
D.8	Sumburgh Papers
D.10	Vaila Papers
D.11	Shetland Library Collection

D.12	Neven of Windhouse Papers
D.16	Irvine of Midbrake Papers
GD.144	Bruce of Symbister Papers
SA.2	Miscellaneous Transcripts and Copies
SC.12/65	Lerwick Sheriff Court, Miscellaneous Papers

SCOTTISH RECORD OFFICE

B.22/8	Edinburgh Burgh Registers of Deeds
C.22	Registers of Retours
CC.8/2	Edinburgh Registers of Commissariat Acts and Decreets
CC.8/8	Edinburgh Registers of Testaments
CC.8/17	Edinburgh Registers of Commissariat Deeds
CC.17/2	Orkney and Shetland Registers of Testaments
CC.17/5	Orkney and Shetland Registers of Commissariat Deeds
CS.1	Court of Session Books of Sederunt
CS.7	Court of Session Registers of Acts and Decreets
CS.15	Court of Session Warrants
CS.96	Court of Session Miscellaneous Productions
CS.290	Registers of Cautions in Suspensions
DI.1	General Registers of Hornings
DI.3	General Registers of Inhibitions and Hornings
DI.47	Edinburgh Registers of Hornings
DI.85	Orkney and Shetland Registers of Hornings
E.2	Exchequer Registers of Signatures
E.41/7	Rental of Yetland, c.1640
GD.190	Smyth of Methven Papers
JC.2	Justiciary Books of Adjournal
JC.6	Justiciary Court Minute Books
JC.19	Justiciary Registers of Bonds of Caution
JC.26	Justiciary Court Papers
NP.1/29	Archibald Millar's Protocol Book
NP.1/36	Thomas Auchinlek's Protocol Book
PC.1	Registers of Acts of Privy Council
PC.6	Registers of Privy Council Acts of Caution
PS.1	Registers of Privy Seal
RD.1	Registers of Deeds
RD.11	Deed Warrants
RH.6	Register House Charters
RH.9/15	Orkney and Shetland Documents
SC.10/1	Sheriff Court Books of Orkney and Shetland

Introduction

The documents in this collection date from the period of the Stewart earls' overlordship in Shetland. The establishment of Lord Robert Stewart, an illegitimate son of James V, as feuar of the earldom of Orkney and lordship of Shetland in 1565, inaugurated over 40 years of stability in administration of the islands. Lord Robert's position was confirmed in 1581, when James VI granted him the titles of earl of Orkney and lord of Shetland (no. 23). These titles were revoked in 1587, when the king reached his majority. However, Robert withstood an attempt to dislodge him, and was able to retain his grant of the earldom. In 1590, a few years before his death, Robert made over the lordship of Shetland to his son Patrick, who became a dominant figure in the northern group of islands for the next 18 years.

Patrick's arrival on the scene marked a turning point in the fortunes of the Stewart earldom. Earl Patrick did not have the administrative capabilities of his father, and was anything but conciliatory towards those who incurred his displeasure. He survived a turbulent start to his period of rule. The late 1590s and early part of the seventeenth century marked an upturn in his fortunes, with the construction of Scalloway Castle, from 1599, and a temporary reconciliation with his enemies. But Earl Patrick's extravagance and foolhardiness caught up with him, and eventually there was such opposition to his local oppressions and disregard of central authority that he was imprisoned in Edinburgh in 1609. This effectively marked the end of Patrick's rule in the north, although it was not until 1615 that he was executed and his titles forfeited. By then the government had taken steps to ensure that an independent power-base would never again be set up in the Northern Isles.

There are full accounts of the careers of Earl Robert and Earl Patrick in two recent biographies, by Peter D. Anderson: *Robert Stewart, Earl of Orkney, Lord of Shetland, 1533-1593* (1982), and *Black Patie, the Life and Times of Patrick Stewart, Earl of Orkney, Lord of Shetland* (1992).

Shetland in the Stewart era

Administration. The main sphere of influence of the Stewart earls was in Orkney, but Shetland formed an important and distinct part of their domain. Shetland had been detached from the earldom of Orkney in 1195, after the earl of Orkney had taken part in an insurrection against the king of Norway. Shetland was thenceforth governed by Norway and Denmark until 1468-9, when the king of Denmark mortgaged his royal rights in both groups of islands to the king of Scotland.

Lord Robert's main establishments in the north were at Kirkwall and Birsay, and his visits to Shetland took place when circumstances permitted, usually in summer. Records show that Robert was in Shetland in 12 of the years between 1568-89, and that Patrick was there in eight of the years between 1590-1608. In addition, Lord Robert's eldest son Henry (Harie), who predeceased him, presided as sheriff-depute in Shetland in 1583 (no. 84). Robert established a house at Sumburgh which Earl Patrick also used (nos. 197, 391). Although Scalloway seems to have been the administrative centre of Shetland since at least the 1570s, it was not until 1599 that Patrick began to build a castle there.

Neither Robert nor Patrick had much success with their deputes, sometimes called 'fouds', in Shetland. Laurence Bruce of Cultmalindie, Robert's half-brother, was overzealous in exercising his duties, to say the least. A royal commission investigated his activities in 1577 (D. Balfour ed., *Oppressions of the Sixteenth Century in the Islands of Orkney and Shetland*, 1859, pp.15-92), and resulted in his suspension. During the 1580s Hew Sinclair of Brough emerged as the leading Shetland landowner in opposition to Laurence Bruce, and became sheriff and foud. However, he and Robert fell out in the late 1580s: Robert imprisoned him and stripped him of his office (no. 200). Subsequently Hew obtained exemption from the Stewart earls' jurisdiction, and the Brough estate became known as a barony.

In a turning of the tables, Laurence Bruce obtained a five year tack of the foudry of Shetland in January 1589 (no. 131). In 1591 Patrick Stewart, now lord of Shetland, came on the scene, and not only harried Hew but expelled Laurence from his jurisdiction. He forced Laurence to flee to the Skerries, small islands off the east Mainland of Shetland, and did not allow him to return until he had paid £1,000 and renounced his tack (no. 353). Laurence Bruce remained at odds with Earl Patrick, and was one of the chief protagonists in his downfall.

When Patrick succeeded his father the office of foud fell into disuse. A sheriff-depute, responsible for Orkney and Shetland, took over local administration, and acted as chamberlain of the lordship rents and revenues as well. In 1593 Patrick Menteith of Fair Isle exercised this office, and in 1594-5 William Bannatyne of Gairsay took over. Patrick quarrelled with both men, and thus added to his troubles. Henry Colville, parson of Orphir, succeeded to the office, but his period of office was brief: he was murdered, allegedly by a gang led by Bannatyne, at Neep in Nesting, Shetland, in July 1596. In 1600 John Dishington was sheriff-depute and chamberlain, and he remained in office until 1603. In 1604 Earl Patrick himself acted as sheriff in Shetland, assisted for a while by Arthur Sinclair of Aith (*CB1*). Between 1606-10 Edward Scollay of

Strynie was sheriff-depute, replaced in 1611 by Thomas Livingstone of Ballintone, last of the Stewart nominees.

There are signs that Earl Robert may not have wished to rely on the traditional system of native parochial bailies—'underfouds'—for local administration. In 1577 he appointed Hew Sinclair of Brough bailie of Nesting, Lunnasting, Whalsay and Skerries for 19 years (no. 176), and in 1589 Laurence Bruce appears as sheriff-depute of Unst, Fetlar and Yell (no. 159). However, Earl Patrick reversed this apparent trend: among his underfouds were William Manson in Gardie in Unst, John Laurenson of Aywick in Yell, Magnus Ollason in Islesburgh in Northmavine, Matthew Robertson in Delting, William Manson in Neep in Nesting, Pole Manson in Hoove in Whiteness, and Magnus Bult in Bressay. Even during Earl Patrick's time there was an increasing tendency to refer to underfouds as bailies, perhaps reflecting a diminution of their traditional functions. Following the downfall of Patrick the privy council of Scotland abolished the 'foreign laws' of Orkney and Shetland (no. 528), and the designation 'underfoud' simultaneously disappears from the record. During the period of the Stewart earls the local officials called 'lawrightmen', originally parochial tribunes of the people (Balfour, *Oppressions*, p.19), suffered a similar eclipse (although the designation lingered on until the eighteenth century).

The Stewart earls' revenue in Shetland consisted of rents and grassums of their estates, taxes from virtually all lands (mainly scat, paid in wadmell, butter and oil, and wattle, paid in money), and fines ('unlaws') from their courts.

Landownership. Many of the documents in this collection deal with the purchase, lease and tenure of lands in Shetland. Earl Robert and Earl Patrick, despite their reputation as greedy land-grabbers, do not seem to have bought or acquired a great deal of land during their tenure of the earldom. Earl Robert's estate in 1589 (no. 156) was very similar to the estates that the Stewart earls' successors managed 40 years later (SRO, E.41/7). The nature of Earl Patrick's acquisitions appears in a 'rentall of the conquest landis in Yetland, conquest be my lord in anno 1604' (no. 383).

A petition to parliament by Lord Sinclair in 1581 (no. 24) marks the last attempt by the Sinclair family, descendants of the erstwhile Sinclair earls, to get back their 'conquest' lands in Orkney and Shetland, lost as a result of inter-family strife which culminated in the battle of Summerdale in Orkney in 1529. Many of these lands became the property of the crown, and were included in the grants to the Stewart earls.

Several Sinclair families, no doubt descendants of the earls, continued to build up (or dissipate) estates in Shetland during our period. We see several of them at work in the present volume: Hugh Sinclair of Brough, especially active in purchasing land in the early years of the seventeenth century; Arthur Sinclair of Aith; the wastrel Francis Sinclair of Uyea. Andrew Mouat of Hugoland and various members of the Cheyne family were also important landowners. Other kenspeckle figures were Laurence Bruce of Cultmalindie, Earl Patrick's enemy, who built the castle at Muness in Unst, and his relative William Bruce, who had estates at Symbister in Whalsay and Sumburgh in Dunrossness. Laurence Bruce's large estate can be seen in a deed of 1610 (no. 503).

Noble families in Norway, whom Shetlanders called the 'lords of Norway', still owned three large estates in the islands, based on the islands of Noss, Vaila and Papa Stour. In 1572 the owner of the Vaila estate, Gorvel Faderdotter, leased it to Robert Cheyne (*RSS*, vii, no. 502). In 1584 the king of Denmark acquired the estate, and leased it to Cheyne for an annual payment of 60 dollars (nos. 60, 85; *Norsk Rigs-Registranter*, ii, 571-2, 581-2). There is a rental of this estate from the 1580s (no. 42). The heirs of Otte Mattson leased the Papa estate to Andrew Mowat of Hugoland in the early 1570s (*RSS*, vii, no. 982). The Rosenkrantz family owned the Noss estate; it was leased to Andrew Gifford of Wethersta in 1605 (no. 401).

There are many references in the documents to smaller landowners, although they often feature as sellers rather than purchasers of lands. A good example is Colbein Ornesone of Symbister in Whalsay, formerly lawrightman in the island, whose mortgages and sales of land to Laurence Bruce and others feature in documents of the 1580s. Despite these survivals, most Shetlanders in our period were tenants.

Arable land in Shetland was distributed among about 700 'towns', and in our period was invariably valued at so many 'marks of land', paying rent in wadmell (cloth) and butter, at so many 'pennies the mark'.

The Church. The biggest church estates in Shetland belonged to the archdeaconry, an ancient institution. During the years 1584-93 there was a long drawn out dispute between two claimants to the archdeaconry. The dispute originated in the demission by Jerome Cheyne in March 1572, on account of feebleness, in favour of Thomas Cheyne (Errol Charters, sect. 1, no. 799; *RSS*, vi, no. 1537). (In fact Jerome continued in possession of the benefice, presumably because Thomas was not qualified as a minister.) Jerome eventually died in 1584, and trouble broke out following a rival presentation by Earl Robert, who claimed the right of patronage, to William Hay (nos. 62-3). To enforce his claim Hay raised an action against Thomas Cheyne, for reduction of his presentation. Proceedings were delayed, as Cheyne was in Geneva, learning to become a minister (no. 87), but eventually the matter came before the commissary court in Edinburgh in February 1588 (SRO, CC.8/2/17-21 *passim*). On 12 July 1588 Cheyne received royal letters allowing him to go to the Netherlands for five years (Count Maurice had made him a councillor in the parliament of Orange: NLS, Adv. MS. 35.5.1). After this we hear no more of the rival claimants until 1592, by which time Thomas had died (SRO, CS.7/139, ff.250-2), when Alexander Cheyne received a presentation from the crown. The dispute eventually went to arbitration in April 1593, and it was decided that Earl Robert was patron of the benefice, and consequently that William Hay had been lawfully presented to the archdeaconry (SRO, RD.1/43, ff.358-62). However, the Cheyne family were able to retain the archdeaconry lands, which Jerome had granted to Patrick Cheyne of Essilmonth in 1570 (*APS*, iii, 616).

Economy and society. Shetland was an agricultural community in our period: a rather poor one, with extensive fishing interests, and relatively complex trading contacts with Scotland, England and Europe. There is a detailed picture of these and other matters in a comprehensive work by Gordon Donaldson, *Shetland Life under Earl Patrick* (1958).

The Records

Local records. The principal collections of family papers containing early Shetland documents are the Bruce of Symbister and Bruce of Sumburgh papers, both in the Shetland Archives, and the fine collection of Mouat family papers at Gardie House in Bressay. Smaller collections in the Shetland Archives include the Vaila papers; and a number of valuable early deeds preserved with Sheriff Court papers, mainly sixteenth and seventeenth century Sinclair of Brough documents. A small group of papers collected by Gilbert Goudie are still preserved in the family house in Dunrossness.

Public records. The texts of a number of early deeds relating to Shetland have survived by being recorded in the books of council and session in Edinburgh. Registration meant that the authority of the court was available for the fulfilment of the undertaking contained in the deed. These Registers of Deeds, as they are known, are extant from 1554. The original deeds were retained as 'warrants' for the register, and some have survived from the period 1580-1611.

Similarly, a considerable amount of Shetland material which would otherwise have been lost has been recorded in the Registers of Acts and Decreets of the Court of Session. This shows that by 1580 Shetland litigants were taking their disputes to the central court in Edinburgh. Indeed, Earl Patrick tried to restrict this practice in 1602, by an act of the lawting (*CB1*, 48). Fortunately, the proceedings of the lawting or sheriff court for 1602-4 have survived; the text, edited by Gordon Donaldson, was published by the Scottish Record Society in 1954.

The central justiciary court dealt with few Shetland criminal cases during this period. One case which did come before it was that against Henry Wardlaw, for the murder of a son of Earl Patrick's shepherd on the isle of Vementry. The case was deserted, presumably because Henry had already undergone trial in the sheriff court, where he was found not guilty (nos. 424, 435; see also Alexander Bruce's chamberlain accounts of Shetland, SRO, GD.190/3/245). It is probably thanks to this case that the Shetland court book for 1602-4 has survived: there is a note in a Court of Session process paper of 1608 that the 'Yeitland court buik' had been delivered to James King in Edinburgh, 'for seiking owt Hendrie Wartlawis process' (SRO, CS.15/123).

No admiralty court records survive from the period 1580-1611 (other than cases dealt with in Earl Patrick's court book). Nor do those of district courts held by underfouds, or local registers of deeds: again, however, a few deeds are recorded in Earl Patrick's court book.

Following the reformation the ecclesiastical courts in Shetland fell into disuse, until the appointment of Jerome Cheyne as commissary in 1584 (no. 58). His successor Robert Cheyne was active until his death in c.1592, but none of his books of record has survived, and he does not appear to have recorded testaments or to have collected the 'quot', one of the principal functions of a commissary. It was not until 1611, with the appointment of Harie Aitken as commissary of Orkney and Shetland (no. 528), that steps were taken to record testaments in Shetland.

Shetlanders, meanwhile, had dealt with matters of inheritance by means of 'schound bills', and deeds of 'upgestry'. Very few examples survive of these peculiarly Shetlandic documents. We have schound bills of William in Hamer in Unst (no. 354), Peter Nisbet of Kirkabister in Yell (no. 409, from a nineteenth century transcript), and James Spence of Midbrake in Yell (no. 431). There are extant deeds of upgestry concerning Haylya Turbensdaughter and Mans Olason in Unst (no. 29), Gutrome Lawrenson in Yell (no. 332, from a transcript), and Ingarth Thomasdaughter in Unst (no. 337). It may be the case that these old practices lingered on longest in the North Isles of Shetland.

In 1599 an act of the Scottish parliament instituted a sasine register for each sheriffdom. This was known as the Secretary's Register, and it is evident from surviving sasines (e.g. nos. 318, 365) that there was a register for Orkney and Shetland. The Secretary's Register was abolished in 1609, and in 1617 the present system of sasine registers began. The first extant register of sasines for Shetland begins in 1623.

The only surviving register of a notary active in Orkney and Shetland during this period is that of Thomas Auchinleck, senior. Most of his work took place in Orkney, and items recorded in Shetland—very rough drafts indeed—mainly date from the period 1585-9.

Some early Shetland deeds are also preserved in the RH.6 and RH.9/15 series in SRO. They were probably rescued by antiquarians in the nineteenth century.

There is a useful summary by Gordon Donaldson of the public records available for students of the history of Orkney and Shetland in vol. ii of *Orkney Miscellany*.

Losses of private records

Shetland has not been fortunate in the survival of its historical records, especially those that were in private hands. This is particularly true of the pre-reformation era, but is true of the early modern period as well.

One of the main losses is that of the papers of the Sinclair earls of Orkney. Many probably survived at the beginning of the seventeenth century: an inventory of Lord Sinclair's charter chest in 1611 referred to 'ane gryit box ... [with] certaine evidentis of Orknay and Yetland made to the erllis of Orknay, Sincleris and utheris thairin contenit speciall all writtin Denche and Duche languages' (SRO, CS.7/259, ff.250-7). Only a handful of early Sinclair documents survived at the beginning of this century—they are printed in *OSR,* i—and some of them cannot now be traced.

Some of the loss was contemporary. Englishmen robbed and despoiled Andrew Mouat of Hugoland of his deeds and other valuables in 1586. An English man-of-war robbed him again in 1590 when he was on a voyage from Norway to Scotland; this time he lost a royal letter and other obligations and bills (no. 184). Dunkirkers burned Muness Castle in 1627, allegedly with the owner's 'haill writs' (*RPC* ii, 184; SRO, CS.7/480, ff.277-9).

A belief that old deeds were indecipherable, especially when they were in poor condition, was another hazard. An inventory of deeds compiled by Thomas Arthurson, c. 1815, refers to early missing Unst writs, 'some of which were in the Norse language ... but when they cam to my hand were so considerably damaged by time and careless keeping that they wer past all perusal and not worth keeping' (SA, D.3/14). In the eighteenth century Helen Neven wrote to David Anderson, her lawyer, that, during a search for a deed, she had 'only found severall peapers that from the badness of the inke and ill care that the men hear who are best aqueant with the old hand can macke nothing of them, and therfore we thought it neadless to send them up to you, ase they are all togeather unlegibill' (SA, GD.144/236/12).

Loss at sea is a recurring theme. In 1761 Helen Neven described how her grandfather was drowned three miles south of Whalsay in 1712, and hazarded a guess that his trunk with his papers went to the bottom with him (SA, GD.144/54). E.S. Reid Tait had a story of a box of books and papers from the sheriff court, saved when a ship carrying them from

Lerwick to Edinburgh was wrecked in Orkney, but subsequently lost in a fire in Kirkwall (where they had been sent for safety!) (E.S. Reid Tait ed., *Hjaltland Miscellany*, i, vii).

Some of these tales may be apocryphal. But there may be substance in one concerning early Quendale estate papers. R. Stuart Bruce, writing to Reid Tait in 1943 (SA, D.6/262/8/5), described how Grierson of Quendale

> had a small room in the house at Quendale, filled with papers. ... These Sinclair papers, being amongst the oldest in Shetland, would have been of the greatest interest. ... Well, old Grierson wanted to clear out this room, and the old ass burned all the papers 'on the green'. When my brother heard of this piece of vandalism, he said to Grierson that he would have given anything to be allowed to see them. The answer was, 'Oh, if I thought you were interested in them, you could have had them for the taking away'.

Reid Tait described how on another—or perhaps the same — occasion a Shetland laird, with help from domestics, carried family papers out of his house, and for three days burned the lot. He also refers to a tale that the Henderson of Bardister and Pettister papers were burned in a fire that lasted for two days: the burn mark extended the width of the gable of the house of Brough, to a height of six feet (*Hjaltland Miscellany*, i, vii).

Even family papers which survived to the present century could be susceptible to loss. A particularly sad example is the Burra Charters, an important collection of early Sinclair deeds. Francis Grant inspected them in the early 1890s, and published abstracts of some of them in the *Shetland News* in 1893-4. J. Storer Clouston made fuller notes of some items, when they were in the offices of Messrs Aitken & Methuen, W.S., Edinburgh, in the early part of this century. Despite extensive enquiries we found no trace of the original documents.

Some early Busta Estate deeds were in existence in the 1870s, when the charter chest was in the hands of Harry Cheyne, W.S., in Edinburgh. Gilbert Goudie examined them, and published one of them (no. 323). There is evidence that the papers at Busta House went for salvage in the Second World War. It is possible that R. Stuart Bruce rescued some early Busta writs, since a few of them are among the Bruce of Symbister papers, now in the Shetland Archives.

Finally, William Chambers, writing in the mid-nineteenth century, reminisced (*My Holidays*, 1867, p.72) how

> about 1823, old deeds of udal tenure were sold as curiosities at bookstalls in Edinburgh at a shilling apiece. They consisted of dingy pieces of vellum scarcely six inches square, with a seal in the corner, and were dated at Bergen in Norway. How these documents should have been brought away from Orkney and Shetland, and how they came to this low pass, instead of being deposited among public records, I am unable to explain. The circumstance is distinctly in my recollection.

Editing the documents.

We began to edit this volume in 1983. Another volume, containing abstracts and texts of documents prior to 1580, is being planned, and perhaps another for documents after 1611, to include land writs up to 1623, when the earliest surviving register of sasines for Shetland commences.

Our main principles in selecting documents for inclusion in the present volume were (a) that they should be of general historical interest, and (b) that they should relate directly to Shetland and/or Shetlanders. We excluded many minor documents, particularly those dealing with legal and ecclesiastical matters, commercial transactions and shipping. Information concerning unused material is available for consultation in the Shetland Archives.

The documents have been arranged in chronological order, with the following provisos:

(a) Documents referred to in inventories have been placed according to the date of the original document;

(b) Registered deeds have been placed according to the date of the deed rather than the date of registration;

(c) Court decreets taken from registers such as the Acts and Decreets of the Court of Session are arranged according to the date of the final decreet (or latest recorded decreet which has been traced), although the action may have been initiated some time earlier.

In the majority of cases we have given an abstract of the document concerned. Occasionally, if the document is important, we give the full text, with a summary in italics as a heading. Where the original document is not known to exist we quote in full the account of it in our source, to obviate further errors. If there is more than one account available we refer to additional material and/or discrepancies in a note.

We have rendered place-names and personal names as in the original documents. (Occasionally names are spelled variously within the same document.) Often, especially in the case of items taken from registers, spellings are wrong. Where appropriate we have given a suggested correct spelling in square brackets, accompanied by *rectius*. Court of Session records of this period are full of inaccurate spellings: not surprisingly, since the busy clerks were unfamiliar with Shetland names and places.

We have noted the *presence*, and not the absence, of seals and 'merchant marks' on documents.

In editing land writs we list the location, nature and amount of land. We do not include the lists of pertinents and attached rights, which are generally stereotyped in form. To retrieve this information readers should refer back to the original documents, whose provenance and call-number are given in footnotes.

We have adopted several conventions throughout the work. We use the spelling 'mark' to denote the measurement of land, in preference to the current usage 'merk'. (Note, however, that authors of some of the summaries we reproduce use the spelling 'merk'.) On the other hand, we use the spelling 'merk' for the unit of currency. We use the spelling 'Yetland' instead of 'Zetland'. We use 'Sir' with a capital letter for knights; 'sir' with a small letter for former Roman Catholic priests.

Finally, until 1600 in Scotland new year's day fell on 25 March. We use a format '3 February 1592-3' to render dates between 1 January - 24 March in the period up to 1599. In original texts dates appear in their contemporary form; e.g. 'Jaj Vc fourscoir threttene yeiris' =1593.

Shetland Documents

1580-1611

1. Stirling Castle, 11 April 1580

Precept for remission to Andrew Hawik of Scatstay for participation in the slaughter of Orne Scrader, sometime indweller in the town of Brame in Dania, committed suddenly (*subito*) in June 1577.

RSS, vii, no.2318. The original entry is in Latin.

2. Hous in Burra, 21 August 1580

'[Disposition by] Eduard Sinclar of Scalloway, with consent of Barbara Mowat, his spouse, to his brother german Arthur Sinclar of Aith, and Margaret Colweill, his spouse, [of] 3 mark of Hous.

'Witnesses: James Sinclair of Brow, and James Sinclair, brother german of Edward and Arthur, etc.'

The original is not known to exist. The above abstract, by J. Storer Clouston, is in OA, D.23, Notebook 4, p.66. Another abstract, by Francis Grant, gives Henry Wardlaw, servant of Arthur Sinclair of Aith, as a witness (OSD, *SN*, 14 October 1893).

3. 5 September 1580

'Charter by Magnus and Thomas Georgeson in favor of ... Laurence Bruce [of Cultmalindie], of 2 merks land, [*blank*] pennies the merk, in Eastness in Northmavine.'

The original is not known to exist. The above abstract is in SA, D.6/194/12 (Inventory of titles of the estate of Busta, in Messrs Greigs' possession, 1840).

4. Gruting, 10 November 1580

Wadset by Magnus Reid of Aith, with consent of Marioun Thomasdochter, his spouse, to an honourable man Laurence Bruce of Cultmalyndies, of 20 marks land, 8 pennies the mark, in Kirkhous in Ayth, with 10 marks land, 6 pennies the mark, in Uphous in Aith, in the parish of Aithsting, redeemable on payment of 60 angel nobles gold in weight, with compensation for any expense sustained by Laurence 'in biging, reparelling, beiting or erecting of the stoiff, houssis and unsettis of my saids landis with the pertinentis, estimeid be the sicht of sex honest men sworne to that effect'. After redemption Laurence shall have the right to lease the lands for a further nine years for payment of a lispund of butter and a shilling of wadmell annually.

As Magnus cannot write he procures the seals of Mr Hierome Cheyn, archdeacon of Yetland, Hew Sinclair of Burgh, and Mr Robert Cheyn of

Valay. Witnesses: Andro Wischett of Melbe, Harie Bruce in Stainswell, Patrik Bruce and Andro Martyne, servants of Laurence, with divers others.

GH. One seal; Magnus Reid's mark.

5. Holyroodhouse, 1 December 1580

Gift to Robert Foulsie, son of Mr Gilbert Foulsie, minister at Kirkwall, for his support for seven years 'at the schole', of the altarage of St Giles of Astay in Yetland, vacant by decease of Mr Magnus Halcro.

RSS, vii, no.2616.

6. 18 December 1580

Disposition by Mans Thomassone, Nicolaus Annersone, Bretha Thomasdochter and Thomas Henrisone, her spouse for his interest, and Ingerith Thomasdochter, and Erasmus Laurencesone, her spouse for his interest, all heirs of the deceased Thomas Annerson of Ronone, to William Manson of Gairdie, their sister's son, of 1 mark land, 6 pennies the mark, in Ronene.

The original is not known to exist. Referred to in an action of removal in July 1617 (*CB2*, p.57).

7. Edinburgh, 31 December 1580

Obligation by Mr Gilbert Foulsie, archdeacon of Orkney, to sir Nicoll Tulloch, vicar of Sandsting, whereby Gilbert undertakes to relieve Nicoll of any action against him by Malcolm Sinclair, or by any other tacksman, for warrandice of the duties of the vicarage of Sandsting.

Witnesses: Gilbert Tulloch, burgess of Kirkwall, Mr James Annand, James Alexander, writer, with divers others.

SRO, CC.8/17/2, ff.342-3.

8. Staindaill in the parish of Sandsting, 7 January 1580-1

Disposition by Katharene Laurencedochter, with consent of William Macheson, her spouse, for his interest, and Erasmus Williamson, her son, to an honourable man Laurence Bruce of Cultmalyndies, of 4 marks land, 8 pennies the mark, of Burraland in the parish of Wallis.

As Katharene cannot write she procures the seals of Hew Sinclair of Burgh, Mr Robert Cheyne of Walay and John Murray in Howland. Witnesses: Harie Bruce, George Gifhart, and Gilbert Makcraiff, with Andro Martyne and divers others.

GH. One seal.

9. Edinburgh (at Jonet Fockhart's booth), 7 January 1580-1

Declaration on oath by Alexander Lawson, in presence of Mr Gilbert Fulsy, superintendent or commissioner of Yetland, that he has learned within the past twenty-four hours that Gilbert, by his letters of monition, had warned Alexander, under pain of excommunication, to use the office of ministry of the parish churches of Northmaven. Alexander protests that (1) Gilbert is not a competent judge because Alexander resigned the vicarage of Northmaven in the hands of the king in November 1578, and since then Alexander has lived in the diocese of St Andrews, (2) Gilbert gave partial counsel in a pronouncement of sentence in July 1579 against Alexander, (3) long before the pronouncement of sentence against Alexander, Gilbert had admitted Mr James Pitcarne to the vicarage in which James has served and still serves, and (4) Alexander never entered on the preaching of the word or administration of the sacraments, knowing himself not qualified or called thereto. Alexander appeals from the said monition to the next provincial synod of the see of St. Andrews, the general synod of the Church of Scotland, or any other competent judge.

Witnesses: James Purdy, Islay herald, James Alexander, sir James Abircrummy, and John Smyth.

SRO, NP.1/29, ff.89-90 (in Latin).

10. 10 January 1580-1

'Umquhill Lawrens Tulloches schownd bill.'

The original is not known to exist. One of the writs taken from Ninian Neven's house in Yell on 24 August 1624 (*RPC*, xiv, p.736).

11. Edinburgh, 18 January 1580-1

Obligation by John Hamilton, burgess of Edinburgh, as cautioner for William Sinclair of Estounres (*rectius* Ustanes), to Alexander Spittell, vicar of Nesting, for the tack duty of the vicarage of Nesting. Alexander, with consent of Adam, bishop of Orkney, commendator of Holyroodhouse, Alexander Kincaid, vicar of Walls, and Walter Callendar, his curators, has set a tack (dated 24 December 1580 at Holyroodhouse) of the vicarage to William for 5 years from midsummer 1580 for an annual payment of 14 old angel nobles gold in weight.

Witnesses: Walter Callendar, Robert Hamilton and Robert Gourlay.

SRO, RD.1/19, f.111.

12. Holyroodhouse, 19 January 1580-1

Gift to Thomas Boyne in Yetland of the escheat of his own goods, fallen to the crown through his being put to the horn for not finding surety to underlie the law before the justice and his deputies in the tolbooth of Edinburgh for participation in the slaughter of Mark Vondroum in Yetland, or for not compearing to that effect.

RSS, viii, no.37. Cf. following item.

13. Holyroodhouse, 19 January 1580-1

Gift to Adam Boyne of the escheat of the goods of Thomas Boyne in Yetland, his father, put to the horn for not compearing before the justice and his deputies in the tolbooth of Edinburgh on 20 January last to underlie the law for participation in the slaughter of Patrick Vinrame.

RSS, viii, no.40. Cf. previous item. A complaint against Lord Robert Stewart in December 1575 mentions 'Thomas Boyane, wha slew ane Patrick Windren in my lord's awn presence, now at his last being at Zetland': Thomas 'being taken and keepit prisoner the space of six vulkis, was put to liberty, and sent to Noroway' (D. Balfour ed., *Oppressions of the Sixteenth Century in the Islands of Orkney and Zetland*, Edinburgh 1859, p.8).

14. Hamber in Ounst, 12 February 1580-1

Wadset by Laurence Hill, with consent of Barbara Erasmusdochter, his spouse, to Laurence Bruce of Cultmalyndies, of 7 marks land, 12 pennies the mark, in Glus, with ½ mark land, 12 pennies the mark, in Barrasetter, in the parish of Northmaving, redeemable on payment of 80 dollars. After redemption Laurence Bruce shall have the right to lease the lands for a further nine years for payment of a lispund of butter and a shilling of wadmell annually 'gif it be requyred'.

Laurence Hill appends his mark and seal, and procures the seals and subscriptions of Mr Robert Cheyne of Valay and Barthill Strang of Voisgarth. Witnesses: Waltir Smyth, underfoud of Unst, Sillvester Fravangord, Harie Bruce, William Smyth, with divers others.

SA, GD.144/21/5. Laurence Hill's mark.

15. Edinburgh, 15 March 1580-1

Decreet of court of session in action at instance of (Robert Cheyne of) Walay against Eduard Sinclair and Thomas (torn) for spoliation on 2 to 6 June 1580 of Robert's lands of Norbie, which he possessed in liferent and had been in his possession for 13 years, and for 'douncasting of twa houssis and awaytaking of the stanis and tymmer'.

The lords of council continue the summons, and ordain the pursuer to have letters to summon witnesses and produce writs.

SRO, CS.7/84, f.201. The folio is torn and partly indecipherable.

16. 26 March 1581

'Ane wedsett rycht of iiij merk land in Tronasetter grantit be Andro Hawick to Petter in Bigga.'

The original is not known to exist. One of the writs taken from Ninian Neven's house in Yell on 24 August 1624 (*RPC*, xiv, p.735).

17. Holyroodhouse, 17 April 1581

Gift to James Tulloch of the prebend of the Cross 'stok' in Dunrosnes, vacant by demission of David Sinclair, for seven years, whereof the yearly rent does not exceed £20. It is certified that James is 'of convenient age to enter in the study of [*blank*], apt and disposit thairfoir'.

RSS, viii, no.222.

18. Edinburgh, 30 May 1581

Contract between Adam Bell of Cruikistoun and Robert Yule, servitor to Laurence Bruce of Cultmalyndies, on behalf of Laurence Bruce, on the one part, and Herman Garetsoun, skipper of the ship the *Quhit Grewhound* of Emdame in Eist Freisland, for himself and his partners, on the other part, whereby Adam and Robert undertake to bring the ship from Yetland to the port of Leith and deliver it and her 'apparelling' to Herman together with 50 old rix dollars. The ship, on a voyage from the port of Cortcimont (?) in Denmark to Emdame laden with malt and other goods, had been taken by Captain William Mowat and John Fardreis, his lieutenant, accompanied by certain Scotsmen, alleged pirates, and brought to Yetland, where the said Laurence, 'not having perfyt intelligence than to the pyrattis, bot upun certaine persuasionis, intromettit with the said ship, hir haill apperalling and maist pairt of the guidis thairin'. It has now been learned that the ship belongs justly to Herman and his partners, who are 'servandis and confiderattis of this realm'. Herman undertakes to renounce all rights of action in the matter, and to constitute Laurence his assignee in all the cargo.

Witnesses: George Littlejohne, Mr Robert Chene of Ure, William Wylye in Copmalindy, Charles Geddy, burgess of Edinburgh, James Borthwick, writer, with divers others.

SRO, CS.7/85, ff.425-8. Cortcimont may be Kertimende, near Odense.

19. Laxfurde, 5 June 1581

Wadset by David Strang, brother german to William Strang of Pettarthie, eldest brother son and nearest heir of the deceased sir George Strang, vicar of Nesting (having power of intromission from said William, and also from Margaret Strang, sister of George, with consent of William Primrois in Dysert, Patrik Strang, youngest brother son of George, Agnes and Gelis Strang, eldest and youngest sisters to George, and James Strang, natural son of George, by letters of procuratory and assignation by the said persons, and the decreet given thereupon by the sheriff of Yetland at Tingwell on 21 June 1569), to the right honourable Laurence Bruce of Cultmalyndeis, of two marks land in Onyarholme in Quhailsaysound, which was wadset to George by Culbane Ormisoun of Sindbister, with power to Laurence to possess the land heritably, 'ay and quhill the said Culbane or his airis lay down to the said Lawrence his airis or assignais the sowm of twentie aucht gulyionis Yetland payment in fat gudis'.

David subscribes and affixes his seal. Witnesses: James Hay, vicar of Unst, Andro Mairtene and John Birstane, with divers others.

SA, GD.144/265/1.

20. Voisgarth, 13 June 1581

Ratification by James Hay, vicar of Unst, to Bartilmo Strang of Voisgeartht, of infeftment by the deceased Mr Francis Bothwell, his predecessor, with consent of Lord Robert Stewart and Adam, bishop of Orkney, to Bartilmo of 12 marks land of Voisgeartht with mansion house, etc., and confirmation thereof under the great seal. Because Bartilmo has no lawful male heirs James undertakes to grant a new infeftment to Bartilmo and his male heirs, whom failing to such other entailed persons as Bartilmo nominates. James ratifies the 'designatioun' of the manse and four acres of glebe land at (torn) of St. Ola and shall make no further claim to the mansion house and land contained in Bartilmo's infeftment, apart from feu duties, because Bartilmo has 'maid coistlie and sumpteous bigging upoun the said landis of Voisgeartht within sax yeiris last bipast, exceiding the doubill availl of the haill landis contenit in his infeftment'. James undertakes to repair the manse designated to him at the kirks of St. Ola sufficiently for 'staiking of ane minister and reidar' to serve at the kirks of Unst, seeing that Bartilmo has promised to supply James at his expense eight dozen fir boards, four dozen 'Rinss spar', and eighteen fir joists, 'quhilk will be sufficient timmer for building and reparing of ane mans to any minister in the countrey'. James acknowledges that the manse and land designated to him at the kirks of St. Ola 'ar the auld accustumat mans quhair the vicars of Unst [*torn*] maid residence in tymes bypast'.

Witnesses: Hew Sinclair of Burgh, John Callendar, with divers others.

SRO, RD.1/20(1), ff.152-3.

20a. Edinburgh, 11 July 1581

Decreet of court of session in action at instance of deceased Mr David Borthuik of Lochhill and Mr Robert Creychtoun of Eliok, king's advocates, and Mr Robert Chene of Unerve [Unerur], against Lord Robert Stewart, feuar and sheriff principal of Orknay and Yetland, Eduard Sincler, William Sincler, William Hendersone, Laurence of Grunyevo, John Skeld, Nicoll Hardwall, James Sincler, Magnus Reid, Arthour Sincler, John Murray, John Smyth, Henry Halcro, Nicolas of Culyevo, James Southerland, Silvester Frangnord, William Allawsoun, William of Gordie, Bothwell in Satyre, Laurence in Grunyesoutter, Magnus of How, Gilbert Coupland, Edward Odsta, George (*rectius*

Garth?) Ulsta, Magnus Nubabak and Colban in Quhalsay, for reduction of decreet, given on 3 June 1578, by Lord Robert, sheriff, and assize, in favour of the said Eduard Sincler, and Andro Wischert, decerning 'the tytle of the sawing of ane last of land in Melbe, viz. the the tua parte extending to tuelf merk lands to apertene to the said Edward Sincler, and the uthir sax merkis extending to the thrid of the said last to apertene to the said Andro'; and for the said sheriff and assize to be punished in their persons and goods for the partial and wilful giving of the said decreet.

The lords of council annul the said decreet 'becaus all clamis, petitionis and libellis aucht and suld be certen and conclude sum certen thing, as alsua all sentences suld be certen and concludand certenlie, conforme to the clame [and] petition quhairupoun the samyn proceidis, and nocht upoun ony uthir caus bot upoun the caussis onlie expremit in the libell; bot it is of veritie that nather the said libell is certen, bot inept, irrelevant and generall, nocht concludand ony certen thing, nor yet is the sentence, decreit and rolment of court foirsaid pronunceit thairupoun certen, nor yet concludand conforme to the libell foirsaid, bot upoun uthir caussis far different frome the caussis and ressones contenit in the said libellit precept intentit and persewit be the said Eduard: for the said libellit precept beiris and contenis the said Eduard to haif ane last or auchtene merk land of the lands of Melbie in Sandnes in heretage, and thairthrow acclamand to haift the rest of the said lands of Melbie, alsweill pertenyng to the lords of Norroway as the uthir uthell lands thairof, as he that is rychteous uthallis man thairof, that is to say heretour and rychtis man of the samyn, that is to say rycht haifar to the reversioun of kyndnes of the rest of the said lands of Melbie, according to the laws of the countrey, concludand thairfoir the said Mr Robert to heir and se Edward decernit to the samyne of the said lands and rycht of the samyne, and he [*i.e.* Robert] to desist and ceis thairfra in all tymes cuming, to the effect the said Edward sould peciablie joiss and bruik the saidis landis, as the said libell at lenth proportis: quhilkis libell being generall in the self, and on na wayis relevant of the law concludand in ony certane part or portioun of the said lands fra the quhilkis the said Mr Robert sould desist and ceis. Nevirtheless the said assysors decernit be thair sentence and decreit the said Eduard to haif titill to the tua pairt, viz. tualf merk land of the said complenaris last of land of the saidis lands of Melbie, and the thrid pairt of the said Mr Robertis last of land, viz. the uthir sax merk land thairof, to apertene to the said Andro Wischert, extending in the haill to ane last of land, to be decernit betuix thame in maner foirsaid, and sua pronuncit ane sentence upoun ane certaine pairt and portioun, na certane portioun being contenit in the said conclusioun of the said petitioun as said is.

'Attoure the saidis assysors be thair pretendit decreit foirsaid decernit the said Mr Robert to tyne his rycht of the said landis, and he that haid contravenit ane act and ordinance maid in our soverane lordis darrest moders lyftyme, and as ane defrauder of the pupillis to quhome he was allegit tutour, and the saidis Edward and Androw to bruik and joiss the said last of land respective in maner foirsaid, as thai that haid conqueist and obtenit the kyndnes thairof fra the auld poss[ess]oures, as the said decreit of the dait foirsaid in the self proportis, and fra the said assysors gifand ane decreit and sentence of ane certane pairt and portioun of the said Mr Robert landis, viz. tua pairtes or tualf merks landis of his last thairof to apertene to the said Eduard, na certane portioun being contenit in the libell as said is, as alsua thairin pronunceing the uthir thrid part of his last of land, viz. sax merks land thairof to pertene to the said Andro Wischert, the samin not being acclamit be him in the libell, nor yit the said Mr Robert beand summondit at any tyme preceding be him to that effect: the said assysors in sua doing hes pronuncit a sentence of a certane portioun *super inserto libello*, and that upoun uthir caussis far different frome the caussis contenit in the libell, as the said pretendit sentence and libell respective in thame self proportis, as alsua he adjugit the thrid pairt of the said Mr Robertis last of land to the said Andro Wischert, quha nevir acclamit the samin, and sua the sentence foirsaid being disconforme utirlie to the libell, the said sentence, decreit and libell of court, with the prossus quhairupoun the samin procedit, ar maist induirlie led, deducit and pronuncit contrair thair awin law and practick judiciallie observit, quhilkis allegeances beand relevand of the law gif the said Mr Robert haid bein sufferit at the first instance for to allege and propone the samin haid bein ane sufficient caus for to haif stoppit farder process, and wald haif obtenit obsolvitur upoun the said pretendit libell, and thairfoir he now proponit the said allegeance, lik as be the tennour heirof he dois now in the secund instance, the samin being verifeit and provin is sufficient to reduce the said pretendit processis, sentence, decreit and rolment of court gevin in favours of the said Eduard and Andro, lik as it wald haf stoppit proces and decreit and it haid bein proponit in the first instance, as said is, as wes cleirlie understand to the said lordis be productioun of the said decreit and proces quhairupoun the samin procedit, and assoilyeis the said sheref and assissors foirsaidis for the punisment contenit in the said summondis, and decernis thame quyte thairfra in tyme cuming for consideratioun moving the saidis lordis, and becaus the said Mr Robert Chene hes consignit and payit to the saidis lords the sowme of xl s., according to thair lait ordinance, thairfoir ordanis letters to be direct to compell, poind and distrenye the said Edward Sinclar his landis and guidis for the said sowme, togidder with the sowme of fourtie pundis as for the coistis and expenssis modifiet be the saidis lords to the said Mr Robert Chene in persute of the said actioun and obtening of this present decreit in forme as effeiris.'

SRO, CS.7/76, ff.346-7; CS.7/85, ff.323-5. It is possible that the clerk has rendered 'samyne' (= joint possession) as 'sawing' (=sowing) at the beginning of the document. 'Samyne' appears later in the document (side-by-side with another 'samyne', meaning 'the same'). See also no. 36.

21. Burghe, 10 September 1581

Wadset by Nicholl Mawnissone, relict of Marioun Petersdochter, to an honourable man Hew Sincleir of Burgh, of 2 marks land, 12 pennies the mark, in Wasterhous in Burgh in the isle of Quhalsay, parish of Nesting, for 80 Yetland 'gulyeounis' in butter, victuals and other duties which he and his deceased spouse 'restis in comptis to the said Hew, of the place of Stroholm, for nonpament' during the time that Nicholl was grieve of Stroholm. Redemption to be at the house of Stroholme.

Because Nicholl has no seal or signet of his own he procures those of famous men: William Mansoun in Neip, Magnus Hansoun of Gillisbrek and Alexander Duff in Skellinstaw. Witnesses: Henrye Keyth, Magnus in How, Magnus in Stroholme, Laes Kneland and Peter Simsoun.

SA, SC.12/65/1/19. The document is unsubscribed.

22. Burgh in Nesting, 20 October 1581

Wadset by Erasmus (blank) in Asweik, guider, tutor and umbothsman to (blank) and (blank) Christofersons, brothers german, his 'oyeisseis', to an honourable man Hew Sincleir of Burghe, of 1½ marks land, 12 pennies the mark, in the town of Glaitnes, parish of Nesting, for 18 'yopeindaills'.

Because Erasmus has no seal or signet of his own he procures those of famous and discreet men: William Sincleir of Ustanes, Henrie Forrester of Lunay and Mans Hanssone of Gillisbrek. Erasmus signs with his hand at the pen led by Peter Symsoun, reader at Nesting. Witnesses: James Dicksoun, Robert Acheissone, Mawnis Burgar, Peter Symsoun, with divers others.

SA, SC.12/65/1/13. The document is unsubscribed.

23. Holyroodhouse, 28 October 1581

Letters by the king, with advice of the privy council, ordaining a charter to be made under the great seal confirming the charter and infeftment of feu ferme by Queen Mary to Lord Robert Stewart, of the lands of Orknay and Yetland, with advocation, donation of kirks, benefices and chaplainries, and of the offices of sheriffship of Orknay, and sheriffship and foudry of Yetland. The king has considered how far the lands lie distant from the rest of the realm, and that he and his predecessors have seldom been there, and that the necessity of justice is daily increasing as the multitude of people grows; considering also the great trouble which the inhabitants suffer by the continual invasion by 'the hieland and brockin men lyand upoun the west and north west pairtis of this realme, and by pirattis and strangearis' which cannot be repressed without the power of a great and noble person continually residing there, and that the king's predecessors have been compelled to sustain a chamberlain for the collection of duties to whom a great portion 'has bein of auld defalkit for the povertie of the tennentis and sterilitie of the grund, besydes the travel and expenssis sustenit be transporting, carriage and hasart of the ferme victuallis', and besides the annual fee which was paid out of the king's revenues to the sheriff of Orknay and keeper of the castle of Kirkwall, tacksmen, ferrymen and officers exceeded £500 yearly in victuals, flesh, butter and mill multures; and also the king has understood that Lord Robert is not able to execute justice adequately without receipt of the casualties and escheats of offenders against the laws and of the 'tollis and custumes of strangearis arryvand'. The king, having fully considered the necessity of the administration of justice, and bearing in mind that the casualties and escheats have been of little or no profit to him, dispones to Lord Robert and his lawful heirs the office of justiciary and the whole casualties, etc., under exception of the great customs of goods and merchandice transported furth of the realm. And further, the king having considered the good, true and thankful service done to his dearest mother and himself by his trusty cousin, and of their nearness of blood; and being of goodwill and mind that Lord Robert should be advanced in honours, creates the tenandry and lordship of the said lands of Orknay and Yetland, etc., the whole superiority of freeholders, advocation, and donation of kirks, benefices and chaplainries, together with the offices of justiciary, sheriffship of Orknay and foudry of Yetland, the whole unlaws, escheats, casualties, wreck and waith, tolls, etc., into one earldom and lordship, to wit the earldom of Orknay and the lordship of Yetland, and ordains Lord Robert Stewart, his heirs and successors foresaids to be called in all times hereafter earls of Orknay and lords of Yetland, and granting to them the title, honour, place and pre-eminence of an earl and lord in all parliaments, etc., and ordains the castle of Kirkwall to be the principal messuage of the said earldom and lordship, to be held by Lord Robert Stewart and his lawful heirs, which failing to return to the king and his successors, for payment of 3,010 merks yearly for feuduty for the said lands, etc., and 1 penny yearly in name of blenche ferme for the offices of justiciary, sheriffship and foudry.

Subscribed by the king.

SRO, E.2/9, ff.98-101. See also *RSS*, viii, no.492, *RMS*, v, no.263, and SRO, RH.6/2610. Ratified by parliament on 29 November 1581 (*APS*, iii, pp.254-6).

24. (*circa* November 1581)

Petition by Henry, now Lord Sinclair, to the king and lords in parliament. Henry is successor to the deceased William, earl of Cathnes, Lord Sinclair, 'quha conqueist certaine landis heretabillie within the boundis of the lordschippis of Orknay and Yeitland, quhilk your graces predicessoris King James the therd ... declarit he [*i.e.* James] had na rycht therto, and be his letter under the privie seill', dated 3 February 1471-2, 'willit that my said predicessour his successoris and thair factoris suld be anserit of the samin without impediment'. By virtue of the said letter William 'bruikit the saidis landis', as did Henry, Lord Sinclair, petitioner's 'guidsir', until his death, 'quhilk wes in the feild of Flowdoun'. During the minority of William, Lord Sinclair, petitioner's father, the said lands, 'and als the landis of umquhile Sir David Sinclair, his eme, to quhom I succeid', were intromitted with by 'officiaris impute be your hienes dairrest guidsir King James the fyft'. James, 'upoun the sute of my said umquhile fader, directit his graces commission to umquhile Oliver Sinclair', dated 21 March in the 28th year of his reign, ' gevand him power to tak cognition quhat possessiouns, landis and rowmes the saidis umquhile Henry, Lord Sinclair, my guidsir, umquhile Sir David Sinclair and utheris our freindis (to quhom I succeid air) had within the saidis lordschippis of Orknay and Yeitland, and, gif my said umquhile fader had rycht therto, to caus him ... bruik the samin'. Petitioner and his father, 'continewing in our persute of our rychtis ... presentit supplicatioun to your hienes darrest moder', declaring that his guidsir, and Sir David, 'conqueist certaine particular landis and rowmes within the iles and boundis of Orknay and Yeitland, ... fra the quhilkis my said umquhile fader wes stoppit and debarrit throwe occasioun and trubill in thai partis'. She directed commission, dated 28 March in the 25th year of her reign, to the sheriff of Orknay, and 'failyeing of him be absens or refuiss, to his lovittis, makand thame shereffis of Orknay and fowdis of Yeitland in that part, chargeing thame to tak cognitioun, be inqueist of the cuntrie, according to the auld ordour observit in thai partis, quhat landis and rowmes ... pertenit to the said umquhile Henry ... and umquhile David Sinclair ... and to retour the samin, and put thame in writ befoir attentik connotaris, swa that efter the sycht thairof hir grace mycht gif infeftmentis ... to my said umquhile fader and me, than his appeirand air'. However, this commission, 'be occasion of civill werris, tuik not effect, quhairthrowe I haife beine and wilbe frustrat of my rycht'. Petitioner therefore beseeches the king and lords to grant commission to (blank), 'makand thame ... shereffis of Orknay and fowdis of Yeitland in that part, to tak cognitioun, be inqueist of the cuntrie, according to the auld ordour observit in thair partis', what lands and rooms pertained to his guidsir and the deceased Sir David, 'and to retour the samin and put thame in writt befoir attentik notaris to your majestie, swa that thaireftir your grace may gif me infeftmentis ... conforme to my said rycht and titill and commissioun grantit be your hienes darrest moder'.

Wemyss Castle. Printed in B.E. Crawford, 'William Sinclair, earl of Orkney, and his family: a study in the politics of survival', in K.J. Stringer ed., *Essays on the Nobility of Medieval Scotland*, Edinburgh 1985, pp.252-3. An endorsement, dated 18 November 1581 at Holyroodhouse, states that 'the lordis of articlis remittis this complaint to begein in to the lordis of sessioune quhome befoir the samyn will get ane ressonabil anser'.

25. Burcht, 20 November 1581

Disposition by Colbein Ormesone of Symbuster, with consent of Johne Colbeinssone, his eldest son, and Christen and Marion Colbeinsdottirs, his apparent heirs, and of Agnes Mawnisdottir, his spouse, to an honourable man and his good friend Hew Sincleir of Burcht, of his 4 ures land in Litilholm in Quhalsaysound and 2 ures land in Claitholm 'afore' Sandweik, all 6 pennies the merk, 'marcheand' with the isle of Quhalsay. If Colbein desires to wadset or sell any of his lands in Symbuster he binds himself to offer them to Hew before any other. If Colbein wadsets or sells the said lands elsewhere in ignorance the disposal shall be null and void unless Hew frees the land and inbrings it to his own use, 'and that be vertew the said land is linallie discendit of the hous and stoik of Burcht'.

Because Colbein has no seal or signet of his own he procures signets of William Sincleir of Ustanes, Henrie Forrester of Lunay and Mawnis Hansson of Gillisbrek. Witnesses: Peter Symson, reader of Nesting, John Amphray of Astay, James Dickson and Robert Achessone, with divers others.

SA, SC.12/65/3.

26. Burch, 20 November 1581

Disposition by Marioun Laurenceisdochter, relict of Mawnis Leslie, with consent of David and John Lesleis, her heirs, to an honourable man and her good friend Hew Sincleir of Burcht, of 6 marks land, 8 pennies the mark, in Grunyeawo, and 1 mark 6 ures, (blank) pennies the mark, in (blank), all in the parish of Wallis, heired by her from the deceased Laurence Brynelson, her father.

Because Marion has no seals proper she procures the seals and signets of Master Jhieremie Cheine, archdeacon of Yetland, Mr Robert Cheine of Vallay, William Sincleir of Ustanes and John Amphray of Astay. Witnesses: Peter Symson, reader at Nesting, James Diksone, Robert Achessone and Edward Thomasson in Garthe.

SA, SC.12/65/1/14. Only one witness subscribes.

27. Hamber, 3 December 1581

Disposition by Nicholas and Thomas Bodelsones, brothers german, to an honourable man Laurence Bruce of Cultmalyndies, sheriff-depute of Yetland, of 1 mark land, 9 pennies the mark, of Sound in West Yell. They assign to Laurence 'the violent profeittis and byrun dewties of the said mark land' withheld from them by Petir in Biggay as possessor for the past 22 years.

Because they have no marks or seals they cause Peter Maxvell, exhorter in Ounst, and Harie Bruce in Staneswell to subscribe in their names, no notary being present. Witnesses: Waltir Smyth, underfoud, Andro Smyth, his son, William Magnussone of Gardy, Williame Smyth of Scraveild, Sewart Fravangord, Walter Makrichie and Johne Mowat.

GH. Marks of William Magnussone, Walter Smyth and William Smyth.

28. Gunneilestay in Brasay, 15 January 1581-2

Disposition by Thomas, Christopher and Gregorius Erasmussones, brothers german, to an honourable man Laurence Bruce of Cultmalyndies, of 3 marks 2 ures land, 8 pennies the mark, of Burraland in the isle of Trundray, heired from the deceased Margarett Irvene, their mother.

Because they cannot write the brothers draw their marks and procure the subscription and signet of William Sinclar of Ustanes. Witnesses: James Sutherland in Quhailsay, David Leslie, Johnne Colving, William Bruce, John Birstane, John Nichoilsone and Andro Martyne.

GH. Marks of disponers.

29. 20 January 1581-2

Deed concerning the upgestry of Haylya Turbennisdochter and Mans Ollasoune, her husband.

The yeir of god 1581 yeir the 20 day Januar.

The quhilk day Haylya Turbennisdochter, moder to Johnne Mansoune in Uphouss, gayff hirselff upgester with hyr husband Mans Ollasoune, father also to the sayd Jhone, and father to Nicolas Symonsonis wyff callet Breta Mansdochter, and thair come in presence of Waltir Smyth and Wilyeam Mansoune in Gardy, onderfoldis of Unst for the tyme, and thair simplicitur refusit to pass in upgestrye amang the rest of hir bairness, and hyr husband quha war also willing to halde thaym in upgestry ever ilk ane for thair awin part after thair powar; in quhais presence and before the saydis judgis comperitt Olla in Torwayll and thayre in lyk maner offerytt hymselff for hys awin part to ressave and hald the said Haylya in upgestrye bot nocht hyr husband; thayrefore the saydis jugiss wyth thair assessowris haiffing god and guid conscience before thair eyis and consedering the gryt inward effectioune and harty luyff of the saydis twa eldrene personnis quha wald nocht ane seperatt fra ane uther; thairfore the saydis judgis with thair assessowris gayff thaim liberty of conscience to gyff thaimselffis upgesteris till ony of thair bairness that thai thocht wald mayst honestlye susteine thaim bayth in bed and buird, quha ryply being advyssitt with thair selffs and of gude jugement did refuyss all the offres of thair bairness and of Olla in Torwell and offerit thaimselffis upgesters tyll Jhonne thair sonne and to Nicoll Simonsone quha haid to hys mareit wyff Breta Mansdochter, the said

Jhonne in Uphouss to hald his fader and moder in upgestrie honestly as becom him to do of the law, and Nycoll Simonsone with his wyff oblegat thaim selffis as become him to do for ane sister with this restrwctioune that the rest of the bairness and all utheris haiffing entress thaironto with thair restrwctioune, that the rest of the bairness with Olla in Torwell sould satysfie and mak thaim guid and thankfull paymentt ever ilk ane respective for thair awin partt, quha also did the same all bot Olla in Torwaill quha also was thair decernit be the saydis judgis to do as the rest.

Now sevin yeir efter the first day of the saidis personnis upgestrie decest at the will of god thair was ane day haldein in Westerhouss and the sayd Olla deit in lyk maner at godis plesour and Bartill Strang, than being onderfold, with certane honest men his assessowris to Wilyeam Mansoune in Gardy, Walter Smyth, Olla in Utterska, Andreas in Garratowne, Thomas in Boudane and James in Sletone(?) in presence of the judge, Nicollas Thomasone quha mareit the saidis Ollais dochter callet Anna Ollaisdochter and Breta Jhonnisdochter and oblegat thaimselffis respective for thair awin partis to frelsay the saidis Jhonne and Nycolas in the fredome of Norweik in thack and pettis ij gullionis to wytt the said Nicolas to satisfie the said Jhone in Westerhouss induring his lyftyme ane gullionis [*sic*] in pettis and thack and the said Breta to fre the saids Nycolas Simonsone in Velsgarth ane halff gullionis [*sic*] and oblegatt thaimselffis never to cum in the contrar of the samyne onder the paine of perjury and violating of our fayth.

In witness of the quhilk we the saydis personnis hes hereonto affixit our markis.

Bartill Strangis [*mark*] mark
Walter Smyths [*mark*] mark
Wilyeam Mansounis [*mark*] mark
Peter Maxwell minister with my hand

SRO, RH.9/15/90. Printed in *Deeds*, no.xiii.

30. Symbister in Quhalsaye, 6 February 1581-2

Wadset by Culbeine Ormesone of Symbister, with consent of Jehannes, his son, and Mariune, his daughter, to an honourable man Laurence Bruce of Cultmalyndies, of 4 marks land, 9 pennies the mark, of the readiest of his lands of Symbister in the isle of Quhalsaye, under reversion of 80 'gulyeonis fatt guid'. Culbeine undertakes not to sell, wadset or set in long tacks any of his two lasts of land of Symbister without the special consent of Laurence.

Because Culbeine cannot write and has no seal proper of his own he gets Williame Sinclar of Ustanes and David Strang of Benestaye to seal and subscribe in his name. Witnesses: James Sutherland in Isebuster,

Christopher in Sandveik, Harie Bruce, Henrie Wardlaw, messenger, and Andro Martyne. (John Colwyn also subscribes as a witness.)

SA, GD.144/28/1. Marks of Culbeine, Jehannes and James Sutherland.

31. Isebuster in Qwalsaye, 6 February 1581-2

Disposition by Magnus Laurencesone in Skea, with consent of Elspett Thomasdochter, his spouse, to an honourable man Laurence Bruce of Cultmalyndies, of ½ mark land, 10 pennies the mark, of Skea in Qwalsay.

Because Magnus cannot write he asks William Sinclar of Ustanes, Henrie Forrester of Lunay and James Sutherland in Isebuster to append their marks and signets. Witnesses: Christopher in Sandweik, Henrie Wardlaw, messenger, Johnne Colving and Andro Martyne, with divers others.

SA, GD.144/265/7. Mark of James Sutherland.

32. Gluss in the parish of Northmaving, 24 February 1581-2

Indenture between Laurence Bruce of Cultmalyndies, on the one part, and Magnus Symoundsone of Glus, with special consent of Olaue, Lawrence, Symound and Michaell Magnussones, his sons, on the other part, whereby Laurence sets in tack to Magnus and his sons 7 marks 6 ures land, 12 pennies the mark, of Glus in the parish of Northmaving, for 19 years, and for further periods of 19 years *in perpetuam*, for payment of 5 lispunds and 1 penny butter, and 5 shillings and 1 cuttle wadmell, with due service at terms of payment 'usit and wount', yearly, and no further duty except 'ane barrell of guid drink with the pertinentis to the bankett anes in the year gif the samyn beis requyred'. Magnus and his sons undertake not to sell, wadset or set in long tacks any part of their lands and uthall of Glus without the special consent of Laurence.

The seals of Laurence, Mr Hierome Cheyn, archdeacon of Yetland, and Andro Giffhartt in Weddirstay are appended. Witnesses: Laurence Gunnasatter, lawrightman of Northmaving, Alester Makbaythsone, officer there, Henry Wardlaw, messenger, Harie Bruce and Andro Martyne, with divers others.

SA, GD.144/21/13. Marks of Magnus, Olaue, Lawrence, Symound and Michaell, and Laurence Gunnasatter.

33. 25 February 1581-2

'Charter by James Magnysone of Qyone, with consent of Synevo Jacobsdochter, his spouse, to Peter Nisbet of Kirkabister, of one merk land in Sellafirth . . .

'Witnesses: Thomas Tholock, James Bogar, and Grigor Peterson.'

The original is not known to exist. The above abstract, by Francis Grant, is in OSD, *SN*, 14 October 1893. According to another abstract, by Gilbert Goudie, 'the seller signs by mark as "James of Swarisetter"' (notebook in Braefield House, Dunrossness).

34. Kirkwall, March (*circa* 1581-2?)

Letters regarding the acquisition of the foudry of Yetland by Hew Sinclair of Broch, Arthour Sinclair of Aith, Williame Sinclair of Oyzea and Andro Mowat of Hewgoland; with response thereto by the inhabitants of Dunrosnes.

Be it kend till all men be thir presentis, we, Hew Sinclair of Broch, Arthour Sinclair of Aith, Williame Sinclair of Oyzea and Andro Mowat of Hewgoland, forsameikill as for the singular weilfair and commoditie of the haill cuntre of Yetland, we have procurit at the handis of our guid maister and lord, my lord erle of Orknay, lord Yetland, the fredome and libertie of the said haill cuntre, in the obtening to us the foudrie thairoff fra the laird of Cultmalindie, and thairby dischergeand and inhibitand him to use the samin for certane yeiris to cum, and forder we ar becumin cautioneris conjunctlie, and hes obligat oure landis, guidis and geir to his lordschip for payment to him of ane thousand pund money betuix this and Lambes nixtocum, thairfoir desiris yow and everie ane of yow, gentill men, commonis and utheris inhabitantis of the said cuntre for the foirnemit causes and considerationis, and for your awin weillis, according to your power and facultie, to fortifie and assist us in paying of the foirsaid soume of ane thousand pund, and the rather for sindre injuries done to yow of befoir, of the quhilk we have our meikill experience, sua thinkis it maist necessar samony of yow as will assist us to your power and releif us of our cautionarie, that ye wald su[*torn*] us ather be your hand wryttis or be your mercheant markis or stampis, and report the samin bak [*torn*] utherwayis we will desist [*torn*].

Be thir presentis, subscrivit with our handis at [Kir]kwall [*torn*] of March [*torn*] yeiris, befoir [*torn*] witnessis: Harie Colvile, chantor of Orknay, Williame S[*torn*].

Ita est Willelmus Fermour notarius publicus testis in premisis manu propria

H. Sinclar of Burche
Arthur Sinclair of Aythe
Williame Sincleir of Uya with my hand
A. Mowat of Howgoland wyth my hand

Gilbart Coupland with my hand at the pen led be the notar underwritin at my command

Ita est Macolmus Sinclar manu propria

The anser of the inhabitantis of Dunrosnes to the premisses as followis: as to the [*torn*] of ony out of office or inputting of ony utheris, thai refar the samin to my lord, to put in quhome his lordship pleissis, onele heirto have thai grantit thair assistance: that quhair as heirtofoir allegit lawis and injustice hes past over thame, that hencefurth sic may be repairit and amendit; and that quhasoevir gettis the superioritie (under my lord) over thame may brek all corrupt custumis and restor the ancient libertie; and all the principallis of the paroche hes subscrivit and sum affixt thair markis as followis. [*The rest of the document is blank.*]

Braefield House, Dunrossness. Copy in SA, SA.2/261/3.

35. Edinburgh, 21 March 1581-2

Decreet of court of session in action at instance of Patrik Chene of Essilmonthe against Henry Halcro, Malcolme Halcro, John Umphray, Erik Asta, James in Scalloway, Magnus there, Magnus Gerthe, Nicoll Thomsoun, Magnus How, Poll Magnussone, Magnus in Ustines, James Kneland, William Sincler of Ustines, Olyver Mansoun, Thomas Mansoun in Overabust, Nicoll Skarpagert, Erik Skarpagerthe, Oliver Husgord, and all other feuars, tenants, parishioners, etc., of the archdeaconry of Yetland, for payment of the fruits thereof. Patrik has a tack, set to him by Mr Jerome Cheyne, archdeacon of Yetland, of the whole benefice with lands and casualties, for 19 years, dated 14 April 1581.

The lords of council decern the defenders to pay to Patrik the teinds and fruits of the archdeaconry for the period of his tack.

SRO, CS.7/88, f.351.

36. Edinburgh, 7 April 1582

Decreet of court of session in action at instance of Mr Robert Chene of Owerwr against Andro Wishart and Edward Sinclair, for removal from Robert's two parts, extending to 12 marks land, of the lands of Melbie with their pertinents, lying within the barony of Geeska and sheriffdom of Yetland, which he holds in liferent, as shown by his infeftment and sasine. Andro and Edward had been warned to remove at Whitsunday 1577.

The lords of council decern the defenders to flit and remove from their respective parts.

SRO, CS.7/89, f.403. See no. 20a.

37. Tingwall, 8 April 1582

'Disposition by Master Hierome Cheyne, archdeacon of Zetland, with consent of Patrick Cheyne of Esselmont, to John Clark, cordiner, in Scalloway banks, and Lilias Bayne [*rectius* Boyne], his spouse, in feu of these lands: "the quoy besyd Scalaway bankis lyand betwixt the lands of my Lord Robert, erle of Orkney and Lord of Zetland" and others. ...

'Witnesses: William Cheyne, Robert Cheyne, reader of Tingwall, Malcolm Halcro and Thomas Tailyeir, and divers others.'

The original is not known to exist. The above abstract, by Francis Grant, is in OSD, *SN*, 14 October 1893.

38. Synbuster in Quhalsay, 7 July 1582

Disposition by Colbein Ornesone of Synbuster in Quhalsay, with consent of Johne Colbeinssone, his eldest son, Christen and Marioun Colbeinsdochtters, his daughters, and Agnes Mawnsdochtter, his spouse, for her interest, to Lord Robert Stewart, earl of Orknaye and lord Yetland, justice general and sheriff principal, of 16 marks land, 9 pennies the mark, in the town of Synbuster in the isle of Quhalsay, pertaining to Colbein heritably, together with the title of reversion of Culbene's lands in the whole town of Synbuster. Colbein binds himself to have this charter rewritten by 'men of law', providing that 'my lord permit me my onlie lyfrent heiroff'.

Colbein and John append their merchant marks and procure those of Mawnis Hanssone of Gillisbrek and Adam Arnat. Colbein subscribes with his hand led at the pen by Peter Symsone, lector of Nesting. Witnesses: Androw Gyfhart, Olaue Culye, George Olauesone and Antonie Laurencesone, with divers others.

SA, GD.144/28/2. Marks of Colbein, Johne, Adam Arnat and Mawnis Hanssone.

39. Symbuster in Quhalsay, 7 July 1582

Disposition by Culbene Ormesone of Symbuster in Quhalsay, with consent of Jehannes Culbenesone his eldest son, and Christiane and Marioun Culbenisdochters, for their interest, to Lord Robert, earl of Orknaye, lord Yetland, of 16 marks land, 9 pennies the mark, of Symbuster in the isle of Quhalsaye, with reservation to Culbene of the landmails, fruits and duties of his said lands for his lifetime only, and with power to Lord Robert to redeem Culbene's other lands in the town of Symbuster previously wadset by him.

Culbene and Jehannes sign with their hands led at the pen by Malcolme Sinclare, vicar of Dunrosnes and notary public. Witnesses: James Sutherland in Isebuster, Adame Arnott of Widlone, Erasmus Smyth of Huiksatter, Olaiue Lie, with divers others.

Instrument of sasine, dated 6 September 1582 (at 1 p.m.). Sasine granted to Andro Mertene, attorney for Lord Robert, earl of Orknaye, lord Yetland, in presence of James Suiderland in Isbuster, Adam Arnot of Wielone, Erasmus Smyth of Huiksetter and Olau Lie, with divers others. Malcolm Sinclar, clerk of the diocese of Orknay, notary public.

SA, GD.144/69/1.

40. Ylsbrughe, 21 July 1582

Ordinance and doom of sheriff court held at Ylsbrughe in the parish of Northmaving, with consent of the parishioners, indicating that Orne Mair, Dutch merchant, had been appointed merchant at Northmaving, and that he had the whole trade of the commons thereof.

The original is not known to exist. Referred to in an action concerning the title and right of the port of Gunyesettervo in Northmaving on 21 July 1603 (*CB1*, p.93).

41. Noss in the isle of Brassay, 8 August 1582

Disposition by gift and tolerance of Robert, earl of Orknay, to Symone Hagarskale, indweller in the town of Hambrughe, of the title and right of the port of Gunyesettervo in Northmaving, for Symone's lifetime.

The original is not known to exist. Referred to in an action concerning the title and right of the port of Gunyesettervo in Northmaving on 21 July 1603 (*CB1*, p.93).

42. 25 August 1582

Rental of property acquired by the king of Denmark from Fru Gorwell Fadirsdotter, widow of Her Laug Brade.

HIETTLANND

Wouge parish

Master Rubbert of Walø, 24 marks land, 8 pennies the mark, pays yearly 8 pund butter, 72 ells wattmell.

Nicolaus Thommisenn of Brocke, 4½ marks land, 8 pennies the mark: 1½ pund butter, 13½ ells wattmell.

Skarffuesettir: 3 marks land, 8 pennies the mark: 1 pund 8 mark butter, 8 ells wattmell.

Svinslannd, 3 marks land, 8 pennies the mark: 1 pund 8 mark butter, 8 ells wattmell.

Niels Olluffsenn of Fotteborge, 36 marks land, 8 pennies the mark: 12 pund butter, 72 ells wattmell.

Gardtt, 3 marks land, 8 pennies the mark: 1 pund 8 mark butter, 8 ells wattmell.

Niels Torbranndsenn of Garsettir, 8 marks land, 8 pennies the mark: 2½ pund 4 mark butter, 24 ells wattmell.

Willum Davittsenn of West Qui, 1½ marks land, 8 pennies the mark: ½ pund 4 mark butter, 4 ells wattmell.

Elvestir, 2½ marks land, 8 pennies the mark: 1 pund 4 marks butter, 10½ ells wattmell.

Dynes Saattir, 2 marks land, 8 pennies the mark: 16 mark butter, 6 ells wattmell.

Fogelø, 27 marks land, 8 pennies the mark: 7 pund butter, 81 ells wattmell.

Gresegaard in Fogelø, 1½ marks land, 8 pennies the mark: 12 marks butter, 4½ ells wattmell.

Sandtzting parish

Kirstenn Jonnsdattir of Rødewick, 6 marks 2 ures land, 8 pennies the mark: 2 pund butter, 18 ells wattmell.

Ostreskiold, 4 marks land, 8 pennies the mark: 1 pund 8 marks butter, 12 ells wattmell.

Rasmus Westreskiold, 4½ marks land, 8 pennies the mark: 1½ pund butter, 13½ ells wattmell.

Kolswick, 1½ marks land, 8 pennies the mark: 12 marks butter, 4½ ells wattmell.

Lauritz and Errick Sellewog, 4½ marks land, 8 pennies the mark: 1½ pund butter, 13½ ells wattmell.

Grytting, 9 marks land, 6 pennies the mark: 4 pund butter, 23 ells wattmell.

Sandnes parish

Master Rubbertt of Norbyegaard, 48 marks 6 ures land, 8 pennies the mark: 16 pund 6 marks butter, 144 ells wattmell.

Ettuort Sinckler of Mielby, 18 marks land, 8 pennies the mark: 6 pund butter, 54 ells wattmell;

Thommis of Hiøgsaattir, 1½ marks land, 8 pennies the mark: 12 marks butter, 4½ ells watttmell.

Pedir Mogennsenn of Siøqui, 1 mark land, 9 pennies the mark: ½ pund butter, 3 ells wattmell.

Jenns Andirsenn of Bustaid, 9 marks land, 8 pennies the mark: 3 pund butter, 27 ells wattmell.

Edsting parish

John Wisker of Borrefiord, 10 marks land, 8 pennies the mark: 3 pund 8 marks butter, 30 ells wattmell.

Haffrø, 3 marks land, 8 pennies the mark: 1 pund butter, 9 ells wattmell.

Lillehoff, 6 ures: 6 marks butter, 1½ ells wattmell.

Gillebertt of Throistad, 14½ marks land, 8 pennies the mark: 4½ pund 8 marks butter, 43½ ells wattmell.

Bastiann of Nusborge, 1½ marks land, 8 pennies the mark: 12 marks butter, 4½ ells wattmell.

Cloistadtt, 6 ures land, 8 pennies the mark: 6 marks butter, 1 ells wattmell.

Wemenderø, 4 marks land: 12 ells wattmell.

Grønnø with Houg, 1½ marks land, 8 pennies the mark: 12 marks butter, 4½ ells wattmell.

Languaskaaill, 2 marks land, 8 pennies the mark: 16 marks butter, 6 ells wattmell.

Hougland, 24 marks land, 8 pennies the mark: 8 pund butter, 72 ells wattmell.

Semennesaatter, 1½ marks land, 1 penny the mark: 18 marks butter, 6 ells wattmell.

Fornordennmaffuid parish

Rasmus of Presthougland, 7 marks land, 8 pennies the mark: 2 pund 8 mark butter, 21 ells wattmell.

Fremgaard, 10 marks land, 6 pennies the mark: 2½ pund 8 marks butter, 20 ells wattmell.

Auffgierde, 1 mark land, 9 pennies the mark: ½ pund butter, 3 ells wattmell.

Andirs Smid of Nuttesettir, 6 marks land, 9 pennies the mark: 3 pund butter, 18 ells wattmell.

Jonn of Borrick, 9 marks land, 8 pennies the mark: 3 pund butter, 27 ells wattmell.

Laxe Kirke parish

Laxeuog, 10 marks land, 9 pennies the mark: 5 pund butter, 30 ells wattmell.

The following properties are found in the northmost part of the country, in both parishes [*i.e* in Unst]:

Olluff of Skaggi, 2 marks 2 ures land, 6 pennies the mark: 15½ marks butter, 4 ells wattmell.

Thommis of Wele, 2½ marks land, 6 pennies the mark: 20 marks butter, 5 ells wattmell.

Thommis of Dale, 1 mark land, 6 pennies the mark: 8 marks butter, 2 ells wattmell.

Hendrick of Papell in Ørrelannd: 2 marks butter, ½ ells wattmell.

Andfind of Klefferwick, 8 marks land, 6 pennies the mark: 2½ pund 4 marks butter, 16 ells wattmell.

Hendrick in Stue, 16 marks land, 6 pennies the mark: 5 pund 8 marks butter, 32 ells wattmell.

Niels of Krogdall, 5 marks 2 ures land, 6 pennies the mark: 1½ pund 4 marks butter, 10 ells wattmell.

Bener of Kleffuerbo, 8 marks land, 6 pennies the mark: 2½ pund 4 marks butter, 16 ells wattmell.

Haldoenn of Mius, ½ mark land, 6 pennies the mark: 4 marks butter, 1 ell wattmell.

Tommis of Badenn, 2 marks land, 6 pennies the mark: 16 marks butter, 4 ells wattmell.

Mogenns of Langhuus, 2½ marks land, 6 pennies the mark: 20 marks butter, 5 ells wattmell.

Gregorrius of Grydgierde, 4 marks land, 6 pennies the mark: 1 pund 8 marks butter, 8 ells wattmell.

Rasmus of Hiøgsteenn, 2 marks 2 ures land, 6 pennies the mark: 18 marks butter, 4 ells wattmell.

Mogenns of Saidlanndt, 3 marks land, 6 pennies the mark: 1 pund butter, 6 ells wattmell.

Hammir benorth

Rubbert of Wouge, ½ mark land, 3 pennies the mark: 4 marks butter, 1 ell wattmell.

South in Jonstt

Simenn of Koilback, 2 marks land, 6 pennies the mark: 16 marks butter, 4 ells wattmell.

Gursaattir, 10 marks land, 6 pennies the mark: 3 pund 8 marks butter, 20 ells wattmell.

Thommis in Holmen, 2 marks land, 6 pennies the mark: 16 marks butter, 4 ells wattmell.

Walter Smid of Waled, 3 marks land, 6 pennies the mark: 1 pund butter, 6 ells wattmell.

Jonn of Suarreuog, 1 mark land, 6 pennies the mark: 8 marks butter, 2 ells wattmell.

Benedigtz of Klepsgierde, 1 mark land, 6 pennies the mark: 8 marks butter, 2 ells wattmell.

Benedigttz of Brewick, ½ mark land, 6 pennies the mark: 4 marks butter, 1 ell wattmell.

The following farms are found in Feteller in Hiettlannd:

Staffenn of Orre, 8 marks 2 ures land, 6 pennies the mark: 1 pund 8 marks butter, 8 ells wattmell.

Rubbirt of Sneborge, 2 marks 2 ures land, 6 pennies the mark: 16 marks butter, 4 ells wattmell.

Rasmus of Øidsettir, 1 mark land, 6 pennies the mark: 8 marks butter, 2 ells wattmell.

Rasmus of Kolbennstofftt, 6 ures land, 6 pennies the mark: 6 marks butter, 1½ ells wattmell.

Olluff Sødirlannd of Sottir, 1 mark land, 6 pennies the mark: 8 marks butter, 2 ells wattmell.

Erich of Eide, 6 marks 2 ures land, 6 pennies the mark: 2 pund 6 marks butter, 12 ells wattmell.

Mogenns of Funne, 2 ures land: 2 marks butter.

Willum of Strand, 1 mark land, 6 pennies the mark: 8 marks butter, 2 ells wattmell.

Helgier in Strandt, 1½ marks land, 6 pennies the mark: ½ pund butter, 3 ells wattmell.

Summa of the above landskyld of Hiettlannd: 136 punds 12½ marks butter and 1,121½ ells wattmell.

Riksarkivet (Oslo), group vii, no.14 (in Danish). Copy in SA, SA.2/182. Printed in L. Daae, 'Om fru Gorvel Fadersdatter og hendes Norske jordegods', *Historisk Tidsskrift* (Norwegian), 3R, vol. 3, 1895, pp.264-8.

43. 12 September 1582

'Contract betuene umquhill Gregorious in Sandfrie and Erasmus Ollasone.'

The original is not known to exist. One of the writs taken from Ninian Neven's house in Yell on 24 August 1624: *RPC*, xiv, p.735.

44. Ayith, 21 September 1582

Disposition by David Strang in Binstay to an honourable man Lourence Bruce of Cultemalyndeis, of 1 mark 3 ures land, 9 pennies the mark, in the isle of Quhalsay.

David affixes his seal, and procures the signet of Johne Murray in Stennydaill and the subscription of Mr Robert Chene of Over Ure. Witnesses: Olay Nicholsone, Charles Demptstar, reader at Aythsting, and Johne Colwyng and Henrie Wardlaw, messenger, servants of Laurence.

GH. According to the docket the land was in Simbuster.

45. Burgh, 13 October 1582

Disposition by Magnus Magnussone in Howland, taking the burden for Anna Magnusdochter, his sister, to an honourable man Hew Sinclare of Burgh, of 1 mark land, 12 pennies the mark, of Cattfirth in the parish of Nesting.

Because he cannot write Magnus draws his 'mark usitt and wount'. Witnesses: Edward Thomassone of Garth, Magnus Burgur, Waltir Ridpeth and Andro Martyne, servant of the earl of Orknay.

SA, SC.12/65/1/16. Marks of Magnus Magnussone and Edward of Garth.

46. Edinburgh, 13 October 1582

Summons of court of session in action at instance of Laurence Bruce of Cultemalindyis against Williame Sinclair of Uyea, for spoliation, on 4 and 5 October 1582, from Laurence's barnyard of Colvadaill in Unst, which had pertained to him in heritage for two years or thereby, of 60 thraves of bere and 120 thraves of oats, with the fodder, valued at £120 and £180 respectively.

SRO, CS.15/36. No decreet has been traced. On 18 May 1583 Manis Colvidell, Rasmus in Colvidell, Manis Rasmussone, Walter Smyth, David Reid, David Flescheour, James Winrhame and James Broun were summoned as witnesses; and on 28 June 1583 Walter Smyth in Unst, William Gardie there, Androw Smyth there, Magnus Colvaddell, Androw Polsoune, Ulay Stephansoun, Silvester, James Broun, John Nicolsoun, John Andersoun, David Reid, Robert Shorthouse, David Flescheour, David Hamiltoun and James Winrhame were summoned as witnesses. On 23 May 1584 the lords of council gave commission to Mr Jerome Chene, archdeacon and commissary of Yetland, Mr Robert Chene of Wallay and James Hay, vicar of Unst, conjunctly, to examine witnesses at Scalloway. On another undated sheet, described as 'the laird of Cultemalyndeis memoriall', Thomas Boyne and James Sutherland in Fetlar appear to be nominated as further commissioners.

47. Kirkwall, 31 December 1582

Assignation by Robert, earl of Orknaye, lord Yetland, to an honourable man Lourence Bruce of Cultemalyndeis, his brother, of a charter by Culbene Ormissone of Symbuster to said Robert, of 16 marks land, 9 pennies the mark, in the town of Symbister in the isle of Quhalsay, dated 7 July 1582 (see nos. 38-9). Robert acknowledges payment by Lourence of 36 angel nobles gold in weight.

Subscribed 'Orknay'. Witnesses: Mr Robert Chene of Walay, Patrik Montetht, Mr Johnne Dischingtoun and Oliver Kennedy, servants of the earl, with divers others.

SA, GD.144/28/9 (parchment) and GD.144/113/25 (paper).

48. Widlon, 10 February 1582-3

Disposition by Erasmus and Michell Lowrensonis of Ovirgill, brothers german, with consent of Maryeoun Lowrinisdochter, their sister, and of Maryeoun Johnisdochter, their mother, and Erasmus Jhonnsone, her present spouse, to an honourable man and their good friend Hew Sinclair of Burghe, of 1½ marks land, 12 pennies the mark, in Sandveik in the isle of Quhalsay.

Because Erasmus and Michell have no seals or signets they procure the signets of Magnus Hansoun of Gillisbrek and William

Mansoun in Neip, together with the merchant marks of Adame Alexanderson in Widlon and Edvard Thomassoun in Garth, and the subscription of Piter Symsoun, reader at Nesting. Witnesses: Robert Atchesoun, Walter Ridpethe, Magnus Firsall and Ener Nicholsoun, with divers others.

SC.12/65/1/15.

49. Cultemalyndeis, 8 April 1583

Assignation by Mr Robert Chene of Wyrie to an honourable man Lourence Bruce of Cultemalyndeis of a wadset by Eduard Sinclair to the said Mr Robert, of 14 marks land, 8 pennies the mark, in Scalloway in Yetland, and 8 marks land, 8 pennies the mark, in Laxfirth in the parish of Tyngwall, dated at Sandness on (blank) 1582. The lands are to be possessed by Mr Robert until Eduard pays him 14 angel nobles. The lands may be redeemed by Mr Robert on payment of £100 to Lourence of which sum Mr Robert acknowledges receipt.

Witnesses: Williame Bruce, Henrie Wardlaw, messenger, and Magnus Flais, servants of Lourence, with divers others.

SA, D.10/12/1.

50. Borday Sound in Norway, 20 June 1583

'[Disposition by] Sunyevo Regnenisdochter, alias Nesbit, to her gudsir's brother Peter Nesbit of Kirkabyster, [of] 2 marks in Suirsetter in Delting.

'Seals of honest and famous men, Donald Frysell of Sandweik, William Spence, son and heir to Henry Spence of Houlland, and David Spenss of Gloup (all still attached. ...). Witnesses: Johne Frysell of Hascoussye, James Nesbit, younger, and Nychell Scott, with others.'

The original is not known to exist. The above abstract, by J. Storer Clouston, is in OA, D.23, Notebook 4, p.66. Clouston illustrates seals of Donald Frysell, William Spence and David Spence. According to a note by Gilbert Goudie the deed bore 'a jotting in Norse on the back: "thez er breff om Sjorsatr"' (notebook at Braefield House, Dunrossness).

51. Skalloway, 26 June 1583

Public instrument narrating that Cristiphor Olauesone in Geill compeared in presence of Malcolm Sinclar, notary public, and, with consent of Peter Michaelsone, his brother's son, made an honourable man Hew Sinclar of Burght assignee to all his goods, with reservation of liferent, in return for good deed and gratitude. Cristiphor undertook not to sell any of his goods without special licence from Hew, who was to stand his good friend in all time coming. Afterwards Peter Olauesone compeared, who, taking the burden for (blank) Olauesone, his brother, Peter Michelsone and Mathew in Geyhous, resigned in favour of an honourable man Hew Sinclar of Burght all title or claim to their lands in the Skeireis, namely: Peter

Olauesone and his brother, 4½ marks land; Peter Michaelsone, ½ mark land; and Mathew in Geyhous, 1 mark between him and his brothers.

Witnesses: William in Neip, Alexander Duf, Magnus in Gillesbrek, Adame in Vidlane, Eduard Sinclar, James Swanie and Walter Redpath, with divers others.

SA, SC.12/65/1/17.

52. 8 July 1583

'Few charter [by Robert, earl of Orkney], granted to Andrew Gifford of Wathersta ..., wherin he reserves for his oun use, 2 or three roums in the house of Wethersta.'

The original is not known to exist. Referred to in T. Gifford, 'A Description of the Isls of Zetland ...', c.1733, p.60 (in library of Society of Antiquaries of Scotland, ms. 563). Cf. T. Gifford, *An Historical Description of the Zetland Islands*, London 1786, p.40.

53. Brow in Dunrosnes, 7 August 1583

Obligation by James Sinclair of Brow to John Hammiltoun, burgess of Edinburgh, for £128 7s. (in settlement of accounts owing to each other, especially of the last 500 merks due by John to Robert, earl of Orknay). In payment James assigns butter (at £8 10s. per barrel), oil (at £6 per barrel), 'oxin or gild kow hyd' (at 16s. per hide), and 'coipman' dollars (at £1 each) to the value of the foresaid sum.

Witnesses: James Dalzell, Williame Thomsoun, burgess of Edinburgh, Andro Marteine, servant of the earl of Orknay, and Adam Sinclair, son of James.

SRO, RD.1/22, f.145.

54. 26 August 1583

'Tack and assedation for the space of 19 years by the earl of Orkney and Zetland in favor of Laurence Bruce of Cultmalindies, his heirs etc., of a piece of land in the room of Scatstay, with houses, etc., in the parish of Delting. ... And on foot of same deed, conveyance of the said tack by the said Laurence Bruce to Andrew Hawick of Scatstay, dated 31 October 1591.'

The original is not known to exist. The above abstract is in SA, D.6/194/12 (Inventory of titles of the estate of Busta, in Messrs Greigs' possession, 1840).

55. Croce Kirk of Dunrossness, 28 October 1583

'[Disposition by] Henry Magnusson of Voe to Arthur Sinclair of Aith, [of] 3 mark (8d.) in Hosweik in Dunrossness.

'Seals: Lawrence Sinclair of Goit and James Sinclair of Brow, and marks of William Androssone of Brek and Roulf in Ringista.'

The original is not known to exist. The above abstract, by J. Storer Clouston, is in OA, D.23, Notebook 4, p.66. A transcription of the document, by Gilbert Goudie, gives Robert Archibald as a witness (notebook in Braefield House, Dunrossness). Goudie illustrates the marks of William Androssone and Roulf in Ringista.

56. Burghe, 1 November 1583

Bond by James Sutherland in Eistbister in Quhalsay in favour of Hew Sinclair of Burghe and his heirs.

Be it kend till all men be thir presentis, me James Suther[land] in Eistbister within the ile of Quhalsay, fouldrie and lordschip of Yetland, with consent and assent of my spous Bessye Williamisdochter, oncoactit [or] compellit or cinisterlie urgit heirto, bot of frie motive and benivolent guid will, for the guid deid done and schawin unto me and my said spous, and to be done, to haif frelie and wrevocablie, bot onye stop or clame to be maid or allegit in all tymes heireftir, be my selff, my said spous or onye utheris in our names, to haif giffin and grantit, and be thir presentis gevis and grantis to ane honorabill man and my speceall freynd Hew Sinclair of Burghe, his eldest sone Harye and thair assignais, for the causes abonewrittin, the fourt pennye of all my guidis and geir, movable and onmovable, present or to cum, and be thir presentis gevis and grantis the said fourt pennye as is abonwrittin, to the said Hew and his aforsaidis, mackand him, his sone entres thairto ather in onye tyme of my lyiff or eftir my deceis, referring the samyn in the said Hewis adoptioun, bindand and obleisand me and my said wyiff and all myn and hiris eftircumaris in straitest forme of obligatioun that may be devysit, and violatioun of myn and hir faythis and famis, never to cum in contrair of this my lauchfull and irrevocable gift or onie poynt thairoff, bot sall warrand, acquyet, manteyn, saiff and defend the said Hew and his aforsaidis and thair assignais haveand thair tytle allanerlie as is abone [*torn*] stop, lett or impediment to be maid be me, my [*torn*] quhatsumevir, and siclyck I the said James bindis [*torn*] presentis to be ane faythfull and trew servand induring the tyme of my lyif to the said Hew and his airis and to nane uther, the king, my lord and my father being reservit, and I the said Hew bindis and ob[*torn*] me and my airis to stand the said James guid freynd and maister a[nd] to do for him in all his honest and leifull causes as becumis ane mai[ster] to do for his servand.

In witness of the quhilk and of ilk poynt abone wreittin I haif drawin heirto my mercheand usit mark, at Burghe the first daye off November Jaj Vc fourscoir thrie yeris, befoir thir witnesses: Edvard Sinclair, taxman of Bulyesetter, Walter Rippett, and David Lasoun, wreittar heiroff, with his subscriptioun manuall at my request and my awen hand led at the pen be him becaus I culd nocht wreit my selff.

[*mark*]
James Sutherland with my hand led at the

pen by David Lasoun at my command
David Lasoun as witness to the premises
Walter Redpaith as witnes

SA, SC.12/65/1/1a.

57. Widlon, 16 November 1583

Disposition by Nicholl Jacobsoun, with consent of Bryid Nicholisdochter, his mother, to an honourable and discreet man Hew Sinclair of Brught, of 1 mark land, (blank) pennies the mark, in Tronasetter in the parish of Lunasting.

Because Nicholl has no signet of his own he procures the signet and merchant marks of Magnus Hansoun in Gillesbrek, Adame Alexanderissone in Widlon and Nicholl Erasmussoun in Levaneip. Witnesses: Edvard Sinclair, tacksman of Bulyesetter, Walter Redpaith, Robert in Gillesbrek, Magnus Makbeythsoun and David Lasoun, with divers others.

SA, GD.144/262/8.

58. Edinburgh, 13 February 1583-4

Bond of caution by Mr Robert Chene of Valay and James Mauchane, burgess of Edinburgh, for Mr Jherome Chene, archdeacon of Yetland, presented by the lords of council to the king to be commissary in Yetland, that Jherome will 'lelelie and trewlie minister in the said office ... to all our soveraine lord liegeis' and account for the quot silver of all testaments confirmed by him and his other intromissions yearly to the commissaries of Edinburgh.

SRO, CS.1/3/2, f.218.

59. Holyroodhouse, 23 February 1583-4

Gift to Mr Jerome Chene, archdeacon of Yetland, of the escheat of the goods of the deceased Margaret Reid of Burgh, who was put to the horn by virtue of letters in the four forms at the instance of Jerome for non-payment to him of the fruits of the archdeaconry, and died thereat.

RSS, viii, no.1871.

60. Edinburgh, 26 March 1584

Letter from James, king of Scots, to Friderick, king of Denmark, etc., on behalf of Robert Cheyn, son of Sir Patrick Cheyn of Essilmonth, who acquired some time ago for himself and for one life afterwards the enjoyment (*usumfructum*) of the lands of Wallay from Goorula Fairs-daughter, relict of the lord of Craigholme, sole heir of her father in said lands, but who now finds that the said lady has surrendered the lands to King Friderick. Although Robert was ready to render the dues yearly, lest he be removed from a possession confirmed for many years past by King Friderick, he thought that he would have easier access to the king if he was commended by James's letters. James asks that Robert may have the lands subject to just conditions, be able to return to his own country and give his attention to the lands, which without cultivation are hardly of any use, and that John Londenau, captain of the castle of Bergen in Norway, who required an increase of 54 thalers in the annual rent, may be stopped from proceedings to the prejudice of Robert's enjoyment of the lands.

Rigsarkivet (Copenhagen): Tyske Kancellis Udenrigske Afdeling, Speciel del: Skotland, pt.2. In Latin. Calendared version in *47th Report of the Deputy Keeper of the Public Records*, 1885, Appendix, p.23.

61. Scalloway, 17 May 1584

'Disposition by William Sinclair of Ustaness to his brother Arthur Sinclair of Aith, of three merks land in Houss, in Burra. ...

'Witnesses: Thomas Bayne [*rectius* Boyne], indweller in Scalloway, Patrik Hog, burgess of Kirkcaldy, and others.'

The original is not known to exist. The above abstract, by Francis Grant, is in OSD, *SN*, 28 October 1893.

62. Edinburgh, 20 August 1584

Presentation of Mr William Hay, son of George Hay of Freuchy (*rectius* Freuchny), to the archdeaconry of Yetland, vacant by decease of Mr Jerome Chene. The bishop of Orknay and Yetland, 'or uther our soverane lordis commissioner in ecclesiasticall caussis within the dyocie of Orknay and Yetland', is directed to examine William and admit him if found qualified to serve as a minister, or in case of his insufficiency to report the same to the king and privy council within six months, that another more qualified person may be presented.

RSS, viii, no.2289.

63. Edinburgh, 24 August 1584

Confirmation of the gift, presentation and collation to Mr Thomas Chene of the archdeaconry of Yetland, vacant by demission of Mr Jerome Chene, with gift of new for life, decerning that the presentation given by the king with advice of the deceased John, earl of Mar, regent, upon the foresaid demission, with the admission and collation following thereupon, shall be good, valid and sufficient to Mr Thomas for possession of the archdeaconry, notwithstanding any objections.

RSS, viii, no.2345.

64. Neip, 28 September 1584

Disposition by Magnus Thomassoun in Kirkebuster, eldest son and one of the lawful heirs of the deceased Thomas in Kirkebuster, to an honourable man Hew Sinclair of Burghe, of his 6 ures of land, 9 pennies the mark, in Kirkebuster in the parish of Nesting, and also 'ane bruther part' of the lands to be inherited after the death of Annye Magnusdochter, his mother, putting Hew in his place as eldest brother 'to lous out' the sisters.

Magnus draws his merchant mark, and procures the signets of William Mansoun in Neip and Alexander Duff in Skellistaw, with the merchant mark of John Mansoun in Grunyeafirth. Witnesses: Magnus Makbeythsoun, Hutcheon Kirktoun and David Lasoun, with divers others.

SA, SC.12/65/1/21. Seals of William Mansoun and Alexander Duff.

65. 3 November 1584

'Charter of wadset by James Sinclair of Brew, to his brother-in-law Arthur Sinclair of Aith, over the land of Brew for an annual rent of £40. ...

'Witnesses: Patrick Hog, burgess of Kirkcaldy, Andrew Watson, Andrew Mowat of Hugoland, Laurence Sinclair of Goat, and divers others.'

The original is not known to exist. The above abstract, by Francis Grant, is in OSD, *SN*, 28 October 1893. According to another abstract, by Gilbert Goudie, Watson's christian name is Alexander (notebook in Braefield House, Dunrossness).

66. Burghe, 20 November 1584

Disposition by Erasmus and Michell Lowrensonis of Ovirgill, brothers german, with consent of Maryeoun Lowrenisdochter, their sister, and Nichoill Olaysoun, her spouse, and of Maryeoun Johnisdochter, their mother, liferenter with them of half the lands underwritten, to an honourable man Hew Sinclair of Burghe, of their 3 marks land, 12 pennies the mark, in the town of Ovirgill in the parish of Lunasting, with power to Hew to 'lous' and redeem all their lands in the town of Overgill wadset or sold by any of their predecessors, and not offered to them as 'rychteous aires and roithismen'.

Because they have no signets of their own they procure those of Magnus Hansoun of Gillisbrek, William Mansoun in Neip and Alexander Duff in Skellinstaw, with the merchant marks of Eduard Thomassoun in Garth and Erasmus in Asueik. Witnesses: Magnus Erasmussoun, Walter Ridpethe and David Lasoun, with divers others.

SA, SC.12/65/1/20. Marks of Edward in Garthe and Erasmus in Asueik.

67. Stoiffabrek in Hildisweck, 12 January 1584-5

Deed comprising: (1) disposition by Nicholl Andersone, and Marion, Bryid, Agnes and Kathereine Andersdotteris, all heirs after their father's mother, with consent of Enar Thomassone in Fyeld and Enar Thomassone of Ure, husbands of Marion and Bryid, to a famous and discreet man Androw Mowat of Hougaland, and his heirs male of the surname Mowat, of their 2 marks land, 9 pennies the mark, in Houssayord, and 1 mark land, 6 pennies the mark, in (blank) in the town of Ure; and (2) disposition by Enar Thomassone of Ure, with consent of Bryde Androisdochter, his spouse, to the said Androw Mowat of 1 mark land, 9 pennies the mark, in Houssayord, and 1 mark land, 6 pennies the mark, in (blank); all forenamed lands lying contiguous in the town of Ure in Eschenes in the parish of Northmaving. The disponers bind themselves not to sell or wadset any of the lands they possess in the town of Ure except to Androw Mowat, and if they do so ignorantly Androw shall have the right to redeem them as if they were his own.

Because they have no seals or signets they procure the signet of Laurence Tulloch of Hildisweck, and the merchant marks of Androu Smyth, Olaue Smyth, Olaue in Videfyeld and Johne in Awisgarth. Witnesses: Olaue Neilssone, Gregorius and Mawnis in Leaskoill, Olaue in Muron, Mawnis in Brekon, 'etc.'

SA, GD.144/21/10. The document is unsubscribed.

68. Edinburgh, 13 January 1584-5

Decreet of court of session in action at instance of Mr Robert Chene of Valay against Andro Mowat of Hugoland, for delivery of an acquittance by Andro Hawik of Skatsta to Robert of all sums of 'money, insycht, plenissing, cornis, cattell, dettis and utheris actiounis and clamis' which Andro Hawik might have craved of Robert by the death of Vincentius Hawik, his father. The acquittance had been subscribed by Andro Hawik and his curator, with consent and authority of Laurence Bruce of Cultemalindy, foud of Yetland, and was in the hands of Andro Mowat.

The lords of council decern the defender to deliver the acquittance.

SRO, CS.7/99, ff.190-1.

69. 15 January 1584-5

'Ane letter of interchange maid be Petter Nisbit of Kircabister with Swane Johnson of Windhous, tuicheing the interchangeing of ane merk land in Setter for ane merk land in Howll.'

The original is not known to exist. One of the writs taken from Ninian Neven's house in Yell on 24 August 1624 (*RPC*, xiv, p.773).

70. Petcorthie, 28 January 1584-5

Tack by Mr William Hay, archdeacon of Yetland, to James Hay, his brother, of the fruits, teind sheaves, landmails, bow teind, boat teind, wool teind, etc., and all lands, holms, skerries, etc., pertaining to the archdeaconry, for 3 years from the date hereof, for £240 yearly.

Witnesses: Mr Robert Wilkie, regent in St Leonard's College, William Barclay of the Rynd, Thomas Barclay, his brother, and Walter Hay.

Erroll charters, section I, no.1068. One seal.

71. Edinburgh, 26 February 1584-5

Decreet of court of session in action at instance of Mr Robert Chene in Valay against Andro Hawik of Skattista, for completion of a blank confirming an obligation by Andro to Robert, by which Andro renounces all title of right or kindness he has to the lands of Valay, Weisdaill, and their goods, in favour of Robert, and also constitutes Robert his assignee in the redemption of all lands wadset by Andro, especially the lands of Skattista, and also binds himself not to wadset or rent out any of his lands and heritages without Robert's consent, and consent of 'his bairns lauchfull, half brethir to the said Andro', and to set no longer tacks of the said lands than are already set. Because the obligation 'wes not sa perfytlie formit as neid requires, thairfoir the said Andro be the tenor of the said obligatioun grantit him to haif ressaiffit ane blank subscrivit be the said Mr Robert, quhairupoun the said obligatioun and contract betuix thame suld haif bene fillit'.

The lords of council decern the defender to exhibit and produce the said blank.

SRO, CS.7/99, ff.299-300. There is an extract decreet in SA, D.10/45, and letters, dated 4 March 1584-5, charging Andro Hawik to comply with the decreet, under pain of rebellion (SA, D.10/46).

72. Edinburgh, 9 March 1584-5

Bond of caution by John Gordon of Petlurg for Mr Robert Cheine, who has been presented by the lords of council 'to the commissarie of Yetland and ilis thairof, that he sall lilie and trewlie minister justice to all our soveraine lordis liegeis', keep the instructions and injunctions given to him by the commissaries of Edinburgh, and account for the quot silver of all small testaments which are confirmed 'ains in the yeir or efter, as he salbe commandit be the saidis lordis'.

SRO, CS.1/3/2, f.255.

73. Holyroodhouse, 9 April 1585

Confirmation of the provision by Adam, bishop of Orknay and Yetland, to Mr William Lauder, minister at the parish kirk of Settlar (*rectius* Fetlar), of the vicarage thereof, with the fruits, etc., as the provision made on 30 April 1563 purports, with the collation and institution following thereupon; and of new gives to William the said vicarage with fruits, etc., manse, glebe and kirkland for life.

SRO, PS.1/52, f.76.

74. Berrie, 25 September 1585 (at 8 a.m.)

Note of assignation by Androw Umphray, elder, at Skalloway bankis, to Androw Umphray, his eldest son, of: (1) the 21 years to run of his tack of 27 marks king's land called Berrie in the parish of Tingwall; and (2) his moveable goods and gear, corn, cattle, oxen, ky, sheep, horses, mares, plenishings, etc., presently in his possession, and also of all goods and gear which 'sall happin to fall to said Androw Umphra elder throw deceis of umquhil Jhone Umphra, his father, and also efter his mother quhen it sall happin', and also all right of lands to be inherited by him from his father, with reservation of 'the use, handling and excressence' of half of the said moveables to Jonatt Jamesoun, his spouse, for her lifetime, providing that she finds caution 'that the stok of the half of the guids intromittit with be hir be furthcumand to hir said sonis utilitie eftir hir deceis'. Androw Umphray, elder, reserves the power to annul the assignations at any time by payment of £10 to his son.

Witnesses: William Sinclair in Skallowa bankis, Robert Wilsoun there and Thomas Auchinlek, notary public.

SRO, NP.1/36, ff.17-8.

75. Ayth, 19 October 1585

Tack by Lawrence Bruce of Cowltmalindeis to William Bruce, his wellbeloved and trusty servant, of his 32 marks land, 9 pennies the mark, in the town of Simbister, with his holm called Winderholm in Quhailsaysound, in the isle of Quhailsay, for William's lifetime, with entry at Allhallowmass 1585, gersum and mail free as his fee for service, 'provyding alwayis the said William remane and trewlie serve me during the space abone wretin and na utherwayis'.

Witnesses: Mr Robert Cheyn of Ure, commissary of Yetland, John Findlasoun, servant of Laurence, and Thomas Auchinlek, notary public.

SA, GD.144/265/3.

76. Lunay, 17 November 1585

Disposition by Mareoun Ollaisdochtir, with consent of Thomas Porteus, her spouse, to the right honourable Lawrence Bruce of Cultmalindeis, of

½ mark land, 9 pennies the mark, in Simbister in Quhailsay in the parish of Nesting and Lunesting.

Mareoun subscribes with her hand led at the pen by Thomas Auchinlek, notary. Because she has no seal she procures those of honourable men: Mr Robert Cheyn of Ure, commissary of Yeitland, and David Strang in Beinsta. Witnesses: Mr Robert Cheyn, commissary of Yeitland, Piter Symsoun, reader at Nesting, David Strang in Beinsta and Thomas Auchinlek, notary public.

SA, GD.144/32/2.

77. Voisgarth, 13 December 1585 (at 10 a.m.)

Note of instrument of sasine in favour of Agnes Mowatt, following on disposition by Bartholomew Strang of Voisgarth, her spouse, with consent of James Strang, his son, of the liferent of 12 marks land of Voisgarth in the island of Unst.

Witnesses: Laurence Bruce of Cultmalindeis, Mr Robert Chein of Ure, commissary of Yetland, Peter Maxwell, minister of Unst, and Thomas Auchinlek, notary public.

SRO, NP.1/36, f.18.

78. Newhouse of Seilyesettir, 13 December 1585 (at 3 p.m.)

Note of instrument of sasine in favour of Cristian Sinclair, in fulfilment of contract between Bartholomew Strang of Voisgairthe and David Sinclair of Huntoun for the marriage of James Strang, son of Bartholomew, to Cristian, eldest daughter of David, of a liferent interest in 36 marks land of Newhouse of Seilyesettir in the island of Unst, with reservation of the free tenement to Bartholomew. Sasine delivered to William Smyth in Scravilt in Bailyeista, procurator for Cristian.

Witnesses: Antony McKessoun in Failyie in Seilyeasettir, Magnus Mansoun in Seitter, Henrik Ulf, burgess of Burrein, and Thomas Auchinlek, notary public.

SRO, NP.1/36, f.18.,

79. House (*aula*) of William Manisoun in Neip, 3 February 1585-6 (at 9 a.m.)

Notarial instrument narrating that Erasmus Ollowsoun, lawful son of the deceased Ollaw Androsoun in Skallesta, with consent of Margaret Nicolisdochtir, his mother, and Agnes Androwsdochter, his father's sister, has renounced in favour of the right honourable Hew Sinclair of Bruche all his right to the lands and 'lows guidis and gere' which may pertain to him by the decease of Androw Ollawsoun in Skallesta, his grandfather.

Because Hew had no writ nor security upon the said disposition, 'bot that the samin wes done befoir certaine famous witnessis convenit for the tyme', Erasmus, with consents foresaid, dispones and assigns his rights to the said lands, etc., to Hew.

Witnesses: William Manisoun in Neip, David Lawsoun, servant of said Hew, Thomas Cheyne, son of Mr Robert Cheyn, commissary of Yeitland, and Thomas Auchinlek, notary public.

SA, SC.12/65/1/22.

80. Bruche, 5 February 1585-6

Decreet arbitral and agreement following submission by an honourable man Hew Sinclair of Bruche, on the one part, and Agnes Androwsdochtir, lawful daughter of the deceased Androw Ollawsoun in Skellista, with consent of Androw Nicolsoun in Skellista, her spouse, on the other part, to the judgement of William in Neip, Alexander Duff in Skellista, Erasmus in Eswik, Alexander Strang in Eiswik and Edward Sinclair in Builyeasettir, concerning the lands and 'lous guidis' which should appertain to Erasmus Ollowsoun, son of the deceased Ollaw Androwsoun, by decease of Androw Olawsoun in Skellista, his grandfather. The said judges find 'that thar wes the tyme of the said umquhill Androw Ollowsonis deceis foure mark land and a half, xij d. the mark, lyand in Skellista within the parochin of Nesting'. Therefore, in accordance with the laws of the country, they decern that 2 marks land and 2 ures appertain to Hew as donator and assignee of Erasmus, and that the other 2 marks land and 2 ures appertain to Agnes, and that the movable goods should be equally divided between Hew and Agnes.

The judges affix their marks. Hew Sinclair signs, and Agnes Androwsdochter and Andro Nicolsoun sign with their hands led at the pen. Witnesses: Alexander Ross and David Lawsoun, servants of said Hew, and Thomas Auchinlek, notary public.

SA, SC.12/65/1/22 (on reverse of no. 79).

81. Holyroodhouse, 16 March 1585-6

Ratification of presentation on 20 October 1584 by Robert, earl of Orknay, of Mr William Hay, son of George Hay of Freuchnye, to the archdeaconry of Yetland, with manse, glebe, kirklands, etc., vacant in the hands of Robert, as patron, by decease of Mr Hierome Chene. The king confirms the presentation, admission, collation and institution of Mr William, and directs the lords of council to grant Mr William letters in four forms causing him to be answered of all teindsheaves, fruits, rents, etc.

SRO, PS.1/53, f.138.

82. Edinburgh, 16 April 1586

Decreet of court of session in action at instance of Alexander Kincaid, brother of Alexander (*rectius* John) Kincaid of Warristoun, against John Murray in Stanisdaill, Edward Sinclair of Scolloway, Christopher Lowrenstoun, Andro Wischart, Olay Christopherson, and all other feuars, tenants, tacksmen, parishioners, and other intromitters for payment of the fruits, rents, teinds, etc., of the vicarage of Wauss, manse, glebe and kirkland thereof. Alexander was provided to the vicarage by Adam, bishop of Orknay, on 21 June 1567, and has been in possession and uplifted the fruits, etc., for the past 18 years or thereby.

The lords of council decern the defenders to pay to Alexander the fruits, etc., of the vicarage, manse, glebe and kirkland.

SRO, CS.7/103, ff.338-9.

83. Edinburgh, 21 April 1586

Summons of court of session in action at instance of Hew Sinclair of Burgh against James Christopherson in Papay, tenant and occupier of 6 marks land in Nether Sound in the parish of Weisdaile, and Ollaw Mansoun of Neboun, tenant and occupier of 3 marks land, 12 pennies the mark, of Gluss in the parish of Northmevin, for removal at Whitsunday 1585.

SRO, CS.15/40. On 2 December 1586 the lords of council admit a protest by the defenders on the grounds that neither Hew nor any in his name had compeared to pursue the summons (SRO, CS.7/109, f.133).

84. Edinburgh, 30 April 1586

Decreet of court of session in action at instance of Mr William Lauder and James Lauder, his son, against Daniell Hawick, for fulfilment of a decreet of court, dated 15 June 1583, before Harie Stewart, master of Orknay, having commission from Robert, earl of Orknay and Yetland, against Daniell, which found that a charter, dated 17 March 1580-1, by Andro Hawick, for himself, and taking the burden for Daniell, his brother, of 9 marks land 'in the southe syde of the ile of Yell', for 46 dollars, granting the same to have been received and paid, 'to be gude and weill gevin'. The charter had been witnessed by Petir Maxwell and Robert Wrycht, and subscribed by Daniell himself, thereby ratifying and approving his brother's selling thereof. Therefore, the court had ordained that the possession already received by James Lauder should stand in effect.

The lords of council decern the defender to observe, keep and fulfil the said decreet of court.

SRO, CS.7/103, f.426. See no. 137.

85. Bruche, 29 July 1586

Precept by Robert, earl of Orknay, lord of Yeitland, and justice general thereof, relating that Mr Robert Cheyn of Ure and Androw Hawik of Scatstay had been summoned at the instance of the tenants of Valay and Valay guidis, in an action of double poinding, to compear before Robert at Skalloway bankis on 22 July instant to exhibit their titles to the said lands. Robert Cheyn had compeared and had produced a letter of tack of Valay and Valay guidis by the king of Denmark, dated 18 October 1584, with a confirmation by the king of Scotland thereupon, together with divers decreets and precepts of poinding in his favour. Androw Hawik had also compeared, and since he had produced nothing that might 'cut away' these titles it had been decerned that the tenants should pay their landmails for the crop 1586 to Robert Cheyn, and annually thereafter. Robert commands his officers to charge the tenants to do so and to poind their goods if they fail, and commands all his underfouds and officers under whose bailliary the lands lie to keep Robert Cheyne in peaceable possession.

SA, D.10/10. According to endorsements the document was produced at courts held at Quhitnes on 14 August 1587 and Skallowaybankis on 30 July 1601.

86. Burravo in Yell, 8 August 1586

Disposition by Olawe, Lorawnce, Mechell and Symond Manssonis, brothers german, with consent of their spouses and heirs, to an honourable man and their good friend Lorawnce Bruce of Cultmaleyndeis, of their 1½ marks land, 12 pennies the mark, in Glus in the parish of Northmaveing.

Because they have no seal of their own they procure those of James Suddirland, Olave Suddirland and Edwartt in Otstay, with the subscription of Pettir Maxuell, minister of Unst. Witnesses: Williame Bruce, Andro Smyth, James Burger and Alexander Isbuster with divers others.

SA, GD.144/66/19 (on parchment, unsubscribed). There is an almost identical document on paper in SA, GD.144/7/32 where the surname of the granters is given as 'Mangnissonis', and Northmaveing is described as a 'foldrie' rather than a parish. The seal of James Sutherland is present.

87. Holyroodhouse, 2 November 1586

Licence to Mr Thomas Cheyne, archdeacon of Yetland, to remain in foreign parts until September 1587, and forbidding action against him in the meantime for non-residence at the kirk of the archdeaconry, as it has not been possible for Thomas to get knowledge of charges and executions made against him at the instance of Mr William Hay, claimant to the archdeaconry, 'especially in consideration of the grit troublis and civile debaitis ovir everie quhair, ather within the realm of France, or in the partis circum-adjacent to the toun of Geneva, quhair Thomas hes resortit and presently dois resort for the attending to guid letters, and speciallie for the trew and sinceir doctrine of Christis evangell presentlie professit within this realm, quhairwith he intends to proffit his subjectis as a proffitable member of Christis kirk'.

SRO, PS.1/54, ff.102-3.

88. Gerde in Redeførd parish, 4 December 1586

Agreement between Aasi Skott and Gilbert Skott, and James Nysbitt, concerning his intromissions with their affairs.

In anno 1586, on the fourth day of December, we the underwritten were in Gerde in Redeførd parish: that is to say Willom Monssøn of Gerde, lawrightman [*laurettis mand*] in Ønyst, and umbothsman for the underwritten brothers Aassi and Gilbert Skott, and with him Salamon Schott and Lauffrens Schott, father-brothers of the before-named Aassi and Gilbert, and with them Peder Nysbitt of Kirckebusted and Jamis Burgar, serjeant [*sergenn*] in Jella, and Mons Nysbitt of Congnesaatther. We make known to all that upon the said day we heard and saw a friendly agreement between Aassi Schott and Gylbert Schott on the one side, and Jamis Nysbitt, their stepfather, on the other side, about count and reckoning [*cont och regenskab*]between them from the time when the said Jamis Nysbitt married the mother of the said Aassi and Gilbert, Kathrina Mathisdaatter by name, both as regards land rent [*landskyld*] and all other matters outstanding between them. And this was their agreement: that the said Aassi should receive and enjoy both his own part and his brother Gylbert Scott's part, from the said Jamis Nysbitt; and since the said Jamis had built a new house [*stoffue*], and other houses, where none were before, for the use of the said Aassi and Gilbert, hence we, the above-named men, judged before God and ourselves, that the said Jamis had done well, and had outlaid and spent more on the said house than he owed them, but since they made a friendly agreement with hand and mouth, the said Jamis would not reckon the highest price, but that each should stand against the other, the houses which he had built and the rent which he owed them, but as for the corn which the said Jamis received and enjoyed with their mother, and which the said Aassi and Gilbert, with their sister, Besi Scott, were brought up on, we, the above-named, found that in whatever year or time the said Jamis Nysbitt shall flit from their land in the said Gierde, then the said Jamis shall work the whole homefield [*winne thett helle tuun*], with his own corn, folk and implements, and thereupon give to the said Aassi, Gilbert and Besi one-half part of the corn, and the other half to himself.

That this be true here under are appended our signatures and seals and marks; and whereas the said Aassi and Gilbert Scott have no seal of their own, they have asked the honourable gentleman and good friend to seal this letter on their behalf, that is, herra Magnus Norsko, minister

[*minister*] in Jella, year and day as stated above. [*Signed*:] I Laurens Skott, with my hand.

SRO, RH.6/2869 (in Danish). Printed with translation in *OSR*, i, no. 74.

88a. 5 December 1586

'Disposition [by] Marjory Firsell, Agnes Firsel, and Magnus Ollason and Olla Manson, and Andrew Firsell, their eldest natural brother, to William Bruce of Simbister, of 2 merks land in Brounigarth.'

The original is not known to exist. The above abstract is from an inventory of writs of John Bruce of Sumburgh, made by Robert Hunter of Lunna, his curator, in 1751 (SA, D.8/235/1, p.9). The entry has been crossed out in ink, indicating that the original was 'thrown away as useless'.

89. Edinburgh and Cultmalindeis, 22 and 23 January 1586-7

Contract between Laurence Bruce of Cultmalindeis, on the one part, and Andro Hawik of Scattistay, on the other part, whereby Andro acknowledges receipt from Laurence of 248 angel nobles, and binds himself to dispone to Laurence his 3 lasts land, 8 pennies the mark, of Scattistay in the parish of Delting, and to obtain ratification of this contract by any other person having right or interest in the land. Laurence binds himself to set the said land back to Andro for a yearly payment of 24 angel nobles, three quarters and a half quarter angel noble, and to subscribe a letter of reversion enabling Andro to redeem the land, on payment of 248 angel nobles at the parish kirk of Tingwell, called Sanct Magnus kirk of Tingwell, or at the parish kirk of Perth if Laurence is not in Yetland.

Witnesses: Mr Oliver Colt, advocate, William Watt, his servitor, James Hay, vicar of Unst, and William Bruce in Symbuster.

SRO, RD.1/41, ff.324-6.

90. Cultmalyndeis, 24 January 1586-7

Letters of reversion by Laurence Bruce of Cultmalyndeis in favour of Andro Hawik of Scattistay, by which Laurence binds himself to redeem 3 lasts land, 8 pennies the mark, of Scattistay in the parish of Delting, on payment of 248 angel nobles by Andro at the parish kirk of Tingwell, or at the parish kirk of Perth if Laurence is not in Yetland.

Witnesses: Mr Alexander Bruce, apparent of Cultemalindeis, Williame Bruce, Henrie Wardlaw, Mr Olipheir Colt, and (torn) Watt, with divers others.

SA, GD.144/65/12.

91. 28 February 1586-7
Deposition by Hew Sinclair of Broch to Johne Broun of Weland and William Fermour, notary, following ordinance of the ministers and elders of Kirkwall, that he has never had carnal copulation with Marjorie Sandelandis and has purged himself unconditionally of the said crime.

SA, SC.12/65/1/23. The document is an extract from the court book of the presbytery of Orknay, subscribed by William Fermour, clerk thereto, and John Brown.

92. Holyroodhouse and Kirkwall, 1 and 30 April 1587
'Mr William Hay, archdeacon of Shetland, with consent of Robert, earl of Orkney and Shetland, and Adam, bishop of Orkney, canons and chapter, sets the said archdeanry in tack to his brother James Hay, vicar of Unst, and to his son for their respective lives, for the yearly sum of £140 Scots, reserving the 9 merks glebe land of Tingwall.'

The original is not known to exist. The above abstract, by Thomas Mouat of Garth, is in GH, in ms. entitled 'Memorabilia Zetlandica', c.1800, p.2. £140 is likely to be an mistranscription of £240: see no.70, *supra*, and obligation by Patrik Cheyne of Essilmonth to William Hay, 9 June 1595 (SRO, RD.1/53, f.43).

93. Holyroodhouse and Kirkwall, 3 and 30 April 1587
Tack by James Hay, vicar of Unst, with consent of Robert, earl of Orknay, and Adam, bishop of Orknay, and provost, canons and chapter of the said kirk, to Arthour Sinclair of Ayth and Margaret Colvile, his spouse, and to Arthour's heir for life, and for 19 years thereafter, of the vicarage of Unst with all duties and teinds belonging thereto, for payment of £120 yearly, with reservation of 12 marks land of Virs at the kirk of Norwik 'to be our manss at the said vicarage in all tymes cuming'.

Witnesses: Walter Callender of Bordie, Alexander Kincaid, vicar of Waillis, Adame Bothuell and Bartilmo Kesso, 'servitoris to the said commendator', with divers others. Subscribed by James Hay, vicar of Unst, Adame, bishop of Orknay and Yetland, Hary Colvill, chantor of Orknay, Thomas Swentoun, chantor of Orknay, Mr Hierem Tullocht, subchantor of Orknay, W. Callendar, 'praefectus Orchadensis ac evangelii minister in Orknay', and Mr William Peirsoun, parson of the Croce in Sanday.

GH. Endorsed on back, under Thomas Auchinlek's subscription, as follows: 'Producit at Skalloway bankis the xv of Junij 1597 and registrat'.

94. Lie in Dunrossness, 25 May 1587
'Charter by James Sinclair of Brew, to his brother-in-law Arthur Sinclair of Ayth, of five lasts of land in the parishes of Whiteness and Weisdale. ...

'Witnesses: Laurence Sinclair of Goit, Robert Tulloch, Robert Ratter, and others.'

The original is not known to exist. The above abstract, by Francis Grant, is in OSD, *SN*, 28 October 1893.

95. Olaberry, 31 May 1587

'[Disposition by] Andro Mowat of Hugaland to his well beloved friend and "maeche" ... Peter Nesbit of Kirkabister, and Bryde Sinclair, his spouse, [of] 2 mark (9d.) in Esterhous of Sellafirth, south part of north parish of Yell.

'Seal of Andrew Mowat of Hugaland.'

The original is not known to exist. The above abstract, by J. Storer Clouston, is in OA, D.23, Notebook 4, p.66. Another abstract, by Francis Grant, in OSD, *SN*, 28 October 1893 states that Andro Mowat had the consent of John, his eldest son, that Berald Mowat, Magnus Mowat and John Nilson were witnesses, and describes the seal.

96. Falkland, 17 June 1587

Licence to Andro Mowet in Yetland 'to joyne him selff in mariage with any parteis quhilk he sall finde aggreable to him within the town of Birrhem in Norraway or ellis quhair within the bounds of the said cuntrey'.

Subscribed: 'James R.' and 'Thirlstane'.

Register of Protections, NLS, Adv. MS. 35.5.1.

97. ' ... in Faitlar', 18 July 1587

Feu charter by Robert, earl of Orknay, to William Stewart, his natural son, of 2 lasts of land of Ayth in (cut away), paying annually a barrel of (butter) and two packs of wadmell, or four old dollars for every pack of wadmell, with precept of sasine (cut away). Reference to tacks which William Sinclair of Uistenes has of the said lands.

Witnesses: (cut away), David Skollaw of Toftis, Walter Bruce, sheriff clerk, Edward Skollaw and Tho(cut away).

SA, SC.12/65/3. Several inches have been cut away from the right hand side of the document, perhaps in cancellation. The year is taken from the docket. The lands were almost certainly in Bressay (see no. 129).

98. Scatstay, 28 July 1587 (at 10 a.m.)

Note of instrument of sasine in favour of an honourable man Laurence Bruce of Cultmalindeis, following on disposition by Androw Hawik of Scatstay, dated 23 January 1586-7 at Edinburgh, with precept of sasine directed to William Bruce as bailie (witnessed by Mr Oliver Colt, advocate, William Watt, his servant, James Hay, vicar of Unst, and William Bruce in Simbister), of 3 lasts land, 8 pennies the mark, of Scatstay. Edward Skollaw, procurator for the said Laurence.

Witnesses: James Irrowing in Scatsta, David Garsoun in Yell and Thomas Auchinlek, notary public.

SRO, NP.1/36, f.13.

99. Holyroodhouse, 29 July 1587

Letters by the king, following his general revocation at the age of 21, ordaining a feu charter to be made under the great seal to Patrik Cheyne of Essilmonth, his heirs male bearing the surname and arms of Cheyne, and assignees, of the lands of the archdeaconry of Yetland, viz., the lands of Celebester, Langtayis and How, in the isle of Sanda in Orknay; the town and lands of 38 marks land of Tingwell and Grista and also 3 marks land of Glesbo, 9 marks land of Satter, 15 marks land of Sowtsatter, 6 marks land of Corkesatter, 9 marks land of Northgarth, 7 marks land in Steinsweill, 12 marks land in Howland, 6 marks land in Howknabrak, 12 marks land in Skalloway, 2½ marks land in Howle, 3 marks land in Tow, 12 marks land of Kebuster, 3 marks land of Weisland, 14 marks land of South Caldcluiff, 2 marks land in Mowsaweill, 15 marks land of Weisgarth, 23 marks land of Urisland, 22 marks land in Gott, 3 marks land in Strand, 3 marks land in Groundiwell, 10 marks land in Belista, 10 marks land in Swynasetter, 3 marks land in Wassettir, 4 marks land in Wadbuster, 7 marks land in Nedir Sound, 14 marks land in Weik, 2 marks land in Schortoun, 2 marks land in Sound, 5 marks land in Settir, 3 marks land in Brindista; 6 marks land in Linksetter in Dunrosnes, 6 marks land in Bleusta, 5 marks land in Ringista, 2 marks land in Croce Ile; 4 marks land in Oxna Ile; 4 marks land in Hildesay; in the parish of Quhyitnes, 12 marks land in Wormadell, 1 mark land in Neisbister, 2 marks land in Eistnes, 3 marks land in Birganes, 5 marks land in Stromnes, 6 marks land in Hugaland, 6 marks land in Hagrista, 1 mark land in Strome; 1 mark land in Halligarth in the parish of Wesell, 9 marks land in Kirkgothie, 3 marks land in Hamirland, ½ mark land in Brek, 3 marks land in Stronfurd, 2 marks land in Browagarth, 1 mark land in Halibuster, 3 marks land in Mustovie alias Scheltoun, 3 marks land in Kekeron, 1 mark land in Dekeron, 2 marks land in Houscurd, 2½ marks land in Tussawell, 1½ marks land in Nethersound, 2 marks land in Overabusk, 1 mark land in Nestbister; 4 marks land in Howgaland in the parish of Burra; 2 marks land in Howgaland in the parish of Tingwall, 2 marks land in Trondera; 2½ marks land in Utrisland in the parish of Nestyne, 3 marks land in Quhalisay alias Selchiskellie; 1 mark land in Bixsetter in the parish of Authsting; 1 mark land in Sepsetter in the parish of Wais; with the sea isles pertaining to the archdeaconry, with fishings of the said lands, as well red as white, as well fresh as in salt water, in all ways in which they can be taken; with reservation to the archdeacon of Yetland and his successors of the present mansion, houses and yards upon the said lands of Tingwell; with licence to Patrik and his heirs to 'big, uphald and inhabit mansionis, biggingis, fortalices and strenthis alsweill batellit as unbattellit' for defence against 'the reif, violence, thift and oppression of thevis, revaris, pirattis and oppressors'. The lands are to be held of the king in 'ane particular tennendry or dominion feuferme and heritage' according to the custom of Scotland, and not to be divided 'amang the [*torn*] kynnsfolk' according to the use or custom of Yetland. Patrik and his heirs and assignees, and their bailies, officers, tenants and inhabitants of the said lands are discharged of all 'fleting, furing and lawting, that is to say to be freed fra all uther jurisdictioun'. The yearly duty for the lands in Orknay is 48 meals bear (or 3s.4d. for each meal), 5 lispunds butter (or 4s. for each lispund) with one cow (or 10s.), and for the lands in Yetland, for every 3 marks land, one lispund butter (or 4s.), and 6 cuttles wadmell (or 2s.8d. for every 6 cuttles), and 5 merks money in augmentation of rental.

SRO, E.2/14, ff.21-3. See also *RMS*, v, no.1314.

100. Houss in Burray, 20 August 1587

Gift by Robert, earl of Orknay, lord of Yeitland, and justice general thereof, to his beloved brother Laurence Bruce of Cultmalindeis, of the escheat of the whole movable goods of Walter Moresoun in Mwnes in Unst, fallen in Robert's hands 'throche ane decreit condampnatour pronuncit aganis the said Walter, at Skalloway bankis the [*blank*] day of August instant', with command to 'all our underfoldis present and to cum to fortefie and concur with the said Lawrence in the lifting of the said escheit guids ... because the said Lawrence hes payit us thankfullie tharfoir'.

GH. One seal.

101. October 1587

'Charter by Andrew Hawick of Scatsta to Malcolm Sinclair of Quendale, vicar of Dunrossness, of 5 merks land in Footabrough and ane merk in Breck, in parish of Walls.

'Witnesses: William Philpe, reader at Walls, and others.

'Sasine given 27th June 1613, in presence of Arthur Irving in Voe, David Nicolson, Andrew Nicolson in Footabrough, and Andrew Thomson. David Hart, N.P., Harry Cheyne, procurator.'

The original is not known to exist. The above abstract, by Francis Grant, is in OSD, *SN*, 17 February 1894.

102. Holyroodhouse, 7 November 1587

Letters by the king, following his general revocation at the age of 21, ordaining a feu charter to be made under the great seal to Hew Sinclair of Burgh, his heirs and assignees, 'efter the forme and manner observit in the realme of Scotland, to wit that onlie ane air sall succeid immediatly efter ane uther thairin, notwithstanding of the contrare custome and lawis observit in Yetland', of the lands called the canons' lands, formerly pertaining to the canons and stallars of the cathedral kirk of Orkney, wherever the same lie within the parishes of Dunrosnes, Burray, Goldberrywik, Quhytnes, Weisdaill, Standsting (*rectius* Sandsting), Delting, Yell, Fetlair and Unst, and now pertaining to the king by the acts of the parliament held in July 1587, with sasine to be given at the ground of Brek in Exinabow in Dunrosnes, paying yearly £20 13s.4d., being £20 'as for the auld maillis usit and wont' and 13s.4d. in augmentation of rental.

SRO, E.2/14, ff.33-4 (annexation of temporalities). See also *RMS*, v, no.1410, and SA, GD.144/71/4. See next item.

103. Brekis, 10 November 1587 (at 3 p.m.)

Instrument of sasine following on feu charter under the great seal to Hew Sinclair of Burgh, dated 7 November 1587, with precept of sasine directed to Andrew Hawik of Scatista as bailie, to an honourable man Oliver Sinclair of Eisthous, procurator for an honourable man Hew Sinclair of Burgh, of the lands called the canons' lands, formerly pertaining to the canons and stallars of the cathedral kirk of Orknay, in the parishes referred to in the said charter.

Done in presence of Leonard Coupland of Oxinsta, John Sutherland, vicar of Sandsting, Henry Smyth, James Mowat, Patrik (*rectius* Peter) Symsone, exhorter at Nesting, and James Kneland, with divers others, and Mr Andrew Robertson and Malcolm Sincleir, notaries public.

SA, SC.12/65/1/24 (in Latin). See previous item.

104. Gildisbrek, 28 November 1587

Agreement between Laurence Bruce of Cultmalindes, sheriff-depute of Yetland, and Colbeine Ornesone in Synbuster, whereby 'Colbein, lyifrenttar of sexteine markis land lyand in the said towin of Synbuster, in face off court, hais frelie and willinglie, uncoactit or compellit, nor yeit sinisterlie urgeit heirto, owergevin all titill of rycht that he hais, had, or may have onto the said xvj markis of land, togidder with all rycht, roith and samaing of the haill towin of Synbuster, oblessand hym his airis and eftercummaris to remove within ten dayis efter the dait heirof', for which Laurence promises 'to stand Colbein his guid freyind, and schaw hym freyndschip and to his bairnis in all his honest and lesum adois'.

Because Colbeine cannot write he has drawn his merchant mark, and requests Peter Symsoun, reader at Nesting, to subscribe in his name.

Witnesses: William Sincleir of Ustanes, Androw Smyth, court clerk for the time, and Peter Symsoun, with divers others.

SA, GD.144/113/16. Mark of Colbeine Ornesone.

105. Edinburgh, 13 January 1587-8

Decreet of court of session in action at instance of Alexander Kincaid, brother lawful of deceased John Kincaid of Warriestoun, against Hew Alcro of Aythsetter, William in Brind, William in Flatabuster, James Sinclar of Brow, John Neving, Arthour Sinclar of Aith, Laurence Lask in the Ile, Magnus in Trosiweick, Harie Smith, Anthonie in Burroland, Magnus in Shanweick, and the other heritors, feuars, tenants, parishioners, and other intromitters of the vicarage of Dunrosnes, for payment of the teindsheaves, boat teinds, emoluments and duties of the vicarage of Dunrosnes. Alexander has a tack of the vicarage for 19 years from May 1587 made to him by Malcome Sinclar, vicar of Dunrosnes, with consent of Adam, bishop of Orknay, and the canons and chapter of the cathedral kirk of Orknay.

The lords of council decern the defenders to pay to Alexander the teinds and fruits of the vicarage for the period of his tack.

SRO, CS.7/113, ff.126-7.

106. Trestay, 24 February 1587-8

Excambion by Eldre Adamesdochter, with consent of Anthane Thomessone, her spouse, and Staphane Mangnissone, her son, to an honourable man and their good friend Lorawnce Bruce of Cultmaleyndes, of 2 marks land, 9 pennies the mark, in Tangowne in Northmaveing, in exchange for 1 mark land, 6 pennies the mark, in Hamber in the isle of Fetlair. Eldre acknowledges receipt of money for the difference (which is 2 marks land of 6 pennies the mark), and if she shall happen to sell her land in Hamber she binds herself to offer it to Lorawnce, 'lyk as he sall do with the landis gottin fra us'.

Because Eldre and her son have no seals they purchase those of James Sudderland, Olawe Sudderland and Eduartt in Odstay. Witnesses: Magnus in Sand, James Strang of Valye and Androw Smyth, with divers others.

SA, GD.144/21/11. The document is unsubscribed.

107. Edinburgh, 24 February 1587-8

Decreet of court of session in action at instance Mr Thomas Cheine, archdeacon of Yetland, against James Hay, for the eviction of Thomas's servants, chamberlains, and others in his name, in July 1585, from the lands of Tingwall and the two isles of Opinvell (*rectius* Oxna?) and

Hildice pertaining thereto, and the lands of Northesetter and Gristra, with the houses, biggings, yards, whitefishing, and pertinents thereof; and for the wrongful occupation, labouring and manuring of the said lands and fishings yearly since then.

The lords of council continue the summons until 4 March 1587-8, and ordain Mr Thomas to have letters to summon witnesses, etc.

SRO, CS.7/114, f.204. No final decreet has been traced.

108. Kirkwall, 4 March 1587-8

Bond of maintenance by Robert, earl of Orkney, in favour of Hew, William, Edward and Oliver Sinclair, sons of the deceased Henry Sinclair of Ewie and the deceased Katherine Kennedy.

Be it kend till all men, be thir presentis, we, Robert, erle of Orknay, lord of Yeitland, forsamekill as throche the occasioun of the mariage accomplisit betuix Sir Patrik Ballentyne of Ewie, knight, and umquhill Katherein Kennedie, relict of umquhill Hendrie Sinclair of Ewie, Hew, William, Edward and Olifer Sinclairis, the sonis and airis of the said umquhill Hendrie and Katherein, ar altogidder frustrat of thair portionis naturall and secluidit fra thair airschipe guidis in greit quantitie, besydis thair landis and kyndlie possessionis tane fra tham in tyme of thair minoritie, and as yit withaldin be the said Sir Patrik to thair greit hurt and wrek, and now the said Hew, William, Edward and Olifer Sinclairis being oblist and bind to us, lyk as be the tennour heirof they bind and obliss tham to concur, fortifie and assist us in all our actionis and adois aganis all deidlie, the kingis majesteis awin propir persoun being exceptit allanerlie, thairfoir to be bindin and oblist, and be the tennour heirof for our part binds and oblissis us to meintein, fortefie and defend the saids Hew, William, Edward and Olifer Sinclairis in all and quhatsumevir thair honest actionis and adois, and specialie in winning and recovering out of the handis of the said Sir Patrik thair airschipe guids quhilk fallis to tham be deceis of ather father or mother, as also thair landis and kyndlie rowmis of Ewie quhilk the said Sir Patrik hes conqueist [*torn*] thair heidis in thair minoritie and les aige, and sall set fordwardis thair actionis thairanent ather in the law or by the law aganis quhatsumever persoun or persounis that sall usurpe in the contrare, the kingis majesteis awin propir persoun being exceptit allanerlie.

In witness quhairof to this our mutuall band, subscryvit with our handis, our signett is affixt. At Kirkwall, the fourt [*blank*] dayis of Marche respective, anno Jaj Vc foure score sewin yeris.

Orknay

OA, D.2/33/13. Endorsement on back: 'The dubill of the band betwix my lord and Edward Sinclair.'

109. Edinburgh, 14 March 1587-8

Decreet of court of session in action at instance of Mr Robert Cheyne of Valay against Androw Stewart, Nicholl Elersoun, Thomas Cheyn in Futurburgh, John Yainesoun, Laurence and Manss Yeanisounis in Grutyr, John Wischert and Olie Natter, Walter Smith in Unst, Thomas Hulnone, Symoun Benedixoun, Manss Quiers, Erasmus Housteane, Schewart in Grudgait, Manss Languss, Holden Meus, Benar Tysbone, Erasmus Cruikdaill, Nicholas Westerhouss, Amphroun Turphingstoun, James Lochheid, Petir Maxwell, Thomas Mansoun in Bodoun, Yeanis in Daill, Ola Cristophersoun, Gregorius in Ska, Skow Williamesoun in Hammer, and Andro Hawik, for payment of the rents and duties of the lands of Valay and Valay goods of the crop and year 1587, and of the outstanding duties for the preceding years. On 2 July 1585, Robert, earl of Orknay, lord of Yetland, sheriff-principal and head foud, had found in an action at the instance of Henrie Williamsoun, Johne Wischert, Sewat Henrysoun, James Andersoun, and the other tenants and occupiers of the said lands, against Mr Robert Cheyne and Androw Hawik, that the said Mr Robert had the best right to the lands of Valay and Valay goods, and ordained the tenants to make payment to him of the rents and duties.

The lords of council decern that letters of horning or poinding be directed to officers of arms charging them to arrest, apprise and distrain the readiest goods of the defenders for the rents and duties of the said lands owing by them to the said Mr Robert.

SRO, CS.7/113, ff.268-9.

110. Edinburgh, 16 March 1587-8

Decreet of court of session in action at instance of Andro Umphray, younger, in Yetland, son of Andro Umphray there, against Andro Umphray, elder, in Skelloway, Ingagarth Adamsdauchter, relict of John Umphray in Skelloway, John Umphray there, Jerome Umphray there, and all other persons having an interest, for payment of the mails, farms, duties, profits and emoluments of the altarage of Sanctgeill in Astray, called the 'stock' of Sanctgeill, at Whitsunday 1588 and yearly thereafter. Andro, younger, has obtained a gift under the privy seal of the said altarage, for his lifetime, for 'his intertenement at the scholes, and that by expyring of sevin yeiris quhairunto Robert Fulsyie wes provydit'.

The lords of council decern that letters be directed charging the defenders to make payment to Andro Umphray, younger, of the fruits of the altarage.

SRO, CS.7/113, ff.273-4.

111. Holyroodhouse, 23 March 1587-8

Letters by the king (understanding that the 'cuntrie of Yetland being gevin throw mariage to his hienes predicessouris be the kingis majestie of Denmark for the tyme, the peple thairof being simple and rude of maneris and wit hes neiver had amangis thame ony perfyt style of richt and securitie of thair landis pertening to thame, bot be nakit and unperfyte formes na wayis aggreable to the forme of rychtis usit and accustumit amangis his majesties legeis of the civill pairtis of the incuntrie of this realme, and his hienes being of mynd to remove the said imperfectioun and barbaritie, and to giff occasioun to the people of the said cuntrie of Yetland to have and use ane bettir forme of ordour of thair heritable richtis and securiteis of thair landis for menes of policie and knawledge amangis thame, and taking away of many questionis and contraversies may happin be generalitie and unperfyte formes of writtis') ordaining a charter to be made under the great seal to Patrik Cheyne of Essilmonth, his heirs male bearing the surname and arms of Cheyne, and assignees, of the heritable gift of the undernoted lands in the parish of Tingwall and foudry of Yetland acquired by the deceased Mr Jherome Cheyne, archdeacon of Yetland, viz., 4 marks land of Frakafeidill sold by Stevin in Sound, with consent of Marioun Johnnesdochter, his spouse; 5 marks land in Daill sold by Henrie Wischert, son and one of the heirs of the deceased Robert Wischert of Melbie; 4 marks land in Daill sold by Laurence in Daill; 2 marks land in Strand sold by Catherene Bie, relict of Walter Strand; 1 mark land in Strand sold by Mawniss Bie; 3 marks land in the town of Strand sold by Thomas Watersoun; 4 marks land in Gott sold by Jeane Leslie; 2 marks land in Lie sold by Jon Sklaitter; 3 marks land in Lie sold by Johnne Bondsone, with consent of his spouse and heirs; 1 mark land in Lie sold by Thomas Watersoun; 4 marks land in Gott sold by Marioun Mawnisdochter, with consent of James Leslie, her spouse; and 1 mark land in Gott sold by Katherene Johnnesdochter, relict of Laurence in Gott, extending in the whole to 30 (*sic*) marks land, which lands were disponed by said Jherome in his lifetime to the said Patrik, his brother's son. The said lands are erected into a free tenandry, with sasine to be taken at the mansion place of Frakafield; and the king, 'understanding the sufficience, honest and modest behaviour of Patrik, his zeal and affectioun he hes and beiris to the propagatioun of the evangell and trew religioun of Jesus Christ', incorporates the advocation, donation and right of patronage of the archdeaconry of Yetland into the tenandry, making Patrik and his heirs male patrons of the said archdeaconry. The lands are to be held of the king and his successors in feu, fee and heritage for ever.

SRO, E.2/13, ff.180-1 (charters). See also: *RMS*, v, no.1502 (this states that scatt and wattle is to be paid according to the rental, in name of feuferm; and one penny in blenchferm for the advocation).

112. Holyroodhouse, 23 March 1587-8

Letters charging the fouds and subjects in Yetland, and strangers resorting thereto, to assist Andro Hawik, admiral-depute in Yetland, under pain of rebellion. Andro has been constituted admiral-depute by Francis, earl of Boithwell, great admiral.

Register of Protections, NLS, Adv. MS. 35.5.1.

113. Holyroodhouse, 8 April 1588

Gift to Andro Umphra, son of Andro Umphra in Skellowa in Yetland, for life, of the altarage of Sanct Gele in Astay in Yetland, called the 'stowk of Sanct Gele', with the fruits thereof, now in the hands of the king on the expiry of the gift to Robert Fulsy, scholar. The gift is 'for upbringing of Andro at the scuillis in vertew and sustenyng of him thairat'.

SRO, PS.1/57, f.97.

114. Holyroodhouse, 3 May 1588

Feu charter by Robert, earl of Orknay, lord Yetland, to Arthur Sinclair of Ayth and Margaret Colving, his spouse, and his heirs male, without division, of 9 marks land in Myn, 22 marks land in Clett, 27 marks land in Papill, and 6 marks land in Houss, 8 pennies the mark, in the parish of Burray, with 2 lasts of land in Northyrland, 8 pennies the mark, in the parish of Dunrosnes. The annual dues are as follows: 4 lispunds butter and 4 shillings wadmell for the lands in Myn; ½ barrel butter and 58 cuttles wadmell for the lands in Clett, with 4 shillings wadmell and 2 pennies (*nummos*) leanger in scatt; 12 lispunds butter and 12 shillings wadmell for the lands in Papill, with 4 shillings wadmell and 4 pennies leanger, with the lands of Sandwik, in scatt; 2 lispunds 16 merks butter and 16 cuttles wadmell for the lands of Houss, and the normal debt of scatt and wattle; 1 barrel butter and 2 packs wadmell for the lands of Northyrland; and 15 poultry fowls for all the said lands in augmentation of the rental, with suit to the three head courts held annually at Scalloway bankis. The precept is directed to James Kintor.

Witnesses: John Cavertoun in Schapinsaw, Alexander Kincaid, Robert Tullocht, and Thomas Auchinlek, notary public.

Sasine given on 29 March 1590 (at 4 p.m.) at North Irland to Arthur Sinclair of Aith and James Sinclair of Brow (procurator for Margaret Colvill). Witnesses: Robert Tulloch, Davide Gowdilokis, Matheu Sinclar, Andro Sinclar and William Mansoun. William Fermour, notary public.

GH (in Latin); seal attached; with sasine on the back. Another version, although subscribed 'Orknay', contains no date nor names of witnesses (Braefield House, Dunrossness: copy in SA, SA.2/261/4).

115. Edinburgh, 15 May 1588

Decreet of commissary court of Edinburgh in action at instance of Mr William Hay against Patrik Cheyne of Essilmonth, tacksman of the archdeaconry of Yetland, by virtue of a tack and factory granted by Mr Thomas Cheyne, his brother, dated 15 April 1587, for production of the demission of the archdeaconry of Yetland by Mr Jherome Cheyne, and reduction thereof. On 15 May 1588 Patrik Cheyne's procurator produces letters executed on John Cheyne in Scallwa, Gilbert Kow in Glak, Nicoll Thomesone and Walter Rois, Andro Cowte in Wischirth, Petir Redall there, David Houpe there, Andro Wishart in Milbie, Andro Allane, mariner, William Philp, Johne Welsche, Alexander Foirman in Worbie and Daniell Hawik, Thomas Andersone in Skalloway, Jerome Umphray there, James in Skalloway, Robert Wilsone there, John Andersone there, James Andersone there, Alexander Thomesone in Laxfurd, Harie Bruce there, John Tait there, Nicolas Smyth in Howland, William Sinclair in Eistnes, Magnus Lowristoun in Kiberstll, Andro Stewart in Fairburg, John Nemo in Stenneddill, Paull Mansoun in Quhitnes, Mans in Wormeddill, Ola Nicolsoun in Twat, John Wishart in Burd, Arthir Erasing in Grot, Mans Halcro in Strander, Mans Bie in Grinwell, Mans Prest, Andro Umphra, John Umphra and Andro Hawik, summoning them as witnesses. Mr William Hay's procurator requests that because most of the witnesses dwell in Yetland a commission should be given for their examination.

The commissaries continue the summons until 16 May 1588.

SRO, CC.8/2/17 (3, 6, 8, and 9 February 1587-8); CC.8/2/18 (21, 22 and 23 February 1587-8, 15 May 1588, 1 and 25 June 1588, 8 July 1588); CC.8/2/20 (5 March 1589-90); CC.8/2/21 (13 August 1590). No final decreet has been traced.

116. Edinburgh, 25 May 1588

Decreet of court of session in action at instance of Hew Sinclair of Strome, William Sinclair of Oistenes, John Umphra, Henry Halcro in Setter, Malcolme Halcro, Erik of Scattista, James in Scalloway, Thomas Boyne, James Boyne, his son, there, and the other tenants and parishioners of the parish kirks of Tingwall, Wisdaill and Quheitnes, pertaining to the archdeaconry of Yetland, against Patrik Cheyne of Essilmonthe, alleged tacksman, on the one part, Mr Thomas Cheyne, alleged archdeacon, on the second part, and Mr William Hay, now archdeacon, on the third part, for decision of the lords of council as to which of the defenders has best right to the fruits of the archdeaconry. On 10 August 1587 the lords of council had ordained Mr Thomas Cheyne to summon the following witnesses, viz., Gilbert Thomsoun in Swynsetter, Jacob Tait in Eisthous, Erastuli in Wedbuster, Nicoll Thomsoun in Howlandis, Nicoll Smyth there, Robert Wilsoun in Scalway, William Sinclair there, John Sinclair there, John Chene, David Thomsoun, Andro Umphray, Edward Sinclair in Melbie, James Southerland in Setter, Alexander Porteous, reader in Bressa, John Umphra there, Hary Bruce in Laxfurde, Gilbert Tow in Glasbo, Thomas Proctor in Ellen, William Moir there, John Cruikshank there, David Waan there, James Brokess, Alexander Ritchie, Gilbert Cheyne alias Keyth in Lichwet, Mr Walter Ogilvie, Mr John Innes, and Mr Thomas Hamiltoun, and to that effect the lords had given commission to John Dennune, minister at Delting, Malcolme Sinclair, minister at Dunrosnes, and Thomas Boyne in Urisland, conjunctly with Mr James Pitcarne, minister at Northemavin, clerk, to pass to Scallowaybank 'all the feriot and law dayis' between 16 and 30 September 1587, to receive the depositions of the foresaid witnesses dwelling in Orknay and Yetland, and these depositions had now been reported.

The lords of council decern the defenders to pay the teinds, fruits, etc., of the crop and year 1582 and yearly in time coming, to Mr Thomas Cheyne, as the party found as having the best right thereto, whereupon Mr William Hay's procurator asked for instruments.

SRO, CS.7/110, ff.163-6, 349-51, 394-5, 461-2, 532; CS.7/115, ff.15-9, 26.

117. Falkland, 18 July 1588

Letter by the king to Andro Mowat of Hougaland taking him and his lands, possessions, kinsfolk, etc., under the king's protection, to be unmolested other than by order of law, with command to the lieges that none of them take upon hand to do or attempt anything contrary, under all highest pain, charge and offence.

SRO, PS.1/57, f.139.

118. Skalloway bankis, 20 July 1588

Disposition by Hendrie Walterstoun, lawful son of Walter Erasmussoun, with consent of Mareoun Magnusdochter, his mother, liferentrix of half of the lands underwritten, and Cristopher in Gunyeuo, her spouse, and of Agnes Walterisdochter, his sister, Ollaw and Jhone Boundsonis, his nearest kinsmen on his father's side, his tutors and curators, to an honourable man Hew Sinclair of Bruche, of 12 marks land in Caldclewche, with ½ mark land in Nether Brewik, in the parish of Tingwall, with precept of sasine.

Hendrie, Mareoun and Cristopher sign with their hands led at the pen by the notary, and Hendrie procures the seals of honourable men: Mr Robert Cheyn of Ure and David Skollaw of Toftis. Witnesses: Jhone Cavertoun in Schapinschaw, Malcum Sinclair, vicar of Dunrosnes, David Skollaw of Toftis, Androw Giffert of Woddirsta and Thomas Auchinlek, notary public.

SA, SC.12/65/1/26. This is an early example of a Shetland disposition containing a precept of sasine.

119. 3 August 1588

'Disposition by Andrew Hawick of Skatstay "to ane honourable man and my guid friend" Arthur Sinclair of Ayth, of 2 merks land in Northmaven.'

The original is not known to exist. The above abstract, by Francis Grant, is in OSD, *SN*, 28 October 1893.

120. Skalloway bankis, 5 August 1588

Disposition by John Wischertt in Burrafirth, tutor and administrator of the bairns of the deceased Matho Wischertt, his brother german, with consent of Elspeit Cheine, relict of said Matho, to Andro Giffertt of Weddersta, of 3½ marks land in Trondevo in the parish of Delting, to be held 'in fie blanch ferme for payment of ane pennie Scots monie ... giff it be requirit allanerlie', with precept of sasine. The lands had been sold by Matho in his lifetime to Andro, but 'na evident nor securitie wes maid afoir the said umquhill Mathois deceis'.

Witnesses: David Moresoun, burgess of Kirkwall, Andro Reid, Gilbertt Mowatt, George Mitchell and William Halcro. Johne Wischertt and Elspet Cheine subscribe with their hands led at the pen by William Fermour, notary public.

SA, GD.144/46/8.

121. 5 August 1588

'Ane acquittance gevin be Robert Sinclair of Lampston [*rectius* Campston*?*] to Swane of Windhous upon the sowme of 24 lib. for 3 yeiris maill of the xij merk land of Setter.'

The original is not known to exist. One of the writs taken from Ninian Neven's house in Yell on 24 August 1624 (*RPC*, xiv, p.773).

122. Usteines, 10 August 1588

Note of renunciation and disposition by William Sinclair, son of the deceased James Sinclair of Houss, to 'my lord of Orkney and his airis', of his right and title of Sanctrinyells Yle, for sums of money paid (unspecified).

Witnesses: Hew Sinclair of Bruche, Alexander Kincaid and Thomas Auchinlek, notary public.

SRO, NP.1/36, f.20.

123. Usteines, 10 August 1588

Note of disposition by Garthraw Olawisdochter, with consent of Poyile Manisoun, her spouse, and Magnus Pitersoun, Mareoun and Katharein Piterisdochteris, her son and daughters, and Margrete Olawisdochter, with consent of Nicole Jacobsoun alias Smyth, her spouse, and their heirs, and Magnus Pitersoun, elder, and Magnus Pitersoun, younger, with consent of their heirs, to Robert, earl of Orkney, of 7 marks land, 8 pennies the mark, in the town of Usteines in the parish of Quhitnes, pertaining to them as uthell land, and ordaining Thomas Auchinlek, notary, 'to mak ane perfyte chartour thairupoun'.

Witnesses: David Skollaw of Toftis, Hew Sinclair of Bruche, Alexander Kincaid and Peter Simsoun.

SRO, NP.1/36, f.20.

124. Usteines, 11 August 1588

Note of renunciation by Elspett Sinclair, with express consent of William Sinclair of Usteines, her spouse, of her right and title of a piece of waste ground in the midtown of Kirkwall which Elspett heired from the deceased Ollaw Sinclair of Brow, her father. Elspett consents that Thomas Auchinlek, notary public, 'sould mak ane perfyt evident', whereupon David Skollaw asked that the renunciation should be made in his favour.

Witnesses: Peter Simsoun, Ollaw Sinclair, brother to William Sinclair of Usteines, and Thomas Auchinlek, notary.

SRO, NP.1/36, f.20.

125. Edinburgh, 13 August 1588

Gift to Sir Patrik Bellenden of Evie, knight, of the escheats of the goods and possessions of David Scola, Malcolme Grote, William Irwing in Saba, Stevin Paplay, Thomas Murray, Andro Bauchope in Edinburgh, Hew Sinclair of Strome, Edward Sinclair, his brother, Andro Giffert, Andro Umphray, David Spens in Skapa, Magnus Cromartie in Kara, Arthor Sinclair in Yetland, Barthill Strang there, James Gib in Kirkwall, Williame Maine, William Moresoun, Thomas Hardie, Thomas Baikie, Gawin Tailyeor, Johnne Fallasdaill, all indwellers in Orknay and Yetland, who have been denounced rebels and put to the horn at the instance of Sir Johnne Maitland of Thirlestane, knight, chancellor, and Sir Lues Bellenden of Auchnoule, knight, justice clerk, feuars of the earldom of Orknay and lordship of Yetland, for non-payment of the mails and duties of the lands and steadings occupied by them for the crop and year 1587, and for 'non rysing, concurring, assisting and pairtaking with the said Sir Patrik Bellenden, his hienes lieutenant of Orknay, in setting fordwart of his commissioun of lieutenandrie the yeir foirsaid, and for thair cuming in armes with displeyit banner in company with Lord Robert Stewart, feuar of the bishoprik of Orknay, against the said lieutenant'.

SRO, PS.1/57, f.171.

126. Skalloway, 15 August 1588

Disposition by Robert, earl of Orknay, lord of Yeitland, to Lawrence Sinclair, eldest son and apparent heir of Arthour Sinclair of Ayth, and his heirs without division, of the isle called Sanctrinyanis Yle, extending to 1 last of land, in the parish of Dunrosnes, with reservation of the liferent to Arthour Sinclair of Ayth and Margrett Colwing, Laurence's father and mother. Precept of sasine directed to James Kintor.

Witnesses: David Skollaw of Toftis, Jespart Smyth and Thomas Auchinlek, notary public.

Sasine given at Sanct Ringanis Ile on 28 March 1590 (at 1 p.m.) by James Kintor at the request of an honourable man Arthour Sinclair of Aith as tutor, guider and administrator for his son Lawrence Sinclair, and also at the desire of Lawrence Lesk, attorney for the said Lawrence Sinclair, in presence of William Fermoir, notary public. Witnesses: Allexander Rannikin, William Williamsoun, David Gowdilokis, Erasmus Sigertsone, Matho Wrycht, Allexander and Lawrence Lesk.

SA, D.10/2/3 (the sasine is on the back).

127. Hous, 16 August 1588

'[Disposition by] David Sinclair of Huntoun, Edward Sinclair of Scalloway, William Sinclair of Ustanes, Olay Sinclair, James Sinclair and Orsilla Sinclair, lawful sons (*sic*) to Laurence Sinclair of Sandes, to their brother Arthur Sinclair of Aith, [of] 21 mark [land] in Hous in Burey. ... This 21 mark was heired from their gudam Mareon of Hous.'

The original is not known to exist. The above abstract, by J. Storer Clouston, is in OA, D.23, Notebook 4, p.66. There is another abstract, by Francis Grant, in OSD, *SN*, 28 October 1893, where it is stated that the land is in 'Hellywick ... in Houss', and that James Kyntoir, Robert Tulloch and Hew Sinclair of Brugh were witnesses. In another abstract Gilbert Goudie places a question mark after 'Hellywic' (notebook in Braefield House, Dunrossness). Both Grant and Goudie give the date as 16 August 1587.

128. 20 August 1588

Nicoll Gregoriowssones charter of j merk half [merk] land in Sandfrie grantit to Andro Gregoriowssone.'

The original is not known to exist. One of the writs taken from Ninian Neven's house in Yell on 24 August 1624: SRO, Privy Council Papers, PC.10/14e (*RPC*, xiv, p.735 incorrectly says 1 merk land).

129. Kirkwall, 15 December 1588

Wadset by Williame Stewart, natural son of a noble and potent lord Robert, earl of Orknay, lord Yetland, to an honourable man Hew Sinclaire of Burgh, of 2 lasts of land, 8 pennies the mark, of Ayth in the isle of Brassay, held by William in feu from his father, redeemable on payment of 500 merks at the kirk of Tingwall in the hands of Andro Mowat of

Hugoland. After redemption the lands shall be set in tack to Hew for 19 years for payment of 2 packs of wadmell and 1 barrel of butter yearly. Precept of sasine.

Because he has no seal Williame Stewart procures those of Johnne Broun and William Fermour, notary in Kirkwall. Witnesses: Edward Sinclair, brother of said Hew, Magnus Paplay, Stevin Paplay, Robert Strang, notary, and William Fermour, notary public.

SA, SC.12/65/3.

130. Dalkeith, 19 December 1588

Ratification of presentation on 30 November 1588 by Robert, earl of Orknay, of James Fulsie, lawful son of the deceased Mr Gilbert Fulsie, minister at Kirkwall, to the altarage and chaplainry of Sanct Geil in Astay in Yetland for seven years, 'in support of his sustentatioun at the scuillis', from the expiry of the other seven years granted by the king to Robert Fulsie, brother of James, 'quhilk is almaist now outrun'.

SRO, PS.1/58, f.100.

131. Edinburgh, 11 January 1588-9

Contract between Robert, earl of Orknay, lord Yetland, and Laurence Bruce of Cultmalindie, whereby Robert sets in tack to Laurence the scatt, wadmell, landmails, casualties and duties of the lordship of Yetland and isles thereof for 19 years from Whitsunday 1589, and also the offices of sheriffship and foudry of the lordship of Yetland, with all fees, etc., for 5 years from Whitsunday 1589. Laurence has paid Robert £1,000 in name of grassum, and binds himself to pay Robert £1,000 yearly at Michaelmas for the period of the tack; and shall administer justice for his period of office 'to all parteis quhome it effeiris according to the laws of the cuntrey, and sall intromett and uptak the unlaws and escheits of court, poynd and distrenyie thairfoir', of which two-thirds shall be for Robert's use, and the other one-third shall be for Laurence's own use for his diligence, travels and labours. As regards the claim of Hew Sinclair of Burgh to have a tack of the scat, etc., with the office of sheriffship and foudry, of which he alleges there are 5 years to run, Robert binds himself 'to do his utter and exact diligence with all possibilitie lauchfull, ather to evict be ordour of law fra the said Hew his taks, rychts and tytills ... or utherwayis sall caus Hew of his awin consent renunce and discharge the same to the effect Laurence may peceablie enter thairto'. If Robert is unable to perform this, then he will grant Laurence £1,000 of the first and readiest payment of the yearly duties which Laurence is obliged to pay for the three isles of Unst, Fetlaire and Yaill, in repayment of the grassum, and he will grant a tack to Laurence immediately on the expiry of Hew's tack on the same terms as above.

Witnesses: John Cavertoun in Schapinschaw, Alexander Kincaid, and Thomas Auchinlek, notary public.

SRO, RD.1/32, ff.216-8.

132. Edinburgh, 22 January 1588-9

Commission of factory by Robert, earl of Orknay, lord Yetland, to Michaell Balfour of Montquhany and Arthour Sinclare of Ayth, giving them power to pass to Yetland and grant feus and tacks of the king's lands of the lordship of Yetland to the tenants, occupiers, etc., in order that Robert may raise funds to obtain a new heritable title and right of Orknay and Yetland, which is at present in the king's hands through revocations, and for which Robert is 'forced to deburss divers and grit large sums of money, not onlie to his majestie, his thesaurar and comptroller, but als to sindrie utheris be his majesties appoyntment and directioun'. The feus and tacks are to be granted 'as maist commodiously may be done' for payment of the 'auld yeirlie wadmaill, butter, oyle, harde fische, skait, watill and utheris dewteis contenit in our rentals thairof ... and payment of tua pultrie foulis yeirlie for every 12 marks land in augmentatioun of our rental', with attendance 'to our heid courtis yeirlie within Yetland as use is'. For every last of land that is feued the commissioners are to obtain composition for grassum of 20 angel nobles 'and mair as thai may guidlie obtene', and for every last of land that is set in tack they are to obtain composition likewise of 18 angel nobles. The 60 marks land in Sowndbroche, Skatnes and Ulsness in the parish of Dunrosnes, the three lasts of land in Northe Lakisffurde and adjacent pertinents, the 27 marks land in Berrie, all the king's lands in the parish of Quhittisnes, the holms of Papa and Thinga beside Skalloway, and the isles and holms of North Havaray, Newmontrie (*rectius* Vementrie), the Skarreis and Musa, with their pertinents, 'sal nawayis be comprehendit in this present commissioun, bot salbe reservit to our selff to be usit and disponit upoun be us at our plesor'. The composition receipts and grassums may be retained by Michaell Balfour, 'for the quhilks he is becum or salhappin becum dettor and cautionar for us', providing that the commissioners shall be accountable to Robert, his heirs and successors, 'of the superplus of the said grassums and intress gif ony salhappin to be'.

Witnesses: Johnne Cavertoun, Thomas Auchinlek, and Alexander Kincaid, servant of Robert, with divers others.

SRO, RD.1/32, ff.230-1.

133. Edinburgh and (torn), 4 and 10 February 1588-9

Obligation by Robert, earl of Orknay and Yetland, to Sir John Maitland of Thirlstane, knight, chancellor, for 8,000 merks for the renunciation by

Sir John into the king's hands of all right and title of his half of the lands of the lordship and earldom of Orknay and Yetland, so that the king may give and dispone the same to Robert and his heirs heritably. Michaell Balfour of Montquhany, Mr John Pitcarne, elder, and Mr Henrie Pitcarne, younger, are cautioners for Robert.

Witnesses: (at Edinburgh on 4 February) George Balfour, prior of the Charterhouse, John Cavertoun, Alexander Kyncaid, Andro Martyne, and Thomas Young, writer; (on 10 February) Mr James Maitland and James Gray, servants of Sir John, and the said Alexander Kyncaid, servant of 'my lord of Orknay'.

SRO, RD.1/32, ff.330-1.

134. Rafirtht in Yell (in church of St. John), 18 February 1588-9

Proceedings and decreet of the commissary court in action at instance of Solamone, Laurence and Oswald Scott, brothers, heirs of the deceased David Scot of Rafirtht, their father ('the first party'), against Magnus Erasmussone, David Barnardsone, and Waltir Mansone ('the second party'), taking the burden upon them for themselves and for 'utheris thair pertineris acclemeris tytill and rycht' to 5½ marks land in the town of Rafirtht, sold to the first party and their father before his decease, as contained in the contract made between the first and second parties on 16 July 1587 at Rafirtht. The first party compeared, and produced the said contract in presence of the second party, and offered to fulfil the same according to the desire of the summons, dated 14 February at Fetlar, which was that the second party should be decerned to receive 35 gudlings in complete payment of 60 gudlings 'as the said contract proportis', or else to allege why they should not. The second party compeared and refused to accept payment, and on being asked by the commissary and his assessors what reasonable cause they had, as there was no special day mentioned for payment, answered that they 'durst not for feir of thair fold'. The commissary, having heard no reasonable cause put forward to the contrary, and 'being weill and ryplie advysit with his assessors', ordained the first party to offer the foresaid sum to the second party, and if they refused, to consign the sum in the hands of Mr Williame Lauder, the vicar. The second party again refused to accept payment, and the 35 gudlings (viz. 3 angel nobles and 10 'copmane dolors'), which together with the 25 gudlings given by the deceased David Scot 'make compleitlie 60 gudlingis', were consigned to Mr William Lauder, and thus fulfilled the contract. The commissary then decerned the second party to receive the foresaid sum of 35 gudlings in gold and silver, in satisfaction and complete payment of the said 5½ marks land in Rafirtht in Yell, conform to the tenor of the contract, within one month, and also decerned that if the said sum remained in the hands of

William 'onlockit' by the second party to the prejudice, hurt and detriment of the first party for one year, then it should be confiscated and held (torn) half (torn), and the said 5½ marks land to pertain heritably to the first party, and the second party's title to the land which they had before the making of the contract to be null and of no avail. The goods and gear of the second party to be poinded for the sum of 43s.4d. 'for expenssis of play'.

SRO, RH.9/15/92.

135. Holyroodhouse, 24 February 1588-9

Precept for feu charter under the great seal to James Hay of Freuchnie, his heirs and assignees, after the form and manner of succession in Scotland, of 24 marks land of Astay in the parish of Tingwall, together with the holm of Tay Holme, and with all scats, commodities and yearly duties which pertained of before to the stouk or prebendary of St Geill of Astay, paying yearly to the king £10 'as the auld dewitie usit and wont', and 6s.8d. in augmentation of the rental.

SRO, PS.1/59, f.37 (in Latin).

136. Trestay, 11 April 1589

Discharge by Mr Williame Laudir, vicar of Yell and Fetler, to an honourable man Lorawnce Bruce of Cultmaleyndes, chamberlain of the bishop's lands and kirk rents of Unst, Fetlair and Yell, of all manner of teinds, such as corn teind, boat teind, bow teind, wool teind, lamb teind and all other small teinds or other duties.

Witnesses. Jhone Pennekwck, laird, Collin Bruce and Andro Smyth, with others.

GH.

137. Edinburgh, 17 May 1589

Decreet of court of session in action at instance of James Lauder, son lawful of Mr William Lauder, vicar of Yell, against Daniell Hawick, for removal from 9 marks land in Southe Lady in Yell. Mr William, on behalf of James, had obtained, at Skalloway banks on 15 June 1583, two decreets before Robert, earl of Orknay, lord of Yetland, and justice general, against Daniell, the one ordaining that the said land pertained to James, and the other ordaining that Daniell should remove therefrom. Daniell continues to withhold the lands from James.

The lords of council decern the defender to remove from the land.

SRO, CS.7/118, f.110. See no. 84.

138. Hous in Burra, 4 June 1589

Feu charter by Michell Balfour of Monquhaney and Arthour Sinclair of Aith, commissioners of Robert, earl of Orknay and Yetland, to Manis Olesoun in Channerweik and Marioun Smyth, his spouse, their heirs and assignees without division, of 6½ marks land, 12 pennies the mark, in Channerweik, presently occupied by them, for payment of the yearly butter and wadmell landmail, with the scat and wattle, and their suit and presence at the head and bailie courts, with service, 'usit and wont'. Precept of sasine.

Witnesses: Andro Balfour, apparent of Montquhany, William Straquhen, William Ormistone, and Andro Edmistone, notary public, with divers others.

SA, GD.144/84/5.

139. Edinburgh, 20 June 1589

Gift to Mr James Pitcarne, vicar of Northmaven, of the escheat of the goods of the deceased Johnne Dynoyne, reader at the kirk of Delteyne, through being born bastard, and dying without lawful heirs or lawful disposition of his goods.

SRO, PS.1/60, f.20.

140. Edinburgh, 20 June 1589

Presentation of Mr Robert Wod to the vicarage of Delting, vacant by decease of Johnne Dinnun, with direction to the commissioner in Yetland to examine the 'qualificatioun and literature of said Robert', and if he is found 'meit to use and exercise the office of ane minister', to receive his confession of faith and oath of obedience.

SRO, PS.1/60, f.21.

141. Northe Strynie, 24 June 1589 (at 11 a.m.)

Note of renunciation and disposition by David Scollay of Toftis to James Skollaw, his son, and Edwarde Scollay, his brother, of the right and title of his lands, burgh lands and field lands, with his movable goods, to be intromitted equally between them, 'incais he sal happen to inlaik now in his vayage to Yeitland; and incais he returne saife that the saids landis and houss guids salbe reddemable to himself upon the payment of ane roisnoble'. David ordains that this renunciation be extended in form of an instrument.

Witnesses: Malcum Grote of Tankirnes, Walter Bruce, Thomas

Swentoun, minister, and Edward Sinclair, brother german of Hew Sinclair of Bruche.

SRO, NP.1/36, ff.20-1.

142. Edinburgh, 2 July 1589

Protest by Mr James Pitcarne, minister and vicar of Northmeving, to the lords of the privy council, regarding the summons, dated 23 January 1588-9 at Holyroodhouse, at the instance of his parishioners of Northmeving, and Johnne Mowatt, son of Andro Mowatt of Hugoland, underfoud of Northmeving, to appear before the council on 17 June 1589 to answer the complaint of troubling and oppressing the pursuers through his avaricious and undecent behaviour, evil life and conversation. The said day being now past, and the pursuers not having appeared, James protests that he should not be held to answer until he is again summoned and his expenses refunded. The lords admit the protest, and ordain that 'in respect of the far distance of his dwelling place and residence, and difficultie of passing in the winter seasone', no new letters should be directed against James before 31 May 1590, and also 'that the caussis of the said complaint aucht first to be cognoscit be the Generall Assembley or utheris haveand commissioun in ecclesiasticall caussis'.

RPC, iv, pp.400-1.

143. Edinburgh, 2 July 1589

Contract between Mr James Pitcairne, vicar of Northmavin, principal, and Alexander Kincaid, vicar of Walls, brother german of the deceased John Kincaid of Wareistoun, and William Hacro of Akeris, cautioners, on the one part, and James Dalzell, elder, burgess of Edinburgh, on the other part, whereby Mr James acknowledges receipt of £200 from James Dalzell for 20 barrels of 'Yetland ulie in beir treis, guid and sufficient merchand wair, without dreg or walter'. Mr James undertakes to deliver the oil to James Dalzell by 11 November 1589 on the shore of Leith, Craill or Dundie, 'haill and frie of chairgis, quhairof he sall mak advertisement to James to ressave the samen in dew tyme'. Mr James shall pay James Dalzell £20 for each barrel not delivered.

Witnesses: Alexander Lawsone, writer, Adame Graham, merchant, burgess of Edinburgh, and John Lawsone, servant of Mr James.

SRO, RD.1/38, ff.113-4.

144. Brunteland, 14 July 1589

Obligation by Mr James Pitcarne, vicar of Northmaven, principal, and John Symsoun, merchant and burgess of Brunteland, cautioner, to Alexander Lawsoun, writer, for £200, payable in equal instalments at Lammas 1590 and Lammas 1591, for the disposition by Alexander to

Ursula Sinclair, spouse of James, of a pension of 15 angels of gold, to be uplifted yearly of the readiest of 'the tua part' of the corn teinds of the vicarage of Northmaven. If James fails to pay the instalments he binds himself to infeft Alexander in an annual rent of £10 for each £100 that lies unpaid, to be uplifted from James's tenement of land in Sanctandrois, now occupied by his father, or from any of his cautioner's lands in Brunteland or Edinburgh, at the option of Alexander, until redemption by payment of the principal.

Witnesses: David Clerk, bailie of Brunteland, Mr Andro Wilson, council's clerk there, Roger Duncansoun, younger, burgess of Edinburgh, and John Lawsoun, servant of Mr James, with divers others.

SRO, RD.1/33, ff.49-50.

145. Mownis, (?) July 1589

Renunciation by Lorawnce Bruce of Cultmaleyndeis, by way of excambion, to his good friend Waltir Smyth of Hamber, of 4½ marks land, 6 pennies the mark, in 'ane plaice callet Westrous in Mowlay' in the isle of Unst, in exchange for the renunciation by Waltir to Lorawnce of 4½ marks land, 6 pennies the mark, in Neddirhoull in Mowlay in the said isle. Lorawnce binds himself to warrant the lands in Westrous 'undir pain of als mekill as gud land lyand als commodiowse'.

Lorawnce affixes his seal, and procures the seals of James Suddirland and Necholl of Culyevo. Witnesses: Robert Yull, Hendrie Warlaw, and Jhone Penniekwck, younger.

SRO, RH.6/3019.

146. Stanidaile, 9 August 1589

Disposition by Robert, earl of Orknay, lord of Yeitland, to his beloved servant Hierome Umphray, and Margrete Morray, his spouse, of 7½ marks land in Utir Sand in the parish of Sandsting, evicted from Nicole Manisoun for theft, and fallen in Robert's hands as escheat, and likewise 1½ marks land there, evicted from Poile Williamsoun for theft, all 12 pennies the mark, for £117 6s.8d. paid to Robert by Hierome. Precept of sasine is directed to Androw Giffert of Woddirsta.

Witnesses: Walter Bruce, Androw Giffert of Woddirsta, Jhone Suddirland, vicar of Sandsting and Aythsting, and Thomas Auchinlek, notary public.

Sasine given at Utir Sand on 9 August 1589. Witnesses: Mathow Robertsoun, Jhone Callendar, Jhone Adesoun, messengers, and Thomas Auchinlek, notary public.

SA, D.10/24/1 (the instrument of sasine is on the back).

147. Condill, 11 August 1589

Feu charter by Michell Balfour of Montquhany and Arthour Sinclair of Ayth, commissioners of Robert, earl of Orknay, lord Yetland, conform to their commission dated 1 January 1588-9 at Edinburgh, to Lawrence Sinclair of Goit and Margaret Leisk, his spouse, their heirs and assignees without division, after the form of succession to lands in Scotland, of the following *pro rege* lands: 10 marks land, 6 pennies the mark, in Ouirscoland (paying annually 3 lispunds 2 pennies butter and 3 shillings 2 cuttles wadmell), 9½ marks land, 6 pennies the mark, in Southerhous (paying annually 3 lispunds 1 penny butter and 3 shillings 1 cuttle wadmell), 16 marks land, 9 pennies the mark, in Mewhous in South Yrland (paying annually 8 lispunds butter and 8 shillings wadmell), 2 marks land, 6 pennies the mark, in Goit (paying annually 4 pennies butter and 4 cuttles wadmell), all in the parish of Dunrosnes, and 3 marks land, 8 pennies the mark, in Brucht in Burra (paying annually 8 pennies butter and 8 cuttles wadmell), with the scat butter and oil yearly, and wattle when it falls, conform to the rental, and in augmentation 7 poultry fowls yearly, and suit at his lordship's head courtis to be held at Skalloway yearly. Laurence is given power 'to flit and remove the dykis thairof and to enlarge the bounds of the corne landis, to birne, ryff and brek furth new landis, to mak new biggins, dykis, tumillis, quyis, toiftis, croiftis, parkis, medows, schawis and uther policie quhatsumevir but contradictione'. Precept of sasine is directed to Jhone Sinclair.

Witnesses: Malcome Sinclair, vicar of Dunrosnes, James Sinclair of Brow, William of Ustines, William Straquhen, and Andro Edmestoun, notary public.

SA, GD.144/27/1. An endorsement by A. Edmestoune states that the document was produced on 8 October 1590; and another by Thomas Auchinlek that it was registered at Skalloway bankis on 15 June 1597.

148. Skallowaybankis, 13 August 1589

Note of renunciation by Magnus Rolland in Sandes in Waiss in favour of William Bruce and Margrite Stewart, and their lawful heirs, whom failing to William's heirs, of 3 ures land, 6 pennies the mark, in Urissetter in Fetlar, for sums of money 'payit be William to me in full landis pryce'. Magnus is to obtain the consent of Bessie Nocollisdochter, his spouse, and is 'content that Thomas Auchinlek, notar, mak ane instrument reversion theirof in maist ample form'.

Witnesses: Mr William Lauder, Osie Scott, and James Frissall.

SRO, NP.1/36, f.21.

149. Skallowaybankis, 14 August 1589

Note of disposition by Erasmus Edwardsoun in Papill in Unst to William

Bruce and Margret Stewart, his spouse, of 2 marks land, 6 pennies the mark, in Papill in Unst. Magnus is to obtain the consent of Ollaw Edwardsoun, his brother, and his heirs, and binds himself to warrant the land, 'and in cais the same be evictit ony wayis, that his twa mark land in Kewis sall warrand the samen'. Thomas Auchinlek, notary, is commanded 'to gif furth ane sufficient chartour thairupoun'.

Erasmus has borrowed the seal of Jon a Skei to be appended thereto, together with his own mark. Witnesses: sir William Tailyour, Hendrie Wardlaw and Walter Redpethe.

SRO, NP.1/36, f.21.

150. Edinburgh, 14 August 1589

Decreet of court of session in action at instance of Laurence Bruce of Cultemalundeis against Daniell Hawik and Andro Hawik, for restitution of his goods and gear spoiled from the place and house of West Burgh in Yell, which belonged to Nicholl Bothwelsone of West Burgh, 'quhair the said Laurence Bruce, complenar, dwell and remanit for the tyme'.

The lords of council continue the summons until 1 November 1589, and ordain Laurence to have letters to summon witnesses, and to produce evidence, etc.

SRO, CS.7/119, f.383. No final decreet has been traced.

151. Skalloway, 15 August 1589

Feu charter by Michell Balfour of Montquhany and Arthour Sinclair of Aythe, commissioners of Robert, earl of Orknay, lord Yetland, conform to their commission dated 1 January 1588-9 at Edinburgh, to Andro Giffert in Wedderstaw and Agnes Robertsone, his spouse, their heirs and assignees without division, after the form of succession to lands in Scotland, of the following *pro rege* lands: 9 marks land, 9 pennies the mark, in South Voxetter (paying annually 4½ lispunds butter and 27 cuttles wadmell), 9 marks land, 10 pennies the mark, in Ylisbuster (paying annually 5 lispunds 8 marks butter and 32 cuttles wadmell), 7 marks land, 9 pennies the mark, in Sandgarth (paying annually 3½ lispunds butter and 21 cuttles wadmell), 5 marks land, 8 pennies the mark, in Toftoun (paying annually 2 lispunds 8 marks butter and 14 cuttles wadmell), 4 marks land, 12 pennies the mark, in Firth (paying annually 2 lispunds 16 marks butter and 16 cuttles wadmell), 6½ marks land, 9 pennies the mark, in Toft in Burnes (paying annually 3 lispunds 6 marks butter and 19½ cuttles wadmell), 2 marks land, 12 pennies the mark, in Midgarth in Burnes (paying annually 1 lispund 8 marks butter and 8 cuttles wadmell), 11 marks land, 10 pennies the mark, in Brekon (paying annually 5 lispunds 16 marks butter and 34 cuttles wadmell), and 1 mark there, 12 pennies the mark (paying annually 16 marks butter and

4 cuttles wadmell), all in the parish of Delting, with the scat, wattle and other yearly service according to the rental, and in augmentation 2 poultry fowls for each 12 marks land, and suit at his lordship's three head courts to be held at Skalloway yearly. Androw is given power to enlarge the corn lands, to remove out or in the dykes, and 'to burne, ryff and brek furth new landis, mak tumulis, quyis and new seatis, toiftis and biggins upone quhatsumevir part of the saids landis, alsweill without as within dyk, in onlaborit as laborit ground'. Precept of sasine.

Witnesses: William Sinclair of Ustenes, William Straquhen, Robert Hermestoune, and Andro Edmestoun, notary public.

SA, GD.144/22/5. An endorsement on the back, signed by Walter Scott, states that the document was produced on 2 August 1597.

152. Southhous in Beinster, 16 August 1589 (at 8 a.m.)

Instrument of sasine in favour of David Strang and Katerine Ferry, his spouse, their heirs and assignees without division, following on feu charter by Michell Balfour of Montquhany and Arthour Sinclair of Ayth, commissioners of Robert, earl of Orknay and Yetland, of 9 marks *pro rege* land in Southhous in Beinster in the parish of Nesting, and 1 mark land in Greiff Skerre, with precept of sasine directed to Jhone Callender, messenger, burgess of Striveling.

Witnesses: Edward Thomesone of Garth, Erasmus Manissone, Manis Symonissone, and others. Andro Edmestoun, notary public.

SRO, RH.6/3020.

153. Kirkabister, 23 August 1589 (at 5 p.m.)

Instrument of sasine in favour of Lawrence Thomesone in Kirkabister and Isobell Cuik, his spouse, their heirs and assignees without division, following on feu charter by Michell Balfour of Montquhany and Arthour Sinclair of Ayth, of 2 marks *pro rege* land of Kirkabister, with precept of sasine directed to William in Neip.

Witnesses: William Sinclair, servant of the honourable (torn) Sinclair of Brucht, Magnus Thomesone, brother german of Lawrence, Magnus (torn)sone in Houssabister, and others. Andro Edmestoune, notary public.

SA, SC.12/65/1/27.

154. Skallowaybanks, 11 September 1589

Note of disposition by Cristean Segar, with consent of Jon Mitchell, her spouse, and Magnus Ollawsoun, her son and apparent heir, to Lawrence Sinclair of Gote, of 2 marks land, 8 pennies the mark, in Kirkhous in Averbie in Levanwik in the parish of Dunrosnes. Cristean instructs Thomas Auchinlek, notary public, to deliver to Lawrence 'ane sufficient chartour thairupoun, beirand ane claus of warrandice according to the use of the cuntrie, and to procure Androw Umphrayis seale to be appendit thairto, and forder is content that Laurence sall redeme samekle of hir sister part of land as hir brethir hes pandsett, the said Lawrence paying for the ayng and uthell thairof'.

Witnesses: Androw Umphray, William Sinclair, Jon Sinclair, his son, Robert Wilsoun, and Thomas Auchinlek, notary public.

SRO, NP.1/36, f.21.

155. Tresta in Fetloir, 2 October 1589

Contract between Laurence Bruce of Cultmalindeis, on the one part, and Hew Sinclair of Bruch, on the other part, for the marriage of Andro Bruce, son of Laurence, to Margaret Sinclair, daughter of Hew, 'with all guidlie haist', to be fulfilled by 15 June 1590. Laurence binds himself to infeft Andro and Margaret, before the completion of the marriage, in all his wadset lands of Scatstay, together with the lands of Sandwik in Yell, the charter and precept to be kept by Hew 'ay and quhill the said band of matrimonie be compleitit in face of halie kirk'. Laurence has received £3,000 in name of 'tocher gude', and because Andro is in Sanctandrois 'at the schole', Laurence binds himself to transport his son with all possible diligence to Yetland by 15 May 1590, 'wind and wedder serveand', and 'in cace ony stay be, as god forbid', then Laurence will repay £3,000 to Hew (or £2,000 if Andro dies). If either party breaks or violates the contract in any point, then he will pay the other party £3,000.

Witnesses: Captain William Sinclair, Johne Pennycuik of that ilk, James Wischart, Mathow Wischart, and Mr Robert Cheyn, commissary of Yetland.

SRO, RD.1/70, ff.62-3. Before 10 August 1599 Hew Sinclair of Burgh obtained letters in four forms charging Laurence Bruce of Cultemalindeis to observe the contract, and litigation followed in the court of session during 1599 (SRO, CS.15/75; see also SRO, CS.290/20 [registered 10 August 1599] and SRO, CS.7/188, ff.72-5 and 119-20). By their decreet on 21 December 1599 the lords of council found in favour of Hew Sinclair, on the grounds that the contract was 'ane trew evident in itself', and that Hew had proved that Andro and Margaret were lawfully married 'be ane persoun haveand functioun in the kirk'. The charter and precept of sasine of the lands in question were consigned at the bar to Hew's procurator, on behalf of Hew and his daughter, and Andro Bruce. The lords decerned that if Andro was not entered into possession of the lands by 20 June 1600 they would find the letters raised by Hew for payment of the penalty to be in order.

156. Leith, 17 October 1589

Letters by the king ordaining a charter to be made under the great seal confirming the feu charter by Michaell Balfour of Monquhanie, commissioner for Robert, earl of Orknay and Yetland, to Michaell Balfour, his second son, of the said earl's lands, called *pro rege*, the king's lands, viz.:

9½ marks land in Southhous in Scatnes, 12 marks land in Newhous (*rectius* Mewhous) in Scatnes, 16 marks land in Scollandis in Scatnes, 2 marks land in Got, 21 marks land 'in the four Tollopes' (*sic*), 20 marks 2 ures land in Lie, 8½ marks land in Oknastay, 4½ marks land in Daill, 11 marks land 'in the four Exingabous' (*sic*), 8½ marks land in Garth, 12 marks land in Quendall, 3 marks 2 ures land in Hildwall, 1 mark land in Ringistay, 1½ marks land in Bacasetter, 2 ures land in Noss, 1½ marks land in Woxburtin [Woxbuttin], 10½ marks land in Troswik, 2 marks land in Clomlie, 6 ures land in Lugasatter, 2 lasts of land in North Yrland, 4 marks land in Eleyeasater, 2 marks land in Wassatter, 2 lasts of land in Sandwik, 18 marks land in Burrowlandis, 1½ marks land in Picgagarth, 18 marks land in Westno, 12 marks land in Burraness, 8 marks land in Cognasburch, 5 marks land in Tow, 1½ marks land in Hellieness, 18 marks land in Aith, 6 ures land in Ockannosetter, all 6 pennies the mark; 14½ marks land in Quendestay, 4 pennies the mark; 10 marks land in Skelberay, 10 pennies the mark; 10 marks 6 ures land in Skousburch, 6 marks land in Olmasettir, 15 marks land in Mawik, 10 marks land in Hoswik, 6 marks land in Viasettir, 12 marks land in Sanday, 6 marks land in Liabutine, 2 marks land in Sater, 8 marks land in Coknesburch, 6 marks land in Oikcramy, 2 marks land in Flattabister, all 8 pennies the mark; 4 marks land in Skousburch, 7 pennies the mark; 11 marks land in Reirweik, 8 marks land in Schonnerweik, 12 pennies the mark, 16 marks land in South Yrland, 1 mark land in Schonnerweik in Westhous [Nesthous], 9 pennies the mark; in the parish of Dunrosnes;

9 marks land in My [Myn], 2 [20] marks land in Clet, 27 marks land in Paphill, 3 marks land in Burch, 7 marks land in Eisterhous in Maill, 9 marks land in Westerhous in Maill, 9 marks land in Branseclait, 6 marks land in Hous, 6 marks land in Cowasatter, all 8 pennies the mark; 4 marks land in Saltberre, 4 pennies the mark; 3 marks land in Burch, 12 pennies the mark; 4 marks land in Oxsnall [Opsuall], 30 marks land in [Easter] Querff, 6 pennies the mark; in the parish of Burray;

14 marks land in Brindistay, 12½ marks land in Sater, 3 marks land in Meikleagarth, 4 pennies the mark; 4½ marks land in Sand, 6 marks land in Outrabister, 6 pennies the mark; in the parish of Golbervik;

3 marks land in Wassater, 6 marks land in Garth, 6 marks land in Scollaway, 1½ marks land in Houll and 2 marks land in Howll, 3½ marks land in Sound, all 8 pennies the mark; 2 marks land in Eisterhous in Hambersland, 2 marks land in South Hambersland, 9 pennies the mark; 13½ marks land in South Laxfuird, 12 marks land in Tronafrith, 18 marks land in Howasettir, 3 marks land in Ureisland, 2 marks land in Sound, all 6 pennies the mark; 2½ marks land in Got, 1½ marks land in Cauldclif, 4 marks land in Ureisland, all 4 pennies the mark; 13½ marks land in Trondray, 7 pennies the mark; 3 marks land in Hugaland, 10 pennies the

mark, 3 marks land in Tow, 12 pennies the mark; in the parish of Tingwall;

3 marks land in Kirbuster, 4 marks land in Hugone, 2 lasts of land in Aith, all 6 pennies the mark; 3 marks land in Howistray, 4½ [4] marks land in Guinneildstay, 4½ marks land in Sater, 8 pennies the mark; 6 marks 2 ures land in Keldabister, 9 pennies the mark; in the parish of Brassay;

1½ marks land in Sand, 3 marks land in Garthishous, 4½ marks land in Silwik, all 12 pennies the mark; 1 mark land in Rawik, 1½ marks land in Wester Skeld, 1½ marks land in Culteswik, 4½ marks land in Tumbling in Twat, 3 marks land in Nosburch, 3½ marks land in Trestay, all 8 pennies the mark, 21 marks land in Westirskeld, 11 marks land in Howland, 1 mark land in Elyeasater, all 6 pennies the mark; 12 marks land in Eisterskeld, 4 marks land in Northhous in Culteswik, 4½ marks land in Hestersater, 12 marks land in Browaland, 4½ marks land in Langasole, 20 marks land in Cloustay, 12 marks land in Onyasound, 9 marks land in Athisnes, 1 mark land in Uphous in Ayth, all 9 pennies the mark; 6 marks land in Southehous in Culteswik, 11 pennies the mark; 8 marks land in Murasater, 4 pennies the mark; 11 marks land in Howland [Howgaland], 1 mark land in Eyeafrith, all 6 pennies the mark; 12 marks land in Brindasater, 10 pennies the mark; 5 marks land in Biggasater, 7 pennies the mark; in the parish of Aithsting and Sandsting;

29 marks land in Quhyteness; 2 marks land in Browatwat, 2 marks land in Curgagarth, 12 marks land in Estadaill, (blank) marks land in Follay, all 6 pennies the mark; 3 marks land in Wattisquy, 12 pennies the mark; 3 marks land in Gronaland, 3 marks land in Ure, 1 mark land in Foutaburch, all 8 pennies the mark; in the parish of Wallis;

4½ marks land in Soimbister, 2 marks 2 ures land in Scaw and 4½ marks land in Scau, all 10 pennies the mark; 1½ marks land in Lewasatter, 4½ marks land in Gillesbrek, 1 mark land in Skelberay and 6 marks land in Uphous in Skelberay, 2 marks land in Laxo, all 8 pennies the mark; 1 mark 2 ures land in Eisterhous, 2½ marks land in Southehous in Isbister, 2 marks 2 ures land in Lie, 1 mark land in Garthishous, 4 marks land in Orgill, 6 marks land in Westhous [Nesthous] in Skelberay, all 12 pennies the mark; 9 marks land in Kirkabister, 4 marks land in Brattabister, 6 ures land in Catfirth, 6 marks land in Laxfirth, all 6 pennies the mark; 3½ marks land in Aswik, 7 pennies the mark; 2 marks land in Kirkabister, 6 marks land in Howland, 9 marks land in Binstay, all 9 pennies the mark; in the parish of Nesting;

9 marks land in Voxater, 18 marks land in Flett, 1 mark land in Kirkhous, 3 marks land in Lie, 3 marks land in Neschon and 8 marks land in Neschon, 1 mark land in Tronasater and Brat [Tronafirth and Bruch], 11 marks land in Burranes, 7 marks land in Sandgarth, 3 marks land in Ingagarth, 3 marks land in Surasater, all 9 pennies the mark; 2 marks land

in Togon, 2 marks land in Skatsta, 36 marks land in Daill, 5 marks land in Tofton, all 8 pennies the mark; 13 marks land in Waddirstay, 2 marks land in Burravo, 2 [12] marks land in Benistay [Buistay], 1 mark land in Hardwell, 9 marks land in North Voxater, 4 marks land in Firth, 1 mark land in Stoud [Skoird], all 12 pennies the mark; 5½ marks land in Brunagarth, 10 pennies the mark; 9 marks land in Trundavo, 7 pennies the mark; 9 marks land in Neschon, 12 marks land in Flotton, 6 pennies the mark; 10 marks land in Ingouting [Gruting], 11 marks land in Brek, 9 marks land in Ilebister, all 10 pennies the mark; 18 marks land in Skatsta, 15 marks land in Gowrfuth [Gonofirth]; in the parish of Delting;

5 marks land in Uyea, 12 marks land in Sandvo, 10 marks land in Fleuagarth, 12 marks land in Burravo, 5½ marks land in Collafirth, all 10 pennies the mark; 9 marks land in Sater, 8 marks land in Collaquy, 5 marks land in Uswik, 2½ marks land in Fublasater, 10 marks land in Glusche, 10 marks land in Burraland, 6½ marks land in Clodusater, 8 marks land in Howll in Sowlam, 1 mark land in Nebon, 2½ marks land in Mure, 1 mark 2 ures land in Ausgarth, all 12 pennies the mark; 1 mark land in Howland, 5 marks land in Wo, 6½ marks land in Swenasater, 7 marks land in Ollaberry, 4½ marks land in Mustasater [Noustasater], 6 marks land in Bardasater, 3 marks land in Glusche, 1 mark land in Hagrasater, 3 marks land in Nebon, 10 marks land in Ulnafirth, 1 mark land in Urafirth, 2 marks land in Bravik Houlland, 4 marks land in Northhous in Tingon, 5 marks land in Aysgarth, all 9 pennies the mark; 7 marks land in Quyfirth, 8 marks land in Vo, 30 marks land in Ollaberry, 2 marks land in Turvasater, 2½ marks land in Huggaland, 8 marks land in Urafirth, 3 marks land in North Hildeswik, 4 marks land in Stoif in Hildiswik, 10 marks land in Bravik, 6 marks land in Fravangord, 18 marks land in Ure, 3 marks in Stow, 8 marks land in Feild, all 6 pennies the mark; 2½ marks land in Swinasater, 7 pennies the mark; 18 marks land in Uphous, 2 marks land in Orabister, 8 marks land in Proshouland [Preshowland], 11 marks land in Atratungon, 8 pennies the mark; 2 marks land in Helveir, 4 pennies the mark; in the parish of Northmaven;

282 marks land in the isle of Unst, all 6 pennies the mark, to wit: 4 marks 1 ure land in Skaw, 6 marks land in Torvoll, 16 marks land in Digrend, 7 marks land in Kirkatoun, 1 mark land in Valisgarth, 2 marks land in Skegga, 2 marks land in Toun, 6 marks land in Croukadaill, 1 mark land in Clisbow, 1 [2] mark land in Bodony, 1 mark land in Mewhous, 1 mark land in Howsten, 1 mark land in Soitland, 3½ marks land in Hamber, 7 marks land in Uragarth, 3 marks 2 ures land in Mydgarth, 6 marks land in Sudernes [Sweinanes], 11 marks land in Row and Maneland, 4½ marks land in Balyistay, 1½ marks land in Wodwik, 1 mark land in Pitasater, 1 mark land in Howland, 4 marks land in Upswall, 12 marks land in Scarpo, 1½ marks land in Ordaill, 3½ marks land in Quhailgarth, 2 marks land in Garth on the south side of the Vo, 3 marks

land in Cliff, 2 marks land in Clegon, 25½ marks land in Colvadaill, 3 marks land in Fravangourd, 12 marks land in Sandwik and Still, 6½ marks land in Hanagarth, 5 marks land in Munes, 2 marks land in Huggaland, 6 marks land in Maland, 6 marks land in Hoverstay, 5 marks land in Sound in Umboith, 11 ures land in Runnon in Garth, 3 marks land in Clipragarth, 1 mark land in Bragnagarth, 7 marks land in Wadbister, 5 marks land in Saxabirnes, 4 marks land in Snarravo, 1 mark land in Hammeir, 46 marks land in Underhoull, 4 marks land in Crosbuster, 3 marks land in Hulnon, 2½ marks land in Garth, 1 mark land in Colvasater, 8 marks land in Caldbak, 1½ marks land in Snaburch, 1 mark land in Vastie [Waslie] 4 marks land in Bigdon, 3 marks land in Sater;

143 marks land in the isle of Fetler, to wit: 20 marks land in Trestay, 43½ marks land in Funye, 15½ marks land in Hubie and 29 marks land in Hubie, 2 marks land in Balyagord, 2 marks land in Strand, 1 mark land in Ulye, 1 mark land in Urie, 3 marks land in Frakkasater, 3 marks land in Urasater, 5 marks 6 ures land in Gruting, 6 marks land in Aith, 4½ marks land in Uskasater;

3 marks land in Wedwik, 12 marks land in Northbrek, 18 marks land in Toft, 3 marks land in Murasater, 2½ marks land in Garth, 1½ marks land in Vachie, ½ mark land in Gudsir, 8 pennies the mark; 6 marks land in Stanissater, 8 marks land in Sandwik, 3 marks land in Kirkabister, 4½ marks land in Wasside [Wassae], 16½ marks land in Nebebak, 1½ marks land in Burranes, 1 mark land in Netherhoull, 5 marks land in Southledie, 2 marks land in Northhous in Sandwik, 2 marks 6 ures land in Ledie, 3 marks land in Hearakle, 2 marks land in Hostonsy [Hoscusay], all 6 pennies the mark; 3 marks land in Wassasere, 3 marks land in Awik, 2 marks land in Arrisdaill, 12 marks land in Samfray, 5 marks land in Sater, 2 marks land in Biggay, 5 marks land in Sound, all 9 pennies the mark; 3 marks land in Quyon, 2 marks land in Burch, 2 marks land in Hamnavo, 2 marks land in Bowasater, 8 pennies the mark; 10 marks land in Graveland, 7 pennies the mark; in the isle of Yell;

And of all other lands called *pro rege* 'alsweill not namit', except the lands reserved in the said commission, to be held by Michaell Balfour, younger, of said Robert, earl of Orknay and Yetland, in feu heritage, under reversion by Michaell Balfour of Monquhanie from said Michaell, his son, by payment of one angel of gold 'quhensoevir it sall pleise the said Michaell, elder'. Sasine to be taken at that part of the 10 marks land of Glusche 'callit the Duitche buithis in Glusche'.

SRO, E.2/16, ff.66-70. Precept in SRO, PS.1/60, ff.121-3. Any significant differences in the precept have been indicated in the entries in square brackets above.

157. Skallowaybanks, at Thomas Sewster's house, 20 October 1589 (at 4 p.m.)

Note of contract of excambion between Lawrence Sinclair of Gote, on the one part, and Hendrie Coupland, with consent of Margret Magnusdochter, his spouse, on the other part, whereby Hendrie renounces in favour of Lawrence his right, title and kindness of their room and lands of Scattishous in South Yrland in the parish of Dunrosnes; and Laurence renounces in favour of Hendrie his heritable right of 9 marks land, 8 pennies the mark, in Northhous of How in the parish of Quhitnes. Each party is to enter to the lands at Allhallowmass 1589, and because 4 marks land of the 9 marks land in Northhous of How is presently under tacks to Magnus Ollawsoun, it is agreed that Hendrie 'sall bruik and possess' 6 marks land, 9 pennies the mark, of the said lands of Scattishous, for the duration of the tacks to Magnus Ollawsoun.

Witnesses: Johne Mowat, apparent of Hugoland, Androw Hawik of Scatsta, Alexander Thomassone in Laxfurde, John Neving of Skousbruche, and Thomas Auchinlek, notary.

SRO, NP.1/36, ff.21-2.

158. Ustanes, 1 November 1589

Wadset by James Sinclair of Brow to William Sinclair of Ustanes, of 14 marks land, 6 pennies the mark, of Haveray, and 3 marks land in Burraland in Trondray, for £100, with one barrel butter for the annual rent thereof to be uplifted out of the said lands.

The original is not known to exist. Referred to in an action for repayment at instance of William Sinclair on 25 August 1604: *CB1*, p.157.

159. Colyevo, Yell, 15 December 1589

Gift of land and goods by Necoll Gottrimson in Culyevo to Marrowne Fersseill, his spouse.

... ... forttowne us to have procreatioun and barnis betux us, then my said spouse to have tein marks of my landis in geft, quhairof iiij marks land, ix pennies the mark, lyand in Keillingsettir, and sax mark lyand in Ure in Fetlar, vj d. the mark, with fyve mark of lous gudis, twelf goullovins to ilk mark, and that during hir lyftyme, retouring eftir hir deceis to the airis lawfullie gottin betuxt us, confermand to the lawes and practtiss of the cowntrie; and thir geftis severeallie and frellie gevin be me as is abowen rehersit to stand in efeck, and the said Marrowne, my forsaid spous, to brouk and joiss and possess the samyn as said is, frellie, quyatlie, weill and in paice, without ony obstikill or impedement to be maid be my airs or asignayis quhatsomevir; lyk as I have downe my uthir delygence in keiping of the said landis and gudis to thair behuff be the help and supportt of my forsaid spous; and thairfor my weill is that the samyn be bruikit be hir as said is, and defendit thairintill be all judges quhome to the samyn sall efear.

In wettnis and for securatie to this my present geft I have apendit my seall, and desyrit maist ernestlie ane honourable mane Lorawnce Bruce of Cultmaylendis, sheriff deputt of Unst, Fetlar and Yell, to subscryve and signat the samyn, with the seall of Willam Mangussone of Gardie, and subsriptioune of Pettir Maxveill, minister of Unst. At Colyevo in Yeill, the xv day off December in anno ane thousand fyve hundreth fourscoir and nyn yeirs. Befor thir wetniss, Daved Spance of Glup, Willame Spance, and Andro Smyth, with utheris dyverss.

L. Bruce of Cultemalyndies,
wytnness.

GH. Only the bottom part of the document is extant.

160. Edinburgh, 20 December 1589

Decreet of court of session in action at instance of Henry Sinclair, grandson and apparent heir of the deceased Oliver Sinclair of Brow, and apparent heir to the deceased Mathew Sinclair, his father, who died in January 1569-70, against James Sinclair, now of Brow, for delivery of writs and evidents of lands which now pertain to Henry, viz.:

Charter and sasine by Orme Manysone of Quindall to the deceased Oliver Synclair, of 6 marks land in Oyngyef(torn) in the parish of Aythsting and Sandsting, together with the instrument of sasine of Mathew Sinklair of the said lands;

Charter and sasine by Benedict, William and James Airlesonis, of the 3 marks land in Borrowland in Tondra in the parish of Tingwall, together with Mathew's sasine of the said lands;

Charter and sasine by Katherene Tullydeif, daughter of the deceased Henry Tullydeif, and Nicoll Halcro, her spouse, for his interest, to Oliver Sinclair, of the 7 marks land in Howgowland in the parish of Quhitnes, and 1 mark land in Hamersland in the said parish, and 1 mark 2 ures land in Northhous in the parish of Dunrosnes, together with Mathew's sasine of the said lands;

Charter and sasine by Marioun Smyth, with consent of Andro Leslie, to Oliver Sinclair, of 5 marks land in Houff, 3 marks land in Hameragart, ½ mark land in Scrapnagart, and 6 marks land in Tow, all lying in Quhitnes in Wesdaill, together with Mathew's sasine of the said lands;

Charter and sasine by Marioun Tullideif, with consent of Gilbert Copland, to Oliver Sinclair, of 6 marks land in Clat in the isle of Burra, and 2 marks land in Tegon in the parish of Onafirth, together with Mathew's sasine of the said lands;

Charter by Oliver Thomesoun to Thomas Kettill, of 2½ marks land in Howiff of Quhitnes, called Sanct Olawes 'presoun', in the parish of Dingwall (*rectius* Tingwall) and diocese of Schetland, together with Thomas Kettell's alienation made to Oliver Sinkclair of the said land, with Oliver's and Mathew's sasine thereof;

Charter of 11 marks land in Tumlin;
Charter of 15 marks land in Girdilstay;
Charter of 12 marks land in Skerrone;
Charter of the lands of Staniswall in Weisdaill;
Charter of 9 marks land in Setter in Weisdaill;

'The rest of the evidentis of saxtein scoir mark of land, being his possessioun the tyme of his decess, with the instromentis and sesing thairupone.'

James Sinclair's procurator denies the points of the summons, whereupon the lords of council continue the process until 15 May 1590, and ordain Henry to have letters to summon witnesses for proof, viz., Malcolme Sinclair in Ness, Lawrence Sinclair of Gott, John Murray of Stennydaill, Mr Robert Cheyne in Ure, Andro Mowat in Uliber, Andro Hawis in Scadistaw, Magnus Reid in Aird, Walter Smyth in the North Illis, Alexander Lister at the Ness, Nicoll Culauuo in Culliuo, and Nicoll Hardwall in Hardwall .

SRO, CS.7/121, f.349, and CS.7/124, f.375; SRO, CS.15/52. No final decreet has been traced.

161. Edinburgh, 27 December 1589

Decreet of court of session in action at instance of Alexander Kincaid against Andro Gyfheart, John Mowat, apparent of Hougaland, Andro Hawik of Scattistay, and the other feuars, tenants and parishioners of the vicarage of Scatza and Delting, for payment of the teinds and fruits of the vicarage for 1589 and yearly during Alexander's lifetime. Alexander was provided to the vicarage on 2 May 1565 by gift and provision thereof under the seal and subscription of Adam, bishop of Orknay, with collation and institution passing thereon, by virtue of which he has been in possession of the teinds, fruits and rents.

The lords of council decern the defenders to make payment to Alexander of the teinds and fruits of the vicarage.

SRO, CS.7/123, ff.54-5; SRO, CS.15/49.

162. Edinburgh, 10 March 1589-90

Obligation by Johnne Umphra in Skallawaybankis, principal, and Patrik Cowan, indweller in Leyth, cautioner, to Johne Howesoun, merchant, burgess of Edinburgh, for delivery of 13 barrels 'gude and sufficient oilyie, Flemis bind', upon the shore of Leith by 1 August 1590. Johne Umphra binds hinself to pay £21 for each barrel not delivered.

SRO, B.22/8/5, f.43. A marginal note, dated 25 November 1591, narrates that Johne Howesoun had granted discharge of the above.

163. (*circa* 1590?)

Disposition by Eduard Thomassone, with consent of Elleine Tailyeour, his spouse, and George Eduardsone, his eldest son, and taking the burden for Dionise Eduardsone, his youngest son, to an honourable man Hew Sinclar of Burgh, of 3½ marks land, 9 pennies the mark, in the town of Garth in the parish of Nesting.

SA, SC.12/65/1/18. The document is unfinished and unsubscribed.

164. (*circa* 1590?)

Wadset by Olaw Sinclair, lawful son and one of the heirs of the deceased James Sinclair of Hous, to an honourable man Hew Sinclair of Broch, of 9½ marks land, 8 pennies the mark, in Wester Quharff in the parish of Burray, ½ mark land in the said parish, and 9 marks land, 8 pennies the mark, in Wolsetter in the parish of Tingwell. The lands are redeemable on payment of 60 angel nobles of gold and weight at the parish kirk of Tingwell. At redemption Olaw shall immediately grant a tack to Hew of the said lands for 19 years, for yearly payment of 8½ lispunds butter (or 4s. for every lispund) and 8½ shillings wadmell (or 2s. for every shilling). Precept of sasine.

Witnesses: Captain Thomas Knichtson, Stevin Paplay, Nicoll Sinclair, Magnus Cragy, burgesses of Kirkwall, and William Fermour, notary public.

SA, SC.12/65/1/25. The document is undated.

165. 22 May 1590

'Feu charter by Arthur Sinclair of Aith, of a rood of land in Scalloway Bankis, on the east side of the town of Scalloway, to his cousin John Sinclair, indweller in Scalloway, and Marion Halcro his spouse. ...

'Witnesses: Andrew Giffhart, Thomas Bayne [*rectius* Boyne] and Robert Tulloch.'

The original is not known to exist. The above abstract, by Francis Grant, is in OSD, *SN*, 28 October 1893. According to a note by Gilbert Goudie the land was on the east side of the 'burn' of Scalloway (notebook in Braefield House, Dunrossness).

166. Edinburgh, 4 June 1590

Bond of caution by James Forbes of Corsinda for Edward Thomasoun in Garthe, Erasmus in Aswik, William McGussoun (*rectius* Magnussoun) in Neip, Allester Tailyeor in Catfurde, Magnus McGillisbreck (*rectius* in Gillisbreck), Adam McOrgill (*rectius* in Orgill), Henry Forester in Lunay, James Andersoun in Nesionis, Robert Hunter in Lie, Erasmus in Mewhous, and the other parishioners and tenants of the parish of Nesting, Newlesting (*rectius* Lunesting) and Quhalsay, that they will compear in the courts of the sheriffship of Schytland, and answer to either William Bruce, on the one part, David Strang in Benestaw, on the second part, Hew Sinclare of Burgh, on the third part, or Laurence Bruce of Cultmalyndeis, on the fourth part, whichever is found by the lords of council to have most right to the vicarage thereof.

SRO, CS.290/9.

167. Edinburgh, 4 June 1590

Bond of caution by James Forbes of Corsinda for Andro in Howle, Martine in Huksiter, Thomas in Coit, Magnus there, and the other tenants and occupiers of the lands of Howle, Coit and Covay in Yetland, that they shall pay their rents and duties for the term of Martinmas 1589 to either Margaret Stewart, relict of William Sinclar of Uya, William Bruce, now her spouse, for his interest, Frances Sinclar, her son, and the other bairns of the deceased William, and James Sinclar of Brow, their tutor, on the one part, or to Hew Sinclare of Burgh, on the other part, whichever is found by the lords of council to have most right thereto.

SRO, CS.290/9.

168. Edinburgh, 10 June 1590

Tack by Alexander Kincaid, vicar of Bressay and Bewrray, with consent of Adame, bishop of Orknay, commendator of Holyroodhouse, and the canons and chapter of the cathedral kirk of Orknay, to Robert, earl of Orknay, lord Yetland, of the vicarage of Bressay and Bewrray, for 19 years from the date hereof, paying yearly duty of £18.

Witnesses: Johne Cavertoun, Walter Callendare of Bordy, Adame Bothwell, and Bartilmo Kello, servants of the said commendator.

SRO, RH.6/3070. Not subscribed by the canons and chapter.

169. Edinburgh, 19 June 1590

Obligation by Alexander Kincaid, vicar of Wallis, principal, and James Nicolsone, tailor, burgess of Edinburgh, cautioner, to Adam, bishop of Orknay, commendator of Holyroodhouse, for the relief of Adam of payment of the tack duty of the vicarage of Nesting, and of all charges of the reader and the third of the said vicarage. Alexander Kincaid is assignee of the tack by Mr Alexander Spittell, vicar of Nesting, to Adam, of the said vicarage for three years from Easter 1590, for yearly payment of 14 angel nobles, dated 16 June 1590.

Witnesses: Walter Callender of Bordie, Malcolme Sincler, vicar of Dunrosneis, Bartilmo Kello, servant of the commendator, Thomas Blakbaird, servant of Malcolme, Adam Bothwell, and divers others.

SRO, B.22/8/5, ff.11-2.

170. Holyroodhouse, 20 June 1590

Gift to Alexander Duff of Terrisoull of the penalty of £40 amerced from Arthour Sinclare of Aith, pledge and surety for Thomas Boyne, now in Skallowaybankis, for the non-entry of Thomas before the justice in the tolbooth of Edinburgh on 16 June 1590, to underlie the law for the cruel slaughter of the deceased Alexander Duff of Torresoull, 'committit upoun set purpois, provisioun and forthocht fellony'.

SRO, PS.1/60, f.147. There are also letters ordaining the gift of the escheat of the goods of Thomas Boyne ('sumtyme in Gibstoun and now in Skellowabanks') to be made to Alexander Duff (SRO, E.2/16). The decreets are recorded on 16 June 1590 in SRO, JC.2/2 and JC.6/3.

171. Holyroodhouse, 21 June 1590

Gift to James Sinclare, lawful son of Malcolme Sinclare of Quendaill, of the prebendary 'callit the Croce Stouk, foundit within the college kirk of Dunrosnes', for his lifetime. The prebendary is vacant on the expiry of the gift thereof for seven years made by the king to Walter Tulloch, and is for the support of James at the schools.

SRO, PS.1/60, f.141.

172. Melbe, 10 August 1590 (at 4 p.m.)

Notarial instrument relating that Yanis in Hugseter, Thomas Reid, William Strawchin, Thomas Benedicsoun and Peter in Melbe compeared at the request of an honourable man Mr Robert Chene of Ore on the ground and biggings of the last of land in Melbe, presently occupied by Mr Robert, as tacksman of David Sinclair of Huntoun, to inspect the houses, biggings and timber thereof. 'After lang avisin[g] thairwith, thai haif upoun thair conscien[ce] praisit the saids houssis and tymmer, being upoun the barnis, byris and all uther houssis belanging thairto, to the sowm of sex gulyeonis and ane half alleinerlie, and thai haif declairit that the stane wark thairof ar altogidder ruinus and in point of tinsall in cais of nocht beitment.' They also deponed that one half of the houses belonged to David Sinclair, and the other half to the lords of Norroway.

Robert took instruments before Lawrence Sinclair, Gilbert Law and Peter Coucas. William Fermour, notary public.

SA, D.10/34/1.

173. Monross, 12 September 1590

Obligation by George Wardlaw, burgess of Monross, to his good friend Hew Sinclair of Burgh, for £460 for merchandise.

Witnesses: William Sinclair, James Wishart, and William Murray, bailie of Monross.

SRO, RD.1/57, f.207.

174. Stainadaill, 5 November 1590

Commission by Patrick, master of Orknay, lord of Yetland, to Johne Awik, to be underfoud of Yell.

Be it kend till all men be thir presentis, we Patrik, master of Orknay, lord of Yetland, etc., conforme to the electione and nominatione of [*illegible*] heall commownis of the yle of Yell, to have maid and constitut our lovit Johne Awik our underfoild within the said yle induring our will; giffand, grantand and permittand full power to hym allane to use, hant and exerce the said office of underfoldrie, nichtbour courtis, to fence and hald decretes and domes, to put to executione wrak, waith and waiff guddis, to caus collect and upgather to our use arestmentis in our names, to mak and lowss, with power siclyk to the said Jhone and his servantis, for quhom he salbe anserable to us, to jornay or chairge in our service, or utheris, our lesome adois, our saidis commownis of Yell; dischairgand all utheris of ony kynd of office ovir thame; and with all and sindre the utheris pointitis, liberteis and just fredomes of auld belonging and appertening to the office of underfoildre allenerlie; and that ay and quhill the said Jhone be dischairgit be us againe, provyding allwayis that the said Jhone mak compt rakning and payment to us of his intromissione quhatsumevir with our wrak, waith and accidentis belonging to us.

In witnes of the premissis, we have subscryvit thir presentis with our hand. At Stainadaill, the fyft of November 1590.

P., L. Yetland.

GH. An endorsement at the foot, signed by Thomas Auchinlek, states that the document was produced at Sanct Jhonis kirk in Yell on 15 July 1607, 'in judicio'.

175. Holyroodhouse, 11 November 1590

Complaint to the privy council by Mr Robert Cheyne of Ur, commissary of Yetland, concerning an assault on him in the kirkyard of St. Gregoreis kirk of Northeavin in Northema on 11 April 1590. Robert had come that day to the kirk to sit in justice in an action raised at the instance of 'ane pure wedow callit Marione Johnesdochter' against Andro Hawik, when the said Andro, with Daniel, his brother, Johnne Strang, William Wilsoun and others came to the kirkyard and enquired why Robert had directed summons against them. Robert had replied that it was to do justice to 'ane pure wedow', whereupon they struck him on the head and shoulders with three swords wounding him on the head and face 'to the effusioun of blude in grite quantitie'.

The lords of the privy council decern that Andro, Daniel and William are to be denounced rebels as they had failed to compear to answer the charge.

RPC, iv, pp.546-7. Letters of horning were raised on 11 November 1590: SRO, DI.47/6 (reg. 27 February 1591).

176. Edinburgh, 7 December 1590

Decreet of court of session in action at instance of Edward Thomason in Garthe, Erasmus in Aswik, Williame Magnussoun in Neip, Allaster Tailyeor in Catfurde, Magnus in Gillisbrek, Adame in Orgill, Henrie Forrester in Lunay, James Sutherland in Nestonis, Robert Hunter in Lie, Erasmus in Newhous, and the other parishioners and tenants of the parish of Nesting, Lunasting, Skerries and Quhalsay, against William Bruce, on the one part, Hew Sinclair of Burgh, on the second part, Laurence Bruce of Cultmalyndie, on the third part, and David Strang of Benestaw, on the fourth part, each of whom claims he is the underfoud of the said parish, and each of whom fines and poinds the pursuers for non-compearance at his court, notwithstanding that the pursuers are only subject to acknowledge one underfoud. The pursuers, being poor tenants and labourers of the ground, dwelling far off in the country of Yetland, may not repair to Edinburgh to make faith to the effect foresaids without their great hurt; neither do they dare hazard to produce this action before Robert, earl of Orknay, foud and sheriff of Yetland, because they understand that the claimants rights all proceed from him, 'lyk it is of veritie' that Robert and his deputes are expressly forbidden by other letters of exemption, granted at the instance of Hew Sinclair, of all proceedings in any actions concerning Hew or his tenants, and the exemption thereanent is presently depending before the lords of council.

The lords of council decern the pursuers to compear and answer in the courts of Hew Sinclair as the party found to have best right to the office of underfoudry 'for ocht that is yit sene', conform to a tack, dated 10 July 1577 at Linlythgow, whereby Robert constituted Hew and his heirs, bailies of the lands of Nesting, Lunasting, Quhailsay and Skerries, for 19 years from August 1577.

SRO, CS.7/126, ff. 332-3.

177. Edinburgh, 7 December 1590

Decreet of court of session in action at instance of Hew Sinclare of Burgh against James Corstorphin in Papay and Oliver Mansoun in Norbie, for removal from 6 marks land, 8 pennies the mark, in the Nethir Sound in the parish of Weisdaill, and from 3 marks land, 12 pennies the mark, of Gluss in the parish of Northmaving, respectively. The lands belong to Hew in heritage, as his infeftment and sasine thereof purport, by virtue of which he had by several precepts warned the defenders to remove at the term of Whitsunday 1585 without effect.

The lords of council decern the defenders to flit and remove from the said lands.

SRO, CS.7/127, ff.346-7.

178. Edinburgh, 12 January 1590-1

Decreet of court of session in action at instance of Magnus Sutherhous in Chalmerweik (*rectius* Channerweik), William Peax, Henrie Smith in Brek within the town of Oxingabu, John Nevene of Skursburgh, Ola Smith in Underbreck, Erasmus in Sound, and the other tenants and occupiers of the canons' lands, which pertained to the canons and stallars of the cathedral kirk of Orknay, within Yetland, against Hew Sinclare of Brugh, on the one part, and Margaret Stewart, relict of William Sinclare of Uya, William Bruce, now her spouse, for his interest, Frances Sinclair, her son, and James Sinclare, his tutor, for his interest, on the other part, for troubling them for payment of the duties of the crops and years 1588 and 1589, and the term of Whitsunday 1590.

The lords of council decern the pursuers to make payment of the duties to Hew Sinclare of Burgh as the party found to have the best right thereto, conform to an infeftment under the great seal of the date 7 November 1587, and instrument of sasine following thereupon under the subscription of Mr Andro Robertsone and Malcolme Sinclare, notaries public.

SRO, CS.7/129, f.94.

179. Vosgarth in Unst, 8 March 1590-1

Deed of gift by James Strang of Grenvaill, son of the deceased Barthillmow Strang of Vosgarth, to Agnes Mowat, of 6 marks land, 6 pennies the mark, in Sowythhous in Garthe benorth the hill in the isle of Unst. Barthillmow had promised Agnes Mowat, his spouse, 6 marks land, 6 pennies the mark, for her good service, but the gift had not been made, nor the place named, during his lifetime. If Agnes, or her heirs, wadset or sell the land they shall offer it to James first.

James affixes his signet, and procures the seals of Petter Nisbit of Kirkabustir and Necholl Gottromesone of Culyevo. Witnesses: Williame Manssone of Garthe, underfoud of Unst, Walter Smyth in Hambour, David Spance and Williame Spance, Waltir Redpeyth and David Copland, with others.

GH.

180. Edinburgh, 11 March 1590-1

Advocation in the court of session of action pursued by Andro Hawik of Scattistay, alleged heir to the deceased Vincentius Hawik, his father, against Mr William Lauder, minister and vicar of Yell, before Robert, earl of Orknay, and Patrik, master of Orknay, lord of Yetland, justice general of the same, and their deputes, 'tuiching the payment making' to Andro of 66 lambs as for one part of the duties and superplus of the bishop's umboths and vicarage of Yell of the crop and year 1560 and each year thereafter, 'doubland unto the year of god' 1589, and for payment to Andro of certain other bishop's umboths and teinds of the said tack of Yell of the crop and years 1561 and 1562

The lords of council discharge Robert, earl of Orknay, and Patrik, master of Orknay, and their deputes, of all further proceeding in the matter, and of their office in that part.

SRO, CS.7/130, f.236.

181. Kirkwall, 13 March 1590-1

Disposition by Ola Sinclair, lawful son and one of the heirs of the deceased James Sinclair of Hous, to an honourable man Lawrence Bruce of Cultemalindies, of 20 marks land, 6 pennies the mark, in Grungyillistay in Brassay, and all other lands in Yetland which he may inherit from his mother Elspett Sinclair, or as heir of his father, 'with power to mak outbrekis, to flit houssis and dyikis to the hill, and to remove tennentis and tennendries als oft as neid beis'. Precept is directed to John Urbie, bailie.

Ola subscribes with his hand led at the pen, and procures the seal of William Fermour, notary public. Witnesses: James Stewart of Gramsay, Walter Bruce, sheriff clerk of Orknay, Andro Giffert of Weddersta, and Henre Wardlaw, servant of Lawrence.

SA, GD.144/253/7.

182. Edinburgh, 2 April 1591

Bond of caution by George Smyth, tailor, burgess of Edinburgh, for Magnus Halcro in Grista, James Cheyne in Burra, Alexander Thomsoun in Laxfurde, William Tait in Tronissettar, Mans in Kirkord, Ola Manssone in Overabust, Boun in Kirkgord, James in Scalloway, and the other parishioners of the kirks of Tingwell, Quhytness and Weisdaill, pertaining in patrimony to the archdeaconry of Yetland, that they shall pay the teinds and duties of the crop 1590 to whichever of Mr James (*rectius* Alexander?) Cheyne, Mr William Hay, or Patrik Cheyne of Essilmonth, the lords of council find has best right thereto.

SRO, CS.290/10. See no. 203.

183. 8 April 1591

Endorsement by Jhon Rottray, macer, that he passed to Schetland 'quhair ane Danskyn schip lay leddin, quhilk wos bruittit to heiv bein laddin be papistis geir, wythin ane vo callit Curtevo of quhilk Jerohin Umquhra was foud thairof', and charged Jerohin to assist Thomas Oggilve. In compliance Jerohin passed with Thomas, requiring Jhon to go with them, to the Danskyn ship, and asked Dyneis Broigger, skipper, where the ship had been loaded. Dyneis testified that he had loaded at the port of Danskyn with 'quhit, certain laistis of barrill, ry, meill, fyf faittis madder, ten schip pund copper, twa greit pecis of bressin artolyerre wyth cannoun, half cannons, quharter cannon, bullat, ane gryt numbar thereof, wyth certan uther furnisyng, quhilk haill guds wythin the forsaid schip pertenit to the Duke of Florens, and bocht wythin the toun of Danskyn be his merchand quha departit out of Danskyn sex hors of tryn(?) aback to Florens, quha frauchtit the forsaid schip to Italie, and he to transport the guids thair throw the straits'. Upon this confession Jerohin Umphra, foud of Curtevo, where the ship lay, and Thomas, thinking the ship 'to be ane of the papistis, and ane of them that was to seig qanever', intromitted with the Duke of Florence's goods, and loaded certain goods therof in his own bark to transport to Scotland, conform to his letter of marque.

The skipper's confession was deponed before Jerohin, foud of Curtevo in Schetland, and Androw Stewart, Androw Mantreis, Jhon of Murray, also fouds thereof, with divers others.

Saltoun Papers, NLS, Ch.15078. Signet attached. Jhon Rottray was acting under royal letters, dated 7 March 1590-1 at Dalkeyth, instructing him to assist Thomas Ogilvy, burgess of Dundee, who had obtained letters of marque 'to rig out certane schippes of weare for taking and intrometting with gudis and geir pertening to persons, professouris of the unioun callit the Halyleague, and in special to the inhabitants of Crottet, Abbaveill and Amyens in the realm of France, be quhome the said Thomas hes been pilleit, and utherwayis hes oft and divers tymes sustenit greit skayth in his persoun and gudis' (Saltoun Papers, NLS, Ch.15077). See also no. 241.

184. Gereis Weycke, 15 April 1591

Supplication by Andrew Mowat, a subject of the king of Denmark, to Queen Elizabeth of England.

It pleaseth your heighnes to understand that I, Andres Motte, esqueyer, retayner, and subjecte under the kynges majestie of Denmarcke, and, for carten causes which god hathe appoynted, dwellinge at this present in his majestie realm of Norway, which am of layte yeres come oute of Shottland, in which place my landes, goodes, and ineritance doth lye and remayn which god hath geyven me to enierett of my progeniteis, gevinge your moste excelent heighnes my greatte sorowe and heavei complaynt to understande that I have benne two seaverall tymes spoyled and robede with Inglysh men dwelling within your majestie realme of Ingland, unto my greate heyndrance and lose of manie houndrthe dolleris. Fyrste, in anno -86 the 12 in Auguste am I robede and spoyled in my dwellinge house called Olleberie in Shottlande bye Inglishe men, the capten beinge named Capten Beare, dwellinge in Ratclyf beseides your majestie citey of London, or havinge his abbydinge in the same place. Which capten hade a shipe called the *Blacke Leyon* of Hull, master tharof called Ellexsander Chapman, dwellynge in Hull, havinge with them an other small barke to thare pennes and haveinge in bothe shipes a greate nomber of men. At which tyme they have not only spoyled my house, but allso have tacken from me in goulde and money and seylver warcke and other goodes the some of two thowsande doleris, beseides my apparell and obligacones and deades, which I woulde not meyse for syxe houndrethe doleris. And now agayn in anno '90 I had occason for to sayll from Norwaye to Shottlande, and from thense to my soffrayne lord and prence the kynges majeste of Skottlande upon sarten matteris I hade for to declare unto his highnes. And beinge come nere to the lande of Shottlande thare came an Ingleshe man of ware upon me and robede me of all that I hade in my shipe, and tocke from me at that present tyme in goulde, selver, and goodes, the some of four thowsande and fyve houndrethe dolleris, besydes a wryteynge which my soffraune lord Kynge Jemes his majestie be fore hade geyven unto me, with sarten other obleygacones and billes aperteyning to my sealf, the which I woulde not meise for a thowsande doleris. Upon vhich saide rover was a roppares sonne of Skarbroughe in Yorckshyar, as nere as I can larnne by my shiper and marineris, which said ropperes sonne hathe a mark in one of his checkes cout with a sorde. And beinge so spoyled and robed two seaveralle times with your majesties subjectes, and havinge by them had suche a greatte lose upon my goodes and monye, it hathe cawsed me to macke my humble sutt and complaint unto my souffrainte lord, the kinges majestie of Danmarke, whoo hathe of his majesties heighenes wryten his lovinge letteres unto your souffrainte majestie in my behalf. And for that I do understand that my souffrainte lord and kynnge his majestie wryteth not so large instrouccones unto your highnes of theise persones as I my self with dyveres otheres can showe and testefye, it macketh me the boulder to present this my humble suppleicacon unto your majestie, moste humble besechinge your heighnes not onlye to geyve me pardon for this my boulde enterprice, but also of your gracious goodnes for my souffraynt lorde and kynge his majesties sacke to be a healpe unto me, whareby I may come unto my ownne agaynne of theise forsaid parsones which have so crewellye meisowsed me, or other wayes to have lawe and justes agaynst them in suche order as it shall seme beaste unto your majesties heighnes. Wryten upon my hows called Gereis Weycke in Norway.

Mowat of Howgland.

CSP (Scotland), x, no.553.

185. Sandy, 18 June 1591

Letter of agreement by Robert, earl of Orknay, to William Sinclair of Ustanes.

William Sinclair of Ustanes, forsameikill as ye and I wes in termis of befoir for the feu gersumis of sevin merk uthell land in Ustenes, quhilk I am willing to do according to our speiking of befoir, quhilk wes thrie aingellis for ilk merk land, quhairfoir ye sall send me the gold with ony man ye pleis and the chartour salbe delyverit to him. Sua reserving all uther thing thairto dois commit you to god.

From Sandy the xviij day of Junij 1591.

Yours Orknay.

CB1, pp.157-8.

186. 24 July 1591

'Sasine in favour of Arthur Sinclair of Ayth, on disposition granted by Nicoll Nicolson, James Nicolson, Katherine Magnusdochter and Herman Manson, her son, of the lands of the town of Scalloway, in the parish of Tingwall; written by William Hermour [*rectius* Fermour], N.P.'

The original is not known to exist. The above abstract, by Francis Grant, is in OSD, *SN*, 28 October 1893. In another abstract, by Gilbert Goudie, Arthur Sinclair is said to receive 'heritable, actuall, reall and corporall possessioun of the said toun of Skalloway' (notebook in Braefield House, Dunrossness).

187. Scallaway banks, 24 July 1591

Feu charter by Patrick, master of Orknay, Lord Yetland, to Robert Wilsone in Scalloway bankis and Margaret Sawllis his spouse, of the tenement of land possessed by them, in length from north to south six score and five feet, and in breadth from east to west 55 feet, 'bounding tuo futtis withowt the syd wall of the said tenement at the east, the full sea and common gatt at the south, the tenement and yeard pertaining to the airs of umquhill John Umphray at the west, [and] the unmanured ground without the head dyk of the said tenement at the north'; with power to them 'to exerce within the boundis of the said tenement all kynd of custum, change, trafeit and merchantdice, sik lyk as anay uther hants or uses within our ... lordschip.' Robert and Margaret are to give at each Hallowmas 'ane half heip of tallou with sex kaponis, and to give thair suit in present to our head courtes to be holden within the parochine of Tingwall, and with service used and wont allenerlie, provyding allwayes that [they] ... prepair for the seat of us or our servands at the banks ane suficient chamber, weill apoyntit, upon our resonable charges and expences.'

Witnesses: Patrick Monteith of the Fair Yle, John Mackinie, James Dicksone and Andrew Edmonstoun, NP, the master's servitors. William Fermour, NP, subscribes as a witness.

The original is not known to exist. The above abstract is from a copy made by Laurence Neven NP at Scallaway Banks, 27 March 1677 (SRO, additional miscellaneous writs, Commissariot of Edinburgh, RH.6 and RH.7, box 1).

188. Skalloway, 31 July 1591

Discharge by Alexander Kincaid, servant of Robert, earl of Orknay, to William Sinclair of Ustenes, for 21 angel nobles of gold and weight. Alexander binds himself to deliver the gold to Robert, and either to obtain a charter of alienation made by Robert to William and his heirs, of the 7 marks land of Ustenes, or else to deliver the gold back to William.

Witnesses: Mr Androw Pitcarne, parson of Westray, and William Fermour, notary public.

CB1, p.158.

189. 31 July 1591

'Wodset charter [by] Andrew Hawick of Scatstay to Arthur Sinclair of Aith and his airs, upon 2 merks land, 9 peneyes the merk, in Voe in the paroch of Delting, with eight merk land in Wadbister, 8d. the merk, in Tingwall paroch ... with ane sasine on the back therof, dated the 7th day of August and year forsaid.'

The original is not known to exist. The above abstract is in a late 17th century Inventory of writs in the custody of Laurence Sinclair of Sandsound (GH). According to an abstract by Francis Grant, OSD, *SN*, 28 October 1893, the wadset was for 50 angel nobles of gold, the document was subscribed at Scalloway, and the witnesses were Laurence Sinclair of Gott, William Sinclair of Ustaness, and William Hermour (*rectius* Fermour), N.P.

190. 5 September 1591

'Wodsett ryght [by] Andrew Hawick of Scatsta to Arthour Sinclair of Aith, upon 8 merks land in Graven, 9d. the merk, redemable for 20 angeles nobeles of gold ... containing ane recept one taille therof for £6 10s.8d., with tuo barrells of butter, declairing the lands not to be redemed untill payment therof, daitted the 28 day of July 1596; with ane precept of saising one the back therof, daitted the 28 July 1592.'

The original is not known to exist. The above abstract is in a late 17th century Inventory of writs in the custody of Laurence Sinclair of Sandsound (GH). According to an abstract by Francis Grant, OSD, *SN*, 28 October 1893, the document was subscribed at Scalloway, and William Sinclair of Ustaness was a witness.

191. Edinburgh, 19 February 1591-2

Decreet of court of session in action at instance of Andro Giffert of Wedderstaw against William Wilsoun, Andro Hawick in Scatstay, Daniell Hawick, his brother, Magnus Olasoun in Neschen, James Aspelene in Tumlene, Nicoll Enersoun in Hardwell, and Cristopher Nicolsoun, for spoliation from Andro of 200 ewes (at £2 each) and 200 year-old sheep (at £1 13s.4d. each) from his lands of Grunasound of Neschen in the parish of Delting on 6 January 1591-2, and of 6 ky (at £12 each) and 10 oxen (at £20 each) from his house of Wedderstay in the parish of Ulnafirth on 8 January 1591-2.

The lords of council continue the summons until 15 June 1592, and decern Andro to have letters to summon witnesses, etc.

SRO, CS.7/136, f.14.

192. Edinburgh, 25 February 1591-2

Decreet of court of session in action at instance of Mr John Lermonth, advocate, procurator fiscal of the commissariat of Edinburgh, against Patrik Stewart, master of Orknay, for impeding Mr Robert Cheyne, commissary 'within the boundis of Orknay and Yetland', from confirming testaments, ministering justice and exhorting his office according to the commission granted to him. For these reasons Mr Robert has made little or no account and payment of his intromissions with 'the cote silver of testamentis within his jurisdictioun, nayther hes exhibite and producit befoir the lordis his registrat buikis according to the injunctioun gevin to him thairupoun'.

The lords of council decern letters to be directed charging Patrik, master of Orknay, to compear before them and find sufficient caution in their presence, under such pains as they shall appoint, that he shall not stop nor impede Mr Robert from using his office.

SRO, CS.7/135, ff.73-4.

193. Edinburgh, 3 March 1591-2

Bond of caution by Sir Patrik Bellenden of Evie, knight, for David Strang in Bewestray (*rectius* Benestay) that he shall compear in the courts to be held by Hew Sinclare of Burgh, who has been found by the lords of council to have the best right to the office of underfoudry, and that David shall desist from all proceedings against the parishioners subject to the said jurisdiction, under pain of £100.

SRO, CS.290/12.

194. Edinburgh, 3 March 1591-2

Bond of caution by Sir Patrik Bellenden of Evie, knight, for Margaret Stewart, relict of William Sinclare of Uyea, William Bruce of Symbester, now her spouse, for his interest, and Robert Sinclare, her son, that they shall desist from molesting and troubling Mans Sutherhous in Channerweik, William Pais, Henry Smyth in Brek within the town of Exnebie, John Neveine of Skowisburgh, Olave Smyth in Elinebrek, Erasmus in Sound, and the other tenants, etc., of the canons' lands, which pertained to the canons and stallars of the cathedral kirk of Orknay, within Schytland, for the mails and duties claimed by them, on the one part, and by Hew Sinclare of Burgh, on the other part, of the crops 1588 and 1589, and term of Whitsunday 1590, if it is found by the lords of council that Hew Sinclare has right thereto.

SRO, CS.290/12.

195. Edinburgh, 3 March 1591-2

Bond of caution by Sir Patrik Bellenden of Evie, knight, for Margaret Stewart, relict of William Sinclare of Uyea, and William Bruce of Symbester, now her spouse, for his interest, that if it is found by the lords of council that they are to make payment to Laurence Bruce of Coupmalindie of arrears of teinds for 5 years of the lands of Uyea, extending to 75 lispunds of butter and 225 cans of oil, together with £4 13s.4d. in expenses, then Patrik shall make payment to Laurence of the monetary equivalent thereof.

SRO, CS.290/12.

196. Edinburgh, 9 March 1591-2

Decreet of court of session in action at instance of Mr William Lauder, vicar of Yell, against Andro Hawik in Scattistaw, and Daniell Hawik, his brother, heirs of the deceased Vincentius Hawik, their father, on the one part, and Mr Frances Cheyne of Cragie, on the other part, for troubling Mr William for payment of certain teinds and bishop's umboths of the vicarage of Yell for the years 1560, 1561 and 1562. Andro and Daniell claim thay have obtained a decreet before the sheriff and foud of Yetland decerning William to pay the said teinds to them; and Frances claims that as donator to the escheat of all goods, etc., pertaining to Andro and Daniell, who have been put to the horn, he has right to the said teinds.

The lords of council decern the pursuer to pay the teinds, bishop's umboths and duties foresaid to Mr Frances Cheyne.

SRO, CS.7/136, f.96.

197. Edinburgh, 28 March 1592

Feu charter by Patrik, master of Orknay, lord Yetland, to William Bruce of Symbester, of the 20 marks land, 6 pennies the mark, of Swounburgh, together with all right and kindness to the 'eyng' of 4 marks land, 6 pennies the mark, pertaining to the 'proves' of Norroway, liand in rig and randell' with the said 20 marks land of Swounburgh, and 'siclik' the 20 marks land, 6 pennies the mark, of Skaitness, in the parish of Dunrosnes, all presently occupied by William and his sub-tenants, with reservation of the right and title of the house and fortalice lately established on the grounds of the said lands of Swounburgh on the south side of the Newhall, together with a yard adjacent thereto, 60 feet broad and wide, at the south-east gable of Newhall, and pasturage of 'tua ky and tua oxin' in the summer on the ground of the said lands of Swounburgh (corn and meadow excepted), together also with the pasturage of 'twentie wodderis within all the boundis of the lokitnes of Skatnes', whenever Patrik or his heirs reside in the house and fortalice of Swounburgh. In his absence William is to have the keeping of the said house and yard, he being answerable to Patrik for the 'insycht, plenischeing and utheris guds and geir that sal be deliverit' at Patrik's departure, and to be free of all pasturage during Patrik's absence. The lands are to be held in feu farm and heritage, paying yearly 13 lispunds 8 marks butter and 13 shillings 2 cuttles wadmell, with the scat thereof 'as for the auld dewtie, usit and wont', together with 3s.4d., and William is to answer three suits at Patrik's head courts in Yetland yearly. Precept of sasine.

Witnesses: James Stewart of Gramesay, Patrik Menteyth of Fair Ile, Thomas Blak and George Trail, servants of Patrik.

SRO, RD.1/38, ff.412-4.

198. (*circa* May 1592)

Supplication to parliament by the possessors of udal lands in Orkney and Shetland, concerning Patrick, earl of Orkney.

My lord commissioner and lordis of articlis of this presentt parliament; unto your grace and lordshipis humblie meines and shawis we your servitors, Laurance Bruce of Cultmalindy, Henrie Sinclair of Towquoy, William Irving of Saba, Robert Sinclair of Camstane, Thomas Cheyne of Walay, William Bruce of Cimbister, John Sinclair of Tobe and Magnus Cromartie of Caray, for our selffis and in name of the remanent our soveraine lordis guid subjectis, heritable possessoris of the udach landis in Orknay and Yetland; that quhair Patrick, earle of Orknay, upon some sinister informatioun made be him that the haill udach landis in Orknay and Yetland wer fallin in nonentrie, hes therupon and upon some other unlawfull groundis purchast ane infeftment of our saids landis, and is myndit to seek the approbatioun and confirmatioun therof in this presentt parliament, that thairby, being claid with the warrand and auctoritie of ane act [of] parliament, he may summarilie, but forme prosceis of law possess him selfe in our haill landis and intruse himselfe therintill; albeit (we doubt not) give your grace and lordshipis understood the nature of our udach landis, and the forme and maner of ther halding, no sick confirmatioun wald be grantit to the said erle; for it is of treuth that quhen the landis of Orknay and Yetland wer under the crowne of the kingis of Norroway for the tyme, the udach landis wer repute as ane part of the propertie of the crown and the possessoris of the earledome bruikit the samin but charter or seasing as heritable rentallaris of the propertie of the crowne for payment of ther scattis, callit in our language the feu dewties,

[and] at the deceis of the possessor and rentallar the entrie of ther aires followed be ane breiff of devisioun callit in Denmark and Norroway ane shownd bill, and is put in executioun be the shereff and his deputis; quhilk forme of halding hes been inviolablie keeped sen syne, alswell during the tyme of the kings of Denmark as sen thir lands fell to the crowne of Scotland, and we and our predecessoris of ther udach landis haiff been in continuall possession theroff according to the tennor of the halding abovewretten, first esteablished in Norroway, allowit in Denmark, and imbracit and ressavit be ane inviolable custome in this kingdome thir fyve agis bygone and mair, and thair wes never any question moved against the forme of our haldings, and the constant and inviolable custome of sa mony ages, without any interruption or process intendit against us or our predecessoris, will never suffer us to fall under the compas of nonentrie, and giff the soverane princes of this kingdome for the tyme had mislykit of the forme of our halding as not agriable to the lawes and customes of this kingdome, ther is no question bot be the authoritie of ane law (all parties being heard) they wald have altered and changit the forme of our haldings, and putt us in suretie be ane new established forme; bot so farr hes the princes of this kingdome been from quarrelling of the nature of our haldings as by taking hold and making ther advantage upon every failyie quhilk happined and fell out agains the condition of our halding, they have approven and allowit our said haldings; for it is ane speciall provisioun and conditioun in our haldings that the non payment of our dewties for thrie termes togidder forfaltis our right and possession, quhairby it is fallen out that many of the udach landis hes fallen in his majesties hands upon this occasion; and farder it is of veritie that quhen this pretendit infeftment wes first purchast be the said earle, we finding our selfes thairin to be verie heavilie grived and prejudgit, we cam unto him and assured him that we wald complaine and seek reparatioun from his majestie, and he fearing (be law) he could not maintaine that pretendit right of his to be guid, he promeisis to us to discharge the samine give we wald pay to him the soumes of money advancit be him in purchasing theirof, quhilk we did; and farder it is of treuth that thir is some lordis in Noroway and Denmark quha bruikis sundrie of thir udach landis in Yetland eftir this same forme of halding, quhais halding the said earle hes nawayes quarrelled and hes omitted ther landis out of his infeftment, and hes only taine him to us whome he thinkis to owirtrow at his pleasur; and sua we being his majesties proper rentalleris, we ought not to be in ane worse condition nor strangers are, and giff this confirmatioun shall passe throw it will so mikle the mair stur up the said earle in most violent courses agains us, and prepaires our utter undoeing and wrack. Heirfor we most humblie beseek your grace and lordshipis that no sick confirmation passe to the said earle in this presentt parliament, and that we may have ane act past in our favoris declaring

that the pretendit infeftment purchast be the said earle of our said udach landis shall nowayes prejudge us in our heritable possessiones, and that the samen sall be no farder extendit but to our feu dewties, quhilk we are content to pay to him or to any other his majesties pleis appoint; and giff it shall pleis his majestie and your lordshipis to alter the forme of our haldingis and to make the samine agreable to the forme of this kingdome, we maist humblie beseek your lordshipis that it be declarit be act of this present parliament that we shall be preferrit to our rowmes and possessiones, and that securities be made to us of the samine, we doing therfor accordingly, and your answer humblie we beseek, etc.

[*A docket?*] The supplicatioun abovewrettin wes given to the lordis of the articles of the parliament haldin at Edinbroughe be King James 6, parliament 12, anno 1592; in the quhilk parliament ane ratificatioun wes made to Patrick, erle of Orknay, of the erldome theroff in ane unprinted act. The forsaid erledome wes ratified of befor to Robert, earle of Orknay, in the 7 parliament haldin at Edenbrough be King James 6, anno 1581.

OA, D.2/33/13 (apparently a 17th century transcription).

199. Scalloway, 10 June 1592

'Disposition by Arthur Sinclair of Aith, for certain sums of money paid to him in his urgent necessity, to Nicoll Garoache, of a piece of ground within the bounds of Scalloway, measuring 16 feet by 40 feet. ...

'Witnesses: Thomas Bayn [*rectius* Boyn?], Robert Wilson and William Hermour [*rectius* Fermour], NP.'

The original is not known to exist. The above abstract, by Francis Grant, is in OSD, *SN*, 28 October 1893.

200. Edinburgh, 7 July 1592

Decreet of court of session in action at instance of Hew Sinclair of Burgh against Patrik, master of Orknay, lord of Yetland, commendator of Quhithorn, for exemption from Patrik's jurisdiction. Hew has been heavily oppressed by Robert, earl of Orknay, father of Patrik, who had taken him captive, 'keipit him in prisoun, pairtley in our cuntrey of Yetland, and pairtley on the sey in ane schip, the space of twentie dayis', and thereafter, without ony form of order, in his own court had accused Hew of many invented and false crimes whereof he was innocent, and refused to let Hew have a procurator or clerk to minute his assertions. Robert had chosen an assize 'of the maist pairt of his awin houshald and domestik servandis quha durst nor wald do na thing bot as thai wer commandit be him'. Although Hew was altogether innocent he, 'at the desyr of sum freindis, wes movit to cum in the said erlis will', and was freed. Thereafter, Robert declared all Hew's goods and possessions to pertain to him as escheat. Therefore, Hew was compelled to come to Edinburgh and purchase letters charging Robert to find lawburrows, and to summon Robert before the council to answer his complaint. Hew also obtained letters to exempt himself from Robert's office and jurisdiction. Nevertheless, Patrik, claiming to have right to the lordship of Yetland made to him by his father has in June, July and August 1591 entered the country of Yetland and taken possession thereof. Robert had granted tacks to Hew of the sheriffship and wadmell of Yetland long before Patrik obtained his right thereto. Patrik has so troubled Hew that he will neither permit him to hold a court within the bounds of Hew's own jurisdiction by his tack, nor suffer him to take up the wadmell, whereby Hew is compelled to charge him with lawburrows, even though Patrik knows that the action of exemption is depending before the lords of council. Hew is informed that Patrik has lately obtained a commission of justiciary and lieutenantry in Yetland, with power 'to heid and hang, put to the horne', and intends, if Hew and other gentlemen in the country who have possessions which Patrik would have, will not give over the same to him, to use this commission to call them and by such form of judgement as he will use not only evict them of their tacks and possessions, but also confiscate their moveables, Patrik being both judge and party, and having command of all the poor men in the country who dare not do but according as Patrik directs them. Moreover, Patrik is minor and not able to exercise such an office and jurisdiction. Therefore Hew and his friends and tenants dwelling on his own lands ought to be exempted from Patrik's office and jurisdiction in all criminal and civil actions concerning Hew in times coming,

The lords of council exempt Hew Sinclair, and his friends, servants and tenants, dwelling on his lands, now and in all times coming, in all actions and causes, civil and criminal, moved or pursued against Hew or his foresaids, before the said Patrik, Lord of Yetland, and his deputes, and discharge the said Patrik and his deputes, of all accusing, calling, unlawing, etc., against Hew.

SRO, CS.7/137, f.310; SRO, CS.15/54 (summons, dated 23 November 1591). Letters of horning had been raised at Hew Sinclair's instance against Patrik, lord of Yetland, on 19 September 1591 (SRO, DI.47/7, ff.113-14): Sinclair stated that the office of underfoudship pertained to him by a gift and disposition granted by Robert, earl of Orknay.

201. Edinburgh, 26 July 1592

Decreet of court of session in action at instance of Hew Sinclair of Burgh against David Strang, for removal from 2 marks of land of Ramstray (*rectius* Beinstay?) in the parish of Nesting. David had been warned to remove at Whitsunday 1590.

The lords of council decern the defender to remove from the land.

SRO, CS.7/137, ff.396-7.

202. 2 August 1592

Decreet of sheriff court of Orknay and Yetland in action at instance of Laurence Sinclair of Goit against the heirs of the deceased Olaw Sinclair, decerning Laurence to have right to the possession of 4 marks land in Uphous in Sandwik, in the parish of North Yell.

The decreet was produced in the sheriff court on 12 August 1617 in an action of removal at instance of Niniane Nevein of Kirkibuster against Donald Fraser in Sandwick (*CB2*, p.63, where the date appears erroneously as 1591 [see SRO, SC.10/1/4, f.52]).

203. Edinburgh, 11 August 1592

Decreet of court of session in action at instance of Magnus Halcro in Greistay, James Chene in Burray, Alexander Thomsoun in Laxfirth, William Tait in Tronissetare, Magnus in Kirkgorth, Ala Mangnusoun in Over Abust, Boun in Kirkgorth, James in Skalloway, and the other parishioners of the kirks of Tingwall, Quhitness and Weisdaill, pertaining in patrimony to the archdeaconry of Yetland, against Mr James (*rectius* Alexander*?*) Cheyne, who claims he has been provided to the archdeaconry, on the one part, Mr William Hay, who also claims he has been provided to the archdeaconry, and who has now been appointed minister at the said kirks, on the second part, and Patrik Cheyne of Essilmonth, tacksman of the archdeaconry, on the third part, for troubling the pursuers for payment of the teinds and fruits of the archdeaconry for the crop 1590. Mr William Hay has purchased letters charging the pursuers to pay the teinds; and Andro Umphray, chamberlain and factor of Patrik Cheyne, has for several years taken up and received the teinds and duties, and has already taken up the great part of the crop 1590, and intends to poind and distrain the pursuers for the balance.

The lords of council decern the pursuers to pay the teinds, rents and duties of the archdeaconry for the crop 1590 and yearly thereafter to Mr William Hay, as the party found to have the best right thereto, conform to the gift of presentation granted by Robert, earl of Orknay, and instrument of collation and institution following thereon, dated 24 July 1585, and the assignation subscribed by Mr James Ritchie bearing the whole archdeaconry of Yetland to be assigned to Mr William for the crop 1591.

SRO, CS.7/139, ff.24-5. See no. 182.

204. Kirkwall, 17 August 1592

Act of deprivation of James Hay, vicar of Unst, Alexander Kincaid, vicar of Wauss, Brassay and Burray, Mr Alexander Spittaill, vicar of Nesting, and either Mr William Hay or Mr Alexander Cheine, whichever is archdeacon of Yetland, from their functions and benefices.

In the synodall assemblie of Orkney and Yetland haldin at Kirkwall upon the seventeine day of August the yeir of god ane thousand fyve hundreth fourscoir tuelff yeiris. The commissioneris deputt be the generall assemblie, to wit Mr Robert Pontt, minister of Sanct Cuthbertis Kirk, and Thomas Swintoun, minister at Kirkwall, with advyse and consent of the haill brethrine off the ministrie of Orkney and Yetland being thair present for the tyme, and also with the concurrance, consent and assistance of my lord Robert, erll of Orkney, Maister Johne Dischingtoun, commiser of Orkney, and Walter Bruce, schereff clerk thair, commissioneris deputt be the kingis majestie; having callit before thame, James Hay, pretendit viccar of Unst, Alexander Kincaid, pretendit viccar of Wauss, Brassay and Burray, Maister Alexander Spittaill, pretendit viccar of Nesting, Maister William Hay and Maister Alexander Cheine, ather of thame pretending rycht to the archideanerie of Yetland; being summond to this day to heir thame, and ilk ane of thame, depryvitt from thair offices and benefices, for non-residence and uther caussis, specifiet in the summondis direct and laufullie exequit aganis thame; and oftin tymes callit comperit nocht, nather be thame selffis nor nane utheris in thair names, to alledge any caus in the contrair. The saidis persones and everie ane of thame beand notoriouslie knawin and provin to be non-residentis, never ane of tham remaining, nor to haif remanit this lang tyme bypast within the boundis or countrey of Yeitland quhare the saidis vicarages and benefices lyis, nor to haif servit the cure thairat be the space of dyvers yeiris; thairfoir the commissioneris, assweill deput be the generall assemblie as be his hieness, with advyse of the haill brethren of the synodall assemblie, hes depryvit and deposit the foresaidis persones and everir ane of thame from thair functiounis and benefices respective foirsaidis, as not residentis and for uther caussis contennit in the summondis raisit aganis thame. Extracted furthe of the buikis of the said synod and commisery be me clerk thairto under subscryvand.

Hibbert Ware Papers, library of the Society of Antiquaries of Scotland, ms. 569. The document is unsubscribed.

205. Scalloway, 23 (?September) 1592

Feu charter by Patrik, master of Orknay, lord Yetland, to Alexander Butter, of the tenement and yard in Scallowa bounded by the tenement occupied by Anny Halcro on the west, the waste ground of Berrye on the north and east, and the (illegible) and common gait on the south, 60 feet broad, and in length from south to north equal with the tenement occupied by the said Anny, with power to win peats, etc., in the east hill of Scallowa, for an annual payment of 13s.4d., suit at the head bailie courts held in the parish of Tingwall yearly, and provision of a sufficient chamber in the tenement for receipt of Patrik's servants on Patrik's own reasonable charges.

Witnesses: Patrik Monteithe of Fairyle, Thomas Blak (?), and (illegible), notary public.

SA, D.10/24/3. An endorsement on the back, signed by Thomas Auchinlek, states that the document was produced at the castle of Skalloway bankis on 30 August 1604 *in judicio*.

206. Scalloway, 26 September 1592

Feu charter by Patrik, master of Orknay, lord Yetland, to William Sinclair, elder, in liferent, and Jhone Sinclair, his son, Marione Halcro, spouse of Jhone, and Henry Sinclair, their son, in fee, of the tenement and yard presently occupied by William in Scalloway, bounded by the tenement occupied by Thomas Boind on the east, the full sea and common gait on the south, the tenement occupied by Jhone Saister on the west, and the loan lying between the said tenement and that occupied by Anny Halcro on the north, in length equal to the head dyke of Thomas Boind's tenement, with power to win peats, etc., in the east hill of Scallowa, for payment of 13s.4d. yearly and 8d. more in augmentation of rental, their suit to the head and bailie courts in the parish of Tingwall, and provision of a sufficient chamber in the tenement for receipt of Patrik's servants on Patrik's own reasonable charges. Precept of sasine.

Witnesses: Thomas Blak, Patrik Mentethe of Fairyle, and Androw Edmestoune, notary public.

SA, D.10/24/2.

207. Kirkwall, 27 January 1592-3

Feu charter by Patrik, master of Orknay, lord Yetland, to Captain Thomas Knychtsone, his servant, his heirs and assignees without division, of 3 marks land of Hoverstay, ½ mark land of Kirkbuster, 6 marks 2 ures land of Keldabuster, 4 marks land of Hewin, 4½ marks land of Gunneilestay, 4½ marks land of Sater, and 33 marks land of Aith, in the isle of Brasay, with power 'to flit dykis and mak outbrekis', and also of the whole scat of the uthail land in the isle of Brasay, both butter and wadmell, to be incorporated with the foresaid lands in the tenandry of Aith (sasine to be taken at the mansion and dwelling place of Aith), under reservation to Patrik of the 'wrack and waith that sall fortoun to cum in the said ile, and the escheittis and unlawis of court that sall fall be occasioun of bluid, thift and uther capitall crymes', for payment yearly of the mails, scat, wattle and duties contained in the rental, together with ½ dollar in augmentation of rental, with suit and presence at the head courts yearly conform to the custom of the country, due service 'usit and wont', and at the entry of every heir payment of 1 angel noble gold of weight in name of doubling of the feu mails. Precept of sasine.

Witnesses: Patrik Menteyth, Williame Bannatyne, Thomas Blak and Andro Mairtyne, servants of Patrik.

From charter of confirmation under the great seal, dated 27 June 1610 (SA, GD.144/24/4; *RMS*, vii, no.313).

208. Holyroodhouse, 5 February 1592-3

Presentation of Mr James Lauder, eldest lawful son of Mr William Lauder in Yetland, to the vicarage of Yell, vacant following the demission of Mr William, with direction to the presbytery of Tingwall, or the commissioner of Yetland, to examine the qualification of James, and if he is found able to discharge his calling and the function of the ministry to admit him thereto, and to receive the confession of his faith and his oath of obedience to the king.

SRO, PS.1/65, f.12.

209. Edinburgh, 3 March 1592-3

Decreet of court of session in action at instance of William Bruce of Simbister against Hew Sinclair of Burgh, Edward Sinclair, his brother, William Sinclair, Thomas Paip, James Oliphant and Oliver Sinclair, domestic servants of the said Hew, for spulyie of the pursuer's house of Symbester in Whalsay in May 1592.

The lords of council continue the summons, and ordain the pursuer to have letters to summon witnesses and to produce evidence.

SRO, CS.7/140, f.284.

210. Edinburgh, 28 May 1593

Decreet of court of session in action at instance of Gilbert Thomesoun in Swynissetter, Magnus Halcro in Greistay, Patrik Cheyne in Burray, Andro Umphray in Skalloway, Robert Cheyne in Stewiniswall, Alexander Thomesoun in Laxfurth, William Tait in Tronnsetter, Magnus in Kirkgorth, Ola Magnusoun in Overabust, Bound in Kirkgorth, James in Skalloway, and the other parishioners of the kirks of Tingwall, Quhytness and Weisdaill, pertaining in patrimony to the archdeaconry of Yetland, against Mr William Hay, archdeacon of Yetland, for suspension of letters of horning obtained by Mr William against the pursuers for non-payment of the duties of the archdeaconry for the crop 1590. Complete payment of the duties has been made by Andro Umphra, on behalf of the pursuers, to James Hay, tacksman of the archdeaconry, with consent of Mr William Hay, for the years 1590 and 1591.

The lords of council suspend the letters of horning purchased at instance of the defender.

SRO, CS.7/142, ff.10-11. There is a bond of caution for the pursuers, dated 25 August

1592, that they shall make payment to Mr William Hay for crop 1590 if they are found liable to pay, in CS.290/12.

211. Kirkwall, 2 June 1593

Note of disposition by Mareoun Reid, one of the daughters and heirs of the deceased Nicole Reid of Aithe, sometime lawman of Yeitland, to John McKenzie, of her sister part of the lands of Howle and Howisguidis in the parish of Weisdale, and her sister's part of 3 marks land of Ayth and 4 marks land in Setter in Aythsting, with the 'haill byrun meillis and dewteis thairof and profeitis of the guids of the samin, togidder with hir haill richt and tytill of quhatsumever utheris lands, guids and movabills scho may air eftir hir said umquhil father and Margret Reid of Bruche'. John undertakes to pay Mareoun half the money which he shall happen to obtain for the said lands, etc., and Mareoun undertakes to leave what is left of this money on her decease to Patrik McKenzie, son of John, for 'his support, to be usit be him as his proper guids'.

Witnesses: James Stewart of Gramesay, and James Monteith of Salcottis.

SRO, NP.1/36, f.30.

212. Edinburgh, 6 June 1593

Decreet of court of session in action at instance of Margaret Stewart, relict of William Sinclair of Uya, and William Bruce of Simbester, now her spouse, against Adam Sinclair of Brow, son and heir of the deceased James Sinclair, for payment of butter, money and grassums due by the deceased James.

The lords of council, considering that the witnesses dwell in Yetland some 300 or 400 miles distant, grant power and commission to Patrik Menteith, sheriff depute of Orknay and Yetland, Mr William Lauder, minister at Yell, Mr James Pitcarne, minister at Northmevin, Peter Maxwell, minister at Wallis, and David Strang of Benestaw, or any two of them, to examine witnesses between 10 July and 10 September 1593 at the Duche booths of Uyasound. The depositions, subscribed by the commissioners, are to be reported by 15 November 1593.

SRO, CS.7/138, f.85, and CS.7/142, f.67.

213. Edinburgh, 23 June 1593

Obligation by Frances Sinclar, son of the deceased William Sinclar of Yoir in Yeitland, to Williame Chaipe, burgess of Edinburgh, for 600 merks for board and provision of meat and clothing for the previous six years. Frances is about to return to his 'awin countrey of Yeitland' and has not the means to satisfy Williame for the sum foresaid.

Witnesses: David Collace of Auchinfousie, Mr Alexander Thomsoun, Thomas Ogilvy, and John Edzer.

SRO, RD.1/71, f.215.

214. Burrawo, 9 September 1593
Discharge by Patrik Monteithe of Fairyle, sheriff-depute and chamberlain of Yetland, to Jhone Awik, underfoud of Yell, of the wattle, landmails and other duties of Yell for 1592.

GH.

215. Edinburgh, 25 September 1593
Obligation by Mr James Lauder, son of the deceased Mr William Lauder, vicar of Yell, and Johne Heriot, baxter, burgess of Edinburgh, his cautioner, to Andro Bauchop, merchant, burgess of Edinburgh, for 3 barrels of Yetland butter packed 'in treis', to be delivered at the shore of Leith by Easter 1594, failing which payment is to be made to Andro at the rate of £20 for each barrel not delivered.

Witnesses: Johne Barnisfather, tailor, William Thomesoun, burgess of Edinburgh, and Mr James Eistoun, notary public.

SRO, RD.1/62, ff.49-50.

216. Dantzig, 15 November 1593 (25 November, new style)
Letter from Jochem Eler, councillor of Dantzig, to Sir William Stewart, lord Pittenweem, relating that in October 1592 a ship called the *Noah's Ark* of Danzig, of 120 lasts fully laden, belonging to himself and his relatives, was stranded in Shetland on the island of Unst. The skipper Zacharias Reymers ran the ship ashore with the full consent and knowledge of William Moneson, the governor, but the governor did not keep his promise, and would not permit them to shelter for more than 36 hours although there was such a storm that the crew could not save more than 5 cannons (*gotiling*), an anchor with the cable, one barce (*barsche*), and 6 barrels of flour, for he had forbidden the inhabitants to come to their assistance, even though the skipper had offered them a handsome reward. The skipper had to give up all that he had saved for 70 thaler, although it was worth six times as much. The lawyer, Admestune, to whom he sold it, gave him a document stating that if he had not given the 70 thaler the skipper and crew would have died of hunger. The governor had also given him a written statement that he intended to keep what had been saved as security until it should be claimed, but he forced the skipper to give up the statement, and so kept the ship and its cargo after the 36 hours had elapsed and the unfortunate crew could not rescue their clothing. A nobleman named Artur Sankler kept the skipper and three

others in food gratis for 14 weeks, for he pitied them so much that, with their own property before their eyes, they should be in such extremity. All this story, as related, the bearer Hans Eler, his son, has sworn to before the court and council, and will give full details to Sir William. And because Jochim has always felt that Sir William, while he was in Dantzig through the war, had been his very good friend he asks him to make representation to the Scottish king to assist Hans, his son, who has full powers to pursue his case against the withholder and user of the stolen goods, that full restitution of the ship and cargo may be made. And if ever any of his people or any of the Scots in Dantzig are in need of help Jochim will always be willing and eager to assist them.

Denmilne MSS, NLS, Adv. MS. 33.1.11., no.15 (in German). See no. 230.

217. Luna, 11 December 1593 (at 2 p.m.)

Instrument of sasine in favour of David Foister and Marione Sinclair, in fulfilment of contract, dated 16 September 1593 at Luna, between Henry Foister of Luna, on the one part, and Laurence Sinclair of Goit, on the other part, for the marriage of David Foister, elder son of Henry, to Marione Sinclair, daughter of Laurence, whereby David, and Marione, his future spouse, receive the house of Luna and 'the first brother part of three of the heall heretage and landis of Luna', with reservation of the liferent to Henry and Katerin Sinclair, his spouse, 'or hir half of the heall during all the dayis of the langer levar of thame twa'. Sasine given by Henry to William Foister, brother german and attorney of David, and to Laurence Sinclair, father and attorney of Marione.

Witnesses: Olla Sinclair, son-in-law of Henry, Magnus in Gilsbrek, and William Makkullo, servant of Patrik, earl of Orknay, lord Yetland. Andrew Edmestoune, notary public.

SA, D.8/46/1.

218. Edinburgh, 17 January 1593-4

Decreet of court of session in action at instance of Jerome Umphra in Sand against Andro Hawick in Scattistay, Daniell Hawik of Southlady, John Strang in Skelberie, David Strang in Benestay, and John Broune in Laxfuird, for spulyie of an eight year old horse worth £40 from the pursuer's lands of Astay in the parish of Tingwall in September 1592, and for loss of earnings from the said horse for five months, in the 'werk, ryding, hyregang and laubour', at 6s.8d. per day.

The lords of council continue the summons, and ordain the pursuer to produce evidence.

SRO, CS.7/144, ff.328 and 332; SRO, CS.15/57 (summons, dated 10 March 1592-3, in which John Rasmusson in Gerth, Magnus Sanderssone in Owknebrek, Sandie in

Owkenbrek, Erasmus in Owkenbrek, and John Williamssone are also summoned to compear as witnesses).

219. Edinburgh, 4 February 1593-4

Decreet of court of session in action at instance of Andro Stewart, Nicoll Eldersoun, Thomas Chein in Futerbrugh, John Yansoun, Laurence and Manis Yansounis in Gruten, and John Wischart, for themselves and in name of the other tenants and occupiers of the lands of Valay and Valay goods, against Andro and Daniell Hawiks, who claim that the lands belong to them, on the one part, and Thomas Chein, son and heir of the deceased Mr Robert Chein of (blank), who claims title to the lands as tacksman, on the other part, for troubling the pursuers for payment of the rents and duties of the said lands. The pursuers had paid the rents and duties in good faith to the deceased Mr Robert Chein for 20 years up to his death in 1591, and since then to Thomas Chein.

The lords of council find that Thomas Chein has the best right to the lands, by virtue of a gift and disposition made by Dame Garveill Fatherisdochter of Geskie, relict of Sir Langbraid of Craigholme, knight, to the deceased Mr Robert Chein, of the said lands, for payment of an annual duty, dated the Thursday after St. Bartilmois Day, 1572, and ratification granted by the regent, dated 3 March 1575-6, and ordain Andro and Daniell Hawiks to cease harassing the pursuers for payment of the rents and duties.

SRO, CS.7/145, f.300. For Robert's title and ratification see *RSS*, vii, no. 502.

220. Kirkwall, 8 March 1593-4

Agreement between Patrik, earl of Orkney, and William Irreving of Sabay, for recovery of ordnance at Fair Isle.

At Kirkwall the viij day off March the yeir of god Jaj Vc fourscoir threttene yeiris; it is appointit, aggreit and finalie endit betuix ane nobill and potent lord Patrik, erle of Orknay, lord of Yetland, on the ane pertt, and William Irrewing of Sabay, on the uther pert, in maner, forme and effect as followis; that is to say the said William Irrewing sall addres him self with all speidfull diligence betuix the day and dait heirof and the first day of Maij nixtocum unto the Fair Ile, and thair be all menis possibill sall win the ordinance that wes tint thair in the Spangyert schip, and sall provid all maner of materiallis meit for that purpois; for the quhilk caus the said nobill lord sall giff to the said William the third part of the said ordinance that sall be win, and the twa part to be furthcumand to the said nobill lord; as also the said nobill lord sall furneis all maner of furnitour, expenssis and chergis for wynning of his twa pertt, and the said William lyikwayis to furneis all cherges and expenssis for wynning of his thrid pert as salbe devisit and set doun be the aviss of bayth the saidis parties;

and heirto thai ar bound and oblist *hinc inde* to observe and keip to utheris.

Subscryvit with thair handis at Kirkwall, the day and yeir forsaid, befoir thir witnes: Harie Colvill, persoun of Orpher, David Kennedy, Captane Thomas Knichtsoun, and William Fermor, notary public.

Orknay.

Miscellaneous Papers, OA, D.8/1/3.

221. Bergen, 'the Virgin Mary's [*blank*] day' 1594

Agreement between Chrÿstenn Jonnsson Forsell, burgess in Berenn, and the honest man Wellem Donnellson Forsell, his kinsman, whereby Chrystenn acknowledges that he has received from Wellem three old dollars and four merchants' dollars (*kópmands daller*) on his property (*paa mÿtt gods*), to which Chrystenn has succeeded heritably after his deceased mother, Merette Wellemsdotter, which lies in his native place (*wdi mÿtt barnnfód*) in Yettland, in Yell; and that he has received this with the condition that his kinsmen, the sons of the said Donnell Forsell, shall be the nearest persons entitled to claim upon his property for the said money, which their deceased father formerly gave to Chrystenn for the part which has heritably fallen to Chrystenn after his deceased father Jonn Forsell, which their father bought of Chrystenn; providing that the land rent which pertains to Chrystenn's part shall come to him until he gets his said money from his said kinsmen, the sons of Donnell Forsell. Wellem Donnellsson Forsell, on his brothers' behalf, acknowledges that if Chrystenn, his kinsman, does not get his money in spring, when he, or any of his brothers come again, then Chrystenn shall have their free leave to sell his land to whatever honest man he himself likes.

Chrystenn sets his signet beneath this his letter patent, and entreats Jackop Spenns to set his mark.

Mandate by Chrÿstenn Jonnsson, burgess in Berenn, to an honourable and right prudent man Wellem Donnellsson Forssell, dwelling in Jettland, giving his full power and authority to Wellem to receive his land rent (*land skÿld*) in Jettland from those parts of land which have heritably fallen to him after his deceased mother, which Wellem shall collect on his account, and he trusts him to pay him when, God willing, he comes next in spring 1595.

The originals are not known to exist. Printed with translations from Danish (by Gilbert Goudie) in *PSAS*, xiv, pp.27-9. The mandate is a separate document.

222. Edinburgh, 25 May 1594

Decreet of commissary court of Edinburgh in action at instance of Margaret Stewart, relict of William Stewart (*rectius* Sinclair) of Oya, and

William Bruce now her spouse, and Mr John Lermonth, procurator fiscal, against Laurence Bruce of Cultmalyndis, chamberlain and tacksman of the bishop's teinds of Unst. Laurence had obtained a decreet against Margaret and William before the deceased Mr Robert Cheyne, commissary of Yetland, for payment of teinds and annual rents, for five years, extending to 15 lispunds butter and 45 cans oil yearly.

The commissaries reduce the decreet given by Mr Robert Cheyne.

SRO, CC.8/2/25.

223. Huip in Stronsay, 21 June 1594

Contract between David Sinclair of Huntoun, on the one part, and Andro Mertine, servant of the earl of Orknay, on the other part, whereby David agrees to set in tack his 18 marks land, 8 pennies the mark, of Melbe in the parish of Sandnes in Yetland, for 9 years from the expiry of the tack which Jerome Umphra presently has of the land. The duties of 'the said last of land' are to be according to the rental, 'exceptand only the ausetter coipe and land sett tirtoun of the same'. If David is moved to wadset or alienate the said land he binds himself to make the first offer to Andro, and not to dispone the land without Andro's consent; and Andro binds himself to 'stand guid friend' to David, and to support him in his honest affairs.

Witnesses: Adam Sinclair of Brow, William Grot, and Thomas Blak.

SRO, RD.1/117, ff.25-6.

224. Scalloway bankis, 15 July 1594

Pardon by Patrik, earl of Orkney, to John in Aweik, for transgressing his commission.

Foirsameikill as John in Aweik hes ignorantlie oversene him self in the administratioun of his office, and hes beine traduced syndrie wayis upone malice, boith for alleged transgressing the boundis of his commissioun and conceilling oft of our casualitie and profeitt (callit the kingis rycht); and eftir sufficient tryell tane be us in his forged accusatioun, we have fundin that all that hes beine laid to his charge in the court hauldin be us at Aweik upone the aucht day of July instant ar bot frivolus and forged inventiounis proceidand of his ignorance; for quhilkis all we ar movit to appordoune him the rather to giff him occacioun to be moir circumspect in tyme cuming, and thairfoir discharges him of all penaltie that he hes incurrit or mycht have incurred at our instance for the same for now and evir, be this present, subscryvit with our hand; to the quhilk our signett is affixt. At Scalloway bankis, the xv day of July Jaj Vc foirscoir fourteine yeiris.

Orknay.

GH.

225. Burgh in Nesting, 8 August 1594

Wadset by Johne Strang, eldest son and one of the heirs of the deceased David Strang of Beinstaw, to an honourable man Hew Sincleir of Burgh, of 1 mark 1 ure land, 12 pennies the mark, in Nesthous in Skeldbrie, and 10 ures feued land in the holm of Greaskerrie be-east Quhalsay, in the parish of Lunesting and Quhalsay, for 8 angel nobles and a gudling. In the event of eviction Hew shall have entry to Johne's heritable and feu lands of Southous in Beinstaw. The lands are redeemable at the parish kirk of Nesting on Whitsunday eve. Precept of sasine.

Johne procures the signets and subscriptions of Mr Alexander Bruce, younger, laird of Cultemalindeis, and Thomas Boyine in Scalloway. Witnesses: Androw Bruce, Olipheir Sincleir, Eduard in Garth, Peter Symsoun, exhorter at Nesting, etc.

SA, SC.12/65/1/29. One seal.

226. Edinburgh, 21 September 1594

Contract between Patrik, earl of Orknay, lord Yeitland, on the one part, and Johne Makesone, burgess of Craill, William Blak, John Bowssie, and George Smyth, commissioners for the fishers, doggers and inhabitants of the burghs of Craill, Anstruther Eastir, and Anstruther Westir and Pettinweme, respectively, assuming responsibility for them and their 'equippages' that fish within the bounds of Orknay and Yeitland, on the other part, whereby Patrik, for himself, and taking the responsibility for the 'haill owthaill men, heretouris, takkismen, persones, vicares, beneficit men and inhabitants' of Orknay and Yeitland (the isle of Westray excepted, so long as it is out of the earl's hands), grants full licence to the inhabitants of the said towns to fish within Orknay and Yeitland, and that they, with their boats and fishers, may freely resort within the said countries (the isle of Westray excepted) for their fishing activities, and to 'big fishearis houssis, skewhoussis', etc., for 'making, paiking, drying and wynning of fische that they sall happin to slay, and to win and to mak thair ulie', lay their boats on the ground, pass through the said countries, buy ale from the inhabitants, etc., providing that: (1) they shall not fish with great lines within the headlands in Orknay and Yeitland; (2) they shall only slay so many small fish within the 'sounds and wrayis [*rectius* voyis]' as is needed for bait; neither they 'nor thair quippage' shall commit any kind of oppression against the said countries and inhabitants by 'landing upon thair holmes and out iyles, slaying of thair wyld fowllis and nestis thairof, taking or slaying of scheip, nolt or uther guidis', without consent of the owners; (3) they shall not oppress any Englischmen, Duchemen or other strangers, or trouble their ships or goods; (4) they and 'thair equippage' who are on land on Sundays shall 'keip the kirk to serve god as they aucht to do'; and (5) they shall not employ countrymen, servants, and their sons without consent of their masters or fathers. The inhabitants of the said towns shall pay Patrik yearly the following duties: (1) for each great ling boat with their 'land lyar', a teind of 50 lings, a ground leave within the flood mark for drying their fish of 1 barrel of small Scots salt, and a ground leave above the flood mark of 12 'keilling' and 12 'skaitt', and in addition each of the said boats which goes to the 'keiling handillingis' shall pay 100 'keillingis'; and (2) for each boat that comes to the 'keiling handillingis' only, with their 'land lyar', a teind of 100 'keiling', a ground leave above the flood mark of a barrel of small Scots salt, and a land leave of 24 'keilling'.

Witnesses: Mr James Melvile, minister at Anstruther Eastir, Harie Colvile, parson of Orphare, William Bruce of Simbister, and William Bellenden (*rectius* Bannatyne) of Gersa.

SRO, RD.1/46, ff.381-3. Printed in *OSR*, i, no.76. There is a contract in almost identical terms, dated 9 December 1581, between Robert, earl of Orknay, on the one part, and Alexander Fermour, burgess of Craill, Alexander Blak and George Traill, commissioners for the fishers, doggers and inhabitants of the burghs of Craill, Anstruther, and Pettinweme and Anstruther bewest the burn, on the other part (SRO, RD.1/20[1] [part 2], ff.347-50).

227. Edinburgh, 25 September 1594

Discharge by Captain William Sinclair, lawful son and one of the heirs of the deceased Henrie Sinclair of Stroyme to Hew Sinclair of Bruche, his elder brother, for 400 merks, being the final payment of a greater sum paid by Hew to William for his 'brother part of the lands of Stroyme and Stroyme guidis, airit be me eftir the deceis of my said umquhil father, and landis price of all utheris landis, takis, roumes and possessiones quhilk I may clame richt unto, lyand within the cuntrie of Yetland and burrow landis of Kirkwall, with my haill tytill and kyndnes of the rowme of Housbie in Stronzay, with all byrane dewteis of the haill landis abonewrettin, and in compleit payment and satisfactioun of all and sundrie my barnis part of geir, lous or fast, utencill and as domicell, quhilk I airit, or at the least fell or suld haif fallin to me in airschip, be deceis of my said umquhil father'.

Witnesses: Laurence Bruce of Cultmalindies, Arthour Sinclair of Aithe, William Bruce of Simbister, and David King, vicar of Bourtrie, writer hereof.

SRO, RD.1/50, pp.556-7.

228. Edinburgh, 23 November 1594

Disposition by Paule Jacquesoun, skipper and part owner of the ship called the *Flieing Hairt* of Edame in Holland, for himself and taking the burden for the other owners, to Patrik, earl of Orknay, lord of Yetland, of the said ship, of the 'burding' of 150 lasts, with her 'ornamentis, appareling and laidining', for 400 Dutch silver dollars. The *Flieing Hairt* was on her voyage from Noroway, where she was ladened with timber, to Holland in September 1594, when she was by the violence of contrary winds driven upon the isle of Yetland, where by the tempestuous blasts and raging storms of wind and weather she was shipwrecked on the isle called Burray, whereat the said skipper was constrained to run her aground, and where she presently lies wrecked. The inventory, subscribed by Paule, states that there are 3,000 'Noroway dails', 47 'dussane of duble ruiff spar', and 30 'peces of aikin tymmer', and also 3 anchors, 3 'cuibbils' (except one cut in two by the violence of the shipwreck), 2 'cordels' (each one 10 fathoms in length), one mainsail with a new main topsail and new foresail ('with ane bonnet and ane foir top saill, blind and missine sailis'), the ship's blocks (full of running tackle), together with her masts and 'floitt boitt' (except her main mast which was 'hewin be the way'), and her other 'furnitour and apparelling necessar'.

Witnesses: Alexander Seggait, merchant, burgess of Edinburgh, Johne Dick, merchant, burgess of Edinburgh, James Lockie, writer, William Bannatyne, servant of Patrik, and Robert Guthrie, servant of Patrik Glasfurd, clerk of Leyth, writer hereof.

SRO, B.22/8/6.

229. Cannongait and Yell, 15 December 1594 and 6 July 1595

Tack by Mr James Lauder, vicar of Yell and Fetlare, with consent of Patrik, earl of Orknay, lord of Yeitland, and of the canons and chapter of the cathedral kirk of Orknay, to his well-beloved William Bannatyne of Gairsay, of the vicarage of Yell and Fetlare, with reservation of the 11 marks land of Lussitter in Yell with 'the housses and biggingis being thairupoun, as for ane gleib and manse to the minister and reidar at the kirk thairof', for the lifetimes of William and his heir, and a further 19 years thereafter. William shall pay to Mr James and his successors a yearly duty of £120 6s.8d.

Witnesses: Mr Thomas Barclay, Andro Martene, Mr George Tod, David Kennedy, Hew Sinclare of Burgh, Edward Sinclare, his brother, and James Lockie, notary public. Subscribed by Hew Sinclare of Burghe, James Lockie, notary public, Eduard Sinclar, Adame Boithuill, prebendary of Sanct Lowrence stouk, Cuthbert Hendersoun, treasurer of Orknay, Mr James Cok, chancellor of Orknay, Patrik, earl of Orknay, Mr James Lauder, vicar of Yell and Fetlar, Hary Colvill, chantor of Orknay, and Thomas Swentoun, archdeacon of Orknay.

SRO, RH.6 (Supplementary, 1591-1600). Seals of the chapter, and Mr James Lauder.

230. Holyroodhouse, 24 December 1594

Decreet in action before the privy council at the instance of Joachym

Eler, Michell Meves, Johnne Bockas, Augustine Eler, Conrad von Bobbart, and Zacharias Reymerche, citizens of Danskene, against Patrik, earl of Orkany, Johnne Forrett of Fingas, and David Hoppringle, burgess of Edinburgh, for restitution on grounds of piracy. In July 1592 a ship of Danskene called the *Ark of Noy*, of which Zacharias was skipper, and the persons foresaid owners, was on voyage to Spain laden with 'knappald, wanscoitt, fathold wode, pype wode, and leid, and being in hir dew course aboute the north ilis of Scotland, wes by grite storme of weddir drevin upoun the coist of Yetland, quhair sho, haveing approcheit to the Ile of Unst, sett saill in Burray firth, of purpois to have refresheit hir equippage with freshe watter, vivers, and utheris necessaris', expecting no injury in view of the peace and amity between the king's subjects and the inhabitants of Danskene. Nevertheless, on 1 October 1592, or thereby, the said ship 'being lyand and rydand richt foiranent the said ile of Unst, and the said Zacharias, skipper foirsaid, with sum of his equippage, haveing cum a-land to ane little village within the said ile, to have refresheit thame and to prepair sum victuallis and uthiris necessaris for thair schip and cumpany, and to have prepairit ane convenient place for thir schip to have lyne in, and thaireftir haveing brocht in thair ship', William Mansoun, underfoud, with other servants of Patrik, now earl of Orknay, accompanied by most of the inhabitants of the isle, pillaged and took away not only the ship, but most of her cargo and fittings, and left 'hir equippage maist miserabillie destitute of all confort and moyane to transport thameselffis in thair awne cuntrey'. In October, Patrik, and in November and December and other months of 1592, Johnne Forrett and David Hoppringle, had intromitted with the ship and goods knowing that the goods were 'strangearis guidis, pilleit in maner foirsaid'. The pursuers seek restitution of the ship and goods, or the prices of the same, the ship being valued at £16,000, the goods at £13,868, and other costs at £3,000.

The king, with advice of the privy council, absolves the defenders from the charge of piracy because the pursuers have failed to prove the points of the summons. The decision is without prejudice to the right of the pursuers to prosecute the defenders before the lords of council and session.

RPC, v, pp.195-7. See no. 216.

231. Burghe, 20 January 1594-5

Wadset by Androw Hawick, lawful son and eldest heir of the deceased Vinsencius Hawick of Skatstaye, to an honourable man Hew Sinclair of Burghe, of 6 marks land, 8(?) pennies the mark, of Trondavo, 4 marks land, 9 pennies the mark, in Burghe in Neschone, 2 marks land, 9 pennies the mark, in Setir, 1 mark land, 12 pennies the mark, in Burranes, 1 mark land, 9 pennies the mark, in Neagerthe, 1 mark land, 9 pennies the mark, in Sandfre, 1 mark land in Mowlaye, all in the parish of Delting; 3½ marks land, 9 pennies the mark, in Sandwick in West Yell; and 3 marks land in Brounatuait, in the parish of Wallis, for 400 merks money, redeemable at the parish kirk of Tingwall on Whitsunday eve. Precept of sasine.

Androw affixes his seal and procures the seals of Henrie Froster, William in Neip, and Magnus Gillisbrek. Witnesses: Adame Alexanderson in Orgill, Nicoll in Neip, Androw Garsetter, and Thomas Paip.

SA, SC.12/65/1/28.

232. Swunburgh, 26 February 1594-5

Wadset by Laurence Strang, son and one of the heirs of the deceased David Strang of Beinstay, to a famous and discreet man William Bruce of Simbister, of 1 mark land, 12 pennies the mark, in Skelbray, in the parish of Lunasting; and 2 ures land, 12 pennies the mark, in Gaill in the Skerreis, for £24. Laurence grants to William 'thre yeiris suspentioun of the same efter the redemptioun thairof onelie'.

Laurence procures the signet of Laurence Sinclair of Goit, minister of Dunrosnes. Witnesses: Adam Sinclair of Brow, Thomas Sinclar, and Thomas Simsone.

SA, GD.144/70/1.

233. Edinburgh, 10 May 1595

Tack by Mr Alexander Spittell, vicar of Nesting, with consent of Patrik, earl of Orknay, lord Yetland, and of the ministers and presbytery of Yetland, to Hew Sinclar of Burghe, of the vicarage of Nesting, for 7 years from Lammas 1595, for payment yearly of 14 angel nobles sufficient gold and weight. Alexander Spittell acknowledges Hew to be the present tacksman of the vicarage, having right to one year's tack thereof from Lammas 1595, by virtue of an old tack set by Alexander Spittell to the deceased Adam, bishop of Orknay, commendator of Holyroodhouse, and thereafter transferred to Alexander Kincaid, vicar of Walls, who thereafter transferred the said tack to Hew, whereby Hew is 'kyndlie' to the said vicarage. Hew shall relieve Alexander Spittell of all charges of the reader and third of the said vicarage. James Achesoun, goldsmith, burgess of the Cannogait, is cautioner for Hew.

Witnesses: Walter Callender of Bordie, Captain William Sincler, Eduard Sincler, brother of Hew, Alexander King, advocate, and Adam Bothwell.

SRO, B.22/8/6.

234. 20 May 1595

Disposition by Wilyeam Mansoune in Gardye, son and heir of the deceased Manse Ornesoune, to his only sister Katherein Mansedochter, now spouse of James Spens, son of the deceased Henrye Spens in Howland, of 1 mark land, 6 pennies the mark, in Setyr in Unst, in complete payment of what she may seek of Wilyeam concerning her father's 'fast guidis'.

Wilyeam affixes his mark, and asks Peter Maxwell to subscribe in his name. Witnesses: Walter Moresoune in Still, Nycolas Hacclay in Hugoland, Manse Antonusone with James, his brother, and divers others.

GH. Mark of Wilyeam Mansoune.

235. 20 July 1595

Disposition by Manse Wilyeamsoune, with consent of Barbara Stephansdochter, his spouse, to a right honourable man Lowrence Bruice of Cultemaleindeis, of 2 marks land, 6 pennies the mark, in Owterska, in the isle of Unst, with ½ mark land, 7 pennies the mark, in the isle of Balta.

Manse purchases the seals of honest and famous men, to wit, James Strang of Voysgarth, Wilyeam Mansoune in Gardie, underfoud of Unst for the time, and David Cowplan in Howland, with the subscription of Wilyeam Bannatyne of Garza, sheriff of Yetland. Witnesses: Peter Maxwell, minister, Walter Rippat, and Jhone Baquhanys.

GH.

236. Scalloway, 4 August 1595

Contract of excambion between Laurence Bruce of Cultmalindies, on the one part, and Mr James Pitcarne, vicar of Northmavene, on the other part, whereby Laurence binds himself to infeft Mr James in 12 marks land, 9 pennies the mark, in Sandwik in Northmavene, with yearly duty of 6 lispunds butter and 6 shillings wadmell, and Mr James binds himself to infeft Laurence in 8 marks land, 6 pennies the mark, and 1 mark land, 12 pennies the mark, in Hildisweik in Northmaven, 2 marks land, 9 pennies the mark, in Freasetter in Nesting, and 4 marks land, 8 pennies the mark, in Saifsetter in Aithsting and Sandsting. In the event of the 4 marks land in Saifsetter lying ley, then Mr James binds himself to infeft Laurence in equivalent land elsewhere. In addition Mr James assigns his tacks in Hildisweik to Laurence.

Witnesses: William Bannatyne of Gairsay, sheriff-depute of Yetland, Hew Sinclar of Burgh, Arthour Sinclar of Houss, Thomas Suonsoun (*rectius* Swintoun), minister at Kirkwall, and James Lockie, notary public.

SRO, RD.1/52, f.72.

237. Dunrosness, 7 August 1595

'[Disposition by] Alexander Vrowing (Irving), son and heir of umquhile William Vrowing of Trondray, to Arthur Sinclair of Aith, [of] 3 merk in Hugaland in Trondray.'

The original is not known to exist. The above abstract, by J. Storer Clouston, is in OA, D.23, Notebook 4, p.66. Another abstract, by Francis Grant, in OSD, *SN*, 28 October 1893, states that Margaret Irving, sister of Alexander, was also a disponer; that the land was 9 pennies the mark; and that Patrick Monteith of Fair Isle, James Kynter, burgess of Aberdeen, Andrew Umphray of Berrie, Malcolm Mouat and others were witnesses, with Andrew Edmondston, NP.

238. Laxfurde, 20 September 1595

Discharge by Williame Bannatyne of Gairsay, sheriff-depute of Yetland, on behalf of Patrik, earl of Orknay, lord Yetland, to Williame Bruce of Symbister, for 5 barrels butter, 10 packs wadmell, and 140 merks, being the full duties of the provost of Norroway's lands for crop 1595.

Witnesses: Thomas Tweddall and Symon Hutoun, servants of William Bannatyne, James Lockie, notary public, and divers others.

SA, D.8/2/1.

239. Ustanes, 9 October 1595

Obligation by William Sinclair of Ustanes to William Bannatyne of Gairsay, chamberlain of Yetland, for 27 angel nobles gold and weight (at £6 for each angel noble), for the umboths of Nesting, Lunesting, Quhailsay and Skeries, due by William to the earl of Orknay for crop 1594. Payment is to be made to William Bannatyne, or to John Arnot, burgess of Edinburgh, in his name.

Witnesses: Arthour Sinclair of Aith, William Low, burgess of Edinburgh, Robert Sinclair, skipper in Leyth, and James Lockie, notary public.

SRO, RD.1/122, f.72.

240. Burght, 17 November 1595

Contract of excambion between an honourable man Hew Sinclair of Burght, on the one part, and Johne Strang, eldest son and one of the heirs of the deceased David Strang, sometime feuar of the 9 marks king's land in Southhous in Beinstay, on the other part, whereby Johne excambs in favour of Hew the 9 marks king's lands, 9 pennies the mark, in Southhous in Beinstay which he has in feu from Michell Balfour of Mountquhanney, commissioner to the deceased Robert, earl of Orknay, lord Yetland, and 1½ marks land, 9 pennies the mark, of heritage in the said town, together with 'the haill rycht, roithe, owthell and samming of the haill last land within the haill toun of Beinstay, baith Southhous and Westerhous', for which Hew binds himself to deliver and warrant to

Johne 9 marks king's land in Skelbre in Lunesting, viz., 4½ marks land in Nesthous and 4½ marks land in Uphous, in feu ferme without gersums, with 4 marks other land pertaining to the king in the said town with payment of gersums, together with 1 mark land, 12 pennies the mark, of heritage in the said town of Skelbre. Johne binds himself to enter Hew in the said lands of Beinstay by 'sloking his awin fyre and kendling the said Hewis with his awin handis befoir the witnessis following'.

Witnesses: Oliver Sinclair of Esthous, Williame Manisoun in Neip, underfoud of Nesting, with his signet affixed, Magnus Hanisoun of Gillisbrek, with his signet affixed, Petir Symsoun, exhorter at Nesting, Hew Tarrell, writer hereof, and Arthour Irving.

SA, SC.12/65/1/31. The word 'owthell' had been omitted and appears in the margin, signed by Hew and Johne.

241. Holyroodhouse, 29 December 1595

Production before the lords of the privy council by Ambrois Lericie, procurator for the Duke of Florens, of an attestation by the magistrates of the town of Danskene, dated 25 April 1592, stating that Anthony Briegers, master of the ship called the *Great Jonas* of Dantzic, having appeared before them, in the matter of certain goods belonging to Ferdinand, Grand Duke of Tuscany, which had been taken from the said ship, had sworn that the ship, having been driven by stress of weather into the harbour of Gritinque Viage in Shetland in the spring of 1591, had been boarded by Jarmirus Unfreii, governor of the island, followed by Captains Thomas Ogilvy and John Roott, both Scots and citizens of Dundee, who, after various ceremonies, the production of letters of marque, and the demand, in the king's name, of a surrender of all the papistical goods in the ship, had proceeded in the most leisurely manner, with threats of overwhelming force if resisted, to seize and unlade the whole cargo of the ship, consisting of specified quantities of wheat, flour, madder, lint, Hungarian and Swedish copper, a barrel of goatskins, one of books, together with some cheese and butter, two cannons, a quantity of bullets and gunpowder, and some ropes and other gear, all belonging to the ship and crew.

RPC, v, pp.251-2. J. MacLeod, 'The Duke of Tuscany and his shipwreck cargo', *SHR*, xv, pp.245-6, prints an inventory of the ship's contents. The affair is also referred to in NLS, Saltoun Papers, MS.17129, ff.11-12, 44-5 and 50-1; *Acts of the Privy Council of England*, xxii, pp.589-90; SRO, CS.7/159, f.189. See also no. 183.

242. Edinburgh, 24 January 1595-6

Disposition by Patrick Chene of Essilmonth to Arthur Sinclair of Ayth, of 3 marks land, 8 pennies the mark, in Wassetter, 4 marks land, 8 pennies the mark, in Wadbuster, 3 marks land, 6 pennies the mark, in Strand, 3 marks land, 6 pennies the mark, in Grenewall, 9 marks land, 8 pennies the mark, in Kebuster, 3 marks land, 6 pennies the mark, in Westland, 22 (23 in precept) marks land, 7 pennies the mark, in Urisland, 15 marks land, 8 pennies the mark, in Burra, 9 marks land, 8 pennies the mark, in Northgarth, 12 marks land, 8 pennies the mark, in Houlland, 6 marks land, 9 pennies the mark, in Outabrek, 7 marks land, 8 pennies the mark, in Nethir Sound, 12 marks land, 6 pennies the mark, in Weik, 2 marks land, 8 pennies the mark, in Trondra, 5 marks land, 6 pennies the mark, in Hugoland in Quhitnes, 6 marks land 6 pennies the mark, in Aythe and Blousta, and 4 marks land, 9 pennies the mark, in Hugoland in Burra, all in the parish of Tingwall. Precept of sasine directed to Magnus Sinclair in Howgoland.

Witnesses: Mr Patrick Chene of Ardoch, Thomas Chene of Ure, William Cruikschank, servant of Patrick Chene of Essilmonth, James Lockie, notary, with divers others.

From charter of confirmation under the great seal (in Latin), dated 17 October 1600 (SA, D.10/24/4). According to Gilbert Goudie there was a sasine among the Scalloway Deeds, dated 1596, 'in Latin, and all frayed into detached pieces' (notebook in Braefield House, Dunrossness).

243. Edinburgh, 26 January 1595-6

Decreet of court of session in action at instance of Thomas Cheine of Ure, son lawful of the deceased Mr Robert Cheine, commissary of Yetland, against Andro Hawik in Skattistay, Manis Elisoun (or Eldersoun) in Nessen, Arthour Irving in Graithe, Henrie Sinclair, John Strang and Magnus Mowat there, for violent eviction of the pursuer and his tenants from the lands of Valay, 'plaice and fisching thairof', in the parish of Walls, on 7 December 1593, and spulyie from the lands on the same day. The pursuer was then in possession of the lands as heir to his deceased father, who had died in April 1591, in the tack granted by Frow Garvell Faderisdochter in Denmark. The goods spulyied were: 12 ky with calves at £10 each; 5 oxen at 20 merks each; 8 yeld nolt at 10 merks each; 400 sheep, whereof 200 ewes, at £1 each; 2 horses at £10 each; 4 mares at £6 each; 3 sows with grice at £3 each; 2 iron pots at £2 each; 2 copper kettles at £3 each; 3 'rouks' of bere, containing 20 bolls, at £4 for each boll with the fodder; 12 reestit mutton 'boukis' at £1 each; 2 kists containing 2 pairs of sheets, 2 pairs of blankets and 2 'koddis' at £10; and 1 new fishing boat at £30. The pursuer produces his evidents and writs, together with the depositions of 'dyverss famous witnesses' conform to the commission granted by lords of council on 7 January 1594-5 to Laurence Bruce of Cultmalindeis, Malcome Sinclar, vicar of Dunrosnes, Andro Giffert of Wedderstaw, John Sutherland, vicar of Sandsting, Jerome Umphray, bailie of Sandsting, John Murray of Stainwell, Andro Wischett of Melby, and John Wischett of Burrafuird, or any three of them, to examine witnesses between 15 March 1594-5 and 25 March 1595 at Skalloway.

The lords of council decern Andro Hawik, Magnus Olisoune (*sic*), and Arthour Irving to have done wrong, and ordain them to restore the goods and gear spulyied or the values thereof, to refund the pursuer £20 for his expenses, and to pay £2 to the lord's collector; and absolve John Strang, Magnus Mowat and Henrie Sinclair, as the pursuer has failed to prove the summons against them.

SRO, CS.7/148, ff.203-4, CS.7/150, f.125, and CS.7/160, ff.47 and 55-6.

244. Burgh (*circa* 1596?)

Tack by Peter Symsone, undoubted vicar of the parish of Nesting, to the right honourable Hew Sincleir of Burgh, of the vicarage of Nesting, Lunesting, Quhalsay and the Skerreis, for 3 years from the date hereof, and thereafter for periods of 3 years throughout Peter's lifetime, for yearly payment of 14 angel nobles. Hew 'hais beine thir dyvers yeiris bygane, lyik as he is yit, takisman of the said viccarage, and hais thankfullie payit to me the dewiteis thairof, sua ration wald that he suld be contenewit takisman of the samin'. Hew has paid Peter a certain sum of money 'for the defence of the patrimonie of the said viccarage'.

Witnesses: William Magnussone in Neip, underfoud of Nesting, Eduard Sincleir in Bulyeasetter, Arthour Symsone, son of Peter, and Hew Tarrald, servant of Hew.

SA, SC.12/65/1/30.

245. Kirkcaldy, 3 May 1596

'Wadsett by Alexander Irwein, mariner and burgess of Kinghorn, one of the heirs of umquhile William Irwein of Tronray, in Zetland, to Arthur Sinclair of Aith, over one merk land in Cultiswik, in Aithsting, and one merk half merk land in Houland, in Tingwall, with consent of Katherine Baird his spouse. ...

'Witnesses: Thomas Call, mariner, burgess of Kirkcaldy, John Robertson, mariner in Burntisland, and divers others.'

The original is not known to exist. The above abstract, by Francis Grant, is in OSD, *SN*, 18 November 1893.

246. Stroholme, 1 July 1596

Wadset by Arthour Sinclair, lawful son and one of the heirs of the deceased James Sinclair of Hous, to the right honourable Hew Sinclair of Burght, of 9 marks 'outhell' land, 6 pennies the mark, of Backay, in the parish of Delting, for 50 angel nobles gold and weight, redeemable at the kirk of Tingwall. At redemption Arthour shall grant to Hew a tack of the land for 19 years, for yearly payment of 3 lispunds butter (or 4s. per lispund) and 3 shillings wadmell (or 2s. per shilling). Precept of sasine.

Arthour signs with his hand led at the pen by Hew Tarrell, and because he has no seal he procures those of discreet men: William Manisoune in Neip, and Eduarde Sinclair in Bilyesetter. Witnesses: Androw Bruce, apparent of Mownes, Hew Tarrell, William Demptster and Henrie Chalmer in Brekis, servants of Hew, with divers others.

SA, SC.12/65/1/32. Seal of William Manisoune.

247. Soundburghheid, 5 August 1596

Obligation by Johnne Wilsoun, younger, burgess in Pittinweme, to his well-beloved friend Captain Thomas Knychtsoun of Aith in Brassay, for £666 13s.4d., payable on behalf of Thomas to Patrik, earl of Orknay.

Witnesses: Captain Robert Grahame of the Scheynis, Alexander Huntare, younger, merchant and burgess in Edinburgh, and Thomas Young, indweller in Kirkwall.

SRO, RD.1/55, f.283.

248. Hardwell, 25 August 1596

Wadset by Nicoll Enarsone of Hardwall to Alexander Isbuster, his son-in-law, of 4½ marks land, 12 pennies the mark, and 3½ marks land, 9 pennies the mark, in the town of Laxo, in the parish of Scatsta, for 17 angel nobles gold in weight and 2 old silver dollars. At redemption Nicoll shall grant to Alexander a tack of the said lands for 11 years, free of duty. The lands are to be held by Alexander in free blench for payment of one penny yearly, if required. Precept of sasine directed to David Diksoune in Scatistay. Nicoll appends his seal and adds his marks, and subscribes with his hand led at the pen by Alexander Bruce, notary public.

Witnesses: Andro Hawik of Scatistaye, John Gray (?), servant of William Tyrie of Busbie, Sanders Mowat, and John Linletter, with divers others.

Sasine given at Laxo on 27 October 1596 (at 2 p.m.) by David Diksone in Scatistay. Witnesses: Lowrence Antonesone in Graven, Magnus Gregoressone, and Lowrence Magnussone in Laxo, with divers others.

Original in possession of Robert L.W. Beveridge, Troon. Photocopy in SA.2/587. Printed in *SHR*, xx, pp.79-81. One seal. The sasine is on the back.

249. Soumburgh, 5 September 1596

Obligation by Captain Thomas Knychtsoun to Johnne Wilsoun, younger, burgess of Pettinweme, following 'compt and rekning' made on the preceding day at Sounburchheid, for 8 lasts of herring, 'guid and sufficient wairis, weill conditionit'.

Witnesses: Captain Robert Grahame of the Schein, Alexander Hunter, younger, burgess in Edinburgh, and Thomas Young.

SRO, RD.1/56, ff.103-4.

250. Edinburgh, 4 November 1596

Decreet of court of session in action at instance of Andro Wisheart in Wallis, Henry Wisheart there, Andro Stewart there, Christopher Lauriston there in Grynyio, Andro Mudie there, James Fraser there, and the other parishioners of Wallis in Yetland, against Andro Edmestoun, on the one part, and Alexander Kincaid, brother of the deceased John Kincaid of Warestoun, for troubling the pursuers for payment of the vicarage teinds of the crop 1595.

The lords of council decern the pursuers to pay the teinds to Alexander Kincaid, who has best right thereto conform to the gift granted to him by the deceased Adam, bishop of Orknay, of the said vicarage for all the days of his lifetime, as the decreet of 16 April 1586 shown to the lords bears.

SRO, CS.7/163, ff.371-2. See no. 82.

251. Edinburgh, 4 November 1596

Decreet of court of session in action at instance of Andro Giffert in Scattistay, Mathow Robertsoun, Nicoll in Hardwell, and the other parishioners of Scatista and Delting, against John Adie, minister, on the one part, and Alexander Kincaid, brother german of the deceased John Kincaid of Warestoun, on the other part, for troubling the pursuers for payment of the vicarage teinds of the crop 1595.

The lords of council decern the pursuers to pay the teinds to Alexander Kincaid, who has best right thereto conform to the gift granted to him of the said vicarage, as the decreet of 27 December 1589 shown to the lords bears.

SRO, CS.7/163, f.372. See no. 161.

252. 18 February 1596-7

'Sasine of Margaret Colvill, from Arthur Sinclair of Aith, her spouse, in 40 merks of Trondray (8d.), bought and conquest by said Arthur and Margaret.

'Witnesses: Poill Manissone in Hoof, bailie of Weisdale, David Sinclair of Burra, Ola and Magnus Vrowing, umquhile heritors of the said lands, Manis in Tow, with others divers.'

The original is not known to exist. The above abstract, by J. Storer Clouston, is in OA, D.23, Notebook 4, p.67. Francis Grant, in OSD, *SN*, 28 October 1893, gives an abstract of the disposition (with same date and witnesses), which is said to be in liferent as a provision for Margaret, and where David Sinclair is said to be bailie of Burra.

253. Leyth, 16 March 1596-7

Obligation by Andro Umphra of Berrie, indweller in Skalloway, to Johnne Wilsoun, burgess of Pettinweme, whereby Andro, who is about to make a mercantile venture in his ship 'to the eistward, or quhair it sall pleis god I gang', undertakes to make 'just compt and rekning' with Johnne of his receipts within forty days of his homeward return. Andro has procuration from Johnne to uplift the following: from Alexander Hunter, burgess of Edinburgh, for the present in Yetland, £874; William Shewin, servant of Arthur Sinclair, 740 ling fish; Johnne Giffert, burgess of Edinburgh, £17; James Kintor's wife, £18; James Kneland's wife; £12; and David Kid of Sanctandrois, for non-deliverance of ½ last of herring, £45. Andro may utilise any 'commoditie, silver or wairis' which he receives from Alexander Hunter, or from 'ony uther contenit within our said procuratorie', during his voyage, and to sell the same 'and to imploy the samin lykas I sall do to my awin'.

Witnesses: William Rig, Samuell Blakburne, Archibald Jarden and James Carmichael, burgesses of Edinburgh.

SRO, RD.1/101, ff.335-6.

254. Leith, 26 March 1597

Obligation by Androw Umphray, indweller in Skallowaybankis, to Johnne Fortoun, younger, merchant and burgess of Edinburgh, for £200, for wine bought and received by Androw. Johnne Pattoun, indweller in Leyth, is cautioner for Androw.

Witnesses: Mr Johne Henrysone, writer in Edinburgh, Patrik Glasfurd, common clerk of Leith, and Thomas Wryght, servant of Patrik.

SRO, RD.1/57, ff.355-6.

255. Quhitisnes in Wais, 18 June 1597 (at 7 a.m.)

Note of sasine given by James Kintore, bailie, to Androw Edmestoun 'upoun the landis of Quhitisnes, according to his feu chartour thairof ... and immediately thairefter the said Androw gaife sesing to Margrete Kintore, his spouse, thairof, indureing hir lyftyme, quhairupoun the said Androw and his spous askit instrumentis'.

Witnesses: David Kincaid and Androw Hawik of Scatsay.

SRO, NP.1/36, f.58.

256. Gierisuig, 20 June 1597

Wadset by Anders Maath of Houckeland in Hietlandt, and his dear wife, an honourable and highborn lady, Else Trondsdaatter of Erisfiordt, to an honourable and discreet man Effuart Sincklair, residing at Bollesetter in Hietlandt, of 12 marks burnt (*march brende*), 8 pennies the mark, in

Øffrebøster, 8 marks burnt, 6 pennies the mark, in Skarpegierdt, and 6 marks burnt, 8 pennies the mark, in Degrand, all in the parish of Wissdal, and 3 marks burnt, 6 pennies the mark, in a farm (*gaard*) called Kirckehuusz, in Daleting parish, which lands are the right odal of Else (*som er min kiere hustruis rette odal*), for 300 rix dollars. The lands are redeemable within three terms: the first by St. John's day, the second by the following St. Olaf's day, and the third by St. John's day in the next year.

Anders and Else affix their seals, and request the learned man Rasmus Joensonn, parish priest at Gierisuig, to affix his seal. Subscribed: A. Mowat off Houcheland, Else Trunsdaatter, and Her Rasmus Jonsønn, minister (*minister*).

Braefield House, Dunrossness (in Danish); copy in SA.2/261/5. Three seals. Printed with translation in *OSR*, i, no. 51.

257. Edinburgh, 30 June 1597

Royal letters charging landlords in Orkney and Shetland to keep good rule.

The kingis majestie, for his hienes bettir obedience, peace, quietnes and gude rule in the cuntrie, answering to justice, and redressing of attemptatis and skathis be the landislordis and landitmen of Orknay and Yetland, and sic as they ar obleist to answer for be the lawis of this realme, actis of parliament and generall band, ordanis letters to be direct chargeing Patrik erll of Orknay, Johne maister of Orknay, Mitchell Balfoure of Monquhany, Laurence Bruce of Cultmalindies, Sir Patrik Bellenden of Evie, Hew Sinclair of Burgh, Arthure Sinclar of Houss, Macolme Grott of Tankernes, Edward Sinclar of Ethie, William Sinclar fear thairof, Macolme Sinclar of Quendell, Thomas Knichtissoun of Brassey, Maister James Pitcarne of [*blank*], Thomas Swintoun of Ranebister, Thomas Bellenden of Stanehous, William Bannatyne of Gersey, Maister Robert Hendersoun of Holland, Henrye Halcro of that ilk, Andro Umphray of Berry, Adame Mudye of Breknes, James Stewart of Grensey, William Stewart of Lykeing, Robert Menteith of Eglissey, Ewmond Sinclar of Flotta, Andro Giffert of Wodersta, James Strang of Voisgairth, William Bruce of Soundburgh, Adame Sinclar of Brow, William Sinclar of Ustnes, Andro Edmestoun of Quhitenes, Henry Sinclar of Towquhoy, Olypher Sinclar of Issinquoy, William Gordoun of Carstane, Mawnis Cromartye of Cara, Edward Scola of Strynie, James Scola of Toftis, James Maxwell of [*blank*], Hew and Robert Halcrois, brether sonnes and aires of umquhile William Halcro of Airkis, Adame Sclater of Burnes, James Murray of Garth, Thomas Murray his gudesone and apperand air, Robert Flett of Howbester, James Stewart of Burray, Frances Sinclar of Uyea, to cum and find sufficient cautioun and souirtie of inlandismen to the contentment of his majestie and lordis of secrete counsale, actit in the buikis thairof, that they and ilkane of thame be thameselffis and all sic personis as they ar obleist to answer for be the lawis of this realme, actis and band foirsaid, sall observe his hienes obedience, keip peace, quietnes and gude rule in the cuntrie, and sall nawyse invaid, trouble, oppres nor persew ony of his majesties subjectis in thair personis, landis, possessiones, guides nor geir, by order of law and justice, ilk persoun under the pecuniall panes following, to be payit to his hienes: that is to say, the saidis erll of Orknay, twentye thowsand pund; the maister of Orknay, ten thowsand merk; and the saidis lardis of Monquhany, Cultmalindies, Evie and Burgh, ilkane of thame, fyve thowsand merk; and als the lard of Tankernes, fyve thowsand merk; the saidis Arthour Sinclar of Houss, the lardis of Ethie, Brassey, Mr James Pitcarne, the lardis of Ranebister, Stanehouse, Holland, Halcro and the lard of Ustnes, ilk ane of thame, twa thowsand merkis; and the remanent personis abonewrittin, ilkane ane thowsand merkis; except Adame Sinclar of Brow, ane thowsand pund; and Henry Sinclar of Towquhoy, ane thowsand pund; Olipher Sinclar of Issaquoy, the saidis fear of Ethie, Macolme Sinclar of Quendell, William Bannatyne of Gairsay, Andro Umphray of Berry, the lardis of Burnes, Grensay, Lykeing, Eglissey and Howbester, quhilkis ar ilkane of thame ane thowsand pund; James Scolo of Toftis, fyve hundreth pund; Hew and Robert Halcrois, fyve hundreth merkis ilkane; Adame Sclater of Burnes, Vc li.; James Stewart of Burray and the said Frances Sinclar of Uyea, ilkane of thame, fyve hundreth merkis; and als that they and all sic as they ar obleist for as said is salbe answerable to his majestie and to justice, and sal satisfie and redres thair attemptattis and skaithis, conforme to the saidis lawes, actis and band, and under the painis contenit thairin, within xl dayes efter the charge, under the pane of rebellioun etc., and gif they failyie, etc., to denunce the dissobeyares.

Sic subscribitur, James R.

SRO, Acta penes Marchiarum et Insularum Ordinem, PC.8/1, ff.32-3. For 'general bands' of this kind see *RPC*, iv, pp.liii-lvi.

258. 9 July 1597

'Charter by Henry Sinclair, son and heir of umquhile Mathew Sinclair of Gruting, to Adam Sinclair of Brew, on the narrative of a submission between them, wherein the arbiters chosen by Henry were Arthur Sinclair of Aith and John Nevin of Scousburgh, and by Adam, Malcolm Sinclair of Quendale and Laurence Sinclair of Goat, the said Adam disponed five lasts of land in Weisdale. ...

'Witnesses: Alexander Bruce, notary, Mr John Adie, minister at Delting, James Knolland and Laurence Sinclair of Goat.'

The original is not known to exist. The above abstract, by Francis Grant, is in OSD, *SN*, 18 November 1893.

259. Skalloway bankis, 10 July 1597

Disposition by Patrik, earl of Orkney, to Lawrence Bruce of Cultmalindeis, of the gift of the escheat of William Schewartsoun.

We, Patrik, erle of Orknay, lord of Yeitland, be the tennour heirof giffis and disponis to Lawrence Bruce of Cultmalindeis, the gift of escheit of the guids and gere pertening to William Schewartsoun, dempt to us for the wrange done be him to Mathow Robertsoun, his fold for the tyme. And that becaus that Mathow Robertsoun hes forgiffin him, for his part, at the lardis request. And thairfoir dischergis our foldis and officiaris of ony trubling or molesting of the said William thairanent. Be thir presentis; subscryvit with our hand at Skalloway bankis, the x day of July 1597.

Orknay.

GH. The endorsement on the back reads: 'The escheit of Wilyame Sewartsone in Caldbak'.

260. Skalloway bankis, 11 July 1597

Mutual bond between Laurence Bruce of Cultemalyndeis, on the one part, and Mr James Pitcarne, vicar of Northmavin, on the other part, in which they forgive each other for all occasions of trouble, envy, hatred and malice that have for long continued between them, except such civil action which either of them has for land or gear against the other. They bind themselves that neither of them, nor their servants, tenants, kin or friends, at any time hereafter, shall invade, trouble and pursue the other, but shall observe and keep firm friendship, good rule and duty, as required by the law of this country, so that they may live in Christian charity so long as God spares their lives. If any kind of controversy shall happen to fall furth between them, they are content that this is friendly received in love and kindly manner before they enter in process. Arthour Sinclar of Aith and John Mowat, apparent of Hugoland, become cautioners for Laurence and James, respectively. In the event of default, the party breaking the bond shall pay £500 to Patrik, earl of Orknay, and £500 to the injured party, and they are content that Patrik, earl of Orknay, shall be judge competent to find which is the defaulting party.

Witnesses: (blank) Levingstoun of Pallintone, Thomas Swentoun, minister at Kirkwall, William Bruce of Symbuster, Mr Thomas Barclay, and Andro Martyne, writer hereof.

SRO, RD.1/114, f.381; SRO, RD.11/52, no.209.

261. Skalloway, 17 July 1597

Wadset by Adam Sinclair of Brow, with consent of Elene Bruce his spouse, to Hendrie Sinclair, eldest son of Mathow Sinclair of Gruting, of lands of Brow, for 30 angel nobles.

The original is not known to exist. Referred to in an action by Patrik, earl of Orknay, lord Yetland, against Adame Sinclair and Elene Bruce, 24 August 1604 (*CB1*, p.153). The wadset was assigned by Hendrie to Patrik on 8 August 1598 (*ibid.*)

262. Quhytnes, 14 August 1597

Doom and ordinance of the lawting court concerning the theft of sheep from the holms of Papay and Hildissay.

At Quhytnes the xiiij day of August the yeir of god ane thousand fyve hunder four scoir sevintein yeiris. The quhilk day as tueching the greit stowth of scheip taine out of my lordis holmis callit Papay and Hildissay, out of the ane sevin scoir and ten or thairby, and out of Papay four scoir or thairby, this last winter, be ressoun that Thomas How, Nicole Easthous, Yanis Olawsoun in How, and Magnus in Vessetter hes confessit, and als being provin that thay wer in the holme of Hildissay takand bait as is alledgit, thairfoir the essyse decernis thame and ilk ane of thame respective to underly the panis contenit in the principall act or decreit maid thairanent, quhilk is committairis of manifest stowth, except that thay had beine drevin thair be storme of wether or obtenit licence thairto, quhilk thai did nocht, and sua culpable of the cryme, thair haill guidis and gere in my lordis will thairfoir; and in tyme cuming ordanis ane gibbett to be placeit in ilk greit holme or yle, and quha so ever beis fund and tryit to enter thairintill, but licence or utherwayis nor as said is, the findair and upgiffar of the samin to have the thrid of thair landis and louse guidis, and my lord the rest as escheit for ever eftir thay be execut or convict thairfoir, and the persoun to be presentit to the scherefe or underfold of ilk parrochin pas them to ane essyse and justefie them incontinent, to quhilk we gife our full power by thir presentis, and siclyk ordanis all the inhabitantis of Quhytnes, Weisdaill and utheris besyd to quyt them that thay have nocht beine in my lordis holmis within this twa yeir, or than to be accuseit thairfoir; and ordanis the brekaris and violateris of thir presentis to be giffin up in dittay ilk yeir be the commonis and foldis of ilk parochin or yle fra this furthe, ilk persoun under the paine of perjurie.

CB1, p.44 (where Vessetter appears as Ressetter: see SRO, SC.10/1/1, f.49).

263. Hay in Dunrosnes, November 1597

Disposition by Garth, Derick and Magnus Mowattis, sons and lawful heirs of the deceased James Mowat in Hai, with consent of Margret Thomasdochter, their mother, to a famous man Malcolme Symoundsone of Culbenisgarth, of 2 marks land, 6 pennies the mark, in Daill and Exingabuth, 'of that four markis land quhilk our said umquhile father airit efter his barne and rais of the stok of Brind', for 36 gudlings in corn, cattle and gold, 'payit and deliverit to our said umquhile father ane grit part thairof affoir his deceis, and the rest to us efter his deceis'.

Because they have no seals of their own they procure those of honourable men: Johnne Nevene of Skousburgh, underfoud of Dunrosnes, and Laurence Sinclair of Gote, minister of Dunrosnes. Witnesses: Alexander Watsone in Goirshous, Thomas Blackbaird in Oxinsta, and Johnne Sinclair of Quhame, lawrightman of Dunrosnes, with divers others.

SA, D.8/3/1.

264. Skea, 21 November 1597

Disposition by Andro Mowatt of Howgoland, with consent of Johne Mowatt, his eldest son and apparent heir, and of Cristian Stewartt, spouse of Johne, to James Mowatt and his heirs male, whom failing to Gilbertt Mowatt and his heirs male, whom failing to the said Johne Mowatt and his heirs, with reservation of the liferent to Andro, of 9 marks land, 8 pennies the mark, in Burrafirth, in the parish of Sandsting; 6 marks land, 6 pennies the mark, in Brownatwat, 6 marks land, 6 pennies the mark, in Stennistwat, 4 marks land, 9 pennies the mark, in Ulvista, 1½ marks land, 8 pennies the mark, in Brabuster, 1 mark land, 9 pennies the mark, in Brek, 3½ marks land, 8 pennies the mark, in Seter, in the parish of Wallis; 4 marks land, 6 pennies the mark, in Howasetter, 3 marks land, 6 pennies the mark, in Grenewall, 1½ marks land, 8 pennies the mark, in Caldcliff, 2 marks land, 6 pennies the mark, in Daill, 1 mark land, 8 pennies the mark, in Skalloway, and 1 mark land, 8 pennies the mark, in the isle thereof called the Brether Ile, 1½ marks land, 8 pennies the mark, in Nesbester, in the parish of Tingwell and Quhitnes; 1 mark land, 12 pennies the mark, in Gletnes, ½ mark land, 9 pennies the mark, in Beinsta, 1 mark land, 12 pennies the mark, in Catford, and 10 marks land, 8 pennies the mark, in Laxvo, in the parish of Nesting and Lunesting; 'togidder with the haill landis of Daill and Daillis guidis, quhairever the samin lyis within the cuntrie of Yetland'. The lands are to be held by James for payment of scat and teinds to the king and the kirk, and of all other customary dues, together with one penny, upon the grounds of the lands of Caldbak, yearly to Andro on Beltane day, if asked. The disposition is in fulfilment of a contract between Andro, on the one part, and Johne and Cristiane, his spouse, on the other part, dated 20 and 21 November 1597 at Collafirth and Skea. Precept of sasine.

Witnesses: Barrold Mowat, Donald Williamson, Magnus Tullo, Magnus Cogill, Andro Mowat, Archibald Sinclair, and William Fermour, notary public, with divers others. Cristiane Stewartt subscribes with her hand held at the pen. Andro Giffhartt subscribes as a witness.

Sasine given at Burrafirth on 23 November 1597 (at 12 noon) by Gilbert Giffert, bailie. Witnesses: Magnus Mowat, George Broun, Nicoll Olasoun, and Archibald Sinclair. William Fermour, notary public.

SA, GD.144/254/3. The sasine is on the back.

265. 24 November 1597

'Wadset by Francis Sinclair, eldest son and heir to umquhile William Sinclair of Uyea, with consent of Robert Sinclair, his brother, and taken burden on him for the remanent heirs, to Jerome Umphray and Margaret Murray, his spouse, of 3½ merks land in Inner Sand. ...

'Witnesses: William Hay, archdeacon of Zetland, Andrew Edmondston, minister of Walls, John Sutherland, vicar of Sandsting and Aithsting.'

The original is not known to exist. The above abstract, by Francis Grant, is in OSD, *SN*, 18 November 1893.

266. Twat, 2 March 1597-8

Obligation by Laurence Bruce of Cultmalindeis to his good friend Arthure Sinclair of Aythe, for 60 angel nobles.

Witnesses: Williame Tyrie, younger, of Busbies, Henrie Wardlaw and Alexander Isbister, with divers others.

SRO, RD.1/79, f.143.

267. Quendell, 16 April 1598

Wadset by William Cheyne, father brother of Patrik Cheyne of Essilmonthe, conform to the commission granted to him by the said Patrik, to Malcolm Sinclair of Quendall, of 27 marks land, 8 pennies the mark, of Gresta, 9 marks land, 8 pennies the mark, of North Setter, 3 marks land, 6 pennies the mark, of Glasbo, 6 marks land, 6 pennies the mark, of Corkasetter, 15 marks land, 6 pennies the mark, in Cauldclift, in the parish of Tingwall; 7½ marks land, 8 pennies the mark, in Kirkgoir, 1 mark land, 6 pennies the mark, in Over Sound, 1½ marks land, 6 pennies the mark, in Nether Sound, 3 marks land, 6 pennies the mark, in Kikrone, 6 marks land, 6 pennies the mark, in Haggersta, in the parish of Weisdaill; 2 marks land, 6 pennies the mark, in Burragarth, 10 marks land, 8 pennies the mark, in Wormidaill, 2½ marks land, 8 pennies the mark, in Ustanes, 1 mark land, 6 pennies the mark, in Wodbester, ½ mark land, 6 pennies the mark, in Hillasetter, 2 marks land, 9 pennies the mark, in Heem and Brek, 2½ marks land, 4 pennies the mark, in Tuslavell, 2 marks land, 6 pennies the mark, in Mousta, 1 mark land, 6 pennies the mark, in Skarpargarth, in the parish of Quhitnes; and 5 marks land, 6 pennies the mark, in Rangista, in the parish of Dynrosnes; for £1,425, redeemable at the Croce-kirk of Dynrosnes on Whitsun eve, to be held of

Patrik in free blenchfarm for payment yearly of one penny on the ground of Ringista on Whitsun eve. Precept of sasine.

Witnesses: Lawrence Sinclair of Got, Alexander Watsoun, Patrik Forbes, Thomas Blakbard, and William Fermour, notary public.

From charter of confirmation under the great seal, 25 October 1600 (*RMS*, vi, no.1081).

268. (June) 1598

Obligation by Lawrence Sinclair of Goit, and James Leslie of Brawik, to Robert Williamesone, burgess of Dysart, for 575 merks, in full payment of 1,150 merks for Robert's ship called the *Lyoun*, the one half paid at Yeitland on (blank) June 1598 on receipt of the ship, and the balance outstanding to be paid by 1 August 1599.

Witnesses: Thomas Auchinlek and William Fermour, notaries, Andro Umphray, and James Kintor.

SRO, RD.1/73, ff.82-3.

269. Edinburgh, 24 June 1598

Decreet of court of session in action at instance of Dame Jean Kennedie, countess of Orkney, against Patrik, now earl of Orkney, for payment to her of the just third of the goods, gear, money and debts, which pertained to the deceased Robert, earl of Orkney, lord Yetland, her spouse, at the time of his death on 4 February 1592-3. Patrik has intromitted with the undernoted goods and gear, and debts, since the decease of Robert, and will not make payment and deliverance to Dame Jean of the just third of the same.

Goods and gear:

In the holms of Vemendrie, Rymswell and other holms in Yetland, being Robert's 'steid rowmes', 7,000 yeld sheep at 30s. per head.

Money received for 'silver maill, wattell and scatt of Yetland' for Whitsunday and Martinmas terms 1592, 11,000 merks.

Wool clipped from Robert's sheep in Orkney and Yetland at Beltane 1592, 60 stones at £4 per stone.

Debts owing to Robert:

'Item, thair wes restand awand the tyme foirsaid the saidis tua yeris [*crops 1591 and 1592*] yerlie to the said Robert, erll of Orkney, lord Yetland, respective be the tenentis and occupyeris of the lands of the lordship of Yetland as is efter delyditt':

'off the iyll of Unst ... auchtein peck xvj cuttill wadmeill of landmaills, and in scatt xxij pack iiij s. wadmeill; in butter for the landmaills nyne scoir lespund ij d. and ob. butter, and in scatt viij^{XX} viij m. iij d., tua pert butter and thrid pert uylie, viij^{XX} gulyeonis in wattill comptand ilk gulyeoun to the fyifth of ane angell, and xxiiij angellis and four dolours for the toll of tua schippis; ...

'of the lands lyand in Yell ... in landmails ten pack xviij s. iiij cuttell wadmeill, in scaitt xij pack xiiij s. of cuttill wadmell, in butter for the landmails v^{XX} xviij leispund iij d. ob., and in scatt vj^{XX} vj m. tua pert butter tua pert oyle, viij^{XX} vj gulyeonis wattill, xxiiij angellis four dolours for the toill of twa schippis lyand thair; ...

'within the iyll of Fetlair in lands maills aucht pack x s. iij cuttill, in scatt xvj pack xviij s. wadmell, in butter for the land maills iiij^{XX} vj leispund iiij d. ob. and in scatt vj^{XX} xviij m., twa pert butter and thrid pert oyll, and iiij^{XX} gulyeons in wattill; ...

'in Northmaben ane uther ill ... in land maills xxx pack ane cuttill wadmell, in scatt xij pack viij s. ij c. wadmell, in butter for the lands mails xv^{XX}ij leispund ob. butter, and in scatt iiij^{XX} xviij m. tua pert butter and thrid pert oyll, in wattill v^{XX} ij gulyeons, xxiiij angellis and four dolours for the toll of twa schippis; ...

'in Deltonyng ane uther iyll ... in land maills xxx pack viij s. vj cuttell wadmell, in butter land maills IJc xxxvj lespund and ane barrell of oyll, in scatt iij^{XX} xviij m. ob., tua pert butter and thrid pert oyll, and in wattill xl gulyeons of meill ob.; ...

'in Nesting in land maills and scatt xxij pack xij s. x cuttıll wadmel, in butter for the land maills iiij^{XX} xiiij leispund iiij d., ane barrell butter, ane barrell ule, and a hundreth and ten fische, keilling and ling, in scatt iij^{XX} x m. ij d., four pert butter and vj pert ule, and xlviij gulyeon in wattill; ...

'in the Walls in ane uther iyll ... in land maills in scatt iij^{XX} viij m. iiij d., four pert butter saxt pert ulie, xxiiij angellis iiij dolours for the toll of twa schippis thair, and xxiiij gulyeons ane meill in wattill; ...

'in Mittingsting [*rectius* Aithsting] in scatt and land maills xxviij pack iiij s. vj cuttill wadmell, in butter for the land maills vj^{XX} xij leispund iiij d., in scatt iiij^{XX} xviij m., four pert butter and sext pert ulie, xij angellis tua dolours for the toll of ane schip thair, and iij^{XX} gulyeonis vj m. in wattill; ...

'in Caitnes [*rectius* Quhitnes] in scatt and land maillis xviij pack xij s. iiij cuttill wadmell, in butter for land maillis iiij^{XX} xviiij leispund x d., in scatt xviij m., four pert butter and vj pert ulie, and iij^{XX} gulyeons in wattill; ...

'in Brassay ane uther iyll ... in scatt and land maills xvj pack xvj s. wadmell, in butter for the landmaills xx leispund, tua barrell butter, in scatt xlviij m., four pert butter and vj pert oyle, and lviij gulyeon in wattill; ...

'in Tingwall ane uther of the iyllis ... in scatt and land maills xxiiij pack tua cuttill wadmell, in butter for the landmaills vj^{XX} lespund iiij d., in scatt vj^{XX} vj m., four pert butter and vj pert oylie, xxiiij angellis four dolours in Laxfurde for toill, and lviij gulyeonis ij m. vj d. wattill; ...

'in Burray ane uther of the iyllis ... in scatt and land maills xiiij pack vj s. iiij cuttill vj d. wadmell, in butter for land maills v^{XX} xiiij leispund iiij d., tua barrell butter, and in scatt xxxij m., four pert butter and four pert ulie, xxiiij angellis four dolours for the toll of tua schippis lyand thair, and iij^{XX}

xiiij gulyeons viij d. wattill; ...

'in Dunrosnes in scatt and landmaills iij^{XX} vj pack tua schilling viij cuttill wadmell, in butter for the landmaills thairof xiiij^{XX} xiiij lespund x d. ob. and four barrell butter, in scatt ix^{XX} xiiij m. viij d., four pert butter and vj pert oyll, xij angellis ij dolours for the toll of ane schip at the Ness thair, and vj^{XX} xiiij gulyeonis in wattill;

'Item thair wes restand awand the tyme foirsaid the saids tua yeir be the haill tenents of Yetland the bischoppis haill umbottis of Yetland, quhilk is the teindis, yerlie the saids tua yeris xvij^{XX} v angellis ane ortt of ane angell and vj dolours;

'Item thair wes restand awand yerlie the saids tua yeris be the awneris of forscoir ten fischearie botts lyand at the Ness, for the teind fische of ilk ane of the saids bottis, the teind of ilk bott extending yerlie to IJc and four dussoun fische, keilling and ling, comptand vj^{XX} to a hundreth, and tua barell salt;

'Item thair wes restand awand the tyme foirsaid the saids tua yeris yerlie be the awners of xxx fischer bottis lyand in Rymmiswell lyand within the said lordship of Yetland, the tend of ilk bott extending yeirlie to IJc iiij dussoun fische, killing and ling, and tua barell salt;

'Item thair wes restand awand the tyme foirsaid of the saids tua yeris yerlie be the tenentis and occupyers of the lands of Foulay ane uther of the iylls within the said lordschip of Yetland, fourtie gulyeons fische, ij pack wadmell; and be the tenentis and occupy[er]is of the Fair Iyll lyand betwixt Orkney and Yetland, IJc xxxij gulyeons.

'Pryce of ilk pack wadmell yerlie the saids tua yeris comptand iij^{XX} cuttill to the pack, and ilk cuttill to thre quarteris of ane elne Scottis, four dolours; pryce of ilk barrell butter yerlie during the saids tua yeris comptand xiij leispund in Yetland the barell and ilk lespund to vj d. butter Yetland compt twentie pund; pryce of ilk barrell ulie xviij lib. yeirlie the saidis tua yeiris; pryce of ilk gulyeon according to Yetland compt is the fyift part of ane angell, fyve pundis Scottis; ilk hundrith fische yerlie the said twa yeris, killing and ling, fyveten pundis; pryce of ilk barrell salt yerlie the said twa yeris, thrie pund; pryce of ilk dolour yerlie the saidis twa yeris, fyiftie shillingis.'

The lords of council absolve Patrik of liability to account to Dame Jean for her terce in respect of the goods and gear, and debts, in Yetland. Patrik had claimed that Robert, his father, long before his death, had set in tack to him the whole rents of Yetland of the crop 1592 for his entertainment in court and service with the king, and for performing and doing of his father's affairs, for yearly payment of 560 angel nobles, whereof Patrik had made payment to his father before his decease, and that by virtue of which Patrik was in actual and real possession of the rents and duties of the lordship of Yetland for the said year. In answer to which Dame Jean had failed to prove that Robert had retained the actual and real possession of the lordship of Yetland by taking up the duties to his own utility and profit to the time of his death.

SRO, CS.7/170, ff.166-8, 458; CS.7/174, ff.25, 103, 162, 431; CS.7/175, ff.242-248. The decreet also deals with Dame Jean's claims to her terce in respect of goods and gear, money and debts, outwith Shetland. The following abbreviations are used: c. cuttell, d. penny, m. meill, s. shilling. Superscript 'xx' indicates a score (e.g. 'v^{XX} xviij' = 118).

270. Symbsuster in Quhailsay, 7 July 1598

Wadset by James Sutherland in Isbuster in the isle of Quhailsaye, with special good will of Bessie Williamesdochter, his spouse, to an honourable man Hew Sinclair of Brught, of his 3 marks land, 12 pennies the mark, in the town of Gairdeishous, for 9 angel nobles sufficient gold in weight, with 1 mark 2 ures land in the easter isles of Quhailsay, called Muyea, 2 ures land in Unyerholme, and 1½ marks land, 12 pennies the mark, in the town of Isbuster, all in the isle of Quhailsay, for the teind lambs of 12 years at four lambs the year, extending to 48 lambs, half ewes and half wedders, with their profits, until James with his 'awin leill win in guidis' redeems the same all in one day.

James draws his merchant mark, and requests William Manisoun in Neip to affix his signet. He also requests Petir Symsoun, minister of Nesting, to subscribe in his name. Witnesses: Olipher Sinclair of Estishous, Hew Tarrel, writer hereof, and Arthour Symsone, with divers others.

SA, SC.12/65/1/33. Mark of James Sutherland.

271. Skalloway bankis, 7 August 1598

Obligation by Malcolme Sinclare of Quendale to his good friend Williame Carmichaell, merchant, for 100 angel nobles gold and weight, which Williame has paid to Patrik, earl of Orknay, lord Yetland, in Malcolme's name and at his command.

Witnesses: Eduard Skollaw of Streynie, John Logane, and Thomas Auchinlek.

SRO, RD.1/65, f.262.

272. Scalloway, 8 August 1598

Excambion between Christopher Lawrensone in Growingsheuo, with consent of (blank), his spouse, and Andro Edmestoune, minister of God's word, whereby Christopher acknowledges having received 20 'gulleonis Yetland payment' from Andro in complete payment of the price of 1 of his 6 marks land, 8 pennies the mark, in Quhitsnes, and exchanges his other 5 marks land in Quhitsnes for 4 marks land, 8 pennies the mark, in Stoiff pertaining to Andro. The 6 marks land in Quhitsnes are to be held by Andro 'in fie blanche for the payment of ane penny yeirlie giff it be requirit; and giff neid be, of the immediat superiour of the lordship of Yetland for the payment of the yeirlie scat allennerlie'. Precept of sasine.

Witnesses: Jerome Umphray, Allexander Laxfuird, bailie of Tingwall, and Jerome Tuaitt, mariner. Christopher subscribes with his hand led at the pen by Alexander Bruce, notary public.

SA, Nicolson Papers.

273. Swynburgh, 12 August 1598

Obligation by Andro Mowat of Howgoland to Patrik, earl of Orknay, lord Yetland, narrating that Andro and the deceased Robert, earl of Orknay, had made a contract whereby Andro would deliver to Robert sufficient oaken timber as would build and complete a ship of 70 feet of length in the keel to have been brought from Norway at Robert's expense in return for 2 lasts of malt. Because Patrik renounces the contract Andro binds himself to deliver to Patrik, or his agent, the undernoted timber: 6 dozen oaken joists, 30 to 32 feet long and 1½ feet 'in the cant'; 2 dozen oaken joists, 18 feet long and 1½ feet 'in the cant'; 100 fir joists, 30 to 32 feet long and 1½ feet 'in the cant'; 1,000 'daills', 14 to 16 feet long and 1½ feet broad; 200 'sparris', 30 feet long and 1 foot 'in the cant'; 5 dozen oaks for 'dures, windies and burdis', 10 and 12 feet long, and 1½ or 2 feet 'in the cant'. The timber is to be delivered, at Andro's expense, to the ship's side in Norway within 15 days of arrival, under penalty of £20 for each work day of delay thereafter through Andro's default.

Witnesses: Thomas Swintoun, minister, William Bruce of Symbuster, Thomas Auchinlek, and Alexander Bruce, notary, writer hereof.

SRO, RD.1/101, f.352.

274. Voisgarth, 21 August 1598

Contract between David Sinclair of Huntone, on the one part, and James Strang of Voisgarthe, on the other part, whereby David, understanding that James and Christiane Sinclair, his daughter, and now spouse of James, were sufficiently infeft in his 18 marks land, 8 pennies the mark, called the great last of land in Melbe, in the parish of Sandische (by virtue of the decreet judicial given in favour of James and Christiane in satisfaction of David's part of the contract of matrimony made between the deceased Bartholomew Strang and James, on the one part, and David and Christiane, on the other part), until David should pay to James and Christiane the sum of £200. David acknowledges receipt from James of £100, for which David sells to James and Christiane, his spouse, the said 18 marks land called the great last in Melbe for £300, of which £200 is allowed for the complete payment of the contract of matrimony. The lands are to be held either in 'fie blanche' of David for the payment of one penny yearly if required, or to be held of the immediate superior of the lordship of Yetland for payment of the yearly scat 'allenerlie'. James binds himself that if David pays him the sum of £300 at the kirk of Balestay in the isle of Unst at Whitsunday, on 40 days warning, he shall resign the lands back to David.

Witnesses: Williame Tyrie, younger, A. Edmestoune, and H. Wardlaw.

SA, D.10/34/2. An endorsement at the foot, written by Thomas Auchinlek, states that the document was produced at Skalloway bankis on 7 August 1599 and registered.

275. Voisgarthe, 21 August 1598

Letters of reversion whereby James Strang of Voisgarthe binds himself that whenever David Sinclair of Huntone, his father-in-law, shall pay him £300 at the kirk of Ballestay in the isle of Unst at Whitsunday, on 40 days warning, he shall resign in favour of David the 18 marks land, 8 pennies the mark, in Melbe, called the great last thereof, in the parish of Sandische, providing that David or his heirs shall not sell or wadset the said land before offering it to James's heirs 'come of ther stok [who are] to have the same for full landis pryce befoir ony uther'.

James affixes his signet. Witnesses: William Tyrie, younger, of Busbie, Henry Wardlaw, servant of the laird of Cultemalindeis, and Andro Edmestoune, minister.

SA, D.10/7. There are abstracts by Francis Grant of apparently related documents no longer known to exist: (1) disposition (lands not specified) in 1599 by David Sinclair of Hunto in favour of James Strang, witnessed by William Tyrie, younger, Henry Wardland, Magnus Norsk, minister, and Andrew Edmonston, minister at Yell; and (2) sasine given at Melbie (Daniel Tullock, attorney) on 6 June 1599 to James Strang, of 18 marks land in 'the Great last of Melbie, called the Sinclair's last' (OSD, *SN*, 18 November 1893).

276. Dunrossness, 24 August 1598

'Wadset by Frances Sinclair, apparent of Uyea, to William Bruce of Symbister, his father in law, of 7 merks land in Deall, in Tingwall, and 1½ merks land in Ska in Quhalsay. ... William Fermour, NP.'

The original is not known to exist. The above abstract, by Francis Grant, is in OSD, *SN*, 18 November 1893. According to an abstract of the sasine (dated 1598), by Gilbert Goudie, Frances Sinclair wadset the land for £100, and the lands were respectively 6 and 9 pennies the merk (notebook in Braefield House, Dunrossness).

277. 26 January 1598-9

Excambion by Ingerith Thomasdochter to William Manssone [of Gairdie] of her 2½ marks land in Sound in Ronene in exchange for 2½ marks land in Gairdoun in the isle of Unst.

The charter was produced in the sheriff court of Shetland on 31 July 1617, in an action of removal at instance of William Manssone of Gairdie (*CB2*, p.57).

278. 20 March 1598-9

'Charter of excambion whereby Laurence Bruce of Cultmalindie exchanges his four merks land in Easter House of Sellafirth, with Peter Nisbet of Kirkabister, for four merks land in Midhouse of Sellafirth in Yell. ...

'Witnesses: Andrew Bruce, William Magnusson of Gairdie, bailie of Unst, John Lawranson of Awick, bailie of Yell. Attested by James of Sivarysetter, lawrytman, David Fouller, James Fryssel, and other divers.'

The original is not known to exist. The above abstract, by Francis Grant, is in OSD, *SN*, 18 November 1893. According to another abstract, by Gilbert Goudie, the deed was subscribed at Sallafirth, and the witnesses affixed their seals, 'impressed on wafers, with their initial on either side' (notebook in Braefield House, Dunrossness).

279. 22 March 1598-9

'The schownd bill of umquhill Daniel Hawick.'

The original is not known to exist. One of the writs taken from Ninian Neven's house in Yell on 24 August 1624 (*RPC*, xiv, p.735).

280. Edinburgh, 7 April 1599

Contract between Frances Sinclair of Uyea, on the one part, and Andro Lawsoun, burgess of Edinburgh, on the other part, whereby Andro lends Frances the sum of 3,000 merks repayable by Whitsunday 1599, failing which Frances binds himself to get himself served heir in the lands of the deceased William Sinclair, his father, and to infeft Andro with a wadset of the same. The lands are as follows: 12 marks land, 12 pennies the mark, in Tegon, 16 marks land, 9 pennies the mark, in Kirkhous, 4 marks and (blank), 8 pennies the mark, in Grorbisnes, 7 marks land, 9 pennies the mark, in Clevogathe, 8 marks land, 12 pennies the mark, in Buistay, 8 marks land, 12 pennies the mark, in Wedderstay, and 1 mark land, 12 pennies the mark, in Husda, in the parish of Delting; 6 marks land, 12 pennies the mark, in Vodlone, 12 marks land, 12 pennies the mark, in Lowning, 4 marks lands, 8 pennies the mark, in Grungyeafurthe, 7 marks land and (blank), 9 pennies the mark, in Dowar, 1 mark land and (blank), 12 pennies the mark, in Skelberrie, and 1 mark land, 9 pennies the mark, in Neip, in the parish of Nesting and Lunesting; 9 marks land, 12 pennies the mark, in Sandsoull, 6 marks land, 12 pennies the mark, in Clodone, 1 mark land and (blank), 12 pennies the mark in Sandwek, 2 marks land, 12 pennies the mark, in Westirhous, 1 mark land, 12 pennies the mark, in Skuaw, 1 mark land, 9 pennies the mark, in Simbester, and ½ mark land, 12 pennies the mark, in Broche, in the parish of Quhalissey; 3 marks land and (blank), 9 pennies the mark, in Bastay, 2 marks land, 8 pennies the mark, in Vassay, 4½ marks land, 9 pennies the mark, in Avek, 3 marks land, 8 pennies the mark, in Howlland, ½ mark land, 6 pennies the mark, in Papell, 4 marks land, 8 pennies the mark, in Grunnasitter, 1½ marks land, 9 pennies the mark, in Kirkabusta, 9 marks land, 8 pennies the mark, in Gossoburgh, 1 mark land and (blank), 9 pennies the mark, in Studdiswek in West Yell, (blank) land, 9 pennies the mark, in Bigsatter, 1 mark land, 9 pennies the mark, in Sellifirth, 6 marks land, 8 pennies the mark, in Gutscheir, 4 marks land, 9 pennies the mark, in Esettaygarthe, and 2½ marks, 9 pennies the mark, in Roffurd, in the parish of Yell; 3 marks land in Skaw, ½ mark land in Utterskaw, 16 marks land in Underhoull, 8 marks land in Lund, ½ mark land in Colvasetter, 1 mark land in Sclettoun, 19 marks land in Ramnagew, 1 mark land in Balyeastay, 4½ marks land in Gunyasetter, 1 mark land in Meuhous, 1 mark land in Bodon, 2½ marks land in Daill, 1 mark land in Sandiwek, 18 marks land in Crosbuster, 48 marks land in Underhull, 8 marks land in Wandstrik, 3 marks land in Mawlall, 1½ marks land in Scolla, 1 mark land in Still, 1 mark land in Midgarth, 2 marks land in Papill, ½ mark land in Torvell, 2 marks and (blank) in Garthe, 1 mark land in Clowdoun, ½ mark land in Setir, 1 mark land in Houston, 9½ marks land in Clevocuster, 84 marks land in Uyea, all 6 pennies the mark, and 2 marks land, 12 pennies the mark, in Baltay, in the isle and parish of Uncet; 1½ marks land in Southhouse in Feinyie, 1 mark land in Russetter, 1½ marks land in Howbye, and 1½ marks land in Toft in Strand, all 6 pennies the mark, in the parish of Fetlor; 2 marks land, 9 pennies the mark, in Wodbustay in Brassay; 3 marks land, 8 pennies the mark, in Aithe in Ailsting; 6 marks land, 8 pennies the mark, in Clatt in Burray; 15 marks land, 12 pennies the mark, in Griddilstay, 6 marks land, 6 pennies the mark, in Schaldernes, 7 marks land, 6 pennies the mark, in Dell, 5 marks land, 8 pennies the mark, in Howlland, 3 marks land, 8 pennies the mark, in Burraland in Trundarie, 1 mark land, 8 pennies the mark, in Eisterhous in Scalloway, 12 marks land, 6 pennies the mark, in Stromfurthe, 6 marks land, 6 pennies the mark, in Haggirstay, 6 marks land, 4 pennies the mark, in North Mustoif, and 1 mark land, 4 pennies the mark, in South Mustoif, in the parish of Quhitnes and Wesdaill; 11 marks land, 8 pennies the mark, in Tombling, 5½ marks land, 12 pennies the mark, in Sand, and 6 marks land, 12 pennies the mark, in Unyeafurth, in Aitsting (and) Sandsting; 6 marks land, 12 pennies the mark, in Reirweik, in the parish of Dunrosnes; and 'the channonis lands in Yetland pertening of befoir to the chanonis and stellars of the cathedral kirk of Orknay'.

Witnesses: Alexander Chaip, James Stewart, servant of Mr John Dempstar, advocate, Alexander Robertsoun, cutler, burgess of Edinburgh, William Sinclair, servant of Mr David Guthrie, advocate, writer hereof, and John Ainslie, notary.

SRO, RD.1/70, ff.120-3.

281. Scallowaybankis, 9 August 1599

Assignation and disposition by Andro Mowatt of Hugaland and Johne Mowat of Olaberrie, his son and apparent heir, to Patrik, earl of Orknay, lord Yetland, of all right, title and claim in and to the isle and holm of Lambay, in the parish of Northmavin, so that Patrik and his servants may plenish the same with livestock and dispone thereupon as they think expedient.

Witnesses: Thomas Swyntoun, minister at Kirkwall, Mr James Pitcarne, vicar of Northmavin, Andro Martyne, servant of Patrik, writer hereof, Johne Makkenzie, servant of Patrik, and divers others.

SRO, RD.1/71, f.271.

282. Skalloway bankis, 21 August 1599

Backbond by Androw Edmestoune, minister at Yell, to his well-beloved friend Thomas Swentoune, minister at Kirkwall, whereby Andro binds himself to pay Thomas the sum of £23 6s.8d. yearly at Whitsunday from 1600, for so long as the £20 for the canons' lands of Yetland and the £3 6s.8d. for the third of St. Michellis Stouk in Yetland shall be assigned to Androw in his stipend by the lords' modifiers for serving in the ministry at Yell or any other part of Yetland. Andro is content that if the tenants and tacksmen pay the £23 6s.8d, to Thomas, 'and report to me the saidis Thomas his discharge thairon, in that respect I hauld me weill content and payit of the yeirlie dewtie thairof; and the said Thomas his discharge salbe as valabill as my awin and sall never cum in the contrair thairof'.

Witnesses: Mr James Pitcarne, minister at Northmaven, Eduard Scolawe of Strynie, and David Kincaid.

SA, SC.12/65/1/34. The document is a copy made by Hew Tarrell of the original, and collated by James Neven, notary public. Thomas Swentoune had been constituted factor, on 11 December 1595, by William Elphinstoune, servant of the king, depute-collector, to uplift the thirds of all the small benefices in Orknay and Yetland (SA, SC.12/65/1/34).

283. Olaberry, 24 August 1599

'Andro Giffairt of Wadderstay, with consent of Agnus Robertson, his spouse, and consent of John Giffairt his eldest son, excambs land with Peter Nesbit of Kirkabister.

'Seal of Andrew Gifford is attached. ... Witnesses: Barrald Mowat in Collafirth, Mans Olasoun in Ailsbroche, Michaell Ollasone in Glus, Nicol in Clodasetter, with divers others. "Subscriptions and signets" of honourable men are said to be appended but are not all there. They include Mathow Robertson in Gerthe, and John Robertson in Nestasetter.'

The original is not known to exist. The above abstract, by J. Storer Clouston, is in OA,

D.23, Notebook 4, p.67. According to another abstract, by Francis Grant (OSD, *SN* 18 November 1893) the lands excambed were 3 merks land in Mowaness in Unst, for 3 merks land in Sursetter in Delting; and Andro Mowat of Hugoland, James (*rectius* John) Mowat, his son and apparent thereof, Mr James Pitcairn, minister of Northmavine, were also witnesses. Clouston illustrates the mark of Mans Olasoun.

284. 8 September 1599

'Ane evident wreattin on paper grantit by ... Mr John Dischingtoun to John Neven, of tua merk ½ merk land in Clibbersweik in Unst.'

The original is not known to exist. One of the writs taken from Ninian Neven's house in Yell on 24 August 1624 (*RPC*, xiv, p.733).

285. Dysert, 26 November 1599

Contract between the right honourable Hew Sinclair of Bruche, on the one part, and William Row, his servant, on the other part, concerning William's intromissions with Hew's goods and gear, whereby William acknowledges that he is due Hew, his master, the sum of £104. Hew discharges William of the said sum, and William binds himself to become servant to Hew for so long a time as Hew thinks expedient, during which time William 'sall remane in the said Hewis service and serve him continualie according to his directioun, sall do his dewetie in all respectis to his said maister in his said service as ane leill trew servand ... sua that gif the said William sall absent him selff fra his said maisteris service without leiff askit and gevin the said William sall be comptit ane perjure and unworthie persoun, and sall serve tua dayis for ilk day he beis absent, and siclyk gif it sall happin the said William passis fra his said maisteris service without licence gevin and grantit ... be the said Hewis awin hand writ', William binds himself to pay Hew the foresaid sum of £104, 'the said William doing his dewtie in all poyntis abonewrittin'. Hew binds himself to pay William 'yeirlie, sua lang as he is in his service, in name of fie, the soume of tuelff pundis, beginand the first yeiris payment and entrie of his service at Martimes in anno Jaj Vc fourschoir nyntein yeiris, quhilk fie he grantis him allredie ressaveit fra the said Hew befoir the hand and dischairgis his said maister thairof'.

Francis Sinclair of Uyea, writer hereof. Witnesses: Lawrence Sinclair, 'son to my Lord Sinclair', Alexander and James Stirkis, and James Scot, taffrowmerall, burgess in Dysert.

SRO, RD.11/38, no.862 (registered in RD.1/82, ff.111-12).

286. Holyroodhouse, 30 November 1599

Gift to Walter Tyrie of Damesay in Orknay of the escheat of the goods of Mr James Pitcairnis, minister at Northmaven, put to the horn at the instance of William Bannatyne of Garsay for not finding lawburrows that

William, his wife and children, shall be harmless and scathless.

SRO, PS.1/71, f.91. Mr James Pitcairn was relaxed from the horn on 17 December 1599 as he had found caution (SRO, DI.47/15, ff.142-3).

287. Simbister, 3 December 1599

Disposition by Magnis Lawrencesone to his good friend William Bruce of Simbister, of ½ mark land, 9 pennies the mark, in the town of Sca in the isle of Quhailsay, heired by Magnis after his deceased brother's sons, George and Magnis Peittersoneis, and now presently manured by Peitter Magnissone in Sca.

Magnis obtains the marks of discreet men: James Sudderland, George Wirk, and Robert Hunter; and subscribes with his hand held at the pen by Johne Young. Witnesses: James Groitt, William Mudy, and Halward Polsone.

SA, GD.144/265/2. Marks of James Sudderland and Robert Hunter.

288. Dysart, 15 January 1600

Obligation by James Sincklair, son and apparent heir of Laurence Sinclair of Gott, in name of his father, to Hew Sincklair of Burghe, for £180 to assist in the payment of 575 merks due in completion of payment for the ship called the *Lyoun*, now pertaining to the said Laurence and James Leslie of Brawik, arrested at the instance of Robert Williamsoun, skipper and burgess of Dysart, for non-payment thereof.

Witnesses: Frances Sincklair of Uyea, Robert Williamsoun, Alexander Stirk, burgess of Dysart, William Row, Magnus Halcro, John Robertsoun, servant of Henry Young, common clerk of Dysart, writer hereof, and Henry Young, notary.

SRO, RD.1/80, ff.371-2.

289. Halyrudehous, 19 January 1600.

Precept of clare constat by Patrik earl of Orknay, Lord Yetland, superior of the lands underwritten, to David Deldell and Arthour Irvine in Fair Isle, bailies, in favour of James Menteyth, heir to the deceased Patrik Menteyth of Fair Ile, his father brother, of (blank) marks land of Fair Ile, 'alswell of that pairt of the samyn haldin be us of his majestie and his predecessores callit the kingis pairt as of that pairt of the same landis quhilk pertenit in temporalitie to the beschoprik of Orknay, callit the beschops pairt', in the lordship and foldrie of Yetland, with the office of bailiary thereof, and lands in Orknay (specified).

Written by Mr James Harley, servant to Richard Cass, writer. Witnesses: Edward Scallow of Stryneis, Thomas Blak, servitor to Patrik, and John Porteous, (blank) to John Leivingstoun of Baldoverane, with others.

The original is not known to exist. Narrated in an instrument of sasine of 9 June 1602 (OA, Baikie of Tankerness papers, D.24/3/53 [18th century copy]), where Alexander Jamieson, attorney for James Menteith of Saltcoittis, delivered the precept to Arthour Irvine, who gave sasine to Alexander, in presence of John Irving (blank) Fairile, James Irving his son there, Clement Irving there, and John and Magnus (blank) there. There are also extant (in OA, D.24/3/52) letters by James Menteith of Saltcoittis, bother son and apparent heir of the deceased Patrik Menteith of Fairyle, with consent of Sir William Menteith of Kerss, 'at quhais instance I am interdytit, for his interes', for sums and deeds paid and done to him by Robert Menteith, his brother german, whereby James constitutes Thomas Sinclar his procurator, for retouring James as heir to the deceased Patrik, of (blank) marks land of Fairyle (designed as above), and lands in Orknay (specified), which lands were held by Patrik immediately of Patrik, earl of Orknay, Lord Yetland; and whereby James subsequently resigns the said lands in favour of Robert Menteith, his brother.

290. Hamer, 10 February (*c.*1600)

Wadset by Jhone Mowat, apparent of Hougoland, to 'my weillovit freind Wilyeam Olasone in Nibon, and his wyff and ayres, [of] all and haill my mark land in Nibon, and that for the sowme of ten auld dolouris; quhilkis sowme of ten dolouris I bind and obleissis me, my ayres, executoris and assignayis thankfullie to content and pay unto the said Wilyeam the sowme forsaid betixt the day and daitt heirof and midsummer nixt to cum; and failyeing thairof the said Wilyeam to bruik and manur the said mark land with the haill landmeillis and deweties thairof ay and quhill the said Wilyeam be payit of the sowme forsaid'.

Witnesses: Mans in Alsburch, underfoud (subscribes 'Magnus Ylisborch' with his mark), Ola, his son (subscribes 'Olay in Ylisburgh, witness'), with divers others.

GH.

291. Holyroodhouse, 4 March 1600

Gift to Hew Sinclair of Burgh of the gift of the escheat of the goods of Frances Sinclair of Uyea, put to the horn at the instance of Andro Lawson, merchant, burgess of Edinburgh, for non-fulfilment of contract dated 7 April 1599 (no. 280).

SRO, PS.1/71, f.163.

292. Reafirthe, 10 March 1600

Excambion whereby Salamoine Scott dispones to Osie Scott in Reafirth, his younger brother, 12½ marks land, 8 pennies the mark, in Reafirth (whereof 2 marks were already wadset to Osie), and Osie, with consent of Sungyevo Smyth his spouse dispones to Salamoine 11 marks land, 6 pennies the mark, in Hammer in the south parish of Unst.

The original is not known to exist. Referred to in an action by Osie Scott against Salamoine Scott, 23 August 1602 (*CB1*, p.43). The date in the text is 10 March 1599.

293. Perth, 29 March 1600

Discharge by James Hay, vicar of Unst, to Hew Sinclair of Burgh, of an obligation, dated 31 October 1587, whereby Hew undertakes to resign the canons' lands of Yetland in the hands of the king in favour of James on payment by James to Hew of 200 silver dollars 'callit yopingdaillis'.

Witnesses: James Nevein, servant of Hew, Mr Robert Nairne, pedagogue to the master of Craufurde, John Craufurde, servant of James, and Mr Robert Nicoll, notary, writer in Edinburgh.

SA, SC.12/65/1/37 (extract of deed registered in Books of Council and Session on 3 April 1600).

294. Scousbruch, 28 April 1600

Disposition by Magnus and Nicoll Mannssone to their good friend Malcolme Halcro of Hosweik, of their 4 marks land, 8 pennies the mark, in the town of Hosweik, in the parish of Dinrosnes, for £116, to be held in blenchfarm for payment of one penny yearly, if required. Precept of sasine. Magnus and Nicoll subscribe with their hands led at the pen by William Fermour, and further have compeared before the said William, notary public and foud of Dunrosnes, 'in ane bailye fencit court and rattifeit thir presentis, befoir the wot of the haill parochin'.

Witnesses: John Neving of Scousbruch, Adem Sinclar of Brow, Magnus of Trosweik, Walter Leisk in Vo, with divers others.

SA, D.8/3/5.

295. Edinburgh, 7 June 1600

Decreet of court of session in action at instance of Cristian Murray, 'iyo' and apparent heir of the deceased William Bolt in Yetland, her 'grandsir', and apparent heir of the deceased Magnus Bolt, brother of the said William, and William Cheyne, her spouse, for his interest, against Adam Sinclair, grandson and apparent heir, at the least apparent heir by progress, of the deceased Aula Sinclair in Yetland, and Hew, William, Malcolme and Marjorie Halcrois there, for production and delivery of the original writs granted to William and Magnus Bolts of the lands of Gerth and Collosetter, and inspection of the bonds made by the said William and Magnus, as superiors thereof, to the said Aula Sinclair.

The lords of council continue the summons, and ordain the pursuers to have letters to warn the defenders to compear, bringing with them the foresaid writs.

SRO, CS.7/190, ff.80-1.

296. Skalloway bankis, 17 June 1600

'Adame Sinclair of Brow, with consent of Helen Bruce, his spouse, in consideration of £1,000 Scots paid his umquhile father James Sinclair of Brow, dispones to Arthur Sinclair of Aith, his mother's brother, 5 lasts of land, as follows: 3½ mark (4d.) in Thislawell, 4½ mark (6d.) in Graven, 2 mark (9d.) in Hammir, 5½ mark (12d.) in Houff in Weisdaile, 3 mark (8d.) in Skarpagarthe, 2 mark (6d.) in Desabrek, 5 mark (6d.) in Skeron, 7 mark (8d.) in Hugoland, 3 mark (8d.) in Houff in Quhitnes, 3 mark (8d.) in Helliasetter, 6 mark (9d.) in Mekill Hugsetter, 3 mark (6d.) in Lytill Hugsetter, 7 mark (12d.) in Houstoun, 9 mark (9d.) in Setter, 2 mark (8d.) in Kicron, 1 mark (8d.) in Hammislatter?, ½ mark (8d.) in Towa, 4½ mark in Hamragarthe (no denomination), 18 mark (9d.) in Staniswo. 5 lasts land in Brow given in warrandice. Malcolme Sinclair of Quendale and Poill in Huiff, foud of Quyhitnes, act as bailies.'

The original is not known to exist. The above abstract, by J. Storer Clouston, is in OA, D.23, Notebook 4, pp.64-6. It has marginal annotations following another copy, noting that the other copy specified 2½ marks in Desabrek and 5½ in Skeron, that Towa was missing, and that 'Hammislatter' = Hammersland. Another abstract, by Francis Grant, in OSD, *SN*, 13 January 1894, states that Arthur Sinclair had paid James Sinclair £1,000 in wadset over the 5 lasts of land in Brew, and a further £1,000 to Adam, himself, in respect of 5 lasts of land in Weisdale and Whiteness. It also gives the names of the witnesses, viz.: Mr John Dischington, sheriff-depute, Andro Edmondston, minister, Robert Tulloch and Robert Scollay, servitors of Arthur, and Thomas Auchenleck, notary public. Grant also gives an abstract of the sasine thereon, dated 4 July 1600, with Hew Halcro of Aithsetter, Malcolm Halcro of Hoswick, John Sinclair 'and others' as witnesses, and with Andrew Edmondston, NP. The relationship between these abstracts, and another, of a disposition dated 7 June 1600, with sasine thereon dated 25 October 1600, printed by Francis Grant (*loc. cit.*), is confusing.

297. Edinburgh, 21 June 1600

Decreet of court of session in action at instance of Robert Monteithe, tacksman of the lands of Fair Isle, against John Pillo and Thomas Patersone, indwellers in Pettenweym, for eviction of Robert from a house and two booths which Robert had possessed as tacksman for divers years, withholding the profits therefrom since the time of eviction, and for spoliation therefrom of 'all and sindra the guidis, geir, insycht, plenissing, salt, treis, barrellis, nettis, lynes and utheris respective libellit'.

The lords of council admit the points of the summons so far as concerns the spoliation to the pursuer's probation, and to that effect ordain the pursuer to have letters to summon witnesses, and to produce evidence.

SRO, CS.7/190, f.118.

298. Culbinsgerth, 11 July 1600

Report of an enquiry by John Neving and William Fermour, underfouds of Dunrosnes, into the marches between Keodo and the 5 marks land of Culbinsgerth.

At Culbinsgerth, the xj day of Julij 1600 yeiris. We, Johne Neving and William Fermour, underfoldis of Dunrosnes, be vertue of the sheref Mr John Dischingtonis commissioun anent the sichting of the marchis betuix Keodo and the v mark landis of Culbinsgerth, we past to the groundis thairof accompaneit with Adame Sinclair of Brow, Lawrence Sinclair of Got, minister, Johne Sinclair, lawrichtman, Lawrence Lesk in Scatnes, Andro Sand [*inserted in place of* Malcolme Halcro, *deleted*], and Magnus in Channerwik, and thair we sichtit and saw the marchis betuix the saidis landis, and culd persaiff na wrang done be ather of Hew Halcro or Malcome in Culbinsgerth, and thairefter we tuik the bodely aith of the said Hew Halcro gif he knew ony wrong done to him thairanent, quha swure in presence of us all upoun the haly evangell that he knew nocht him self dampnefeit in ony point, bot onlie wes desirous to knaw his marchis and to lat his bairnis understand the samen; and thairefter we tuik the depositiounis of thir aigit witnesis following, that is to say Thomas in Bramer, Marcus in Bramer, Erik in Gord, William Persoun, Magnus Adamsoun in [*torn*], William in Brind, Magnus in Vasgerth, and Ola Adamsoun in Claphoull, quha being sworne, ilk ane of thame se[*torn*]lie examinat deponis as followis: Thomas in Bramer, ane man of lv yeir of age, deponis be his grit aith that he knawis na wrang done be ather of the saidis perties to utheris, bot all marchis and meithis continew and standis in that samen forme and effect as he and his predecessoris hed seine of auld, past memorie [of] man; Marcus in Bramer, ane man of lx yeiris deponis ut supra; Erik in Gord, ane man of iij^{XX}x yeiris, deponis ut supra; William Persoun, ane man of lv yeir, deponis word by word ut supra; William in Brind, ane man of iij^{XX} yeiris, deponis ut supra, with this additioun that he wes at the sichting of the grund afoir with John Smyth and Gilbert Coupland, foldis for the tyme, at the requist of umquhill Nicoll Halcro, father to the said Hew, than persewer, and na falt found, bot ordenit all marchis to stand as thair foirbearis hed sett doun of auld, past memorie of man; Magnus in Blosto, ane man of Jc yeir, Magnus in Vasgerth, ane man of iij^{XX}x yeir, deponis word be word as this last depositioun; Ola in Claphoull, ane man of Jc yeir, deponis as this last depositioun, and mair that he hes beine four severall tymis at the sichting of this grund, and to this hour na wrang found to be done, and continewalie ordenit all marchis to stand as they stand of auld. This we the foirfolkis abone writtin testifeis to be of treuth. Be this our subscriptionis as followis, day, yeir and place foirsaidis.

Johne Sinclair, Lawrence Lesk in Scatnes, Magnus in Channerwik, and Andro Sand, with our hands at the pen led be William Fermour, notar publict, at our commandis.

William Fermour, noter public and fold of Dunrosnes, with my hand.

John Neving, with my hand
at the pen led be William
Fermour, notar publict.

A. Sinclair of Brow.

L. Sinclair of Gote.

Producit at Skalloway bankis the xxiij day of Julij 1600 in judicio:

The juge and the essyss ratefeis and apprewis the tryell and diligence abone wretin in all poyntis according to the tennour thairof; and ordanis the parteis to keip thair possessionis as they did befoir according to the tryell foirsaid; and in the meintyme absolvis the parteis abone wretin of ony cryme or penaltie quhilk can be laid to thair cherge thairanent for ony thing knawin as yit.

Thomas Auchinlek, scriba.

SA, D.8/5/1. Superscript 'xx' indicates a score (e.g. 'iij^{XX}x' = 70).

299. Skalloway, 23 July 1600

Wadset by Androw Hawik of Scatsta to his good friend William Bruce of Symbister, of 1½ marks land, 12 pennies the mark, in the parish of Lunesting, for £31 6s.8d., to be held in blench ferm until redemption, for payment of one penny yearly on Whitsun eve. Precept of sasine.

Witnesses: Henry Wardlaw of Clousta, Andro Steill, and Alexander Bruce, writer hereof.

SA, D.8/4/1. The lands were probably at Skelberrie (the endorsement on the back reads: 'Androw Hawik, Skelberrie').

300. Skalloway bankis, 26 July 1600

Instructions to John a Ewik, foud, and Androw Edmestoun, to collect £5 6s.8d. for each last of land in the isle of Yell.

John a Ewik, fold, and Androw Edmestoun, ye sall nocht faill to pas and collect the summe of v li. vj s. viij d. Scottis monie for ilk last of the haill landis within the yle of Yell, and speciallie of the uthell, bischop, king, lordis of Norrowayis, and all sort of kirk landis and uther, acording to the number and quantitie of the lastis, and for tryell of the quantitie thairof ye sall tak advyse of Piter Nisbeit, Gilbert Nisbeit, Osie Scott, William Spens, James in Swaresetter, and John Nevebak; and in cais of [*torn*] of thair absence ye sall try the quantitie of the lastis your selff [*torn*] with thame that ar present, as ye salbe anserabill thairfoir; and in the [*torn*] of none payment to poind everie man acording to his awin pairt without ony exceptioun, and report payment thairof to my Lord with all possibill diligence; as ye will anser thairupon. Subscryvit with my hand at

Skalloway bankis, the xxvj day of July 1600.

Mr Jhan Dischingtoun.

GH.

301. 11 August 1600

'Charter of wadsett by Christopher Laurenceson, with consent of his two sons, John and Laurence Christophersons, to Arthur Sinclair of Aith, of 3½ merks land in Braebister, in parish of Walls. ...

'Witnesses: Alexander Pringill, David Kirkcaldy, William Fermour, NP.'

The original is not known to exist. The above abstract, by Francis Grant, is in OSD, *SN*, 13 January 1894.

302. Hous in Burray, 21 August 1600

Contract between Arthour Sinclar of Aith, on the one part, and William Sinclar of Ustaness and Elizabeth Sinclar, his spouse, on the other part, whereby William and Elizabeth wadset to Arthur and Margaret Colvill, his spouse, 24 marks land, 8 pennies the mark, in Ustaness, in the parish of Quhytness, for 27 angel nobles sufficient gold and weight, together with £17 3s.4d. lent to them by Arthur. Precept of sasine.

Witnesses: Mr John Dischingtoun, sheriff and chamberlain of Yetland, David Sinclar of Huntoun, Patrik Hog, burgess of Kirkcaldy, and Robert Scollay, servant of Mr John, with divers others.

SRO, RD.1/256, ff.424-6.

303. Setter in Quhalsay, 26 August 1600

Disposition by Robert Williamsone, with special consent and good will of Sinyeavo Peterisdochter, his spouse, and all their lawfully begotten heirs, to an honourable man Eduard Sincleir of Setter, of 1 mark land, 12 pennies the mark, in the town of Skaw, in the isle of Quhalsay.

Because he has no seal or signet Robert requests Peter Simsoun, minister at Nesting, to subscribe in their names. Witnesses: Robert Sincleir, apparent of Brugh, Gilbert Gifhart, and Hew Tarrell, with divers others.

SA, GD.144/69/13.

304. 17 November 1600

Bill of 'upgaistry' by Brita Androisdochter, 'at the sycht of the fold and certane neutrall honest men', whereby her lands in Houll in Unst are divided between her children, viz. to Laurence Androisone, 2 marks 5 ures land, and to Sinevo and Ingagarth Androisdochters, 2 marks 5 ures.

Referred to in an action by Laurence Androissone against Mans Williamsone and Andro Strang, 7 October and 2 November 1620 (*CB2*, pp.83, 85).

305. Brantshamerland, 16 January 1601

Disposition by Marioun Thomasdochter, and Magnus Sutherland, her spouse, for his interest, with special consent of Androw Gareauch, her lawful son, to the right honourable and her good friend Hew Sinclair of Brugh, of 1 mark uthell land, 12 pennies the mark, under Westirhous of Beinstay, in the parish of Nesting. Precept of sasine.

Because they have no seals they procure those of honourable and discreet men: William Mansoun in Neip and Edwart Sinclar in Bulyesetter. Witnesses: George Sinclar in Friesitter, David Strathauchane, Hew Tarrell, James Neven, notary public, and James Davidsone, writer hereof, servants of Hew.

SA, SC.12/65/1/38. One seal.

306. Valey, 18 January 1601

Disposition by Johne Wischert of Burrafirth to the right honourable Hew Sinclair of Burght, of 1½ marks uthell land, 12 pennies the mark, in Orgill, in the parish of Lunesting. Precept of sasine.

Because he has no seal Johne procures the seal of an honourable man Thomas Chene of Valey. Witnesses: Thomas Chene of Valey, Alexander Chene, his brother german, Peter Symsone, minister of God's word at Nesting, Robert Murray, apparent of Stanidaill, Robert Wricht in Skalloway, Laurence Strang, servant of Thomas, James Nevein, notary public, and James Davidsone, servant of Hew Sinclair. Hew Tarrell, writer hereof.

SA, SC.12/65/1/39.

307. Stanidaill, 20 January 1601

Disposition by Agnes Walterisdochter to the right honourable Hew Sinclair of Burght, of 2 marks uthell land, 9 pennies the mark, in the town of Cauldclif, in the parish of Tyngwall, and ½ mark uthell land, 9 pennies the mark, in Brabister, in the parish of Wallis. Agnes also ratifies all dispositions by Henrie Waltersone, her brother, the deceased Marioune Magnisdochter, her mother, and Christopher Laurencesoun in Grunyevo, her father-in-law, for his interest, and by herself, to Hew, of the town and last of land, 9 pennies the mark, of North Cauldclif, in the parish of Tyngwall. The lands are to be held in free blench as any other uthell land is possessed. Precept of sasine.

Because she has no seal Agnes procures the seals of discreet men:

Thomas Chene of Valey and Johne Murray of Stanidaill. Witnesses: Andro Hawick of Scatstay, Olipher Sinclair of Estishous, Williame Sinclair of Rewict, Peter Symsoun, minister of God's word at Nesting, Gilbert McCreithe in Eister Skeld, Johne Wischert, underfoud of Sandsting, and James Davidsoun. Hew Tarrell, servant of Hew Sinclair, writer hereof.

SA, SC.12/65/1/40.

308. Stroholme, 19 February 1601

Disposition by Johne and David Nikolsones to the right honourable Hew Sinclar of Burgh, of 1 mark uthell land, 9 pennies the mark, in Hewon, in the parish of Quhytnes and Weisdaill, with ½ mark uthell land, 6 pennies the mark, in the holm called Hodg, adjacent to the holm called Hoy, in the mouth of Weisdaill Vo. Precept of sasine.

Because they have no seal they procure the seal and stamp of an honourable man Williame Sinclar of Ustenes. Witnesses: Arthour Quhyt in Trestay, Hendrie Chalmer in Brekis, Nicoll Johnesone in Houfe in Weisdaill, James Nevin, notary public, Hew Tarrell and James Davidsone, writer hereof, servants of Hew Sinclar.

SA, SC.12/65/1/41.

309. Stroholme, 19 February 1601

Disposition by Nicholl and Magnus Johnesoneis to the right honourable Hew Sinclair of Burght, of ½ mark uthell land, 6 pennies the mark, in the holm called the Hodg, adjacent to the island of Hoye, in the mouth of Weisdaill Vo, in the parish of Weisdaill and Quhytnes, for yearly payment of one penny, if required. Precept of sasine.

Because they have no seal they procure the seal of an honourable man Williame Sinclair of Ustines. Witnesses: Arthour Quhyt in Trestay, Henrie Chalmer in Brekis, Johne Nicholsoun in Stroholmesfirthe, James Neven, notary public, James Davidsoun and Hew Tarrell, writer hereof, servants of Hew Sinclair, with divers others.

SA, SC.12/65/1/42.

310. Burght, 5 March 1601

Disposition by Agnes Androwisdochter, with consent of Androw Nicholsone in Skellinstay, her spouse, to the right honourable Hew Sinclair of Burght, of 2 marks 2 ures uthell land, 12 pennies the mark, in Skellinstay, and 1 mark land, 9 pennies the mark, in Gairthe, in the parish of Nesting. Precept of sasine directed to Williame Mansoun in Neip, underfoud of Nesting.

Because they have no seals or signets they procure those of honest and discreet men: Eduard Sinclair in Bilysetter and Williame Mansoun in Neip. Witnesses: Petir Symsoune, minister at Nesting, Williame Mansoune in Neip, Eduart Sinclair in Bilyesetter, (torn) in Brenshamersland, Arthour Symsone in Brattabuster, James Davidsone, servant of Hew Sinclair, and James Neven, notary public, with divers others. Hew Tarrell, servant of Hew Sinclair, writer hereof.

SA, SC.12/65/1/43. One seal.

311. Burgh, 26 March 1601

Disposition by Ungyea Anthonisone to the right honourable Hew Sinclair of Burgh, of 1 mark uthell land, 12 pennies the mark, of Mewis in Burgh, in the isle of Quhailsay. Precept of sasine.

Because he has no seal he procures the seals of discreet men: William Mansone in Neip, underfoud of Nesting, and Magnus Hansone in Gilsbrek. Witnesses: William Dempster, wright, David Strathauchane and Johne Sutherland, masons, Alexander Wallis, and James Davidsone, writer hereof, all servants of Hew Sinclair, and James Neven, notary public, with divers others.

SA, SC.12/65/1/44. Two seals.

312. Burgh, 28 March 1601

Disposition by Moungo Cristopherisone, Sinne Cristopherisdochter and Erasmus Cristopherisone, her spouse, for his interest, with consent of Marioun and Cristiane Olawesdochteris, and Olaw Erasmissone, spouse of Cristiane, to the right honourable Hew Sinclair of Burgh, of 1½ marks uthell land, 12 pennies the mark, in Gletnes, and ½ mark uthell land, 9 pennies the mark, in Southhous in Beinstay, in the parish of Nesting. Precept of sasine.

Because they have no seals they procure the seals of honest and discreet men: William Mansone in Neip, underfoud of Nesting, and Magnus Hanisone in Gilsbrek. Witnesses: David Strathauchane and Johne Sutherland, masons, David Dicksone, grieve in Biggay, Alexander Wallis, James Davidsone, writer hereof, and James Neven, notary public, all servants of Hew Sinclair, with divers others, to wit Frances Nicolsoun.

SA, SC.12/65/1/45. One seal.

313. Goat, 16 April 1601

'Charter by Laurence Sinclair of Goat to Arthur Sinclair of Aith, of 6 merks land in Cleat in Burra. ...

'Witnesses: James Sinclair, his eldest son, William Sinclair, also his son, and William Fermour, NP. Seal attached bearing a chevron between three mullets.'

The original is not known to exist. The above abstract, by Francis Grant, is in OSD, *SN*, 13 January 1894.

314. Cappasetter in South Yell, 18 May 1601

Excambion whereby Hew Sinclair of Burght transfers to his good friends Daniell and David Beaes, and Bryid Laurencedochter, their mother, in liferent, his 12 marks uthell land, 8 pennies the mark, in Seater in the isle of Yell, the north part thereof, in exchange for 12 marks uthell land, 8 pennies the mark, in Stapnes, and 5 marks land in Stanisland, in the parish of Wallis. If Bryid, during her lifetime, or Daniel and David, sell or wadset the land in Seater they bind themselves to make the first offer thereof to Hew. Precept of sasine for the land in Seater.

Witnesses: Francis Sinclair of Uyea, Frances Nicolsoune, Hew Tarrell, writer hereof, and James Neven, notary public, servants of Hew, with divers others, Petir Johnesoun of Cappasitter, and James Patersoune.

SC.12/65/1/47.

315. Cappasetter, 19 May 1601

Excambion by which Hew Sinclair of Burght transfers to his good friend Petir Johnesoun in Cappasetter his 3 marks uthell land, 9 pennies the mark, in Sandwick in (blank) Yell, in exchange for 3 marks uthell land, 9 pennies the mark, in the isle of Biggay. If it shall happen, god forbid, that Petir falls in poverty whereby he is forced to sell or wadset the land in Sandwick, then he shall dispone the land to Hew, and to none others, for land's price. Precept of sasine for the land in Sandwick.

Witnesses: Francis Sinclair of Uyea, Francis Nicolsoun, Hew Tarrell, writer hereof, and James Neven, notary, servants of Hew Sinclair, Arthour and Thomas Quhytis, mariners, with divers others.

SA, SC.12/65/1/48. One seal.

316. Overhoule, 19 May 1601

Disposition by Bryid Olawisdochter, with consents of James Lauder, her spouse, for his interest, and of Williame Olawissone, her brother, and Katherene Olawisdochter, her sister, to the right honourable and her good friend Hew Sinclair of Burght, of 1 mark uthell land, 6 pennies the mark, in the holm called Onyerie in Yelsound at the north-west end of Biggay, in the parish of Yell. Precept of sasine.

Because she has no seal she procures the seal of an honourable man Garth Johnesone and David, his son. Witnesses: Arthour Quhyte, skipper, Francis Nicolsone in Biggay, Hew Tarrell, writer hereof, David

Strathauchan, William Dempster, James Neven, notary public, and James Davidsone, servants of Hew Sinclair, with divers others.

SA, SC.12/65/1/46.

317. Browarrie in the Skerreis, 14 June 1601

Disposition by David Eraismussone in Hucsetter to the right honourable Hew Sinclar of Burght, of 1 mark uthell land, 9 pennies the mark, in Hucsetter in the isle of Quhailsay. Precept of sasine.

Because he has no seal he procures the seal of an honest and discreet man William Manisone in Neip, underfoud of Nesting. Witnesses: Magnus Sutherland in Brenshamerisland, Magnus Eraismussone in Wadbuster, David Strathauchin, servant of Hew, Nicholl Manisoun in Houle in the Skerreis, and James Neven, notary public. Hew Tarrell, servant of Hew Sinclair, writer hereof.

SA, SC.12/65/1/49. One seal.

318. Sowmebu 28 June 1601

Disposition by William a Brind in Cunnesburghe to an honourable man Williame Bruce of Symbister, of 3½ marks uthell land, 12 pennies the mark, in the town of Scheldesetter, in the isle of Quhailsay, for payment of one penny yearly in name of blench ferm upon Whitsun eve, if required. Precept of sasine directed to David Rasmussone in Huiksetter.

William a Brind procures the seal of an honourable man Mr Thomas Barclay of Cowplahillis, and affixes his own mark. Witnesses: Mr Thomas Barclay of Cowplahillis, Andro Steill, servant of William Bruce, William Bruce, his son, Mathow Magnussone in Watsgarthe, and Alexander Bruce, notary public, writer hereof.

Sasine given on 8 January 1607 (at 4 p.m.) to James Sincler, attorney for Williame Bruce of Symbuster. Witnesses: Alexander Fordyce, servant of William Bruce, Magnus Ollasoun and Johnne Magnussone in Scheldesetter, Ninian Rasmussoun in Huiksetter, Alexander Bruce, notary public, and George Blak, servant of Alexander; 'and ordains thir presentis to be registrat in the buikis of secretarie of Orknay and Yetland, thairin to remane *ad perpetuam rei memoriam*'.

SA, GD.144/20/1 (disposition) and GD.144/69/14 (sasine).

319. Grunyeafirthe, 1 July 1601

Disposition by Magnus, Johne and Bartilmew Laurencesones to the right honourable Hew Sinclair of Burghe, of 1 mark 6 ures uthell land, 8 pennies the mark, in Grunyeafirthe, in the parish of Nesting. Precept of sasine.

Because they have no seals they procure the seals of honest and discreet men: Eduard Sinclair in Billysetter, Williame Manisone in Neip, underfoud of Nesting, and Magnus Hanissone of Gillisbrek. Witnesses: Francis Sinclair of Uyea, James Neven, notary public, Hew Tarrell, servant of Hew Sinclair, writer hereof, Nichol of Windes, Erik and Magnus Johnesone in Uphous in Grunyefirthe, with divers others.

SA, SC.12/65/1/50. Seal of Williame Manisone.

320. Edinburgh, 3 July 1601

Decreet of court of session in action at instance of James Strang of Wasgarth against Frances, Robert and James Sinclairs, sons and heirs of the deceased William Sinclair of Uyea, and Adam Sinclair, their tutor, for his interest, for fulfilment of a decreet obtained by the deceased Barthilmo Strang, father of said James, against the said William Sinclair, at Scalloway bankis on 21 June 1582, for payment of the kirk umboths of the isle of Uyea for the years 1578, 1579 and 1580, of 15 barrels of butter and 45 cans of oil for each year, and of decreet of transferring dated at Scalloway 2 August 1595.

The lords of council decern letters to be given in all the four forms charging the defenders to fulfil the aforesaid decreets.

SRO, CS.7/196, ff.144-5; SRO, CS.15/81 (summons, 4 July 1600).

321. Burghe, 10 July 1601

Discharge by Thomas Suentoun, commissioner of Yetland, to the right honourable Hew Sinclair of Burghe, of 1 barrel butter for the teinds of the lands of Stroholme, payable yearly to the archdeacon, for the crop 1600, assigned to Thomas as part of £100 for his commissioner's fee. Thomas binds himself to keep Hew scatheless of all claims, especially by Patrik Cheine of Essilmonthe, present possessor of the archdeaconry.

Witnesses: Mr William Haye, archdeacon of Yetland, Petir Symsoune, vicar of Nesting, James Neven, notary public, and Hew Tarrell, servant of Hew Sinclair, writer hereof, with divers others.

SA, SC.12/65/1/51.

322. Aberdene, 17 July 1601

Obligation by Francis Sinclair of Uyea, and James Sinclair, apparent heir of Laurance Sinclair of Goit, to Patrik Ross, burgess of Aberdene, for delivery of 15 barrels 'meit butter guid and sufficient stuff, merchandwair, weill packit in beir frie [*rectius* trie?] bind' (or £30 for each barrel not delivered), upon the shore of Scalloway by 1 August

1601; providing that if Francis and James pay Patrik the sum of £234 3s.6d. before 3 August 1601, 'then we to be free of the said butter and price thairof'.

Witnesses: Patrik Davidsone, Patrik Leslie, burgess of Aberdene, and James Knollis, writer hereof.

SRO, RD.1/370, f.210.

323. Bergen, 27 July 1601

Disposition by Herlüff Lauritzon, burgess in Bergen, to Andrew Smith in Noderseater, of 5 marks land in Findeland in Hillswick Bay.

I, Herlüff Lauritzon, burgess in Bergen, acknowledge and make known to all by this my open letter, that whereas the deceased Anne Mogensdotter, burgess here in this same city, in her full health, with well resolved mind and purpose, and with the advice and consent of her family, brother-in-law, and good friends, has sold and transferred from herself and her heirs, and to the honest man Annders Smidt, residing at Noderseater in Hellisuig 'toon' [*bÿgtun*], 5 marks land in Findeland, lying in the foresaid Hillisuig 'toon' in Hettlandt, giving annually 10 pennies butter and 10 pieces [*str.*] in land rent, as witnessed more fully by their contract of sale, here appended; and whereas the forenamed Anne Monsdotter's brother-in-law, named Siuord in Urim in Haranger, has requested and ordered that I should speak with the forenamed Anders Smidt about the money which still remains unpaid under the forenamed contract, and receive the same on his account, because he cannot remain here and wait for the forenamed Annders Smidt's coming here from Hetlandt; and whereas the forenamed Annders Smidt has, in the presence of good people, made up with me on behalf of the forenamed Siuord and paid willingly and without further quarrelling and contention on the foresaid Siuord's behalf, the sum which remained; therefore, all the land rent which up to this day was due from him, as also the money which was promised for the same land under their contract, is now, the least with the greatest, all paid and satisfied, according to the wording of other documents, which have been found after the said Anne Monsdotter's death, and have been delivered up to me. Therefore, I cede and convey, on the aforesaid Siuord of Urim's behalf, to the forenamed Anders Smidt and his heirs, the foresaid 5 marks of land in Findelandt, free and indefeasible, as property in proper udal right [*frj og frellseligue for rett odals gods*], to enjoy, use and possess, with all right and privilege, which the forenamed Siuord or his heirs could have thereto in any way; and I, the forenamed Herloff Lauritzon, shall be his surety for all further demands of the foresaid Siuord and his heirs in every way.

For the confirmation of the truth whereof, I have appended my signet underneath this my open letter, and in the usual way have requested these honest men to seal it in testimony along with myself, namely, Jon Maen, Anders [*blank*] and Johan Sandersson. Done at Bergen the 27th July 1601.

The original is not known to exist. Printed with translation from Danish (by Gilbert Goudie) in *PSAS*, xiv, pp.32-3.

324. Scalloway bankis, 30 July 1601

Decreet of sheriff court of Shetland in action at instance of Thomas Chein of Valay, against the tenants of 10 marks land in Laxo.

At Scalloway bankis the penult day of July 1601. The quhilk day annent the actioun and cauis persewit be Thomas Chein of Valay againis Lourence in Graven, Manis Uraving, Thomas Andersone, and remanent the tennentis and occupiaris of the ten mark land in Laxo within the parochin of Delting, for possessing the said Thomas thairwith as partis and pertinentis of the lands of Valay and Valay guids, wrangouslie grippit and possest be tham, with the byrun girsumes, dettis and dewiteis thairof, induring the space of ix yeiris last bypast, as at mair lenthe in the lybellit precept reasit and executit this day, of the dait the xiiij day of the monethe of July instant is contenit. Compeirit Androw Hawik of Scatstay and alledgit that na actioun sould proceid aganis the saidis tennentis bot onlie aganis myselff as titular of the landis of Valay and Valay guidis. Compeirand the said Thomas and alledgit that the said Androw sould nawayis be harde to alledge ony rycht to the said landis of Valay and Valay guids; in respect that he hes beine hiddertill denudit of all rycht and possessioun thairoff, and to verificatioun of samen produceit ane tack and assedatioun sett be Georwall Fathers Dochter of Geidinsk, the relict of umquhil Sir Langhe Brage of Crogholme, knycht, to umquhil Mr Robert Chein of Ure, his father, upoun the saidis haill lands of Valay and Valay guids and thair pertinents, induring all the days of his lyftyme and efter his deceis to ane of his eldest lawful airis; In [*torn*] contenit in the said tack of the dait at Lwne in Skone upoun Tysday eftir Sanct Bartilmes Jaj Vc lxx[*torn*] yeiris, and siclyk produceit twa severall preceptis subscryit be umquhil Robert, erle of Orknay, lord of Yeitland, of the daittis, the ane at Brughe, the xxix day of July the yeir of god Jaj Vc fourscoir sax yeiris, and the uther at Skalloway bankis the thrid day of July the yeir of god Jaj Vc auchtie sevin yeiris, finding the said umquhil Mr Robert to have best rycht and tytill to the saids lands of Valay and Valay guids, and thairfoir to be anserit of the land meiles, girsumes, dettis and dewiteis thairof of the crope and yeir of god fourscoir sax yeiris, and siclyk yeirlie and termelie in tyme cuming; Unto the quhilk it wes alledgit be the said Androw Hawik that na possessioun sould be grantit to the said Thomas ay and quhill he enterit him selff to the said umquhill Mr Robert, his father, according to the conditioun sett down in the principall tak and assedatioun maid to his said father and him upoun the saidis landis, and lykwais produceit dyverssis and sindrie wreitis upoun the saidis landis desyring him to be possest thairin according to the tenour thairof; Quhilkis altogidder in [*torn*] of my lord beand referrit to the interloquitor of the essyss thay altogidder beand ryplie advysit thairwith finds the said Thomas Chein to have best rycht and tytill to the foirsaidis haill lands of Valay and Valay guids with the pertinentis [*torn*] ony thing alledgis or produceit in his contrair as yitt; and thairfoir decerns the said Androw Hawik to decist and ceis fra all trubling or molesting the said Thomas and his tennentis thairto; and ordainis the said Thomas to be enterit and possest thairwith, and to be anserit of yeirlie dettis, girsumes and dewiteis thairof fra this furthe according to his rychtis and tytillis of the samen, and nane otheris; And ordainis precepts and executoriall to follow thairupoun in forme as effeiris. Extractum de libris vicecomitatus Yeitlandie per me Thomam Auchinlek eiusdem, etc., tempore scribam.

Thomas Auchinlek, scriba.

SA, D.10/1/9. See no. 85. The following appear at the foot and on the verso of the document:

'Mr John Dischingtoun, sheriff depute of Yetland; To my lovittis underfoldis quhairsumever within the mainland and ils of Yetland, our officaris in that part, conjunct and severallie, speciallie constitut, greting; forsameik[ill] as it is complenit to me be Thomas Chein of Valay, that quhair he hes [*torn*] ane decreit befoir the sheriff of Yeitland and his deputtis decerning him to be enterit and possest in all and [haill] the lands of Valay and Valay guids quhairever the samen lyis within the cuntrie of Yeitland, and to be anserit of the girsumes, landmeilis, dettis and dewiteis thairof in all tyme cuming, as at mair lenthe in the foirsaid decreit of the dait at Skalloway bankis, the penult day of July last bypast is contenit; heirfoir I charge you straitlie and commands that incontinent this my precept seine, ye pas, enter and possess the said Thomas Chein in all and haill the foirsaids haill lands of Valay and Valay guids in all pairtis quhair the samen lyis, be slokin of the fyris quha wrangouslie posesis the samen, and kendle and enter the said Thomas thairunto, to the effect that he and his subtennentis may peciablie bruik and possess the samen in all tyme cuming according to the said decreit in all poyntis; And that ye discherge Androw Hawik and all utheris his subtennentis that thay nawyis truble or molest the said Thomas in peciable possessioun thairof fra this furthe, ilk persone under the paine of Jc lib; As ye will anser thairupoun. Subscryvit with my hand; At Skalloway bankis the thrid day of August 1601.

'Mr Jhan Dischingtoun.

'Upoun the tent day of August the yeir of god within writtin, I, Androw Vischert, bailyie of Waiss, past at command of the precept within writtin, and enterit and possest Thomas Chein of Walay in the lands of Norby, and all uther lands, guids and geir, according to the decreit and precept [*torn*] specifyit. And this I did befoir thir witnessis: Magnus Rasmussone in Melby, Ola Sinkler in Norby, and Androw Stewart, with uthers divers.'

'Underfoldis and officars of the mainland and yles of Yetland; I command yow be thir presentis, to pas and tak tryell quhat landmails, debtis and dewties of Valey and Valey guids ar restand awand to Thomas Chene of Valey of this and crope 1605 yeiris, all yeiris preceiding, and siclyik yeirly and termelie in tyme cuming, during his tak and richtis of the saids landis, conforme to the decreit and precept within writtin; And quhat ye find justly restand ather be probatioun, confessioun or wrete; that ye caus him and his factors be pait thairof within tenor of law, under the paine of poinding; and as neid beis that ye poind and distrenyie thairfoir; and mak arrestments at his instance thairanent, and minister justice to all ... according to the law; as ye wilbe anserabill thairfor upoun the execution of your officis, quhairanent thir presentis salbe your warrand. Subscryvit be me. At Scalloway bankis, the 6 of September 1606.

'Eduard Scollay.'

325. August 1601

'Charter of wadsett by Francis Sinclair of Uyea, and as taking the burden on him for Robert, James, Margaret and Katherine Sinclairs, his brothers and sisters, in favour of Andrew Giffart of Woddersta, over 8 merks land in Buista, 8 in Woddersta, 1 in Hoversta, in the parish of Delting, and 2 in Unzeafirth, in Aithsting, for seventeen score five pounds, sixteen shillings and eight pence. Precept of sasine directed to John Mowat, apparent of Howgaland. ...

'Witnesses: Adam Sinclair of Brew, William Bruce of Symbister, William Sinclair of Ustaness, Andrew Umphray of Berrie, Thomas Auchenleck, notary, and Thomas Auchenleck, younger, his son, writer thereof, and Patrik Ross, burgess of Aberdeen. Sasine annexed, dated 21st July 1602.'

The original is not known to exist. The above abstract, by Francis Grant, is in OSD, *SN*, 13 January 1894. There is a briefer abstract of this wadset in SRO, CS.7/468, f.399, where the date is stated to be 2 August 1601, 'Housda' replaces Hoversta, and the date of the sasine is given as 24 July 1602.

326. Burray, 23 August 1601

'Charter by John Johnsone in Sound in Gulberwick, with consent of Barbara Robertsdaughter, his spouse, to Arthur Sinclair of Aith, and Margaret Colville, his spouse, of a half merk land lying in Burraland in Trondra. ...

'Witnesses: Thomas Barclay of Paplay, John Symsone, burgess of Burntisland, Thomas Sinclair in Orkney, Robert Tulloch in Maill, James Sinclair of Norbister, and Patrik Hog.'

The original is not known to exist. The above abstract, by Francis Grant, is in OSD, *SN*, 13 January 1894.

327. Scalloway bankis, 4 October 1601

Discharge by William Ballentyne of Garsay to Edward Sinclair in Bulyeasetter of: (1) 'full compt, raknyng and compleit payment' of the rents, teinds, etc., of the vicarages of Yell and Fetlair, whereof William is principal tacksman, and Edward, his tacksman, for the years 1596, 1597 and 1598, 'be payment maid to me yeirlie be the said Edward of fourscoir fourteine angell nobillis sufficient gold and wecht'; (2) the wadmell of Yeitland for 1595, sold by Edward to William's use as chamberlain, of 350 auld dollars and 'ane ort of ane dolour'; (3) 16½ angel nobles and 1 dollar owing to William by Orne Nebebak in Burravo and 'that mascope', 13 angel nobles owing to William by Elizabeth Kennedy and Hendry Forrester, 4 angel nobles 'and gund' owing to William by Yaine

Bankis, 5 'gund' owing to William by Hendry Bremer, 17 gudlings 4½ shillings and 'ane gund' owing to William by Yaine Mair, and 2 angel nobles and 1 dollar owing to William by Androw Stewart, conform to their obligations; and (4) an obligation by Mr James Lauder of 3½ angel nobles, an obligation by James Lauder, his servant, of 1 angel noble for which Mr James was cautioner, an obligation by William in Gardeis of 1 angel noble 'of the rest of the wattell of fourscoir fourtein yeiris crope', an obligation by Ramnikin Buisok of 6 gudlings, an obligation by Hermon Suemanis of 25½ angel nobles, an obligation of Herman Gruning and 'that moscrope' of 2 gudlings, and an obligation of William of Skeldberrie of 12 angels, which obligations had been delivered by William to Edward in 1595 for collection, 'quhairoff he gat na peyment, and therfoir at the making heirof hes deliverit me thame agane'.

Witnesses: Andro Umphrey of Berry, Allexander Thomassoun in Laxfurd, Patrik Hog, burgess of Kirkcaldie, and John Ross, mason in Scalloway.

CB1, pp.104-5.

328. Edinburgh, 5 November 1601

Decreet of court of session in action at instance of Thomas Cheyne in Ur against Andro Hawick in Skattista, Alexander Isbuster in Hardwell, Andro Wishart of Nevie, Olla Cristophersoun in Papa, Andro Mowat of Hewgoland, James and Barrell Mowatis, his sons, John Strang of Kewnrar, David Strang, his brother, Andro Ewing, William Sinclair of Ustaness, and Laurence Sinclair, his son, for violent eviction from the town and lands of Norbie, and spulyie thereof.

The lords of council continue the summons, and ordain the pursuer to have letters to summon witnesses for proof and to produce evidence.

SRO, CS.7/198, ff.230-1.

329. Brucht, 28 December 1601

Obligation by Frances Nicolsone to an honourable woman Jeane Bruce, spouse of Hew Sinclar of Brucht, for £30, to be paid by 1 January 1602, failing which together with ½ barrel oil by Lammas 1602.

Witnesses: Peter Symsone, minister at Nesting, William Magnussoun in Neipe, and Arthour Sympsoun.

SRO, RD.1/162, f.286.

330. Burghe, 30 December 1601

Disposition by George Work, with consent of Katherene Culye, his spouse, to the right honourable Hew Sinclair of Burghe, of 4 marks land, 12 pennies the mark, in Nesthous, and 2 ures land, 12 pennies the mark, in Gairdeishous, all lying in the town of Isbuster in the isle of Quhailsay; together with 10 ures uthell land, 6 pennies the mark, in the isle of Muyea, and 2 ures uthell land, 6 pennies the mark, in Unyearholme, in the easter holms of Quhailsay. Precept of sasine.

Because George has no seal he procures the seals of honest and discreet men: Williame Manissone in Neip, underfoud of Nesting for the time, and Magnus Hanissone of Gillisbrek. Witnesses: William Manissone in Neip, Petir Symsone, minister at Nesting, James Sutherland in Quhailsay, George Sinclair in Friasetter, Thomas Mowat, and Hew Tarrell, servant of Hew Sinclair, writer hereof, with others.

SA, SC.12/65/1/52; SA, GD.144/265/10. The two dispositions are similar, both being written by Hew Tarrell, and subscribed by the same persons. The first document has seals of William Manissone and Magnus Hanissone.

331. 31 December 1601

'Disposition in wadsett by Adam Sinclair of Brew, with consent of Helen Bruce, his spouse, and Laurence Sinclair, his eldest son, fiar thereof, to Arthur Sinclair of Aith, of 4 merks land in Esthouse, and 1 in Westerhouse, in the town of Flattabister and parish of Dunrossness, in consideration of 16 angel nobles of gold. ...

Witnesses: Patrick Hog, burgess of Kirkcaldy, John Bruce, servitor to said Adam, and Robert Wilson in Scalloway.'

The original is not known to exist. The above abstract, by Francis Grant, is in OSD, *SN*, 13 January 1894.

332. Northbrek, 18 January 1602

Deed of upgestry by Gutrome Lawrensone in favour of James Spens of Midbrek.

To all and sindre to quhas knawledge this present sall come, we, Guthrome Lawrentsone, forsmucle as I am now agit, feble, and nocht able to sustain my selff, nethir hes any cynsman that is able to resaive me in upghaistrie, hes therfoir at ye making of thir presents, come in presence of Andro Edmessoune, vicar of Yell, Jhone Laurensone, foild of Yell, James Ollasone of Swaresetter, lawrichtman, James and Gilbert Nisbetts, and dyvers utheris witnesses, and their of my awin fre will in my great neid be reasone of auge, seikness and inhabilitie become and enterit upgaister to my favorable and gud frennd James Spens of Midbrek and his airis during all the dayis of my lyftyme; Lyk as I, be the tenor of this present writ, for the caussis foresaids enters and becomes upgaister to the said James and his aris during all the dayis of my lyftyme as said is, to be honestlie and well cled, and fed at bed and bowrd as becomes ane man of my calling, lyk as the said James has obliged hym to do in presence of the witnesses abouve writen; For the quhilk I, the said

Gutrome, at the place and tyme of the making hereof, have giffin and delyverit over in the handis and possessione of the foresaid James Spens all and sindre my cornis, cattell, gudds and gair, movable and unmovable, thatte war in my possessione, together with the soumis, debtis, richt or titill that is myne or be law pertenes to me or micht pertene to me; And in speciall be the tenour heirof has giffin, grantit and deliverit, lyk as I be the tenour heirof giffs and frelie deliverit to the said James and his airs all and heall my heretable four mark lands and ane half, vj d. the mark, lying in North Brek within St Ollaw his parochin [*word lost*] uthall richt with and having crofts and tofts, yards, ground, pertinentis pertaining that may be knawen to pertain thereto befoir, to be bruikit, jusit and possessit be hym and his airis forevir heirafter; Reservand lyferent of ane of the said four mark and ane half to Margaret Lawgusy, my spous, to be manurit be hir to hir proffitt during all the days of her lyftyme alleinaerlie, and after her deceis to returne to the said James and his airis in perpetual heritage, but contradictions, obstacles, impediment or againe calling quhatsomevir; And I, the said Gutrome, binds and obligis me to hald firme and stable this present upgaistrie, conforme to the custome and law in the cuntre under the pane of [*blank*] and perpetual infamie.

In witness quhairof, because I cannot writ myself I have cawsit Andro Edmestoune subscryve this present writ, and for want of ane seall of my awin has procurit the seal of the foresaid Johne Lawrensone, baillie, James Ollasone, lawrichtman, and Nicol Guthromesone of Cullivo, to be hung hereto; At Northbrek, the 18 day of Janauar 1602, befoir the witnessis above written. Gutrome Lawrenson, with my hand led tuchand the pen be Andro Edmestoune, minister of godd's word and vicar of Yell, because I cannot wret.

Ita est Andreas Edmestoune de
speciali mandate dicti entromitto

The original is not known to exist. The above 19th century transcription is in SA, D.16/392/71.

333. Kirkwall, 28 January 1602

Contract between James Menteith of Saltcoittis, with consent of Robert Menteith, his brother german, on the one part, and Andro Umfra of Berrie, on the other part, whereby James sells to Andro their '*pro rege* mark land' of Fair Isle, 'alsweill that part of the samen commonlie callet the kinges landis, as that part thairof quhilk pertenet in temporaletie to the bischoiprik of Orknay callet the bischoipes landis', together with the office of bailiary of the said lands. The lands formerly belonged to the deceased Patrik Menteith of Fair Isle, father brother of James and Robert, in feuferme and heritage, and now pertains to James, as Patrik's heir, by virtue of a precept of clare constat granted to him by Patrik, earl of Orknay, lord Yetland, dated at Halyruidhous on 29 January 1599(-1600).

James grants to Andro in warrandice his feued lands of Eglissy and room of Work, in Orknay. Andro binds himself to pay James and Robert £2,000. If either party 'failye or brek to utheres in the sustenand heidis abonewrittin quhairthrow the partie brokin unto salbe moveris or compellet to registrat thir presentes, rais letteris ... as god forbid, in that cais the partie breker salle content and pay to the partie kepar and observear quhatsumever the soume of ane thousand pundis money foirsaid, and that nocht as ane penaltie thairfoir bot as ane liquidat soume presentlie modefeit be thame with thair awin consentis as for intress, coist, skaithe and dammage to be sustenet be ather of tham thairthrow', with the exception that if James peaceably enters Andro to the uplifting of the duties of the said lands of Fair Isle of the crop 1601, then James and Robert shall be exonerated of the foresaid sum of £1,000 and shall not be astricted thereto.

Witnesses: Patrik Ros, merchant, burgess of Aberdein, James Rettray, burgess of Kirkwall, John Menteith, Mr Walter Douglas, servant of said Robert, and David Arthour, notary public, writer hereof.

SRO, RD.1/88, ff.333-5.

334. 10 March 1602

Excambion between Agnes Thomasdochter, with consent of Laurence Farquhar, her spouse, and William Manssone (of Gairdie) of 2½ marks land in Sound in Ronen, in the isle of Unst, in exchange for 2½ marks land in Upiswall in Unst besouth the voe.

The deed was produced in the sheriff court on 31 July 1617 in an action of removal at the instance of William Manssone of Gairdie (*CB2*, p.57).

335. Burghe, 12 March 1602

Wadset by Olipher Sinclair of Estishous to the right honourable Hew Sinclair of Burghe, of 6 marks land, 6 pennies the mark, in Haggristay, in the parish of Weisdaill; 6 marks land, 6 pennies the mark, of Wodbuster, and 8 marks land, 9 pennies the mark, in Kirkgoir, in the parish of Quhytnes, under reversion of 77 old silver dollars. Precept of sasine.

Olipher subscribes with his hand, and because he has no seal he procures the seals of honest and discreet men: David Forster of Luney, and William Magnussone in Neip, underfoud of Nesting. Witnesses: Francis Sinclair of Uyea, Laurence Sinclair, son of William Sinclair of Uistines, James Neven, notary public, and Hew Tarrell, servant of Hew Sinclair, writer hereof, with others.

SA, GD.144/272/3.

336. Soundbrughe, 29 March 1602

Contract between William Bruce of Simbuster, on the one part, and Jhone

Boquhannan for himself, and as commissioner for Jhone Sinclair, skipper at Skalloway bankis, on the other part, for payment to William of £113 and 22 auld silver dollars, with an ort of a dollar, for fish, herring, oil, butter and other wares. Payment to be made by 1 July 1602, failing which 'it sould be lesum to William to mell ... with all thair reddiest guidis, gere', etc.

The original is not known to exist. Referred to in an action by William Bruce against Jhone Boquhannan on 21 July 1603 (*CB1*, pp.95-6).

337. Gardie in Unst, 10 May 1602

Deed of upgestry by Friea Rasmeisdochter to William Manssone of Gardie, in respect of her mother Enggegerth Thomesdochter.

Be it kend till all men be thir presentis, me, Friea Rasmeisdochter to haif ovirgiven and transferit, and be the tenour hierof ovir geveis and transferris my mother Enggegerth Thomesdochter, with all and haill hir landis and herittag, viz. tua mark and ane half, sax penneis the mark, lyand in Ronin in Sound, and ane mark and ane half in Gardone, all within the south perischoune of Unst and lordschip of Yeittland, to my guid freind William Manssone of Gardie his airis and assignayis, togedder with all my haill guids and geir, movabill and unmovabill, apertteining to me or that heirefter may be found to aperttein to me; and I the said Freia and my hisband Ingillbrycht Nickellsone granttis us weill conttent, sattisfeit and thankfullie payit for our guid will and ovirgevin of our said mother to the said William and his airis in opgester; to be bruikit, joissit and possessit be the said William and his airis for now and ever, and that of upgestrie, be verttew of ane lawdabill coustome and form of the cunttrye of upgesterie, quhair with express conssent of my haill barrnis I am become lawfull upgester to the said William, to be sustenitt in meat and claith all the dayis of my lyftyme; rattiffieing, confirmyng and apreving the forsaid gift gevin to the said William and his airis to stand firme and stabill without ony revocattioun or bak calling quhatsumever, and for the better sicurittie and veriffiecattioun to the said William and his forsaidis.

Becauss I culd nocht writt my selff I haif procurit the seallis off famous and discreit men, viz., Mangnis Thomasone of Ronin seall, with the seall of Nickell Aiklay of Hugaland, and Malcome Mowatt off Wadbusteris seall, and with the subscriptioun of Jhone Arschair, to be affixit and sett to this present evedent. At Gardie in Unst, the tent day of May 1602; beffor thir wittnesis forsaids and under subscryveand, with utheris dyverss.

Friea Rasmeisdochter, with consent of my hisband Ingillbrycht Nickellsone, with our handis led at the pen be me Jhone Arschair, becaus we culd nocht writt our self.

Jhone Arschair, wittnis to this premessis.

GH. Two seals affixed.

338. Meidbrak, 10 June 1602

Disposition by Enggerth Olayisdother, with consent 'of the aires gottin betuixt Rasmeis Poullsone and me', to her good friend James Spence of Meidbraik, of her ½ mark land, 6 pennies the mark, in Setter, isle of Unst, 'of the said James awin uthall ... with the enge, uthall and reversioun, roth and samyn of the aforsaid half mark land ... and that for full lands pryse payid and delyverit to me and my forsaid bairnis in our greit urgent nessyttie and neid: the quhilk half mark I offerit to the barrnis father britther becaus thai aclameit maist rycht to haif lousit it, and they againe war nocht the men that mycht do the same be ressoun of scarsity'. The lands are to be held in free blench, for payment of one penny Scots on Whitsun eve if asked. Precept of sasine.

Enggerth subscribes with her hand led at the pen by Jhone Arschair, and because she has no seal proper or mark of her own she procures with great instance the seals of William Manssone of Gardie and Nickell Guttrumsone of Culyawo. Witnesses: Malcome Mowat of Wadbust[er], (torn) of Wadbuster, with divers others.

The original is not known to exist. The above 19th century transcription, abridged here, is in SA, D.16/392/71/79. The two seals were affixed; an illustration of that of William Manssone accompanies the transcription. According to an abstract of the document, made by T.W.L. Spence of Uyea from the original in 1878 (SA, D.12/155/11) the second witness was 'Magnus [*blank*]sone off Wadbuster'.

339. Meidbreak, 10 June 1602

Disposition by Jainnit Jhonesdochter, with consent of the heirs begotten between her and Mangnis Rasmeissone, to her good friend James Spence of Medbraik, of 1 mark land, 6 pennies the mark, in Gardone, in the isle of Unst, for £16. The land is to be held by James in free blench for payment of one penny on Whitsun eve, if asked. Precept of sasine.

Jainnit subscribes with her hand led at the pen by Jhone Arschair, and because she has no mark or seal she procures the seals of William Manssone of Gardie, Mallcom Mowatt of Wadbuster and Nichell Guttrimsone of Cullyavo. Witnesses: Mallcom Mowatt, Mangnis Anttonessone of Wadbuster, with divers others.

SA, D.6/1/1.

340. Medbraik, 10 June 1602

Disposition by Friea Rasmesdochter, with consent of her spouse and all her heirs, to her good friend James Spence of Medbraik, of 2½ marks land, 6 pennies the mark, in Snabroch, and ½ mark land, 6 pennies the mark, in Gardoun, in the isle of Unst. The lands are to be held by James in free blench for payment of one penny on Whitsunday eve, if asked. Friea acknowledges that 'the said Rasmeis maid condittioun in his lyftyme to the said James that gaif that he sellit or wadsett his land of Snabroch to ony man, that the said Jameis suld haif the first pan offer of the samyn, as the said James' chartour of excamying will tesstifie and beir wittnes'. Precept of sasine.

Friea subscribes with her hand led at the pen by Jhone Arschair, and because she has no seal of her own she procures the seals of William Manssone of Gardie, underfoud of the isle, and Nickell in Cullyavo. Witnesses: Malcome Mowat of Wadbuster, and Mangnis Anttonessone of Wadbuster, with divers others.

GH. Seal of William Manssone.

341. Edinburgh, 10 June 1602

Decreet of court of session in action at instance of Elizabeth Sinclair, relict of James Sinclair of Hous, and William Sinclair of Ustenes, now her spouse, for his interest, and William and Arthour Sinclairis, lawful bairns of said James, against Thomas Cheyne of Walay, son and heir of the deceased Mr Robert Cheyne, commissary of Yetland, and Adam Sinclair, son and heir of the deceased James Sinclair of Brow, for reduction of decreet, given at Wisdaill on 8 November 1587, by Mr Robert Cheyne, commissary foresaid, against Elizabeth Sinclair and the other pursuers foresaid, decerning them to pay the deceased James Sinclair the sum of 462 gudlings 5 shillings of hard fish.

The lords of council continue the summons, and ordain the pursuers to have letters to warn the defenders to compear, and bring with them the said decreet.

SRO, CS.7/252-3.

342. Weddersta, 23 July 1602

Wadset by Johnne Mowat, apparent of Howgoland, with consent of Andro Mowat of Howgoland, his father, to his good friend Magnus Cogill, of an annualrent of 8 lispunds butter and 8 shillings wadmell from their 12 marks land, 12 pennies the mark, in the town of Enisfirthe, in the parish of Northmaven, for the sum of £100 old silver dollars. The land is to be held by Magnus for payment of one penny yearly at the feast of Whitsunday, if required. Redemption to be within the kirk of Ollaberrie at Whitsunday or Martinmas on forty days warning. Precept of sasine directed to Magnus Ilesburghe, foud of Northmaving.

Witnesses: Andro Giffert of Weddersta, Mr James Pitcairne, vicar of Northmaven, James Mowat, son of the said Andro, and Alexander Bruce, notary public, writer hereof.

Sasine given on 24 July 1602 (at 4 p.m.). Witnesses: Andro in Hagersetter, Patrik Mowat and Robert Kirknes, servants of Andro Mowat of Howgoland, Allester Cogill, servant of Magnus Cogill, Andro Nicolsoun, Lowrence Magnussone in Enisfirthe, Christopher Magnussone in Gunyessetter, Alexander Bruce, notary public, and George Blak, his servant.

SA, GD.144/277/28. The sasine is on the back.

343. Edinburgh, 31 July 1602

Decreet of court of session in action at instance of Laurence Bruce of Cultmalindeis against Ollaw Sutherland in Fettler, for putting a herd of old swine in Laurence's pasturage of Halyeisness, which devoured 40 of Laurence's lambs there, and also for chasing a black 'stude' mare, which was 8 years old, with her 'staig and followar', over a craig whereby they perished.

The lords of council continue the matter, and ordain the pursuer to have letters to summon witnesses, and to produce evidence.

SRO, CS.7/195, f.448.

344. Scalloway bankis, 22 August 1602

Contract between Johne Menteith, merchant, on the one part, and Andro Edmestoun, minister at Yell, on the other part, whereby Johne binds himself to deliver to Andro, at the port of Burravo in Yell, 12 chalders 'guid fresch dry and sufficient Orknay beir ... be the run beir tre thrie schakkis to the barrell', before 2 February 1603. Andro binds himself to pay Johne 1½ silver dollars 'for ilk run beir tre full haveand thrie schakkis, ane auld silver dolour and ane half in form'; with payment 'at the delyverie of the said victuall the equall just half of the principall in ulie and silver, the ulie at vij dolouris or thrie angellis as the said Andro sall chois, and the uthair half in money or wairis foirsaid upone the pryce mentionat' to be paid before Whitsunday 1603.

Witnesses: Mr James Pitcairn, vicar of Northmaven, James Kintor, burgess of Aberdene, and John Hekfuird.

SRO, RD.1/177, f.138.

345. Skalloway bankis, 24 August 1602

Decreet arbitral by 'the jugis and amicable compositouris underwretin' in the actions and claims of debt by James Kintoir, on the one part, and William Sinclair of Ustaness, on the other part, whereby William is ordained to pay James £40 by Allhallowmass, and likewise to pay James and his wife £16 18s.11d. within fifteen days.

Subscribed by: William Bruce of Simbuster, Androw Mowat of Hougoland, Jhone Mowat, apparent of Hougoland, and Jhone Nevein of Skousbrughe at the pen led by Jhone Mowat. Thomas Boynd, judge.

CB1, p.49.

346. Skalloway bankis, 26 August 1602

Decreet arbitral by William Bruce of Simbuster, Edward Scollay of Strynie, and Thomas Boynd in Skallaway, arbiters chosen for the part of William Sinclair of Ustanes, Arthour Sinclair of Ayth, Andro Hawik of Scatstay, and Hierome Umphray in Sand, arbiters chosen for the part of Edward Sinclair in Bulyeasetter, whereby William is decerned: (1) to pay Edward 48 dollars which he disbursed in William's name to Herr Yanisoun, Herr Gabriell and certain other burgesses of Birroun, for his relief of 100 dollars contained in an obligation which they had of William; (2) to pay Edward 25 silver dollars which he paid to the wife of Herr Pear in Phanais in William's name for the relief of a golden chain which she had of his in wadset; and (3) to pay Edward 20 silver dollars and ½ dollar (outstanding on an account of 93 silver dollars and ½ dollar) by Whitsunday 1603. The other undecided actions and controversies anent grassums, teinds and landmails claimed by William from Edward are continued until 15 November 1602, when both parties, with William Neipe, foud of Nesting, are ordained to compear at Skalloway bankis. William and Edward are decerned to pass to the sheriff-depute to obtain his precepts for summoning all teind payers and other necessary witnesses to compear on the said day for proving of either of their allegations. Alexander Bruce, notary public, writer hereof.

CB1, pp.138-9.

347. Skalloway bankis, 29 August 1602

Obligation by Andro Umphray of Berrie to Patrik, earl of Orknay, lord Yetland, for 3,000 merks. Patrik has obtained a decreet against Robert Menteyth, brother german to James Menteyth of Salcoittis, decerning Robert's goods and gear in Orknay and Yetland to be escheat to him for certain crimes, enormities and contempts. Because Andro is in debt to Robert for 3,000 merks for his right of Fair Isle disponed to Andro, which is arrested at the hands of Bernard Stewart, donator to the said goods as a part of Robert's moveables, therefore Andro binds himself that if the said sum is found to appertain to Patrik and his donator as part of Robert's moveables, by virtue of the said decreet, at the sight and judgement of John Arnot, merchant, burgess of Edinburgh, John Levingstoun, agent to Patrik, Mr Alexander King, and the rest of Patrik's procurators, then Andro will pay the said sum to John Arnot in name and behalf of Patrik by Martinmas 1602, and shall report John Arnot's acquittance and discharge thereupon to Patrik and his donator.

Witnesses: William Bruce of Symbister, William Carmichell, merchant, Edward Scollay of Strynie, and Robert Scollay, writer hereof.

SRO, RD.1/91, f.430. In August 1601 Robert Menteith had deforced John Sinclair, the earl's officer, in execution of his office of poinding the lands of Fair Isle for 12 gulyeons of fish owed by Robert to Patrik, earl of Orknay, for the feu duty for crop 1601. Robert was pursued by the earl before Malcolm Groat of Tankerness, his bailie depute, in the Place of the Yards (in Kirkwall), and for non-compearance and non-defence Robert was convicted of the crime of deforcement, and his moveable goods and gear in Orknay and Yetland were escheated to the earl, on 24 January 1602. This sentence was annulled by the court of session on 29 January 1607 (SRO, DI.3/6, ff.238-40; DI.3/7, ff.84-6; CS.7/224, ff.259-61).

On 3 December 1602, in an action raised by Andro Umphray in the court of session, it was decerned by the lords of council that Andro should pay James Menteith of Saltcoittis £2,000 for the *pro rege* lands of Fair Isle, with £1,000 'for entres coistis, skaythes and dampnage', conform to a contract, dated 28 January 1602, between James and Andro. The lords of council discharged Patrik, earl of Orknay, and Bernard Stewart, his donator, of all further charging, horning, poinding or troubling of Andro in the said matter (SRO, CS.7/203, ff.94-5).

348. Hous in Burray, 22 September 1602

'Contract made at Hous in Burray. ... It is contracted and finally endit betwixt honourable and discreet men, that is to say, Arthur Sinclair of Ayth, on the one part, and James Sinclair of Norbister, on the other, in manner following, viz., the said James has sold ... without redemption ... to the said Arthur, all and haill his four merk land, six pennies the merk, lying within the ile of Halveray, parochin of Burray and sheriffdom of Zetland, acquired by him from umquhile James Sinclair of Brew, quhilk was wadset by his father umquhile Olave Sinclair of Brew to Laurence Sinclair, umquhile father to the said James Sinclair of Norbister. ...

'Witnesses: George Williamson, Gilbert Cantlie, indweller in Scalloway, David Sinclair, fowde of Burray, Patrick Hog, burgess of Kirkcaldy, who subscribes on behalf of James Sinclair of Norbister, because he could not write.'

The original is not known to exist. The above abstract, by Francis Grant, is in OSD, *SN*, 13 January 1894.

349. Edinburgh, 24 November 1602

Bond of caution by Laurence Bruce of Cultmalundie for Adam Sinclair of Brow, anent murder of Matho Sinclar of Nes.

The quhilk day Laurence Bruce of Cultmalundie become pledge and souirtie for Adam Sinclar of Brw that he sall compeir befoir our soveraine lordis justice or his deputtis the thryd day of the nixt justice air of the sherifdome of Orknay and Yetland, or soner upoun fyfteine dayes wairning, and underly the law for furnesing, flitting, furing and supporting of the principall actouris and crewall murtheraris of umquhile

Matho Sinclar of Nes, under the painis contenit in the actis of parliament.

SRO, JC.19/3. For Matho Sinclair's murder see nos. 358, 361 and 429, and *CB1*, pp.28, 31, 38 and 42-3.

350. Edinburgh, 1 December 1602

Decreet of court of session in action at instance of Hew Sinclair of Burgh against Margaret Stewart, relict of William Sinclair of Uyea, and William Bruce of Simbaster, her spouse, for reduction of decreet arbitral given by Patrik, earl of Orknay, lord Yetland, Laurence Bruce of Cultmalindies, and William Bannatyne of Gairsay, on 26 April 1593, following submission dated 25 April 1593, for reconciliation of all malice and trouble between the parties. Margaret and her spouse were decerned to renounce all right and title of kindness which they had to the canons' lands of Yetland in favour of Hew, and Hew was to pay William Bruce 400 merks by 25 December 1593 or else to infeft Margaret in an annualrent of 40 merks to be uplifted from his lands of Axnabow and Skowisburgh, or any other of his best-held lands of Yetland, and also to grant William a tack of the canons' lands of Lowasetter for 19 years, grassum free, for payment of the yearly duty contained in the old rental; and as concerning Hew's heritable right of the lands of Howll and Margaret's liferent right thereof, together with Hew's heritable right of 1½ marks land of Burgh in Quhalsay, which was then debatable between the parties, the arbiters reserved the same to the decreet of the sheriff principal of Orknay and Yetland and his deputy; together with reduction of whatsoever decreet, given by Mr John Dischingtoun, commissary of Orknay, following thereon.

The lords of council continue the summons, and ordain the pursuers to have letters to warn the defenders to compear, and bring with them the said submission, decreet arbitral, and decreet given by the commissary.

CS.7/204, ff.106-7. For further information see *CB1*, pp.40-1, 107.

351. Burghe in Nesting, 4 December 1602

Wadset by William Froster of Lie in Quhailsay to the right honourable Hew Sinclair of Burghe, of 7 marks land, 9 pennies the mark, in the town of Sursetter, in the parish of Delting, and 1½ marks land, 8 pennies the mark, in Langaskoill in Tuait, in the parish of Aithsting, for 94 gudlings Yetland payment. Redemption is to be at the house and place of Burghe at Whitsunday or Martinmas, on forty days warning, in four parts as follows: 'the ane part fourth part in lous buttir lispunds, the uther fourth part in bullis of ulie, the thrid part in hard fisches, and the fourth part in fresche fisches, togidder with ane barrel ulie in pakit guidis'. Precept of sasine.

William asks Petir Symsone, minister at Nesting, to subscribe for him with his hand touching the pen, and because he has no seal he procures the seals of honest and discreet men: Williame Manisone in Neip, underfoud of Nesting, and Magnus Hanisone of Gillisbrek, father-in-law of William Froster. Witnesses: Petir Symsone, minister foresaid, Arthour Symsone, his son, Francis Nicolsone, Williame Demptster, and Hew Tarrell, servant of Hew Sinclair, writer hereof, with others.

SA, SC.12/65/1/53. Seals of Williame Manisone and Magnus Hanisone.

352. Burghe in Nesting, 4 December 1602

Wadset by Magnus Hanissone of Gillisbrek to the right honourable Hew Sinclair of Burghe, of 6 marks uthell land in the town of Gillisbrek, in the parish of Lunesting, 'now occupyit with my awin pleuche, and that under reversioun of sax scoir sax gudlingis Yetland payment, to be payit severalie in four partis, at twa termes, half at the ane terme and half at the uther, to wit, the ane fourth part in lous buttir lispunds, the uther fourth part in lous bullis of ulie, the thrid part in hard fische, and the fourth part in fresche fische'. The lands are to be held 'be all rycht marchis auld and devysit as the samen lyis in lenthe and breid, rig and rander, throch the said toune of Gillisbrek'. If Magnus fails to pay the annual duties then his other lands in the said town are to be comprehended in the wadset. Redemption is to be at the house and place of Burghe at Whitsunday or Martinmas, on forty days warning. After redemption of the first half Magnus shall have entry to 3 marks of the said 6 marks 'and be dischargeit of the half annuallis, to wit ane half barell ulie and fyve gudlings hard fische'. Precept of sasine.

Magnus affixes his signet, and procures the signet of a discreet man, William Manisone in Neip, underfoud of Nesting. Witnesses: Peter Symsone, minister of Nesting, Arthour Symsone, his son, Francis Nicolsone, William Demptster, and Hew Tarrell, servant of Hew Sinclair, writer hereof, with divers others.

SA, SC.12/65/1/54. Seals of Magnus Hanisone and William Manisone.

353. Edinburgh, 21 December 1602

Decreet of court of session in action at instance of Laurence Bruce of Cultmalindie and Andro Bruce of Scatsta against Patrik, earl of Orknay, lord Yetland, and Mr John Dischingtoun, commissary of Orknay, for exemption from their jurisdiction. The grounds of complaint are as follows:

In 1592 when Laurence was tacksman of the wadmell of Yetland, by virtue of a tack made to him by the deceased Robert, earl of Orknay, and which had several years to run, Patrik violently intruded himself in Laurence's possession of the wadmell, and pursued Laurence for his bodily harm and slaughter with 600 men 'boden in feir of weir'. Laurence, who was then at the haven of Laxfirth collecting the wadmell, was pursued by sea and land until he escaped 'to ane out iland of Yetland callett Skaries'. Patrik would not allow Laurence to return until he renounced the tack, and paid Patrik £1,000, which Laurence did through fear for preservation of his life. Since then Patrik has intromitted with the wadmell of Yetland, which is worth in yearly rent the sum of 3,000 merks or thereby.

Since Whitsunday 1599 Patrik has forced the pursuers' hinds, servants and labourers of the mains of Aythe, Hillisweik, Tresta, Munes and Scattista, and the tenants of their other lands in Yetland and the isles thereof, to come to his castle of Skalloway, and there compelled them to bear stones and timber, to make and bear mortar, and to use all kind of labour and work at the castle, at their own expense, for eight days at a time, as often as pleased Patrik, without provision of meat or drink, so that the poor men by often resorting there were 'altogidder wraikit and depauperit, and ane greit number of thame fameschit for laik of veveris', with the consequence that many of them left Laurence's service, and his mains and lands were laid waste for lack of tenants and labourers. Patrik has raised new taxes and imposts upon the lands of Yetland, and in 1599 and 1600 compelled the tenants to pay one angel noble for each last of land, the whole lands of Yetland being 1,400 lasts of land, and for non-payment of these unlawful and extraordinary taxes poinds and comprises their possessions.

When Laurence came out of Yetland to Orknay in April 1602 to attend to his affairs Patrik, without any form or order of law, apprehended Henrie Wardlaw, tenant and domestic servant of Laurence, who had accompanied his master. Henrie, for relief of his cautioner, entered himself in ward in the castle of Skalloway on 23 June 1602, and although Henrie was subsequently put to liberty 'the said erle be ane number of his souldeoris serchit and socht the said Henrie', and having apprehended him re-entered him in ward on 19 August 1602, when he was detained in prison in 'the lach volt of the jame' of the said castle. Patrik then put Henrie to an assize, first of the gentleman of the country who found him not guilty, and, not being content therewith, to an assize the next morning of the common ignorant people of the country, who also found him not guilty. Patrik, disappointed of his intent, kept Henrie in ward in the said vault until six o'clock in the evening on 31 August 1602 when, the gentlemen of the country having returned to their own homes, he commanded Henrie to be brought forth of ward, and appointed Barnard Stewart, his master stabler, James Crawfurd and William Robertson, his domestic servants, to wait on Henrie coming out. Patrik went to the 'castell heid' to watch, and had Henrie 'not with sett seleretie eschewit and wan the hous of John Buchanane adjacent to the said castell and cloisit the yett and durr thairof behind him', he would have been bereft of his life. With Patrik watching from the castle walls the said persons climbed in over the back dyke of the close, but as they could not get entry to the house wherein Henrie had escaped they cried for fire to burn the chamber where he was. Henrie for very just fear rendered himself in their wills, and came out unarmed on promise of safety. While Henrie was speaking to Barnard Stewart and James Craufurd, beseeching them to save his life and to do him no harm, the said William Robertson, servant of Barnard, came behind Henrie and, expressly against their promise, struck him with a double musket staff on his head, whereby the staff was broken in two, 'and thairwith fellit the said Henrie and dang him cauld deid to the grund', and besides that gave him many strokes, to the great effusion of his blood. All this had been done despite letters obtained by Henrie from the lords of council, which had been executed against Patrik on 15 August 1602, commanding Patrik to desist from all fencing and holding of courts and proceedings against Henrie until 24 November 1602.

The lords of council exempt the pursuers, and their hinds, men, tenants and servants, from the offices, judgements and jurisdiction of Patrik, earl of Orknay, and Mr John Dischingtoun, and their deputies; and discharge the said defenders of all summons, calling and pursuings of the pursuers, their hinds, men, tenants and servants, and of molesting, troubling or of any proceedings, criminal or civil, against them in all time coming.

SRO, CS.7/203, ff.157-9. On 27 July 1605, in an action at the instance of Laurence Bruce, the lords of council decerned that Patrik, earl of Orknay, had contravened lawburrows, on account of his actions against Henrie Wardlaw as narrated above. On 30 January 1606, Patrik, in an appeal against this decreet alleged that 'Henrie being charged to underly the law for the slauchter of umquhile Nicoll Magnussoun, and for his compearance to find caution, and in respect of his refusal to find caution was tane and put in ward, and eftir his finding of caution to compeir to underly the law, he wes put to libertie, and the day appointit for his trial, that day comperit the said Henrie and producit the said letteris discharging the juge of all forder proceding, quhilk wes willinglie obeyit, and immediatelie in jugement, and in proud contempt of our soverane lord and the juges sittand in jugement, put his fingeris in his mouth and thairwith spanging his thowme and fingar togidder, with the sound of his mouth utterit contemptibill langage sayand he defyit the Lord Orknay and his deputtis, and eftir the pronunceing of the saidis wordis he ran furth of jugement, and the juges haifing directit the officaris of court to tak and apprehend him for his proud contempt, he offerit thame straikis and wald not be tane and entir in ward bot be violence, in the quhilk caus albeit the said officaris had strakin him thai did na wrang'. The appeal was refused by the lords of council (SRO, CS.7/219, ff.131-4, 316-7; SRO, DI.3/14, ff.111-2).

354. 1603

Schound bill of William in Hamer.

Ane schound and divissioune [of] William [in] Hamer in anno 1603 [*torn*] within the perischen [*torn*] and lordschip off Yeitland.

At Maland in Unst, ane schound and divissioun hald [*torn*] parttíes underwritten quhilk ar to say, on the ane part Mathow Skowsone,

[Rasmeis], his brother, with thair sister Breitta, and Petter Rasmessone for his [entres], Agnis Williamsdochter and hir spous William in Maland for thair entreis, all the [*torn*] in Hameris barrinis and airis forsaid [*torn*] certteine honest fam[*torn*] discreit men to sit upone the said [*torn*] divissioun off sick landis mowabill, gudis and geir as pertinyit to the forsaid William in Hamer, submitting thameselffis, and sworne be the faith off thair bodyies and tinsall off [thair] gudis and geir airit heirintill, to [*torn*] deliverance [*torn*] men, to wit, James Strang in Woisgerth, Walter Gray in Cliff, David Copland in Howland, with owtheris dyveris.

The inwettour off the landis, guidis and geir:

Item, in the first, fyve mark in Hamer and iij mark in Swenes, ane mark in Hagadall, thre mark in Grutgert, ane mark in Guidon, and iiij mark and vj uris in Cliperisweik, vj uris in Dersetter, ij mark half mark in Balayasta, ij mark in Balltone, ane mark half mark in Daill, all vj d. the mark. Item, the divissioun heiroff, to Mathow Skowissone and his brother Rasmeis and thair sister Breitta, v marks in Hamer, ane mark in Sweinaness, vj uris in Hagadaill, ij mark in Ballyasta, ane mark in Ball[tone], and the said Breitta sall air bot the ane ane mark in Suenaness [in hir partt] off airschip, or ellis the pryce off the mark land; and to Petter Erasmusoun, the father brother sone, in his partt off land, iiij mark [vj] uris in Cliperweik, with ij uris in Hagadaill, ane mark and half in Daill, and half mark in Ballt[one], with vj uris in Dertsetter, be reassoun he gat na kyndneis off his [*torn*] in his lyfftyme or yeit nane off [his] mawaboll guidis, and the said [Petteris sister] sall haiff ane mark land, or ellis the pryce of ane mark land, as the brother can best spair; item, to Agnis Williamsdochter in hir [partt] off land eftir hir father, thrie mark land in Grutgerth, [ane] mark in Guidon, ij mark in Sweness, ane half mark in Sweness, ane half mark in Ballttla, with ane half mark in Ballazasta, with the haill half off the stoff of Hamer be ressoun scho the said Agnis was not sua wiell haldin in [other thingis] as the laiff off the airis; and as for the uther mawabill guidis or geir ewerrie ane off this partties his content off all maner of thingis continnit heirintill under the painis afforsaid; and for the mair [degnittie and strenth] heiroff we thir partties forsaid his desyrit and requyrit with greit instance thir honest and discritt men to sitt thair seallis or markis, [*torn*] day, yeir and place forsaid.

Willyame [*mark*] Manssone off Gardie
James [*mark*] Strang in Woisgerth
Walter [*mark*] Gray in Cliff
David [*mark*] Copland in Howland
[Jhone] Arschair with my hand

SA, D.6/1/2. The document is in poor condition, and has been badly repaired. Some reconstruction of the text has been attempted.

355. Edinburgh, 20 January 1603

Decreet of court of session in action at instance of Hew Sinclair of Burghe against James Corstorpherson in Papay, occupier of the pursuer's 6 marks land, 8 pennies the mark, in the Nether Sound in the parish of Weisdaill, and Olipher Mansoun, occupier of the pursuer's 3 marks land, 12 pennies the mark, of Gluss in the parish of Northmaving, wrongously occupied by the defenders since the warning made by Hew to them for removal at Whitsunday 1585, 'the space of saxtein yeris last bipast', for payment of the profits which Hew might have had from the lands for the said period of 16 years.

The lords of council continue the summons, and ordain the pursuer to have letters to summon witnesses, etc.

SRO, CS.7/204, f.260.

356. Goit in Dunrosnes, 27 (torn) 1603

Disposition by Thomas Symoundsone of Loiphell, for himself and as administrator of the bairns of the deceased James Symoundsone, his brother, to a famous discreet man Laurence Sinclair of Goit, of 3½ marks land, 6 pennies the mark, out of 6 marks land in Lophell, in the parish of Dunrosnes, for payment by Laurence of £70 (viz., £32 16s.8d. to the deceased James during his lifetime, and £37 3s.4d. to said Thomas). Precept of sasine.

Thomas subscribes with his hand at the pen led by William Fermour, foud of Dunrosnes and notary public; and procures the seals of said William and (torn)ing of Skousbrogh. Witnesses: Patrick Forbes, merchant, son of (torn), (torn)ar, vicar of Dunrosnes, Johnne Steinsone, officer, Walter Copland, David Butter, and Gregor Olavesone, with others.

SA, GD.144/268/17. One mark.

357. Bruch, 30 January 1603

Obligation by Andro Bruce of Sanduik and Williame Bruce of Symbester to be cautioners for the sons of the deceased Hew Sinclair of Bruch.

Be it kend till all men be thir presentis, me Andro Bruce of Sanduik and Williame Bruce of Symbester, forsamikill as umquhill Hew Sinclair of Bruch at his letter will ordenit Hew Sinclair, his lawfull sone, to be maid assignay to the thre thowsand merkis monie that is laid upoun Francis Sinclairis landis within the cuntre of Yetland, and to the malis, fermes, dewties and gersumis thairof, and to all annuelrentis of the samin quhill the lawfull redemptioun thairoff, and Harie Sinclair, his uther lawfull sone, to thre thowsand merk money laid upoun James Prymrois landis, burges of Edinburgh, or at the leist in his possessioun, and to the profittis and annuelrentis thairof, be the space of [*blank*], and Allexander Sinclair, his youngest sone, to thre thowsand merk and proffittis thairoff upoun the laird of Phillorthis land, as the securities maid to the said umquhill Hew Sinclair be the saidis personis at lenth beris. Quhilk assignatiounis Robert Sinclair, now of Bruch, hes confermit and ratefeit to his saidis brether, and denunceit him and his of all richt and titill that he hes or may haif thairunto for ever, as thair securities maid be thame thairupoun of this present dait at lenth beris. And becaus Jane Bruce, mother to the saidis Hew, Harie and Allexander Sinclairis, lawfull sonis to the said umquhill Hew Sinclair, thair father, is nominat be her said umquhill spous, and constitut be the said Robert Sinclair, now of Bruch, tutrix, curatrix, gydder, governour and lawfull administratour to all hir awin bairnis gottin betuix hir and the said umquhill Hew, thairfoir we the saidis Andro Bruce of Sanuik and Williame Bruce of Symbester be thir presentis becumis cautioneris and souerties conjunctlie that the foresaidis sowmes of money laid upoun thair land and annualrentis thairof particularlie abonespecifeit sall be fourthcumand to everie ane of the saidis thre bairnis and to thair airis, executouris and assinayis heretablie, quhill the lawfull redemptioun thairof at thair perfit aige of twentieane yeiris compleit, allowand to everie ane of the saidis bairnis induring thair minoritie in halding of thame at sculis and uther verteous educatioun, sic yeirlie dewtie and sowmes of monie as thair said mother will tak upoun thair conscience, and be the modificatioun of the narrest of thair father kin. And to this effect the said Jane Bruce bindis, obligattis and astrictis hir and thair landis, guidis and geir in speciall warrendice of our said cautionarie incace of failye (as god forbid) and quhat expenses, dampnege or interest we the saidis cautioneris sall happin to sustene in defalt of the said Jane, and dampnege of the saidis bairnis, that scho sall refound the samin in agane to us the saidis cautioneris, togidder with the sowme of [*blank*] as for ane liquidat sowme sett doun and modefeit be us perties abone writtin; and forder bindis and oblisses us the saidis perties abonewrittin and everie ane of us for our awin perties to reforme thir presentis to utheris alsoft as we the saidis cautioneris sall require the said Jane thairto, quhill we be sure anent our said cautionarie be the avis of men of law and of judgment, and ordenis this present to be registrat in the buikis of counsall, and the authoritie to be interponit thairto and to haif the strenth of the decreittis or actis with executiouns of horning, poinding, wairding, aresting and comprising to pas heirupone in forme as efferis, and the horning to pas upone ane simpill cherge upoun vj dayis warning, and the executioun of the ane nocht to prejudge the uther, and to this effect nominatis [*blank*] procuratouris or ony ane of thame to compeir befoir the saidis lordis and consent to the registring heiroff *promittendo de rato* etc.

In witnes heiroff we the saidis cautioneris and the said Jane hes subscrivit thir presentis with our handis at Bruch, the penult day off Januar the yeir of god Jaj sex hundreth and thre yeiris, befoir thir witnesses: Arthour Sinclair of Aith, Williame Tyrie of Busbies, Edward and Oliver Sinclairis, father brether to the said Robert, Peter Symsoun, minister, Hew Tarrell and William Fermour, notar publict, and writter heiroff, with Johne Sutherland, minister, and Francis Nicolsoun.

Frances Nicolsone, witnes — Andro Bruce with my hand — W. Bruce of Simbester with my hand

Jane Bruce with my hand at the pen led
be the notar under writtin at my command
becaus I can nocht write my selff.

Ita est Wilelmus Fermour notarius publicus
in premissis testantibus meo signo
et subscriptione normalibus

Williame Tyrie yownge[r] witnes
J. Sutherland witnes
Hew Tarrell witnes to the premises
Henrye Colville witnes

Arthur Sinclar of Aithe witnes
Edward Sinclair witnes
Olipher Sinclair witnes

Producit at Soundbrughe the twentie day of Junij 1604 befoir my lord in judicio: William Bruce denyis that ever he subscryvit the samin

Wilelmus Fermour, notarius publicus, testis in premissis manu propria

Thomas Auchinlek, scriba

[*Docket*:] The guidman of Burghs obligatioun.

SA, SC.12/65/1/55. For the vicissitudes of this document see *CB1*, pp.109-10, 133-4 and 147-50.

358. Edinburgh, 23 February 1603

Decreet of court of session in action at instance of Adam Sinclair of Brow against Patrik, earl of Orknay, and Mr Johne Dischingtoun his depute, Thomas Auchinlek, clerk of court, Robert Sinclair of Campstane and Edward Sinclair, brother to the deceased Mathew Sinclair. Adam has divers possessions and lands in Orknay and Yetland, expecially the lands of Browe and links thereof. Patrik resolved to possess them, and sundry times summoned Adam to compear before him and his deputes, under pretext and colour of law, to trouble him in his person and goods. Adam being ready at all times to suffer trial by law, Patrik, frustrated of his evil intention, in August 1602 summoned Adam, by a pretended precept directed by Mr Johne Dischingtoun, sheriff depute of Yetland, as 'ane of the furnesaris, faltaris, freindis and supportaris' of the murderers of Mathow Sinclair of Ness (which murder took place on 27 June 1602), 'immediatlie eftir and befoir hait blude', to compear before Patrik and his deputes to underlie the law for the said murder. Although the pursuer is 'maist innocent' thereof, and had compeared 'and offerit himself in redie to abyd tryell', Patrik committed him to ward in his castle of Skalloway, and while he was in ward 'causit gif furth greit dome and sentence againis him', decerning all his lands, goods and gear to pertain to the said earl, and to remove himself furth of the country within 15 days, to remain banished therefrom under pain of horning.

The lords of council suspend the letters of arrestment, poinding, horning and others raised at the instance of the earl of Orknay against Adam, until the letters are produced.

SRO, CS.7/207, ff.99-100. See no. 349.

359. The kirk of Lunay, 6 March 1603

Disposition by Mathew Forrester of Vodlone, son of the deceased Henrie Forrester of Lunay, with consent of Jane Kennadie, his spouse, to David Forrester of Lunay, his brother german, of 4 marks land, 9 pennies the mark, in the town of Lie benorth the voe of Olnafirth, for consideration of 2 marks land, 12 pennies the mark, in Vedlone in Lunesting, and other good deeds, gratitudes, movable gear and money received from his brother David. Precept of sasine.

Mathew procures the signets of famous and discreet men, Androw Haweck of Skatstay, William Magnussone in Neip, foud of Nesting, with the merchant marks of Magnus Hanssone of Gillisbrek, and William Forrester of Lee, his brother german. Mathew subscribes with his hand led at the pen by Peter Simsoun, minister of Nesting. Witnesses: Robert Magnussone in Kirkabuster, Antonie in Fluyagarth, and David Strang.

SA, D.8/4/2.

360. Edinburgh, 10 March 1603

Obligation by Frances Sinclair of Iwyea, and Robert Sinclair his brother, to John Deanes, bailie of Hawik, in their 'grit strait and necessitie', for 200 merks, repayable by Martinmas, failing which they undertake to infeft John in an annualrent of 20 merks from Frances's lands of Underhoull and Croisbuster. For John's greater security Frances deposits with John: (1) a feu charter by the deceased Lord Robert Stewart to the deceased William Sinclair, and Margrat Stuartt his spouse, of the lands of Umberhoull, dated 25 February 1574-5; (2) an infeftment by James Hay, vicar of Unst, with consent of the deceased Adam, bishop of Orknay, of 'the said' lands of Vinstrik, dated 12 and 13 January 1578-9; and (3) a sasine written on paper, 'under the note' of David Andersone, notary, whereby the deceased Robert, bishop of Orknay, commendator of Kynlos and Beulie, constituted Mr Malcolme Halcro assignee to the reversion of the lands of Crosbuster.

Witnesses: William Douglas of Mar, John Castellaw, writer, David Libertoun, burgess of Edinburgh, John Gilmour, writer, and Alexander Sempill, writer.

SRO, RD.1/271, ff.73-5.

361. Holyroodhouse, 2 April 1603

Precept for a remission to Frances Sinclair of Uya, Robert Sinclair, his brother, Laurence Sinclair, son of William Sinclair of Ustaness, James Sinclair, son of Laurence Sinclair of Gott, and John Bruce, sometime servant of Adam Sinclair of Brow, for the slaughter of Mathew Sinclair of Ness in June 1602.

SRO, PS.1/74, f.8 (in Latin). See no. 349.

362. Northbrek in North Yell, 15 April 1603

Disposition by Thomas Olaiffsoune, with consent of his wife and bairns, to Jamys Spens of Mydbrek ('I grantis me to have ressavit frome my guid freind ... in my gret urgent neid and necessitie quhen I haid nathing to sustein my wyf nor bairnes in maill, corne and uthir neidfull wairs, and sundre detts payet unto uthir to quhome I wes endettit'), of 1½ marks land, 6 pennies the mark, in the 'twne' of Northbrek, parish of North Yell, 'quhilk I heretable airit eftir my sayd [*rectius* fader?]'.

Thomas 'requyrit with instans' the seals of honest men: Nicollis Guttromsone of Culyevo, Jhone Lawrensone of Aweik, bailye of Yell, Jamys of Swarisseter, lawrightman, and appends his merchant mark. Witnesses: Jamys Nisbet, Gilbert Nisbet and Daniell Nisbet, 'wyth wthirs beand present for the tyme'.

The original is not known to exist. The above abstract is from a 19th century transcription (SA, D.16/392/71/79). Jamys Nisbet subscribed as follows: 'Jeg Jacob Nisbet for namen'. Thomas Olaiffesoune signed with his hand touching the pen. There is an illustration of Thomas Olaiffsoune's mark, and of three others, with the transcription. Another transcription (SA, D.12/155/11) is accompanied by illustrations of two seals.

363. Thowrhous in North Yell, 20 May 1603

Disposition by Walter Iryeounsone, indweller in Torhous in North Yell, with consents of his wife and bairns, and also with consent of Nicollis Guttromsone of Culyevo, his father's brother, 'quha did reffues me for the present', to his 'ryght truest and best beloved freind' James Spens of Mydbrek ('in my gret neid and necessitie quhen I had na thing to sustein my wyff nor famelie'), of 1 mark land, 7 pennies the mark, in Torhouse, parish of North Yell.

Walter 'hes requyrit maist ernestlie' the seals of honest men: Nicollis Guttromsone of Culyevo, John Lawransone of Aweik, bailie of Yell, James of Swareseter, lawrightman. Witnesses: James Nisbet, Gilbert Nisbet and Danyell Nisbet, with others.

The original is not known to exist. The above abstract is from a 19th century transcription (SA, D.16/391/6/1). Jamys Nisbet subscribed as follows: 'Jeg Jacob Nisbet for navna'. Walter Iryeounsone signed with his hand touching the pen. The transcription is accompanied by illustrations of Walter's mark, and of the three seals.

364. Bergen, 22 May 1603

Declaration by the mayors and councillors of Bergen anent sale of 12 marks land in Brolandt.

We, the mayors and councillors of Bergen in Norway, notify and make known by this our open letter that in our town hall on 22 May 1603 there came before us Ibbe Jorgennssen, poor-law inspector for the house below the cathedral in the same place, with full powers on behalf of Anna, widow of Oluff Hagenssen, who is now in the said poor-house, together with the honest and well esteemed man Rennertt Woig, councillor and town bailiff [*byfougid*] in Bergen, with authority on behalf of the children of the said Oluff, on the one part, and Edwardt Zinckler of Bollestad in Hietland, and Jacob Petterssen, servant of Rubertt Zinckler of Borg in Hietland, on the other part, concerning 12 marks burnt in a land [*jord*] called Brolanndt, in the parish of Sannduig in Hietland, of which the said Oluff Hagenssen had inherited one half from his deceased father Hagenn Jonssenn, and the other half from N. Jonnssenn, his father's brother, and that they have agreed in this way, both parts friendly, before us as follows: that the said Rennertt Woig and Ibbe Jorgennssen, on behalf of the said Anna, widow of Oluff Hagenssen, and their children, have sold, conveyed and made over to the said Rubertt Zinckler, and his brothers and sisters and their heirs [*hannds syskinne och theris arffuinger*], the said 12 marks land in Brolandd, to enjoy, use and keep it in a firm and immovable bargain to everlasting odal possession and property [*euindelig odell och eyendomb*]; and the said Rennertt and Ibbe also acknowledge that they have received and collected from the said Rubertt Zinckler's proxies all that came of their bargain, which is 100 rix dollars, both for the bargain and the cost of the deed of conveyance: so they are thanking them for good payment, on condition that they compensate the writ [*haandschrifft*] they have given for the arrears. And we decide that the said Rennertt and Ibbe, on behalf of the said Anna, [widow] of Oluff Hagenssen, shall have no further lot, share or portion in the said 12 marks land in Brolanndt after this day in any way; and thereafter they have handed over to the said Eduardt Zinckler and Jacob Petterssenn all letters and evidences they have had thereupon here in Bergen.

In confirmation of this the said Renertt Woig and Ibbe Jorgenssenn, each by their own hand, have signed here beneath. And in further witness hereof we have let hang here underneath our ordinary privy town seal.

SA, D.11/190 (in Danish). Seal. Sannduig is an error for Sandsting.

365. Sowmeburghe, 6 July 1603

Disposition by Hew Halcro in Cunnesburghe to his good friend Williame Bruce of Symbuster, of his mark uthell land, 9 pennies the mark, in the town of Symbuster, in the isle of Quhailsay, for payment yearly of one penny at Whitsun eve. Precept of sasine directed to George Blak.

Hew Halcro subscribes with his hand led at the pen. Witnesses: Walter Richie, servant of John Arnot, burgess of Edinburgh, Robert Forbes, brother german of Patrik Forbes, merchant at Dunrosnes, James Grote, servant of Malcolme Sincler of Quendale, and Alexander Bruce, notary public, writer hereof.

Sasine given on 9 January 1607 (at 9 a.m.). Witnesses: James Sincler, Alexander Fordyce, servant of William Bruce, Magnus Ollasoun in Huiksetter, Andro Yeanesoun, Vincentious Christophersoun in Symbuster, and Alexander Bruce, notary public; 'and ordanis thir presentis to be registrat in the buikis of secretarie of Orknay and Yetland, thairin to remaine *ad perpetuam rei memoriam*'.

SA, GD.144/28/6 (disposition) and GD.144/49/57 (sasine).

366. Skalloway bankis, 22 July 1603

Obligation by Dame Margaret Levingstoun, countess of Orknay, having special power of Patrik, earl of Orknay, her spouse, for taking order with his affairs during his absence in England, to Mr James Stewart, brother german of Patrik, for 6,000 merks, payable by Whitsunday 1604, with £500 in expenses. Patrik was addebted to James for 10,000 merks, of which he has lately made payment of 4,000 merks. Arthour Sinclar of Aith, Mr James Pitcarnis, vicar of Northmaven, Robert Sinclair of Brough, Androw Gifard of Waddersta, Laurance Sinclar of Got, Olivir Suddirland, foud of Fetlar, John Neven of Scousbrugh, David Kincaid, Mr William Hay, archdeacon of Yetland, Androw Edmonstoun, vicar of Yell, and Alexander Thomasoun, foud of Tingwall, act as cautioners.

Witnesses: Andro Mairtine, servant of Patrik, writer hereof, Mr Thomas Levingstoun, treasurer of Glasgow, Alexander Stewart, servant of Patrik, James Levingstoun, Patrik Bog, Walter Richie, and Alexander Bruce, notary public.

SRO, RD.1/134, ff.96-7.

367. Skalloway bankis, 27 July 1603

Obligation by Mr William Hey, archdeacon of Yetland and minister of

God's word at Tingwall, to his good friend Edward Sinclair of Bulyeasetter, for £100.

Witnesses: Hierome Umphray of Sand, Andro Edmistoun, minister of God's word at Yell, Piter Simson, minister at Nesting, George Ogstoun, servant of William Bannatyne of Gairsay, writer hereof, and William Bannatyne, with divers others.

CB1, pp.137-8.

368. 30 July 1603

'Charter of wadsett by John Mowat, with consent of Andro Mowat, Hugoland, his father, and Christian Stewart, his spouse, for seven score auld dollars, together with 25 pounds, making in all 200 auld dollars, to Arthur Sinclair of Aith, of an annual rent of 70 auld dollars of silver to be uplifted from 15 merks 6 ures land in Sullom, in the parish of Northmaven, and 3 merks in Turvisetter and 4 in Swinasetter in the said parish, by the said Arthur Sinclair and Margaret Colville, his spouse, during the not redemption. ...

'Witnesses: Thomas ..., commissioner of Yetland, Mr James Pitcairn, and others.'

The original is not known to exist. The above abstract, by Francis Grant, is in OSD, *SN*, 13 January 1894. An annualrent of 70 auld dollars seems improbably high.

369. Scalloway and Kirkwall, (blank) and (blank) August 1603

Contract between Thomas Swentoun, minister of Kirkwall, with consent of Agnes Hobroun his spouse, on the first part, and Mr James Pitcairne, minister of Northmaven, with consent of Ursula Sinclare his spouse, on the other part, for the marriage of John Swentoun, eldest son of Thomas, and Margaret Pitcairn, eldest daughter of James. Thomas binds himself to infeft John in the 8 penny land of Burgar in Evie, the lands of Damesay, with reservation of liferent to Walter Tyrie and Marion Wauch his spouse, a tenement in Kirkwall, between the lands pertaining to the treasury of Orknay on the north, the lands pertaining to James Murray of Gairth on the south, the common 'calsay' on the east, and the sea called the Oyse of Kirkwall on the west, reserving to Thomas and Agnes their franktenement and liferent thereof; failing which the 3 pennyland of Fealquhoy in Evie, 2½ pennyland in Kingshouse in Haray and 2½ pennyland in Bimbusta. James binds himself to infeft John and Margaret in his 41 marks heritable land in Yetland, all 6 pennies the mark, with reservation of liferent, and to pay Thomas 1,200 merks money in name of tocher good.

Witnesses: John Monteithe, merchant in Kirkwall, Walter Tyrie of Damesay, Laurence Dempstartoun, merchant, Mr Thomas Barclay of

Coplahillis, Andro Admestoun, minister at Yell, Mr Gilbert Mowatt and Andro Pitcairne.

SRO, RD.1/105, ff.462-3.

370. 1 August 1603

'Sasine ... on disposition by Robert Wright in Scalloway to Arthur Sinclair of Aith, of a tenement in Scalloway.

'In presence of Adam Boyne in Scalloway, and others. Alexander Bruce, NP.'

The original is not known to exist. The above abstract, by Francis Grant, is in OSD, *SN*, 13 January 1894.

371. Voisgarth in Ownst, 15 August 1603

Discharge by David Sincleir of Huntoun in Orknay to his beloved friend Thomas Chene of Valay, and Thomas's contracted spouse Agnes Strang, of payment for the reversion and title of right of the 18 marks land, 8 pennies the mark, called the great last, in Melbie.

Witnesses: Patrik Hog, writer hereof, minister of Fetlar, John Archear, Robert Bunt, tailor in Ownst, and John Sincler, son of David, with divers others.

SA, D.10/17/3.

372. Voisgarth in Ownst, 16 August 1603

Precept directed by David Sincleir of Huntoun to Androw Wischert, foud of Wais, to pass to the 18 marks land, 8 pennies the mark, called the great last of Melbe in Sandnes, and give sasine thereof to Thomas Chene of Valay, and his contracted spouse Agnes Strang, conform to the tenor of the contract between the deceased James Strang, on the one part, and the said David, on the other part, dated 21 August 1598 at Voisgarth, and conform to the assignation made to them of the said contract by David and his daughter Christine Sincler, relict of the said James, taking the burden for the other heirs of the said James.

Witnesses: Patrik Hog, minister of Fetlar, writer hereof, John Archer, Robert Bunt, tailor in Ownst, and John Sincleir, son of David, with divers others.

Sasine given on 23 April 1604 (at 10 a.m.) to Thomas Chene and George Blak, attorney for Agnes Strang, spouse of Thomas. Witnesses: Magnus Rasmussone in Melbie, Rasmus Blans there, Robert Wischert, son lawful of Andro Wischert, foud of Wais, and Alexander Bruce, notary public.

SA, D.10/17/3. This precept and the sasine are on the back of the discharge dated 15 August 1603 (no. 371). See also no. 274.

373. Garderhous in Aithsting, 27 August 1603 (at 10 a.m.)
Instrument of sasine in favour of Arthour Sinclair of Aithe, following on wadset by John Wishert, foud of Aithsting and Sandsting, of 4 marks uthell land, 12 pennies the mark, in Gairderhous in the parish of Aithsting, and 5 marks land, 8 pennies the mark, in Burrafirth, under reversion for £235. Robert Tulloch, procurator for Arthour Sinclair.

Witnesses: James Esspleine and Olla Yelt, officers in Aithsting and Sandsting, Nicoll Yeanesoune in Gairderhous, William Magnussone in Inner Sand, Alexander Bruce, notary public, with Thomas Angusone, his servant.

Transumpt made in 1625 by Alexander Bruce, notary public, in process Wischart v. Sinclair, SRO, CS.15/186 .

374. Quendaill, 6 September 1603
Obligation by Andro Giffert of Waddersta to his good friend Alexander Kincaid, vicar of Waills, for £300, payable by 15 June 1604, with the provision that if Andro pays Alexander £204 before 1 May 1604 then he shall be free of the forenamed sum of £300.

Witnesses: John Sutherland, vicar of Sandsting, William Fermour, notary, Malcolm Sinclair of Quendaill, writer hereof, with others.

SRO, RD.1/206, f.119.

375. Soundburgh, 5 October 1603
Contract between William Bruce of Simbester, on the one part, and Robert Sinclair, lawful son of William Sinclair of Uyea, and commissioner for Frances Sinclair, on the other part, whereby Robert dispones to William, 42 marks land of the north part of Uyea, with the little island called Half Grunna lying eastward from the isle of Uyea, with the island lying south-east from the isle of Uyea called Wodderholme, in the parish of Unst, under reversion of 300 merks. Robert, by his commission dated 26 July 1603 at Leith, has power of Frances to uptake his mails and duties of his lands in Yetland, and also to borrow 400 merks upon 16 marks land of Kirkhous, 42 marks land in Uyea, and 9 marks land in Clovacast, in the isle of Unst. Robert and Frances undertake to get themselves heritably infefted in the said lands.

Witnesses: William Fermour, notary public, Lawrens Sinclair, minister of God's word, Andro (illegible), writer hereof, Hutcheon (illegible), John Fermour, son lawful of William Fermour, Alexander Fordyce, and William Fordyce.

SRO, RD.1/113, ff.84-87.

376. Quendell, 15 November 1603
Excambion between Malcum Sinclair of Quendell and the honourable

Arthour Sinclair of Ayth, whereby Malcum exchanges his 2½ marks land, 8 pennies the mark, in Northbrogh, in the isle of Burray, which he bought from Marioun Olavisdochter, for Arthour's 2½ marks land, 8 pennies the mark, in Cumlaweik, in the parish of Dunrosnes. Precept of sasine.

Witnesses: Laurence Sinclair of Got, minister at Dunrosnes, Thomas Blackbaird, and Johne Sinclair of Quhame, officer.

Braefield House, Dunrossness. Photocopy in SA, SA.2/261/6.

377. Edinburgh, 12 January 1604

Bond of caution by Andro Bruce of Scattistay for Nicoll in Grobisnes, Nicoll in Clovicast, John Giffert in Busta, Andro Giffert in Wodersta, Mathow Foister in Wodlen, Magnus in Gellesbrig, Magnus in Uphous in Crwinfirth, Bartill there, Magnus in Dowar, Thomas Cowplen in Skelberrie, William Mansoun in Neip, Robert Hunter in Sanctthows in Quallschay, Walter in Wassay, John in Evict, Magnus in Howland, Nicoll in Papell, Petir Neisbet in Kirkibuster, Crespeit Cullane in Gossuburch, William Firsall in Bogsetter, Erasmus in Guidshir, Lowrence Mathesoun in Gransetter, William Bruce younger in Underhoule in Unst, Walter Rippeth in Rannigo, Ola Sutherland in Still, William Bruce elder in Uya, Thomas Lawder in Roseta, Captain Thomas Knichtsone in Aith, John in Stromefirth, John Sutherland in Unyefirth, Magnus Smith in Bustie, Magnus Nicolsoun in Stanis and Wisdaill, and the remaining tenants and occupiers of the undernoted lands, viz., 12 marks land, 12 pennies the mark, of Pegra, 16 marks land, 9 pennies the mark, of Kirkhous, 4 marks land, 8 pennies the mark, of Groisnes, 7 marks land, 9 pennies the mark, of Clevagath, 8 marks land, 12 pennies the mark, of Bustey, 8 marks land, 12 pennies the mark, of Wedderstay, in the parish of Dalting; 1 mark land, 12 pennies the mark, of Hisda, 6 marks land, 12 pennies the mark, of Wodland, 12 marks land, 12 pennies the mark, of Loening, 4 marks land, 8 pennies the mark, of Drunyeafirth, 7 marks land, 9 pennies the mark, of Dowar, 1 mark land, 12 pennies the mark, of Skelberrie, 1 mark land, 9 pennies the mark, of Neip, in the parish of Nesting and Lunesting; 9 marks land, 12 pennies the mark, of Sand Sodell, 6 marks land, 12 pennies the mark, of Clodone, 1 mark land, 12 pennies the mark, of Sandwek, 2 marks land, 12 pennies the mark, of Wasterhous, 1 mark land, 12 pennies the mark, of Skaw, (blank) marks land, 9 pennies the mark, of Skumbester, ½ mark land, 12 pennies the mark, of Bruche, in the parish of Quhalissay; 3 marks land, 9 pennies the mark, of Bastay, 2 marks land, 8 pennies the mark, of Quhassay, 4½ marks land, 9 pennies the mark, of Avek, 3 marks land, 8 pennies the mark, of Howland, ½ mark land, 6 pennies the mark, of Papell, 4 marks land, 8 pennies the mark, of Grunnaster, 1½ marks land, 9 pennies the mark, of Kirkabusta, 9 marks land, 8 pennies the mark, of Gossoburch, 1 mark land, 9 pennies the mark, of Staiddisuokin in Wast Yek, (blank) marks land, 9 pennies the mark, of Bigfat, 1 mark land, 9 pennies the mark, of Seltisfirth, 6 marks land, 8 pennies the mark, of Gutscheir, 4 marks land, 9 pennies the mark, of Esetaygarthe, 2½ marks land, 9 pennies the mark, of Ruffine, in the parish of Yell; 3 marks land of Skaw, ½ mark land of Utterskaw, 16 marks land of Unddohoule, 1 mark land of Sclettoun, 19 marks land of Ramnagew, 1 mark land of Balyestay, 4½ marks land of Gunrasetter, 1 mark land of Meuhous, 1 mark land of Bedone, 2½ marks land of Daill, 1 mark land of Stisodik, 18 marks land of Toobuster, 48 marks land of Underhull, 8 marks land of Windstrik, 3 marks land of Mowlaw, 1½ marks land of Stilla, 1 mark land of Still, 1 mark land of Midgath, 2 marks land of Papill, ½ mark land of Torwell, 2 marks land of Garth, 1 mark land of Cowdone, ½ mark land of Seter, 1 mark land of Houstoun, 9½ marks land of Clevacuster, 84 marks land of Uyea, all 6 pennies the mark, and 2 marks land of Baltay, 12 pennies the mark, in the parish of Unce; 1½ marks land, 6 pennies the mark, of Southhous in Seinyie, 1 mark land, 6 pennies the mark, of Russetter, 1 mark land, 6 pennies the mark, of Dowbye, (blank) mark land, 6 pennies the mark, of Howlie, 1½ marks land, 6 pennies the mark, of Coft in Strand, in the parish of Fletter; 2 marks land, 9 pennies the mark, of Wodbuseay in Brassay; (blank) marks land, 8 pennies the mark, of Wthie in Alsung; 6 marks land, 6 pennies the mark, of Clatt in Burray; 15 marks land, 12 pennies the mark, of Girdilstay, 6 marks land, 6 pennies the mark, of Schaldernes, 5 marks land, 6 pennies the mark, of Adell, 5 marks land, 8 pennies the mark, of Howland, 3 marks land, 8 pennies the mark, of Barrabquhan in Tundrad, 1 mark land, 8 pennies the mark, of Eisterhous in Scalloway; 12 marks land, 6 pennies the mark, of Stromfirtie, 6 marks land, 4 pennies the mark, of Northmas(illegible), 1 mark land, 4 pennies the mark, of Southmiscuif; 11 marks land, 8 pennies the mark, of Tomling, 1½ marks land, 12 pennies the mark, of Sand, 6 marks land, 12 pennies the mark, of Unyeafurth; and lands called the canons' lands lying in Yetland, that they shall pay their duties for the crop 1603 to either Frances Sinclair of Uyea, or to Robert Sinclair, his lawful brother, or to James Sinclare, his brother, or to Margaret Sinclar, their sister, and William Bruce in Underhoill in Unst, her spouse, for his interest, or to Robert Sinclar, eldest lawful son of the deceased Hew Sinclar of Burgh, or to Hew Sinclar, second lawful son of the said deceased Hew Sinclar and Jean Bruce, his spouse, whichever is found by the lords of council to have the best right thereto.

SRO, CS.290/25.

378. Birsay, 20 February 1604

Instructions anent peats to be led to the castle of Scalloway.

Apud Birsay xx° day of Februar 1604.

The rentall of the peattis quhilkis ar to be cassin, win and led to my lord's houssis presentlie, 1604, as followes:

Item, it is appoyntit that the mid parochin and south parochines of Dunrosnes sall cast, win and leid to my lord's houssis ten faddom of peattis, conteining xx fute of hicht, xvj fute of breid, and xiiij fute of lenth, and the peattis to be thrie quarteris deip.

Item, the north parochin of Dunrosnes is appoyntit to cast and win upon the hill of Skalloway, everie thrie last of land, ane faddom peattis, in hicht, lenth and breid forsaid, quhilk will extend to viij faddome peattis being xxiiij last of land.

Item, Burray lyikwayes ilk thrie last of land to cast, win and stak upon the hill betuix Skalloway and Brassay, ane faddome peittis in lenth, hiecht and breid forsaid, viz. xxj last of land extends to vij faddome peattis.

Item, Brassay appoyntit lyikwayes to cast and wyn upoun that samen hill sevin faddome peattis of the quantitie forsaid, beand xxj last of land, and stakit be thame thair.

Item, Tingwall parochin being lyikwyes xxx last of land is appoyntit to cast, wyn and stak upon ane dey place of the said hill, x faddome peattis of lenth, breid and hiecht forsaid.

Item, it is appoyntit that the parochin of Quhytnes and Weisdaill sall leid to the castell of Skalloway v faddome peattis of the lenth, breid and heicht forsaid.

Item, the parochin of Aithsting and Sandsting is appoyntit to leid to the castell fyve faddome peattis of lenth, hiecht and breid forsaid.

Item, the parochin of Wais is appoyntit to leid five faddome peattis of the hicht, lenth and breid forsaid.

Item, Delting parochin appoyntit to leid sex faddome peattis of the hicht, lenth and breid forsaid.

Item, Nesting parochin vj faddome peattis of the hicht, lenth and breid forsaid.

Item, Northmaving to leid to the said castell fyve faddome peattis in lenth, breid and hicht forsaid.

And that everie ane of the fowdis caus this be put to executioun in dew tyme of yeir, under the paine of ane hundreth li., and that they charge ilk ane of the tennentis to this effect under the pain of ten punds.

Alexander Bruce ye sall delyver to the fowdis presentlie thir preceptis and charge thame to observe the contentis thairof under the paines thairin contenit. With certificatioun thair unlawes sall nocht be unliftit in caice ony of thaim [*word missing*?] Thir presents salbe your warrand, and thairfor sie it done.

SRO, GD.190/3/233/1. The document is unsubscribed. There is a transcription of another version in an appendix to a rental of Shetland written down about 1640 (SRO, E.41/7).

379. Edinburgh, 15 March 1604

Decreet of commissary court of Edinburgh in action of divorce at instance of Androw Bruce, son of Laurence Bruce of Cultmalindies, against Margaret Sinclair, daughter of Hew Sinclair of Burgh. The marriage had taken place in November 1597 and had been solemnised by Petir Symesoun, reader, by virtue of which the parties gave the use of their bodies to the other in mutual company and society, at bed and board, as becomes married folks, until 1 July 1598, when Margaret withdrew herself from the pursuer, and gave the use of her body in the filthy crime of adultery to Adam Cowie, son of (blank) Cowie, piper in Kirkcaldie, and that in the chambers and house of her father's house of Burgh and thereabouts, with Adam 'useing hir as hamelie in all respecttis as gif scho had bene his lawfull spous', whereby the pursuer claims that she has made herself divorced from him. The following witnesses had been summoned: Mathow Forrester in Luliskerrie, Androw Steill, James Davidsoun, James Liddell, Francis Nicolsoun, William Dempstar, Hew Tarrell, David Pitcairne, William Wilkie, John Michell in Raitt, William Row, George Schevin, James Wischart, and John Stirk. Of these the undernoted had been examined by the commissaries on 26 May 1602 and admitted to give evidence: Androw Steill, who declared that he had no master at present but had served William Bruce in Yeitland for the past two years for a yearly fee of £10 and a stand of clothes, and that since leaving his service 12 weeks previously he had been up and down the country selling 'schone, banats and uthir chapman wairis', and also declared that he had been servant to the laird of Cultmalindies some years previously, and on enquiry had replied that the cloak about him was his own and that he was worth in free gear £30; James Davidsoun, who declared that he was presently servant to the laird of Busbie for a yearly fee of £10 and a stand of clothes, and that he had never been servant to the laird of Cultmalindie, but had served Androw Bruce 4 years previously; James Davidsoun, who declared that he had been in service with Hew Sinclair for 4 years and had taught Hew's bairns for his meat and clothes but had no other fee of him, and had left Hew's service at Lammas last and had been in Kaitnes since.

The commissaries decern Margaret Sinclair to be separated and divorced from Androw Bruce, and that Androw 'to be frie to marry quhair he best pleiss in the lord as gif the said Margaret war naturallie deid', and that Margaret to forfeit all infeftments of conjunct-fee or liferent given to her in contemplation of her marriage.

SRO, CC.8/2/32 (26 May 1602), CC.8/2/33 (29 July 1602, 20 November 1602, 24 December 1602, 26 January 1603), CC.8/2/34 (15 March 1604). The marriage contract, dated 2 October 1589, had already given rise to litigation (SRO, CS.15/75; SRO, CS.7/188, ff.72-5, 119-20).

380. Kirkwall, 29 March 1604

Contract between Patrik, earl of Orknay, lord Yetland, on the one part, and Patrik Ross, merchant, burgess of Abirdene, on the other part, whereby Patrik, earl of Orknay, sells to Patrik Ross 200 packs of wadmell to be delivered by Midsummer 1604 by the earl's tenants, servants and chamberlains at the port of Laxfuird 'usit and wont'. Patrik Ross binds himself to pay John Arnot, sometime provost of Edinburgh, on behalf of the earl, 20 merks for each pack, by Martinmas 1604 (or £10 for each pack by 8 October 1604).

Witnesses: Mr Thomas Levingstoun, treasurer of Glasgow, Barnard Stewart, Andro Mairtene, and Robert Scollay, servant of Patrik, earl of Orknay, writer hereof.

SRO, RD.1/123, ff.150-1.

381. (April 1604?)

Duties payable to William Bruce for fishing lodges, etc., at the Nes.

Information of the dewteis quhilk William Bruce ressaivis yeirly at the Nes fra the strangeris doggaris and utheris thair resorting in April 1604.

It is testifeit be Jhone Watsoun, Thomas Hunter and William Baine, all indwellaris in Craill, that thai pay for ilk dogar ludge thai hald of William Bruce in Dunrosnes in Yetland, xx s. silver, ane barrell of collis, and 6 dry keling; and all the rest of the cost syd men payis alsmekle for all thair ludgis yeirlie; and all the dogaris of Fischaraw payis to the said William Bruce for ilk ludge thai hald of him yeirlie, xxx s. silver, ane barrell of collis, aucht keling, ane handlene, and ane leid; and all the merchantis ludgis that dryis fyshe one the schoir payis four poundis; the broustaris payis part four poundis, and sum payis sax poundis yeirlie.

Item, to remember that the doggaris of Fischerraw payis yeirlie xxx s. monie for everie bot, and thair is xviij bottis at Sondbruch this present yeir 1604, besydis uther litill commoditeis.

SRO, GD.190/3/233/2.

382. Northbreck in North Yell, 20 May 1604

'[Disposition by] Olaiff Torwallsone or Torwaldsone, indweller in Northbreck, with consent of bairns and nearest of kin ... to James Spence of Midbreck ... ½ mark, 6d. the mark, in Northbreck, in presence of Nicollis Guttromsone of Cullyvoe, Thomas [*rectius* John] Lawransone, bailyie of Yell, James (Ollafsone) of Swarisseter, lawryghtman, before witnesses: James Nisbet, Gilbert Nisbet, Daniel Nisbet.'

The original is not known to exist. The above 19th century abstract is in SA, D.16/392/71/71. The document may well have been dated 20 May 1603: see nos. 362 and 363.

383. 21 June 1604

Note of lands in Shetland conquest by Patrik, earl of Orkney, in 1604.

Rentall of the conquest landis in Yetland conquest be my lord, in anno 1604. 21 Junij 1604.

Item, the landis of Got perteining to Laurence Sinclair, wodset to his lordship for xx li. of annualrentis on reversioun of IJc lib., begining the first termes payment thairof at Lambes nixt 1604.

Sex mark land in Exina', disponit be Andro Edmesburt in St. Androis to my lord under reversioun of Jc lib. jd. Ane tak or few chartour of the buith quhair the said Andro duellis. This extrie bocht to Malcome Sinclair in 1605, and ordanes to crave the dewtie for all yeiris preceiding, togidder with the dewtie of the excambit land sen the excambion gottin fra Francis Sinclair.

Item, xv mark land in Laberla, xiij mark in Burra and Trondray, disponit to his lordship be William Sinclair of Ustanes.

Item, iij mark land in Conyegairth in Weisdaill decernit be umquhill Hew Sinclair fra his lordship, quhilk now is cum in agane.

Item, xij markland in Lie in Whalsay, disponit to his lordship be David and Andro Forresteris. Compositioun for thift.

Item, ij mark, ix d. mark, in Overscalloway, disponit be the said David. Coft.

Item, ix mark, vj d. mark, in Got in Tingwall parochin, disponit be Gilbert Thomassone to my lord under reversioun of Jc xxvj li. Unjust.

Item, j mark, xij d. mark, in Gardehous, disponit be Hwlion Gilbertsone, with consent of Jon Wishert, to my lord heretablie. Ane unjust unlaw.

Item, j mark land in the said toun of Gruitting, disponit heretablie be Magnus Jonsoun in Cultsweik to my lord.

Item, xxxj mark land in Yell, Fetlar and Hascosey ar disponit to my lord four yeiris syne be the airis of umquhill Mr William Lawder. And knowis not whidder the samen be rentallit or not as yit.

Item, vj mark ½ mark land in Yell and Fetlar, disponit to his lordship be Gutheron Thomsone and Thomas Manssone, and knowis not whidder it be rentallit or not.

The haill channonis landis rentallit.

And of iiij mark land in Luciter excambit to James Spence, sone and air of umquhill David Spence in Gloup.

Item, vij mark land in Ustanes, evictit fra William Sinclair.

Item, iij mark land in the yle of Unst, fallin in escheit for thift in Crosbuster.

Item, xiiij mark land in Hammer in Unst, assignit and disponit to my lord be Osea Scot.

Item, ix markland in Southhous in Beinsta, j markland in Greifskerrie in

Nesting, disponit to my lord be Jon Strang and his brother.

Robert Sinclair of Uyea, his brother part of land perteining to him within the countrie of Yetland, disponit be him to my lord.

Ane annualrent of ij barrell butter, disponit be Mr James Pitcairne to my lord furth of the landis of Gildersta and Cheldernes, or out of any of his best haldin landis in Yetland, under compositioun of Jc old silver dollouris and the byrun annualrentis thairof restand sen the dait of the first charter of wodset, viz. twa barrellis butter yeirlie.

The original is not known to exist. This transcription, in the handwriting of Andrew Smyth, chamberlain of Shetland, is an appendix to a rental of Shetland written down about 1640 (SRO, E.41/7). The original was obviously annotated at a later date or dates ('this extrie bocht ...', 'ane unjust unlaw', etc.), and Andrew Smyth has transcribed the annotations as well. Some renderings of words and names ('extrie', 'Laberla') suggest that the original was difficult to read.

384. Soundburgh, 22 June 1604

Assignation by William Synclare of Ustaness to Patrik, earl of Orknay, of: (1) £100 and annualrent thereof, extending to 16 barrels butter, owing to said William out of the 15 marks land of Halvaray and 3 marks land in Burraland in Trondray, wadset to William by the deceased James Synclare of Brow; (2) 78 gudlings owing by said James to William, being 48 gudlings for the price of 2 oxen, and 30 gudlings for the hire of the oxen for 16 years; and (3) 144 gudlings owing by Adam Sinclare of Brow, son and heir of James, being 84 gudlings for the hire of oxen, and 60 gudlings for the price of 4 'outyok' oxen. The sums extend in the whole to 222 gudlings fish and 16 barrels butter, 'comptit in gold' to 108 angels 2 gudlings, and £100. If Patrik 'prevaillis nocht' in obtaining the abovewritten sums, then William consents to Patrik having access to sufficient of his lands of Ustaness as may pay him completely of the said sums. Precept directed to Johne Synclare in Garthe and Patrik Ross in Aberdeen for giving sasine to Patrik of the lands of Haveray and Burraland in Trondray.

Witnesses: Thomas Swintoun, minister, archdeacon of Orknay, Laurence Sinclare of Gott, Thomas Auchinlek, William Fermour, Alexander Bruce, notary, Andro Martene, and Robert Scollay, servant of Patrik, writer hereof.

SRO, RD.1/107, f.145.

385. Castle of Skalloway, 30 June 1604

Disposition by Patrik, earl of Orknay, lord of Yeitland, in fulfilment of a contract of excambion between him, on the one part, and Herman and Thomas Magnussonis, brother sons and heirs of the deceased Magnus Nicolson in Trondray, on the other part, of the same date, whereby Patrik exchanges his 6 marks king's land, 8 pennies the mark, in Overskalloway, in the parish of Tingwall, for their 7½ marks land, 8 pennies the mark, in the north end of the isle of Trondray, in the parish of Tingwall. Precept of sasine directed to David Kaid in Scalloway bankis.

Witnesses: Patrik Ross, merchant, burgess of Abirdein, John Ross, mason, David Kaid, Thomas Auchinlek younger, Thomas Auchinlek elder, notary public, with Alexander Bruce, notary public, and Robert Scollay, writer hereof.

Braefield House, Dunrossness. Photocopy in SA, SA.2/261/7. There is an abstract of the sasine following thereon, dated 4 February 1608, in OSD, *SN*, 27 January 1894.

386. 6 July 1604

'Sasine ... on charter by Robert Sinclair, for himself, and as commissioner for Francis Sinclair of Uyea, his brother german, son to umquhile William Sinclair of Uyea, in favour of William Bruce of Symbister, of 22 marks of arable land called the north half of Uyea, with the equal half of the same called (?the south half), dated 9th October 1603. Alexander Bruce, NP.'

The original is not known to exist. The above abstract, by Francis Grant, is in OSD, *SN*, 27 January 1894.

387. Urafirthe, 12 July 1604

Letters of interdiction by Robert Sinclair of Brughe, eldest son of the deceased Hew Sinclair of Brughe. 'Forsameikill as I haife beine haiffelie hurt and prejugit be the consale and opinionis of diverse personis ... sen the deceise of my said father, be ressoun of my tender yeiris and laik of knawledge and discretioun to governe the samin ... and now takand guid consideratioun of my oversycht thairin', Robert undertakes that he will not 'tak ony doing' in matters concerning his lands, heritages etc. without the advice of his uncles Patrik, earl of Orknay, and Edward Sinclair.

Witnesses: Thomas Swentoun, minister at Kirkwall, Mr James Pitcarne, minister at Northmaving, Hew Halcro, fiar of that ilk, Edward Scollay of Strynie, Edward Sinclair, brother german to Robert Sinclair of Campstaine, Thomas Auchinleck, notary public, and Robert Scollay, writer hereof.

CB1, p.152.

388. Graveland, 13 July 1604

Assignation by Mr James Pitcairne, vicar of Northmaving, to Patrik, earl of Orknay, lord of Yetland, of 100 old silver dollars and the annualrent thereof, extending yearly to 2 barrels butter 'merchand wair, full pacquit in Brenner treis', owing to Mr James by William Synclare of Ustanes, since the date of the wadset charter to Mr James by William, with consent of Elspeth Synclare, his spouse, and Laurence Synclare, their eldest son, which annualrent should have been uplifted yearly from 15 marks land, 12 pennies the mark, in Girdilstay, and 6 marks land in Chaldernes, in the parish of Tingwall; and likewise constitutes Patrik his assignee in the remaining heads and clauses of the said wadset charter and precept of sasine, dated 16 May 1599 at Urafirth. Precept of sasine directed to Malcolme Halcro in Linksetter.

Witnesses: Thomas Swintoun, minister at Kirkwall, Andro Edmestoun, minister at Yell, Thomas Auchinlek elder and Alexander Bruce, notaries, Thomas Auchinlek younger, and Robert Scollay, writer hereof.

SRO, RD.1/107, ff.149-50.

389. Lie, 23 July 1604 (at 12 p.m.)

Instrument of sasine in favour of Patrik, earl of Orknay, lord Yetland, following on disposition by William Forrester of Lie, of 12 marks uthell land, 12 pennies the mark, of Lie, in the isle of Quhailsay, to be held of the immediate superior by Patrik for payment of one penny in name of blench ferme at Whitsunday, if required, with precept of sasine directed to William Magnussone in Neip, foud of Nesting. The charter, dated 21 July 1604 at Burghe in Nesting, was witnessed by Edward Scollaw of Strynie, Edward Sincler of Marasetter, Andro Merteine, Thomas Auchinlek elder, notary public, Thomas Auchinlek younger, his son, Alexander Bruce, notary public, and Robert Scollaw, servant of Patrik, earl of Orknay, writer hereof, with divers others.

Sasine given in presence of Magnus Thomassone in Kirkabuster, Merteine Pitersone in Burghe, Henrie Work there, Rasmus Ollasoun in Levasetter, and Alexander Bruce, notary public.

SRO, RH.9/15/83.

390. Scalloway bankis, 23 July 1604

Disposition by Arthour Synclare of Ayth, with consent of Margaret Colvile, his spouse, to Patrik, earl of Orknay, lord Yetland, of 3 marks land, 9 pennies the mark, of Hewgoland, 26 marks land, 8 pennies the mark, of Inner Trondray, and 17 marks land, 8 pennies the mark, of Burraland, all in the isle of Trondray, together with the right and kindness of all other lands previously disponed by way of excambion to Patrik by Olaw and Peter Urovingis, and Hairmon and Thomas Magnussonis, to be held by Patrik of the immediate superior thereof for yearly payment of one penny at Whitsunday in name of blench ferme, if required. Precept of sasine directed to John Wischart in Burrafirth.

Witnesses: Thomas Swintoun, minister at Kirkwall, Mr James Pitcairne, minister at Northmaving, Edward Scollay of Strynie, Andro Martyne, and

Robert Scollay, servant of Patrik, writer hereof.

SRO, RD.1/107, ff.151-2.

391. Scalloway bankis, 5 August 1604

Contract between Patrik, earl of Orknay, lord Yetland, on the one part, and William Bruce of Symbustar, with consent of Margaret Stewart, his spouse, and Robert Bruce, his eldest son and apparent heir, on the other part, whereby William resigns the feu charter made to him by Patrik, of 20 marks king's land, 6 pennies the mark, of Soundburgh, with the 'sameying' of the 4 marks land, 6 pennies the mark, called provestis lands, lying rig and rendal with the foresaid 20 marks land of Soundburgh, and the 20 marks land, 6 pennies the mark, of Scatnes, in the parish of Dunrosnes, as at more length contained in William's infeftment granted by Patrik on 28 March 1592 at Edinburgh; with entry to Patrik at the date hereof, with the corn and crops growing on the lands of Soundburgh, and the crop or duties of the lands of Scatnes which the occupiers are obliged to pay for the same. William shall also resign to Patrik all right and title he and his spouse have in the 46 marks land, 6 pennies the mark, of Underhoull, in the isle of Ounst, with entry at Allhallowmas 1604; and further William shall discharge Patrik of the contract between them dated 24 July 1593 at Howbie in Yetland, and keep Patrik scatheless of the yearly payment of 5 barrels butter and 10 packs of wadmell, with the grassum and all other duties which Patrik was obliged to pay for the lands called the provestis lands to any person in Denmark or Norroway by virtue of the foresaid contract. In return Patrik shall grant William a feu charter of the 2 lasts of land of Sandweik, amounting to 36 marks land, in the parish of Dunrosnes, to be held of Patrik for the yearly payment of the duties contained in the rental, with due service 'as use is'; and discharges William of the yearly duty of 20 angel nobles which he is obliged by virtue of the foresaid contract to pay to Patrik for the provestis lands in Yeitland, the first year's discharge to begin for crop 1605. Patrik also discharges William of all action which Patrik has against him by virtue of the contract made between him and the commissioners of the burghs in Fyffe in name of the 'doggaris and fischaris thairof', and shall relieve him of that part of the contract made between him and the foresaid commissioners and 'doggaris' anent their lodges in Soundburghheid, the said 'doggaris' paying suchlike yearly duty to Patrik as William was in use to get of before. William shall at the date hereof deliver to Patrik or his servants the keys of the lodges and all other houses upon the lands of Soundburgh. Patrik shall also discharge Margaret Stewart and William of the action raised by Patrik against them for non-entry to the lands of Uyeo so far as concerns her liferent of the same. Patrik shall deliver to William as many cattle, oxen, horses and sheep upon the ground of the lands of Sandweik, or the prices of the same by the estimation of four honest men equally chosen, as William leaves at Soundburgh; and likewise at the sight of the same men shall content and satisfy William for the 'insicht and plenissing' that is within the house of Soundburgh, excepting the fixed work only, so that Patrik may use them as he pleases in time coming. Patrik shall enter and possess William with the said lands of Sandweik, the crop growing upon the ground, and with the goods, gear and plenishing of the same; and shall relieve him at the hands of Malcolme Synclare, vicar of Dunrosnes, of the duties of the teinds which William was obliged to pay him yearly for the lands of Soundburgh and Scatnes.

Witnesses: Thomas Swintoun, minister at Kirkwall, Edward Scollay of Strynie, Thomas Auchinlek, notary public, Andro Martyne, servants of Patrik, Robert Scollay, writer hereof, servant of Patrik, David King, bailie of Hoy and Walls, and Alexander Bruce, notary public.

SRO, RD.1/107, ff.143-4. There is an extracted copy in SRO, RH.9/15/79.

392. 8 August 1604

'Sasine ... on charter of wadsett by John Mowat of Howgaland, with consent of Andro Mowat, his father, to Arthur Sinclair of Aith, and Margaret Colville his spouse, of an annual rent payable out of 16 marks 6 ures land in Ska, in Northmaven, dated 20 July 1604.

'Witnesses: Andrew Gifford of Woddersta, Andrew Umphray of Berrie, Hierome Umphray of Sand, and others. James Neven, NP.'

The original is not known to exist. The above abstract, by Francis Grant, is in OSD, *SN*, 27 January 1894.

393. Scalloway bankis, 11 August 1604

Contract between Patrik, earl of Orknay, lord Yetland, on the one part, and Andro Umphray of Berrie, on the other part, whereby Andro binds himself to pay John Arnot, burgess of Edinburgh, on behalf of Patrik, the sum of 1,000 merks before 1 November 1604, and to deliver to Patrik an acquittance of the said sum before 11 November 1604. And likewise, in the event of Robert Menteyth not obtaining a reduction of that decreet, pronounced in Kirkwall, for the deforcement of John Synclare, officer at Dunrosnes, and other clauses contained therein before Whitsunday 1606, Andro binds himself to pay Patrik £2,000, or else to make such disposition or resignation as Patrik shall require of the lands of Eggilsay and Worke, which are disponed by James Menteyth of Saltcoittis and Robert Menteyth to Andro in clause of warrandice of the lands of Fair Isle before there was any right or security made by them to William Stewart of Lyking thereof, and shall deliver to Patrik the contract made between the said James Menteyth and Robert Menteyth, on the one part, and Andro, on the other part, with all infeftments following thereupon, and shall put Patrik in 'his rycht rowme and place of the same'; for which cause Patrik binds himself to receive Andro tenant to the lands of the Fair Isle in the same manner as the deceased Patrik Menteyth of Fair Isle was infeft of before, providing always that Andro exhibits to Patrik the infeftment made by Patrik to the deceased Patrik Menteyth thereupon, so that it may be confirmed.

Witnesses: Thomas Swintoun, minister at Kirkwall, Edward Scollay of Strynie, Andro Martyne, and Robert Scollay, servant of Patrik, writer hereof.

SRO, RD.1/107, ff.150-1. On 21 February 1606 the lords of council considered an action apparently arising from this contract. In a decision recorded by Haddington (Morison, *Decisions*, p.16481) it appears that Umphray claimed that the contract was null, 'because it was extorted by fear and dead-dome; because the earl having caused send this Vinfra [*sic*] to him to his castle in Zetland, presented to him this contract ... and commanded him to subscribe it, which the said Andro Vinfra refused, wherewith the said earl was so offended, that with terrible countenance and words, and laying his hand upon his whinger, he threatened with execrable oaths to bereave this Vinfra of his life, and stick him presently through the head with his whinger, if he subscribed not, and so for just fear he being compelled to subscribe it, the same was null'. In response the earl alleged 'that the same could not come in the way of exception, especially because there was no fact nor deed libelled, but only boisterous words which could not be thought just fear'. The lords 'found the exception of fear very relevant'.

394. Ustanes, 14 August 1604

Disposition by Robert Sinclare, one of the lawful sons and heirs of the deceased William Synclare of Uyea, to Patrik, earl of Orknay, lord Yetland, of his brother's part of land, with the iands lying within the isle of Uyea, and whatsoever other lands which he might inherit through the decease of his father, and shall be laid to his brother's part 'be ane shewnd and devisioun of the same according to the lawis of the countrey', to be held by Patrik in free blench ferme of the immediate superior thereof, for yearly payment of one penny at Whitsunday, if required. Precept of sasine.

Witnesses: Laurence Sinclare, son of William Sinclare of Ustanes, John McKenzie, Androw Martene, servants of Patrik, John Broun, servant of Androw Martene, and Robert Scollay, servant of Patrik, writer hereof.

SRO, RD.1/107, ff.146-7.

395. (Torn) 1605.

Excambion between Edwarde Sinclair of Marrasetter and the honourable Robert Sinclair of Burghe, his brother, of 2 marks land, 8 pennies the mark, in Degrand 'within the toune' of Everrabuster in the parish of Weisdaill, and 2 marks land, 9 pennies the mark, 'in the toune' of Flett in Olnafirthe, parish of Delting, for 3½ marks land, 12 pennies the mark, 'in the toune' of Marasetter in Quhailsay, foudry of Nesting.

Edward Sinclair affixes his own signet, and procures that of Williame Manisone in Neip, foud of Nesting for the time. Witnesses: Peter Symsone, (torn) Nesting, Edwarde Syncler in Bulyesetter, Hew Tarrell, servitor of Robert Sinclair, writer hereof, Arthour Symsone, and Henrie Sinclair, 'son to said Eduarde', with divers others.

SA, GD.144/51/22.

396. Uyea in Unst, 8 January 1605

Disposition by Thomas Tulloch of Fiblesetter, taking the burden for Bessie Laing, his spouse, to Robert Sinclair, his son-in-law, and Issobell Tulloch, his daughter, and present spouse of Robert, of 8 marks land, 12 pennies the mark, in the town of Fiblesetter, and 2 marks land, 12 pennies the mark, in Odisnes, in the parish of Northmaven, for payment of one penny yearly in name of blench ferme on Whitsunday eve, if desired. Precept of sasine directed to David Androsone in Laxo.

Witnesses: Magnus Norsk, minister of God's word at Unst, James Sinclair in Uyea, and Alexander Fordyce in Uyea, writer hereof.

SA, GD.144/278/22 (certified copy of principal charter by Patrik Sands, notary public).

397. Urafirth in Northmaven, 23 January 1605

Contract of excambion between James Mowat, lawful son of Androw Mowat of Hougoland, with consent of John Mowat, his brother, on the one part, and Mans Mowat in Burrafirth, on the other part, whereby James dispones to Mans 4 marks land, 9 pennies the mark, in Ulvista, 3 marks land, 8 pennies the mark, in Brabister, and 1 mark land in Breck, all in the parish of Walls, and ½ mark land, 12 pennies the mark, in Houffe in Weisdaill; and Mans, with consent of Cristiane Irving, his spouse, and taking the burden of his heirs, dispones to James, 9 marks land, 8 pennies the mark, in Eastburrafirth, in the parish of Aythsting.

Magnus Mowat signs with his hand led at the pen by Mr James Pitcairne, vicar of Northmaven. Witnesses: Mr Gilbert Mowat, vicar of Delting, James Nevin, Androw Pitcairne, George Brown, and Olaw Ilsbrocht.

SRO, RD.11/65/500 (reg. 9 February 1609).

398. 31 May 1605

'Coppie of umquhill James Strang of Wosgarth his schound.'

The original is not known to exist. One of the writs taken from Ninian Neven's house in Yell on 24 August 1624 (*RPC*, xiv, 736-7).

399. 7 June 1605

'Precept by John Laurenceson of Aywick, fowde of Yell, in virtue of a commission direct to him by Patrick, earl of Orknay, Mr Andrew Edmondston, minister of God's word in Yell, William Magnusson in Gairdie, Ola Sutherland, bailie of Fetlar, James Sutherland, his son, James Olasone, lawrightman of Yell, William Spence of Houlland, James Spence of Midbrake, and James Cargil in Colvasetter, for making a just division among the heirs, male and female, of umquhile Peter Nisbet of Kirkabister, his lands and goods. ...

'Witnesses: William Tyrie of (Queyon?), Andrew Edmondston, minister at Yell, and others. Ninian Neven, NP.'

The original is not known to exist. The above abstract, by Francis Grant, is in OSD, *SN*, 27 January 1894. See nos. 402 and 409.

400. Gairdie, 15 July 1605

Extract decreet anent a lamb marked by David Jameson belonging to Ritchie Forbes in Willing.

At Gairdie the fyfteine day of Julij 1605

Quhilk day anent the ditty giffin up, bearing that David Jameson had markit ane lamb of Ritchie Forbes in Willing, quhairin tryall being tane it is fund that the foirsaid lamb wes markit be him negligentlie, and how schone that com to his knawledge incontinent thairefter he com to William Gairdie, fold for the tyme, and exponit the veritie thairof to him, and offeris ane uther in place thairof to be giffin for the uther, as the said fold testefeit upoun his quentiene. Thairfoir decernis the lambis to be inbrocht to my lordis use, and the said David Jamesoun to be frie of all stowth thairanent for ony thing knawin as yit; And ordanis that nane repruif him thairfoir fra this furth, ilk persoun under the paine of xl lib.

Extractum
Thomas Auchinlek, scriba.

SA, D.16/389/48/1.

401. Skalloway bankis, 22 July 1605

Tack by Andro Giffart of Woddersta, assedator of the lands of Noss and Noss goods, to Patrik, earl of Orknay, of 21 marks land in Ustaness, in the parish of Quhytisnes, which belongs to the said Noss goods, occupied presently by William Sinkclair of Ustanes, for 19 years, with entry at Allhallowmass 1605, for payment yearly of 9 lispunds 8 marks butter and 9 shillings 2 cuttells wadmell. Andro discharges Patrik of the yearly duty and grassum of the said lands which he might have claimed of Patrik's father by virtue of his former tack.

Witnesses: Edward Scollay of Strynie, Andro Martine, Robert Scollay, servant of Patrik, writer hereof, and Thomas Auchinlek, notary public.

SRO, RD.1/115, ff.140-1.

402. Kirkwall, 7 August 1605

Commission by Patrik, earl of Orkney, lord of Yetland, to the underfoud of Yell, to hold the schound of the deceased Peter Nisbit.

Patrik, erle of Orknay, lord of Yetland, schireff principall and justice generall of the same, to our lovit Johne Aveik, underfold of Yell, greiting: it is our will and we command yow that ye convein ane sufficient number of honest nychtbouris at the heid bull and principall hous quhilk perteinit to umquhill Peter Nisbit, upon sic lauchfull dayis as ye think expedient, all pairties haifand entres beand lauchfullie wairnit thairto as use is in siclyke causes, and thair that ye hauld ane schuind and divisioun of all the landis and louse guidis quhilkis perteinit to the umquhill Piter the tyme of his deceis, amangis his neirest and lauchfull airis, and outred ane brother for ane brother, and ane sister for ane sister, baith in landis and louse guidis, the debtis of the defunct beand first payit, according to the lawis of the cuntrie and justice, and under the paine of fourtie pundis as ye will anser to us thairupon, anent the quhilk we commit to yow our full power, be this present subscryvit with our hand at Kirkuall, the vij day of August 1605.

Orknay.
A. Martyne.

Braefield House, Dunrossness. Photocopy in SA, SA.2/261/8. See nos. 399 and 409.

403. Skalluway bankis, 9 August 1605

Disposition by Magnus Magnussone alias Linklet in Gott, taking the burden for Marione Jhonesdoghter, his spouse, to his good friend Allexander Thomasone, of 4 marks land, 6 pennies the mark, in the town of Got, in the parish of Tingwell. Precept of sasine directed to Malcolme Halcro in Linksetter.

Witnesses: Thomas Auchinlek younger, Gilbert Cantlie in Skalluwa, David Sinclere, foud of Burray, Allexander Bruce, notary public, and Johne Georgesone, writer hereof.

Sasine given at Gott on 27 September 1605 (at 8 a.m). Witnesses: William Lincleter in Urisland, Williame Tait in Tronnafirthe, Alexander Bruce, notary public, and John Georgesoun, servant of Alexander.

SRO, RH.9/15/88. The instrument of sasine is on the back.

404. Dunrosnes and Burly, 10 and 30 August 1605

Contract between Arthour Sincler of Aith, on the one part, and Mr Thomas Berclay of Colplahillis, his son-in-law, on the other part, whereby Arthour acknowledges receipt of £2,200 from Mr Thomas, and binds himself, with consent of Margaret Colvill, his spouse, and Laurence Sinclair, his eldest son, to infeft Mr Thomas in the lands of Stenswall, extending to five lasts land, 8 pennies the mark, in the parish of Woisdeall, under reversion for the said sum of £2,200. For warrandice Arthour shall infeft Mr Thomas in 2 lasts land of Hous.

Witnesses: Malcolme Sincler of Quandell, Harie Colvill, Robert Tulloch, William Fermour and James Nevin, notaries public, and James Davidsoun, writer hereof (at Dunrosnes); and (blank) Monypennie, son of the laird of Pitmillie, Henrie Colvill, brother of Margaret Colvill, and Robert Tulloch (at Burly).

SRO, RD.1/134, ff.54-5.

405. Scalloway bankis, 28 August 1605

Obligation by Magnus Olawsoun of Ilsbrughe, as principal, and Andro Giffart of Weddersta, Mr James Pitcairne, vicar of Northmaving, and Andro Edmestoun, vicar of Yell, as cautioners, to Alexander Bruce, servant of the earl of Orknay, for £400, to be paid by 31 July 1606. If Magnus, or his cautioners, pay £240 before 30 June 1606 then they shall be relieved of payment to Alexander of the foresaid principal sum.

Magnus Ilsbroch subscribes with his hand at the pen led by William Fermour, notary public. Witnesses: Malcum Sinclar of Quendaill, Edward Scollay of Strynie, William Fermour, notary, Nycoll Synclar, and Thomas Auchinlek younger, writer hereof.

SRO, RD.1/121, ff.340-1.

406. Kirkwall, 23 September 1605

Obligation by Adam Sinclar of Brow to Patrik, earl of Orknay, lord Yetland, for £1,000. For the more sure payment Adam binds himself to infeft Patrik in his lands of Brow, in the parish of Dunrosnes, under reversion for the said sum.

Witnesses: John Makcartnay, merchant in Edinburgh, James Traquair younger there, Thomas Lentrone, citizen in Sanctandrois, and James Jak, notary public, writer hereof.

SRO, RD.1/118, f.211.

407. Skalluway bankis, 23 September 1605

Wadset by Allexander Thomasoune in Laxfurd to Patrik, earl of Orknay, lord Yetland, of 4 marks land, 6 pennies the mark, in the town of Gott, in the parish of Tingwell, for payment of one penny in blench farm at Whitsunday eve, if required. The land is redeemable by 30 June 1606 for £80, failing which the heritable right of the same shall properly appertain to Patrik. Precept of sasine directed to Nicoll Thomassone in Vegnisgarthe.

Witnesses: Captain Thomas Knightsone, Patrik Ross, merchant and burgess in Abirdeine, Allexander Bruce, notary public, and Jhone Georgesone, writer hereof.

Sasine given to George Blak, procurator for Patrik, earl of Orknay, at Gott on 28 September 1605 (at 9 a.m.). Witnesses: Magnus in Gott, Rasmus in Gott, Johnne Georgesoun, and Alexander Bruce, notary public.

SRO, RH.9/15/89. The instrument of sasine is a separate document.

408. Edinburgh, 8 October 1605

Service of Robert Sinclare of Burgh, as heir of the deceased Hew Sinclare of Burgh, his father, in the lands of the barony of Burgh, viz., 36 marks land of Burgh, 33 marks land of Glaitness, 6 marks land of the great isle of Glaitness, 4 marks land of the little isle of Glaitness, 12 marks land of the great isle of Linga, 4 marks land of the little isle of Linga in Quhailsay Sound, 4 marks land of Friasetter, 6 marks land of Vassa, 1 mark land of Asweik, 1 mark land of Skellesta, 2½ marks land of Hussabuster, 3 marks land of Kirkabuster, with 1½ marks land of Levaneip, 1 mark land of Skelberrie, 3½ marks land of Newing, 2½ marks land of Grunyefirth, 3 marks land of Cleit in Quhailsay, 6 marks land of Sandweik, with another 3 marks land there, 2½ marks land of Huksettar there, 2 marks land of Levasetter there, 6 ures land of Ska there, 1 mark land of Marasetter there, ½ mark land of Burgh alias Eisterhoussis there, 30 marks 2½ ures land of Skerreis, in the parish of Nesting; 4½ marks land of Howff, with another 2 marks land there, 3 marks land of Hammagarth, 1 mark land 6 ures land of Houscoir, 4½ marks land of Skapagarth, 1 mark land of South Kirkgar, 6 marks land in Sound, 2 marks land of Cova, in the parish of Weisdaill; 3 marks land of Neisbuster, 2 marks land of Hammer, 1 mark land of Uphous, 1 mark land called Turnereis in Ustines, in the parish of Quhytenes; 12 marks land of Unyefirth, 2 marks land of Twait in Langoskaill, 2 marks land of Samlesetter, in the parish of Sandsting and Esting; 12 marks land of Browaland, 5 marks land of Curcagarth, 9 marks land of Setter, 4 marks land of Fowdasburgh, 6 marks land of Melbie in Sandnes, 6 marks land in Garmatwait, 1½ marks land of Seter, in the parish of Wallis; 6 marks land of Howland, 3 marks land of Gluss, in the parish of Northmaven; 12 marks land of Bewsetter, 15 marks land of Culbaneisburgh, 8 marks land of Hame and Hoversta, 2 marks land, in the parish and island of Bressa; 4 marks land of Burra, 3 marks land of Wedirsta, 8 marks land of Lingaholme, in the parish of Delting; 4 marks land of Sandweik, 1 mark land of Clet, in the parish of Burra; 9 marks land of (blank), in the isle of Unst; 1 mark land called Unholme, holm called Linga in Yelsound, united in the barony of Burgh;

and also 18 pennies land of Howsbie, with the island of Auskarrie, in the island of Stronsay, parish of Sanct Nicolas in Orkney; 3½ marks uthell land, 9 pennies the mark, in the town of Garth, in the parish of Nesting, acquired from George and Dionise Eduardsones, heirs of the deceased Eduard Thomassone; 2 marks 2 ures uthell land, 12 pennies the mark, in Skellinstay, and 1 mark uthell land, 9 pennies the mark, in Garth, in the parish of Nesting, acquired from Agnes Androisdochter in Skellesta.

SRO, C.22/3, f.163 (in Latin). There is a precept from chancery, 13 November 1605, for giving sasine of the lands in the barony of Burgh, in SA, GD.144/81/1.

409. Netherhouse of Kirkabister in North Yell, 10 October 1605
Schound bill of Peter Nisbet of Kirkabister.

'At the Netherhouse of Kirkabister, within the parish of North Yell, the tent day of October the year of god 1605 years; the schownd, ranking and division haldin after umquhile Peter Nisbet of Kirkabister of his lands and moveable goods devydit conform to the law amangst his usuale aires maill and femaill; that is to say Magnus and James Nisbet, Clara and Janet, brothers and sisters german borne to him of umquhile Catherine Tulloch, his first spouse; William, Gilbert and John Nisbets, brothers german, with Marion, thair sister, aires borne to him of umquhile Catrein Spence, his second spouse; Daniell and David Nisbets, Catrein, Ursula, Grizell and Agnes, brothers and sisters german, borne to him of umquhile Breta Sinclair, his last spouse: amongst the quhilk airis the divisioun underwritten was maid be John Laurensoun in Aweik, bailie of Yell, according to the commission and precept direct specially to him of ane noble and potent lord Patrik, earle of Orknay, lord Yetland, etc. to that effect; accompanyit with the honest men efter following, Andrew Edmestoune, minister of god's word at Yell, Olave Sutherland, bailie of Fetlar, William Magnussoun of Gardy, James Olavsoun, lawrichtman of Yell, William Spence of Houlland, James Spence of Midbreck, James Sutherland, lawful sone to the said Ola, James Burger and Jasper Culen, officiars, all sworne the gret aith but fear or favour to ministrat justice equallie to the parties.

'Summa Terrarum:

'Imprimus, in Netherhouse of Kirkabister, 12 marks, 9 pennies the mark; in Overhouss there, 9 marks, 9 pennies the mark; in Scammadaill, 4 marks, 6 pennies the mark; in Cunningsetter, 6 marks, 9 pennies the mark; in Sellafirth, 9 marks, 9 pennies the mark, and 6 ures; in Flugga [*rectius* Hugea? *see below]*, 1 mark, 6 pennies the mark; in Burranes, 4 marks, 9 pennies the mark; in Lumbister, 6 marks, 9 pennies the mark; in Bigsetter, 5 ures; in Hammer in Unst, 4 marks, 6 pennies the mark; in Bowaness, 1 mark, 6 pennies the mark; which lands above written being reducit to 6 pennies the mark for better devision thereof will extend to 70 marks, 6 pennies the mark.

'Summa bonorum movabilium:

'Item, 9 kyne quayes. Item, 3 stirks. Item, 40 yewis with lambs following. Item, 5 angell nobills, and in Osea Scot his hands, 6 angells. Item, 16 dollouris. Item, ane silver belt, pryssit 16 shillings, ane silver cross, four shillings, ane silver spune, pryssit 4 shillings, ane silver quhissell, ane pair silver clasps, 2 shillings, ane silver spune, two shillings. Item, 2 kettles, 6 potts, three pair of taings, and iron girdle, ane brand iron. Item, 6 tin plates, 2 pair of nebloomes, 6 tin canis, 2 washing potts, three uther potts, twa iron crocks, 3 chandleiris, ane last [*blank*] 3 [*blank*] ane ark, ane watter milne furnishit, ane feather bed, 7 bolsters, 3 beds, 3 pair blanketts, 4 braquells, ane pair of scheets. Item, ane jak, ane masher, and pair plate sleives, ane gun and sword, ane ell and doublatt, ane pair of breks, ane sow with 4 gryss, 7 geise ... ane auld sixairn boit ...

'Divisio terrarum unicuiq secundum:

'Item, to Magnus, his eldest air maill of the first marriage: in Netherhouse in Kirkabister, 6 marks, 6 pennies the mark, and in Scammadaill, 7 ures. Item, to James, his brother german: in Cunningsetter, 6 marks, 6 pennies the mark, and 7 ures. To Clara: in Netherhouss in Kirkabister, 3 marks, 6 pennies the mark, and in Scammadaill, 3 ures 1/2 ure. Item, to Janet: in Overhous, 3 marks 1 ure, and in Bigsetter, 2 ures. Item, to William, as eldest air maill of the second marriage: in Northhouss in Kirkabister, 6 marks, 6 pennies the mark, and in Scammadaill, 7 ures. Item, to Gilbert: in Overhouss there, 6 marks, and in Scammadaill, 7 ures. Item, to John: in Burranes, 6 marks, and in Overhouss in Kirkabister, 7 ures. To Marion: in Netherhouse in Kirkabister, 3 marks, and in Scammadaill, 3 ures half ure. Item, to Daniell, as eldest air maill of the last marriage: in Easterhouss in Sellafirth, 6 marks 7 ures, and in Hugea, 1 mark. To David: in Hammer in Unst, 4 marks, and in Sellafirth ... Item, to Catreen: in Overhouss in Kirkabister, 3 marks, and in Scammadaill, 3 ures half ure. To Ursula: in Sellafirth, 2 marks 6 ures, and in Lumbister, 5 ures half ure. Item, to Grissell: there also, 2 marks 6 ures, and in Lumbister, 5 ures half ure. To Agnes: in Kunningsetter, 2 marks one ure, in Bowanes in Unst, 1 mark, in Lumbister, 6 ures, and for ... 6 marks her portion equall with the rest, the brothers oblige them to mak fue to her in Lumbister, ane ure half ure lands. Item, the gold, silver and silver wark, with the moveable goods and domicile, were divided equally be the said fold and his assessors to ilk brother and brother, and to ilk sister and sister, according to the law, use and practice of the cuntrie, and ilk ane made out and out ... thairwith as well as of thair ... as their ... And all claimaris present maid out thairwith, viz. to John Magnussone and his brother, twa yewis within full [*blank*] of thair claim which this was contentit. To Magnus Johnsone for a discharge simpliciter of his claim ... To Gregorius in Burranes, 12 shillings. To Osla and Nicoll Nisbets, half mark land in Kunningsetter, and to Schewart Androsones aires in Basta, 6 shillings. Item, it was claimit be James Nisbet, the second son of the first marriage, that his umquhile father was restand to Magnus, his brother, and him, with their sisters, of umquhile Catrein Tulloch, the half of the moveables which was in the said umquhile Peter his possession the time of the decease of the said Catrein Tulloch, thair mother, together with the yeirlie profit and bygain comoditie thereof sine the time foresaid. As also was claimit certaine lambs pertaining to him and in his father's possession divers years bygane with the bygane profits thairof, quhilk was given to him be umquhile sir James Follesdaill, his gudfather. For absolving the first part of the said claim was producit ane discharge given be Magnus, his elder brother, taking the burden upon him for the time for the said James and his heall sisters, containing ane absolute discharge of all and whatsumever he for himself or they might acclaim of thair said umquhile father or his aires, be virtue of the said umquhile mother her deceis ... of house or fast gear. As the samyn of the dait at ... the 25 January 1600 years at main length purports. And as to the claim of the lambs be riscievit not, as certain number of thaim now living was 18 bi the ... it was repellent except that they satisfyit him with twa yowis with lambs for ane discharge simpliciter thairof ... Attenr was given to him for sum debt payit to him for his umquhile father in Norraway 5 ures land in Bigsetter.

'Item, fersomuckle as at the beginning of this schownd and ranking the heall aires of the first twa marriages murmurit against the gift given to the said umquhile Peter Nisbet, thair father, to the said umquhile Breta Sinclair, his last spouse, and to the aires begettin between him and her, forsameikile as efter good reasoning and mature deliberating it was found to be aprovit and allowit in the heall first aires of befar ane to be tham as the letters maid be tham thairupon under thair subscription manuall purportit. They all with ane voice and ane ... all was content and understandit it should stand for the said Breta and her aires as the letter of gift maid thereupon to her purportit and never to be reclainit be tham nor none of thair aftercomers under the paine of ... and defamation. Quhilk by the judge and assessors forsaid was given for doom.

'A. Edmonstoune, minister.
With my hand.

'Nn. Neven,
pro tempore scriba.'

The original is not known to exist. The above transcription, by Francis Grant, is in *SN*, 1 and 8 January 1898. See nos. 399 and 402.

410. November 1605

'Charter by Francis Sinclair of Uyea, and James Sinclair, his brother german, to William Bruce of Symbister, their father-in-law, of 3 merks and 1 merk in Balzesta, and 2 merks in Mewlay, in island of Unst. ...

Witnesses: James in Balzea, Gilbert Williamson. Alexander Bruce, NP. Sasine annexed, dated November 1605.'

The original is not known to exist. The above abstract, by Francis Grant, is in OSD, *SN*, 27 January 1894.

411. Cannogait, 11 November 1605

Contract between Patrik, earl of Orknay, lord Yetland, on the one part, and William Bruce of Symbestar, on the other part, whereby the contract between Patrik and William, dated 5 August 1604 (no. 391), is annulled. Patrik shall grant of new to William 20 marks land of Soundburgh, together with all right, title and kindness of the 4 marks land called the provestis landis, lying runrig with the said lands of Soundburgh, and 20 marks land of Scatnes, with reservation of the right and title of the house lately built by Patrik on the ground of the lands of Soundburgh, on the south side of the Newhall, together with a yard adjacent thereto at the south-east gable thereof, and pasturage of 2 ky and 2 oxen in the summer, and pasturage of 20 wedders within the boundary of the lokitnes of Scatnes, at the times when Patrik resides at the foresaid house and fortalice of Soundburgh. In Patrik's absence William shall have the keeping of the house and yard, and be answerable to Patrik for the plenishings, etc., and be free of all such pasturage. The lands shall be held in feu farm and heritage for yearly payment of 13 lispunds 8 marks butter and 13 shillings 2 cuttles wadmell, with the scat and wattle thereof 'usit and wont', together with 3s.4d. for the old feu duty and augmentation, and also giving three suits at the head courts in Yetland yearly. Patrik undertakes to remove himself, his tenants, servants, chamberlain, and especially Malcolme Sinclair, and all other possessors of the lands of Soundburgh, Underhoull, Scatnes and provestis lands, and to enter William by 25 November 1605, and to deliver to him the corns which grew upon the ground of Sumburgh this present year and which were put in the barns and barnyards thereof. It is agreed that Patrik shall have full right to receive and uplift the whole profits and commodities of all Orknay and Caithnes fisher boats, with privileges of lodges to the said boats upon the ground of the lands of Soundburgh for their ground leave yearly during the time of the fishing, to be built above the sand mark by the said fishers conform to use and wont, and William binds himself to give them ground leave to that effect, and for upholding of the said lodges to cast 'fuill and devot' on the ground of Soundburgh or Scatnes according to use and wont, and Patrik shall cause the fishers to keep William's corns, meadow and grass from all destruction and scathe that may befall thereto by the said fishers and their goods, and by occasion of making of 'unlaid gaittis and passages' through the said corns, meadows and grass which were not there before. Patrik and the fishers are to pretend no right or interest in the lands of Soundburgh by reason of the privilege foresaid, but only to the fishers' lodges and that during the summer season only. William binds himself to renounce in favour of Patrik the 2 lasts of land in Sandweik, and to enter Patrik in possession thereof with the corns thereupon as soon as William is entered in possession of Soundburgh; and forasmuch as William paid Patrik 20 angel nobles or 160 merks money for the lands called the provestis lands before the contract of 1604, William now binds himself to pay Patrik the said sum yearly so long as he shall possess the said lands called the provestis lands, but if William is evicted from the said lands by any person then he shall no longer be obliged to make payment of the said 20 angels.

Written by Harbert Dwne, servant of Mr James Harlaw, writer in Edinburgh. Witnesses: James Sinclair of Murkill, Hew Halcro fiar of that ilk and James Annand, servant of Patrik.

SRO, RD.1/113, ff.132-8. There is an extracted copy in SA, D.8/6. The feu charter in favour of William Bruce of Symbister is dated 15 November 1605 (*RMS*, vi, no.1679).

412. Kirkwall, 20 January 1606

'Charter by James Chalmer, brother german to Magnus Chalmer in Setter, sometime servitor to Patrick, earl of Orkney, to William Bannatyne of Gairsay, in name of Isobel Pollok, his spouse, and John Bannatyne, his son, of a tenement in Scalloway. ...

Witnesses: William Carmichael, merchant, Daniel ... , NP, James Jack, NP, Oliver Kennedie, Andro Bruce of Westermail in Burray, Captain Adam Loutrain [*rectius* Allan Lentrain], bailie in Kirkwall, Thomas Young, merchant, and others.'

'Sasine dated 15th September, 1608: compeared Alexander Johnstoun alias Laxford, bailie for James Chalmer [*designed as above*], holding a precept of sasine in his hands, and passed to the tenement of land in Scalloway, having the burn of Scalloway on the east, and Thomas Boyne's tenement on the west; also compeared Mr Andrew Umphray of Berrie, attorney specially constitute by Isobel Pollok, spouse to William Bannatyne of Gairsay, and Mr Walter ..., attorney for John Bannatyne, her second son, proceeding on charter by the said James Chalmer to the said Isobel Pollok, in liferent, and John Bannatyne in fee, said tenement to be held of the earl. [The precept is] written by George Ogstoun, servitor to William Bannatyne of Gairsay. Witnesses: Andrew Bruce in Westermail in Burra and others.

Sasine given in presence of Mr Robert Ramsay, minister of Walls, Henry Steinson, merchant, Edward Scolla, sheriff deput of Orkney, Malcolm Halcro, Mans Halcro in Ollaberry, Nicoll in Walsett, and James Neven, NP.'

The originals are not known to exist. The above abstracts, by Francis Grant, are in OSD, *SN*, 27 January 1894.

413. Edinburgh, 23 January 1606

Decreet of court of session in action at instance of Laurence Bruce of Cultemalyndie, Andro Bruce of Scatsta, Andro Giffert in Waddersta, John Mowat, apparent of Howgaland, John Giffert in Boista, Edward Sinclair in Neschin, Andro Haik in Scatsta, Olla Cull in (blank), Alexander Isbister in Hardwell, Iner Nicolsoun in Burrowness, John Wilsoun there, and Magnus Irwing in Laxo, and the other parishioners of Delting, against Alexander Kincaid, on the one part, who alleges he has been provided of old to the vicarage of Scatza and Delting, and Mr Gilbert Mowat, on the other part, who alleges he has been provided to the vicarage by Patrik, earl of Orknay, lord Yetland, for troubling the pursuers for payment of the vicarage teinds and fruits of the crop 1604.

The lords of council decern the pursuers to pay the teinds and fruits to Alexander Kincaid, who has best right thereto conform to a decreet of the lords of council given in his favour of the date 27 December 1589.

SRO, CS.7/218, ff.253-4; SRO, CS.290/26 (5 March 1605).

414. Edinburgh, 30 January 1606

Decreet of court of session in action at instance of Malcolm Sinclar, Thomas Cheyne, Harie Cheyne, Christopher Lauristoun, Walter Scot, Andro Wischart, Andro Stewart, and the other parishioners of Wallis, Wallay and Foulay, against Alexander Kincaid, servitor of John, commendator of Halyrudhous, on the one part, who alleges he has been provided of old to the vicarage, and Robert Swyntoun, on the other part, who alleges he has right to the teinds of the vicarage, for troubling the pursuers for payment of the teinds of the crop 1604.

The lords of council decern the pursuers to pay the teinds to Alexander Kincaid, who has best right thereto conform to the gift granted by Adam, bishop of Orknay of the said vicarage on 21 June 1567.

SRO, CS.7/218, ff.286-7; SRO, CS.290/26 (25 April 1605).

415. Edinburgh, 17 February 1606

Testament of Hew Sinclare of Burgh

The testament dative and inventar of the guidis, geir, sowmes of mony and dettis pertening to umquhile Hew Sinclare of Burgh within the parochin of Nesting and sherefdome of Yetland in Orknay the tyme of his deceis, quha deceisit in the moneth of December the yeir of god 1602 yeiris, faythfulie maid and gevin up be Jane Bruce, his relict spous, in name and behalf of Laurence, Hew, Hary, Alexander and Dorathie Sinclares, thair laufull bairnis, executors datives decernit to thair said umquhile fader be decreit of the commissar of Edinburgh, as the samyn decreit of the dait at Edinburgh the [*blank*] day of Februar the year of god 1606 yeiris at lenth proportis.

In the first the said umquhile Hew Sinclare of Burgh had the guidis, geir, sowmes of mony and dettis of the availl and prices eftir following pertening to him the tyme of his deceis foirsaid, viz., item, upoun the ground and landis of Burgh, 12 wark horssis, price of the pece ourheid £6, summa £72; item, mair upoun the said ground and landis, 16 milk kye and yeild, price of the pece ourheid £10, summa £160; item, mair upoun the said ground and landis, 10 oxin, price of the pece ourheid £12, summa £120; item, mair upoun the said ground and landis, 300 yowis and yeild scheipe, price of the pece ourheid £1, summa £300; item, in the barne and barneyard of Burgh, 23 bollis beir, price of the boll with the fodder £5, summa £115; item, mair, ane fischer bot with four airis, price £12; item, mair, ane uthir fyschear boit of sex airis, price thairof £18; item, mair, ane uthir boit callit the *Hew*, haveing fyve airis, price thairof £30; item, upoun the ground and landis of Beinstay, 12 milk ky and yeild, price of the pece ourheid £10, summa £120; item, mair thair, 4 oxin, price of the pece ourheid £12, summa £48; item, mair thair, 6 wark horssis, price of the pece ourheid £6, summa £36; item, mair in the said barne and barneyaird, 12 bollis beir, price of the boll with the fodder £5, summa £60; item, mair thair, ane fischar boit of four airis, price thairof £12; item, mair thair, ane uthir boit of sex airis, price thairof £18; item, upoun the ground and landis of Garth, 12 milk ky and yeild, price of the pece ourheid £10, summa £120; item, mair thair, 4 oxin, price of the pece ourheid £12, summa £48; item, 4 horssis, price of the pece ourheid £6, summa £24; item, mair in the said barne and barneyaird, 12 bollis beir, price of the boll with the fodder £5, summa £60; item, upoun the ground and landis of Sandwick in Quhailsay, 8 ky, price of the pece ourheid £10, summa £80; item, mair thair, 4 oxin, price of the pece £12, summa £48; item, 2 horssis, price of the pece £6, summa £12; item, mair thair, 60 scheipe young and auld, price of the pece ourheid £1, summa £60; item, ane fischear boit thair with four airis, price thairof £12; item, ane uthir boit thair with sex airis, price thairof £18; item, upoun the ground and landis of Mekill Linga in Quhailsay Sound, 200 scheipe, price of the pece ourheid £1, summa £200; item, mair, 20 stottis and quoyis of tua yeir auldis thair, price of the pece ourheid £4, summa £80; item, upoun the ground and landis of Skairis, 10 ky milk and yeild, price of the pece ourheid £10, summa £100; item, 4 oxin price of the pece £12, summa £48; item, mair thair, 60 scheipe, price of the pece ourheid £1, summa £60; item, in the saidis barnes and barneyairdis, threschin and unthreschin, 12 bollis beir, price of the boll with the fodder £5, summa £60; item, 600 salt fische, keling and ling, price of the hundreth £20, summa £120; item, mair, ane fyschir boit of sex airis, price thairof £18;

item, mair thair, ane uthir boit of four airis, price £12; item, upoun the ground and landis of Flewgairth, 200 scheipe young and auld, price of the pece ourheid £1, summa £200; item, upoun the ground and landis of Strolme and Linga, 16 ky, price of the pece ourheid £10, summa £160; item, mair thair, 12 oxin, price of the pece ourheid £12, summa £144; item, mair thair, 6 horssis and mares, price of the pece ourheid £6, summa £36; item, mair thair, 20 yowis, price of the pece ourheid £1, summa £20; item, 3 fischer boittis, price of the pece £12, summa £36; item, upoun the ground and landis of Bigay, 6 ky, price of the pece ourheid, £10, summa £60; item, mair thair, 3 oxin, price of the pece ourheid £12, summa £36; item, mair thair, 40 scheipe, price of the pece ourheid £1, summa £40; item, mair thair, ane fyschear boit, price £12; item, upoun the ground and landis of Colbinsburgh in Brassay, 4 ky, price of the pece ourheid £10, summa £40; item, 4 oxin, price of the pece ourheid £12, summa £48; item, mair, 2 wark horssis, price of the pece ourheid £6, summa £12; item, upoun the ground and landis of Swynnessettaris Brut, 50 scheipe, price of the pece ourheid £1, summa £50; item, in the toun of Burgh, 28 barrellis of butter, price of the barrell £20, summa £560; item, 16 barrellis of oyllie, price of the barrell £18, summa £288; item, mair, 120 of gulyennis of hard fische, price of the gulyenn £1, summa £120; item, 26 packis of wadmell, price of ilk pack £10, summa £260; item, mair, 6 daiker of hydis, price of the daiker £15, summa £90; item, 20 bollis of greit salt, price of the boll £1, summa £20; item, mair, 16 hering nettis, price of the nett 10 merks, summa 160 merks; item, in utencilis and domicelis with the abuilyementis of his bodie, by the airschip estimat to the sowme of £100 mony.

Summa of the inventar: £4,727 13s.4d.

Followis the dettis awin to the deid:

Item, thair was awin to the said umquhile Hew Sinclare of Burgh, of Thomas Schewin in Valley, the sowme of £80; item, be Olla Suderland in Fitlar, 38 gulyennis of hardfische, price of the gulyenn £1, summa £38; item, be Mathew Forrester in Lunasting, £160 mony.

Summa of the dettis awin to the deid: £278.

Summa of the inventar with the dettis: £5,005 13s.4d.

To be dividit in thrie partis, deidis part is £1,668 11s.1d.

Quhairof the quot is componit for £60.

We, Mr Johne Arthour, etc., understanding that eftir dew summoning and laufull warning maid be forme of edict oppinlie as effeiris, etc., we decernit thairintill as our decreit gevin thairupoun beiris, conforme to the quhilk we, in our soverane lordis name and auctoritie, makis, etc., quhairupoun Laurence Sinclare [*rectius* Bruce] of Coupmalundie is becum cautioun, etc., as ane act beiris.

SRO, CC.8/8/41, ff.97-8.

416. Norbie, 25 February 1606

Wadset by Mathew Forrester to Olave Sinclair, his brother-in-law, of 3 marks land, 9 pennies the mark, in Clowstay, in the parish of Aythsting, for £48. Precept of sasine.

Mathew subscribes with his hand at the pen led by John Sutherland, vicar of Aythsting and Sandsting. Witnesses: Mr James Pitcairne, vicar of Northmaving, Mr Gilbert Mowat, minister at Delting, Mr William Hay, and James Mowat.

SA, D.16/389/4.

417. Bakasound, 18 July 1606

Disposition by Rasmes Olaysone, heritor of ½ mark land, 12 pennies the mark, in Sand, in the parish of Sandsting, to his well-beloved friend Jarome Umphray of Sand, of his 'rycht and kyndnes bayth of landis and lous guidis', with power to Jarome 'to call, follow and perschew for my haill airschip and bairnis part of gair'.

Because he has no signet Rasmes causes his master Johnne Oleffsone of Mustard to set his signet hereto. Witnesses: Eduard Sinclair of Bulyeseter, Hary Chyne, Jarome Tait, skipper, Henrie Sinclair, with divers others.

SA, GD.144/186/27. Jarome Tait's mark.

418. Skalloway bankis, 24 July 1606

Contract between Andro Umphray of Berry, on the one part, and Janet Jamesone, his mother, liferenter of Berry, on the other part, whereby Janet renounces her liferent and conjunct fee lands in the mainland of Yetland, disponed to her by the deceased Andro Umphray, her husband, and surrogates Andro, her son, in her place, and binds herself to leave to him after her decease the 'haill insicht, plenissing, moveable goods and gear that sall appertene to her at her departure, the abulyement of her awin body only exceptit'. Andro binds himself to pay Janet, his mother, yearly for her lifetime, the sum of £100, together with 1 barrel salt beef, ½ barrel salt mutton, 6 reestit muttons, ½ barrel meat butter, 1 barrel salt fish, 3 dozen dry fish, ½ barrel herring, and 4 lispunds wool, at her own dwelling house in Aberdene, or at the dwelling house of James Neven or William Makertny in Leyth. If the said sum of £100 and gear is not able to sustain Janet 'in the rank of ane honest woman' then Andro shall pay her as much more as four honest friends chosen equally between them estimate that she ought to have. In the case of non-payment Andro binds himself to repossess Janet in the rooms of Houll, Berry, Astay and Burvein 'in als guid ane estait and als weill plenissit as they ar for the present'.

Witnesses: Jherome Umphray of Sand, Gilbert Giffert in Sandes, James

Neven, indweller in Leyth, writer hereof, Walter Thomesone, burgess of Aberdene, and Hendrie Lindesay, mariner in Dundy.

SRO, RD.1/157, ff.257-8.

419. Burghe, 7 August 1606

Disposition by Lawrence Sinclair of Gott, to James Sinclair, his eldest lawful son, and Cristiane Sinclair, spouse of James, in fulfilment of matrimonial contract, of 21 marks udal land and 2 marks feued land of Gott 'with the manor place, onsettis and plenesing presentlie thairupone', 20 marks udal land of Nether Scoland 'with the plenesing presentlie thairupone, reservand to me induring my lyftyme as is heireftir reservit', 9½ marks feued land of Southhous in Scatnes, 14 marks udal land and 10 marks feued land in Over Scoland, 1½ marks udal land of Tolhoip, 1½ marks udal land in Lie, 6 marks udal land of Lobell, 1 mark udal land of Daill, 14 marks udal land of Midbrek in Exingabow, 1 mark udal land in Northbrek there, 1 mark udal land of Ringista there, all 6 pennies the mark, 7 marks udal land, 12 pennies the mark, in Galone in the Fair Ile, all in the parish of Dunrosnes, with reservation to Lawrence during his lifetime of 'the east tofall of the maner place of Gott, the haill est lugeis in the nes withe the houssis of Wirkie and haill remanent landis abonewreattin, exceptand onlie the saidis twentie thre mark land of Gott and twentie markis land of Nether Scoland with the plenesing, maner place and pertinentis thairof abonewreattin, exceptand befoir exceptit'. Precept of sasine directed to James Wischert, burgess of Dysert, to be given on the lands of Gott by deliverance to James and Christiane of 'erth, stane, ane rip of corne, and the kruk of the yett of Gott'.

Lawrence affixes his proper seal of arms. Witnesses: Androw Bruce of Sandvick, James Sinclair of Rapness, James Neven, indwellar in Leithe, Petir Symsone, minister at Nesting, and Hew Tarrell, servant of Robert Sinclair of Burghe, writer hereof.

SA, SC.12/65/1/56.

420. Soundburgh, 27 August 1606

Discharge by Walter Ritchie, servant of Sir John Arnote of Berswik, knight, to Magnus Olawsone of Ilisburgh.

Be it kend till all men be this present letter me Walter Ritchie, servitor to Sir John Arnote of Berswik, knycht, and haveing full power and commission of my guid freind David Dewar, burges in the Cannongate, to compone, transact and aggrie with Magnus Olawsone of Ilisburgh and his cautioneris of sic sowmes of money as thay wer bind be thair letters obligatoris beiris to Alexander Bruce, servitor to the erle of Orknay; and David Dewar beand lawfullie constitute assignay; be the tennour heirof grantis me to have receavit fra the handis and delyverance of the said Magnus the sowme of threttein scoir four punds guid and usuall money of the realme of Scotland, and that in compleit payment of the haill sowme contenit in his obligatioun aggreit and componit be me according to my commissioun thairanent, quhairof I hald me weill content, satisfeit and payit, and exhoneris, quytcleamis and frielie discharges the said Magnus and his saids cautioneris of the foirsaid sowme of threttein scoir four punds for now and ever, in toikin quhairof I haif deliverit to the said Magnus the registrat obligatioun with ane assignatioun maid be Alexander Bruce to that effect and the letters of horning; and gif neid beis I sall report ane sufficient dischairge of the said David Dewaris to that effect.

Subscrivit with my hand at Soundburgh, the xxvij of August the yeir of god Jaj VJc and sex yeiris. Beffoir thir witnessis: William Bruce of Simbester, William Fermour, fold of Dunrosnes, Alexander Murchesoun, Alexander Fordyce, with utheris.

Williame Fermour, notar publict, witness

W. Ritchie with my hand
W. Bruce of Simbister, witnes
Allexander Murquhosone, witnes

SA, GD.144/61/27.

421. Cultmalindie, 2 November 1606

Obligation by Adam Sinclair of Brow to the right honourable Laurence Bruce of Cultmalindies, for £804 13s.4d. Adam binds himself to make payment by 8 November 1607, and for security suspends and discharges the reversion granted by Laurence to him for the redemption of 10 marks land, 6 pennies the mark, in the isle of Havray, in the parish of Burray, and 4 marks land, 9 pennies the mark, in the town of Rairwik, in the parish of Dunrosnes, so that Laurence shall possess the foresaid lands until Adam pays him the said sum of £804 13s.4d., together with the sum of 200 merks contained in the reversion.

Witnesses: Mr Alexander Bruce, fiar of Cultmalindies, Robert Sinclair in Peill, Henrie Wardlaw, messenger, and David Rollok, notary, writer hereof.

SRO, RD.1/138, ff.348-9.

422. Cultiswick, 15 November 1606

Disposition by Elene and Guthroun Olavesdochteris in Cultiswick, with consents of their husbands Magnus and Olave Johnesones, to their good friend Jherome Umphray of Sand, of ½ mark land, 12 pennies the mark, in the town of Uttersand, in the parish of Sandsting. Precept of sasine.

The granters subscribe with their hands at the pen led by Johne Sutherland, minister of God's word at Aythsting and Sandsting. Witnesses: William Sinclair of Rawick, Gilbert Mattreyth in Quhytisnes, William Wilsoun in Wester Skeld, Nichole Johnson in Gruting, Malcolme Sutherland, Olav Yelt, Robert Watsoun, and Patrik Broun, cooper.

SA, GD.144/9/22. Marks of William Sinclair, William Wilsoun and Olav Yelt.

423. Cultiswick, 15 November 1606

Disposition by Magnus Olavesone in Hestinsetter to his well-beloved friend Jherome Umphray of Sand, and Margaret Murray, his spouse, of ½ mark land, 9 pennies the mark, in the north last of Cultiswik, parish of Sandsting, for payment yearly at Whitsunday to the superior of the country of one penny, if required. Precept of sasine.

Magnus subscribes with his hand at the pen led by Johne Sutherland, minister at Aythsting and Sandsting. Witnesses: William Sinclair in Rawik, Gilbert Mattrayth in Quhytisnes, William Wilsone in Wester Skeld, Nichole Johnsone in Gruting, Malcolme Sutherland, Olave Yelt, and Robert Watsone, with Patrik Broun, cooper.

SA, GD.144/19/18.

424. Edinburgh, 6 December 1606

Summons at instance of Magnus Jacobsoun in the isle of Vemendrie, as father, Erasmus Magnussone and (Nicoll) Magnussone, as brothers, with the remaining kin and friends of the deceased Nicoll Magnussone, and Sir Thomas Hamiltoun of Monkland, king's advocate, for his interest, against Henry Wardlaw in (blank), servant of Laurence Bruce of Cultmalindie, who with his complices in December 1601 set upon the said Nicoll on the lands of Vemendrie, and with 'ane gritt rung or battone, sword or dager, hurt and woundit him in his heid, legis and armes, and strak him thairwith crewallie to the eard, and be the said straikis and woundis maist crewallie and schamefullie and tyrannouslie slew and murdreist the said umquhile Nukall under silence and clud of nycht, and thaireftir kaist him ower ane craig in the sea, sua that nane sould haif suspectit him to haif done sa villanus a murthour, bot that he had drownet him self desperatlie and wilfullie'.

Henry Wardlaw is charged to find caution to the justice clerk that he shall compear before the justice in the tolbooth of Edinburgh on 13 January 1607, and underlie the law for the said murder.

SRO, JC.26/4/6. In the diets of the justiciary court Henry Wardlaw vigorously protested his innocence and after several adjournments the action was deserted on 7 January 1608 (SRO, JC.2/4, ff.151, 162, 163, 167, 182 and 204; SRO, JC.26/5/2). According to a bond of caution by Laurence Bruce of Cultmalindie, on 13 July 1602, Nicoll Mansoun, the youngest son of Magnus in Vemendrie, was shepherd to 'my lord of Orknay' (SRO, JC.19/3). See no. 435.

425. Houss in Burray, 11 January 1607

Obligation by Frances Sinclar of Uyea to Laurence Sinclar of Houss, whereby Frances acknowledges receipt of £300, and binds himself to deliver to Laurence a charter upon his 16 marks land, 9 pennies the mark, in the town of Kirkhous in Olnafirth, in the parish of Delting.

Witnesses: Robert Tulloch in Northbister, Hew Sinclar, son of James Sinclar of Maill, and Niniane Neven, son of Johne Neven of Skowsbruch.

SRO, CC.17/5/1, ff.32-3. The deed warrant is extant (OA, SC.11/5/1607/2).

426. Hamnavo, 26 January 1607

Disposition by Bodwell Erasmussone to the honourable William Bruce of Symbister, of ½ mark land, 8 pennies the mark, in Hamnavo. Precept of sasine.

Bodwell subscribes with his hand led at the pen by Andro Edmestoune, minister of Yell. Witnesses: Jhone Edmestoune, Allexander Murkesone, Jhone Lawrensone, bailie, and James Ollasone, lawrightman.

SA, D.8/7/1.

427. Hamervo, 27 January 1607

Contract between William Bruce of Symbester, on the one part, and Manes Thomasone in Hamervo, on the other part, whereby William sets in tack his udal lands in Hamervo, 'and samekill as he may get to by or to possess in the foirsaid towne, togidder with four mark cloaster land, for full deutie usit and wont, to be payit yeirlie be the said Manis and his eftercummiris for all the spaice and termes of fyve yeris nixt and immediatlie to follow heireftir; And because the said Williame haid his plenissing upone the said rowme, he hes set to the said Manss fyve guid and sufficient ky, togidder with fourtie yewis and yeir auld hogis with fourtie scheipe, viz. twentie-four yowis guid and sufficient and sextein hogis, with ane sufficient utyoik oxe, with ane sufficient oxe backeoutyeok, ane horss, ane meir with ane fole at hir fote, ane gaite thrie yeir auld, and tua getts yeris auld, foure brode geis, ane ganner, ane hen, nyne leispound beare and sextene leaspound aeittis, tua mekill kistis, ane lytill kist, ane meit buird and burd triestis, fyve pair of meassis and tua clokis, tua speiddes, ane sufficient cutter and sock, ane guid and sufficient girss sye with ane uthir thak sye, ane pleuche at eardreis with sky mischell; Quhilk haill geir abonewreittin I the said Manss grantis me presentlie to haif ressavit, bindin and obleiss me and my aris and eftercummeris to thankfullie delyver bakagane ilk beist of the lyk valedetie and guidnis as I haif ressavit the samen, upone the fyftein day of Apryle to the said William Bruce or any in his name; And sall fodir the foirsaids kye and oxin to pleuche be rassin as the said William hes done unto me at the full iche of the outrynning of my takis, and premonition to be made be ather of the saidis parteis fourtie days befoir the feist of Hallowmes at the said tyme of ichew; And the rest of the geir callit plenissing sall delvyer as guid as I haif ressavit it, and sall pay yeirlie to the said William and his foirsaidis, for the profeitt of his fyve kye, ten guid and sufficient leaspound butter, and for the hyre of his said tua oxin yeirly, gulyeonis usit and wont, and for the profeit of his scheipe sall pay yeirlie twelff guid and sufficient slauchter muttone with ane leaspond woll, and for the profeit of his geis, sex geis yeirlie, and for the profeitt of his swyne, ane slauchter tua yeir auld swyne yeirlie, quhilkis failyeand bindiss and obleiss me, my aris and assignayis to pay to the said William and his foirsaids the hiest mercat price thairof, and obleiss me to be ane thankfull tennent to my maister and his servandis as guid ocaseon sall urge thame. Forder it is specallie agreit upone betuix the tua parteis that the said Manss sall nether sell ... nor dispone his udell landis in Hamirwo bot to the said William and his foirsaidis for full landis pryce, gif it sall happin the said Mans or his foirsaidis to cum in sic necessetie; And nane of the parteis to cum in the contrair heirof under the pane of all thair movable guids and geir, and tinsill of the samin the ane halff to the king and the uther halff to the persewer; Promesand be the faith and treuth of thair bodeis to hald firme and stabill'.

Andro Edmendstoun, 'wrytar of Yell and notar', subscribes for Mans. Witnesses: John Edmeistoun, Alexander Murequhowsone, writer hereof, John Awick, foud of Yell, James Suarisetter, and Gearth in Brugh.

SRO, RD.1/148, ff.157-8. 'Hamervo' is an error for Hamnavoe, in South Yell (and cf. next item).

428. Hamnevo, 29 January 1607

Disposition by Manss Thomassone to William Bruce, of ½ mark land, 6 pennies the mark, in Murresetter, and ½ mark land in Hamnevo in Yell. Precept of sasine.

Manss requires Allexander Murquhowsone to subscribe in his name. Manss Thomassone and Christifer Jonissone affix their marks. Witnesses: James Sinclair, (torn) Vowrk, and Ola Bodwelsone.

GH. Marks of Manss Thomassone and Cristifer Jonissone.

429. Edinburgh, 10 February 1607

Decreet arbitral by Andro, Lord Stewart of Ochiltrie, Walter, lord of Blantyre, George Sincler of Mey, and David, bishop of Ross, arbiters chosen by Patrik, earl of Orknay, lord Yetland, and Adame Sincler of Brow, in terms of submission, dated 30 January 1607, anent all actions, causes, quarrels, controversies and debates standing between them. The arbiters decern that Adame discharges Patrik of all debts, actions of spulyie, etc., raised by Adame against Patrik, and that Adame shall pay Patrik the sum of £1,000, for which causes Patrik shall enter Adame to the actual real and peaceable possession of his lands and possessions of Brow whereof he was in possession when he was exiled from Yetland, excepting the tack and steading of Sandweik, by 31 March 1607, under pain of £1,000, and that the decreet of banishment given and pronounced by Patrik against Adame for participation in the alledged slaughter of Mathow Sincler is null and void, and ordains Patrik 'to delyte the samen out of the buiks of office'. The arbiters ordain the obligation made by Adame to Patrik, for £1,000, dated 23 September 1605, to be discharged, and ordain all writs consigned by Adame for obtaining of suspension to be given up to him, and of all other bonds, obligations, and actions of spulyie which Patrik can or may lay to the charge of Adame, and especially that (1) an assignation by William Sincler of Ustaness of £100 with an annual rent of 1 barrel butter furth of the isle of Havarie granted by the deceased James Sincler of Brow, (2) an assignation by Henrie Sincler of Gruitting to Patrik of 13 angel nobles with an annual rent of £18 granted by Adame, and (3) an assignation by David Wilson of Skalloway banks to Patrik of an obligation for £160 owing by Adame to Robert Wilsone, father of said David, be discharged. Patrik is to fortify, maintain and defend Adame in his lawful affairs and business.

Written by David Heart, writer in Edinburgh.

SRO, RD.1/131, ff.61-4.

430. [10] February 1607

'Disposition by Francis Sinclair of Uyea to Laurence Sinclair, appearand of Houss, of land in Olnafirth. ...

'Witnesses: Malcolm Sinclair of Quendale, Mr James Pitcairn, vicar of Northmaven, Mr Gilbert Mowat, and Gilbert Cantlie, writer thereof.'

The original is not known to exist. The above abstract, by Francis Grant, is in OSD, *SN*, 27 January 1894. According to another abstract, in a late 17th century Inventory of writs in the custody of Laurence Sinclair of Sandsound (GH), the document was a wadset of 16 merks land, 9d. the merk, in Kirkhouse in Olnafirth, for the sum of 500 merks. The date is also taken from the latter abstract.

431. 13 March 1607

Schound bill of James Spence of Midbrak.

The schound and rakning haldin efter James Spence of Midbrak, the xiij of March 1607.

Stuborne that they salbe oblisit na thing to him, and ordanis the land to pas in devisioune.

Devisioune:

Item, it is decernit to Katrin Manissdochter the relict of the said umquhill Jamis the equall half, conforme to thair contract matrimoniall: viz. xxj mark half mark land layand in [*torn*] all pertinentis, in Snawbruch iiij mark, in Setter iiii mark, in Collvasetter ½ mark, in Vatqui ½ mark, in Torwes iiij mark.

Item, to Georg as eldist brother iiij mark in Houland, twa mark ½ in North Brak, in Kirkatoune ij mark ij uoris.

Item, to David, the youngist brother, in Northbrak vj mark ½, in Kirkatowne j mark j uour, and in Gardone j mark.

Item, to Maruwne, thair sister, iiij mark ij uoris layand in Kirkatewne in Unst.

Item, forsamekill as be the said Katrines lyfrent the haidbull is in hir handis, ordanis the said Georg, efteir the deces of the said Katrin his mother, to his haid bull in Midbrak d[*torn*]d to pass frome the ij mark ½ in Northbrak to his brother David to be his haid booll, and the said Georg to have twa mark ½ mark of the redeist of the said Katrinis layfrent thairfor, as also ordanis the said Katrin, Georg and David, upone thair expensis, to upmak sick houses in Northbrak to the said David as is in Midbrak.

The inventarie of the movabill guddis and gaeir:

Item, ten oxin iij there [*sic*] yeir awld, xiij ky, iij quoyokis thrie yeir awld, iiij quoyokis twa yeir awld, vj [*blank*], fayve wark horsis, iiij merris yung and auld, four lambe of teind in Yell, ane lamb ½ in Setter in Unst. Item, of yeld schip, ane sex haring bot at viij lib., x buchtis of lynis at iij gullionis; Item, ane half barrall ule at vj gullionis; Item, xij barrall of vyet aitis at xxiiij gullionis; Item, aucht barrall of beair at xxiiij gullionis; aduce [*rectius* adhuc?] in Setter four barrell eattis at viij gullionis. The insicht comprysit to viij gullionis.

[*torn*] to the deid:

Fetlar: Item, awin be Willam of Hamer, ij gullionis; [*torn*]l Jhonesone in Urie, ij gullionis; N[*torn*] Gibhouse, j gullion; Olla Grigorussone in Daill, j gullion; Marioune Eklagarth, ½ gullion, Johne Litillaland, ½ gullion; Lowaranc in Daill, j gullion.

Unst: Henray Willamsone, xij gullionis; Olla Snawabroch, j gullion ½; Androw in Gardie, ix s.

Yell: Gilbirt Nisbit, iij gullionis; Nicoll in Volasta, iij gullionis.

Mainland: Androw in Sellsetter for ane bot, vij gullionis; Thomas in Houland in Northmavin, j gullion ½.

Dettis awine be the deid:

Item, to Jaspart in Birroune, xl gullionis; to Marioune Lawrencdochter, viij gullionis; to Yane the marchant, ix gullionis; to Thamas in Daill, j gullion ½; to Martin Mowat, v s.; to Janat in Snarravo, j gullion; to Olla

Turvollsone, j gullion; to Lowrance in Burro, j gullion; to Olla Urovingsone, ij lispund butter, ij shilling wadmell; to Olla Clougone, j gullion ½.

Anent the clame of half mark land laying in Ure in Fetlar, acclemit be Georg Spenc frome Willame Spenc and [*torn*] airis of umquhill David Spenc, quhilk half merk land wes gifin in airschip to the said umquhil James, togiddir with the bayru[n] landmaillis; forsamekill as Jamis Spenc now of Gluip and Walter Scot cravis the [*illegible*] land maillis in Kirkatoune awine for four yeiris, and forsamekill as the said land lay lei, yet the said Geo[rg] decernit to allow ij gullionis to the said Jamis, and ordanis William Spenc and the forsaid airis to pay sax gullionis of bayrunnis for the said half mark in Ure, and to bay ane thrid of ane mark of land to the said Georg.

Item, as for devisioune of the gair, it is apoyntit that the airis maeill, viz. Georg and David, have thair he[*torn*] extending to iij^{XX} gullionis ilk ane, as Arthour Phriser thair brother in law hes resevit, and tharefteir to pairt the rest in halveris, viz. to Kattrin thair mother in layferent the ane half, the uther half to keip equalie amangis them, ane brother for brother, and the sister ane sister pairt, at the sicht of th[*torn*] above wretine.

J. Edmonstoune [*torn*] of Yell
A. Edmestoune
minister at Yell
as witnes

W. Scot, witnes
J. Sutherland, witnes
[*illegible*] Swarisetter
Daniell Nessbet
[*illegible*]
[in witness]

SA, D.12/19/1. The document is badly torn: some reconstruction of the text has been attempted.

432. Edinburgh, 14 March 1607

Decreet of court of session in action at instance of Henry Wardlaw, messenger, servitor to Laurence Bruce of Cultmalyndeis, against Patrik, earl of Orknay, lord Yetland, James Esplane, his officer, Magnus Bryngalsoun in Efert, Nicoll and John Magnussounis, his sons, Olay Sutherland, underfoud in Fetler, for wrongous eviction, on 18 July 1604 and remaining days of said month, from the town and lands of Cloustay which Henry had in tack from Laurence Bruce of Cultmalyndeis, and spulyie of the following goods and gear: 25 bolls oats, price of the boll with the fodder £5; 25 bolls bere, price of the boll with the fodder £7; 10 milk ky with 5 calves, price of each cow £13 6s.8d. and price of each calf £2; 5 young ky of 4 years old or thereby which all had calves, price of the piece £12; 12 oxen, price of each £20; 3 young ky of 3 years old and more, price of each £8; 3 young oxen of 3 years old, price of each £12; 90 ewes with their lambs, price of each with their lamb £2; 20 gimmers, price of each 30s.; furth of said lands of Cloustay, 3 mares with 3 foals, price of each with the foal £12; one young mare, price thereof £5; 3 work horses, price of each £10; furth of the isle of Fetler, spulyied from the pursuer, 2 mares with their foals, price of each £12; one horse, price thereof £10; furth of the town and lands of Cloustay, 6 brood geese with 2 ganders, price of each 13s.4d.; 16 fathoms of old peats 'standand stakit in the hous over yeir', price of each fathom 30s.; 24 men's day work of new peats, 'castin and win', price of each man's day work 30s.; 16 men's day work of hay mowing, price of each man's day work £3; 2 boats with 3 oars on either side, price of each boat £20; and about 400 set great-line hooks to slay fish with, price of each score £1.

The lords of council find and declare Patrik, earl of Orknay, to have done wrong in the eviction and spulyie, and decern Patrik and James Esplein, his officer, to restore to the pursuer the foresaid goods and gear; and further absolve the defenders, apart from Patrik, earl of Orknay, for the eviction of the pursuer from the lands of Cloustay and others foresaid; and likewise absolve Magnus Bryngalsoun in Efert, Nicoll and John Magnusounis, his sons, and Olay Sutherland, underfoud in Fetler, from the points of the summons so far as concerns the spoliation of the goods and gear.

SRO, CS.7/229, ff.43-7. The action had been first brought before the lords of council on 12 June 1605; on 20 February 1606 the pursuer had been granted letters to summon witnesses, viz. James Wischart, Alexander Mylne, James Neving, Alexander Thom, and Thomas Reid (SRO, CS.7/215, f.274, and CS.7/216, ff.233-4). On 25 June 1607, Patrik, earl of Orknay, was put to horn at instance of Alexander Bruce, fiar of Cultmalindie, assignee of Henry Wardlaw, for non-fulfilment of the decreet (SRO, DI.3/24, ff.316-20). On 11 February 1608 Patrik undertook to remove Magnus Olasoun, and Nicol and John Magnusouns, his sons, from the town and lands of Clousta, extending to 24 marks land, 9 pennies the mark, in the parish of Aythsting and Sandsting, and to enter Henry Wardlaw and Margaret Buchanane, his spouse, there (SRO, RD.1/145, ff.103-4).

433. Quendall, 1 May 1607

Obligation by Harie Cheine of Stopnes to Malcome Sinclair of Quendall, for 64 angels of gold and weight in complete payment of the 1605 crop of the vicarage of Waillis, according to Harie's tack and intromission therewith; and also for complete payment of the butter and wadmell landmails of the 1606 crop with the bowteind of the said year. Harie binds himself to pay 32 angels by Lammas 1607, and the other 32 angels by Lammas 1608.

Witnesses: Robert Blak, James Sinclair of Goit, and Mr Robert Swentoun, minister at Waillis, writer hereof.

SRO, RD.11/72 (reg. 9 May 1610). On the back is a receipt, dated 14 April 1609 at Quendell, by Malcolm Sinclair of Quendill to Hary Chene of Stepnes for £184 in part payment of the sum abovewritten, leaving £200 owing in complete payment of the 64 angels; witnessed by James Sinclair, son of Malcolm, Thomas Blakberd, and Oliver Sinclar.

434. 6 May 1607

'Charter by [*blank*] Tornysdaughter of Ennisfirth, lawful spouse to Andrew Mouat of Hogoland, with full assent and consent of her said spouse, in favor of James Mouat of Burrafirth, her son in law, of ... 5 merks land in Braehoulland, in the parish of Northmavine.'

The original is not known to exist. The above abstract is in SA, D.6/194/12 (Inventory of titles of the estate of Busta, in Messrs Greigs' possession, 1840).

435. Edinburgh, 21 May 1607

Decreet of court of session in action at instance of Patrik, earl of Orknay, lord Yetland, and Thomas Auchinleck, his clerk of court, against Henry Wardlaw, servant of Laurence Bruce of Cultmalindeis, for suspension of letters charging the pursuers to deliver to Henry extracts of two decreets of court whereby Henry was found not guilty of the slaughter of Nicoll Magnussoun, son of Magnus Jacobsone, shepherd of the isle of Vehemendrie. Henry had alleged that on 19 August 1602, in a court held by Patrik in his castle of Skalloway, Andro Hawick, procurator fiscal, had pursued him for the alleged slaughter, and that he had been found not guilty by an assize of which Arthure Sinclaire of Aythe was chancellor; and that on the next morning Patrik had called a new assize of which Andro Mowat of Hougaland was chancellor, and caused Alexander Thomassone in Laxfirth, his procurator fiscal, pursue Henry again for the said slaughter, and that, as of before, he had been found not guilty. However, the pursuers allege that Henry Wardlaw was never pursued by Patrik, earl of Orknay, for the said slaughter, nor yet was there ever any court held by him thereanent in the castle of Skalloway, nor was Thomas Auchinleck ever clerk to any such court, and that the said letters and horning contained therein should be suspended. The defender offers to prove that he was challenged for the murder and slaughter foresaid before the earl of Orknay and his deputes in August 1602, and that having then entered upon panel in the castle of Skalloway, he had been put to the knowledge of an assize, and was pursued by Magnus Jacobsoun, father to the said Nicoll, being present in judgement, with Andro Hawick, procurator fiscal for the earl of Orknay, the said earl of Orknay being present in judgement and assisting Mr John Dischingtoun who was judge in the said matter, and that he was found not guilty.

The lords of council declare that they will examine Edward Scolay, who in August 1602 was cautioner for Henry, that he should enter before the earl of Orknay to underlie the law for the said crime, and also examine Thomas Auchinleck who was clerk in the said matter ex officio, before they give answer; and therefore ordain letters to be directed charging Edward Scolay and Thomas Auchinleck to compear on 20 November 1607, to answer such things as shall be enquired of them 'anent the clenging' of Henry at the castle of Skalloway, and also to answer such other things as shall please the lords to enquire of them, and likewise ordain letters to be directed charging Thomas Auchinleck to exhibit on the said day all his minutes concerning the said matter, under pain of rebellion; and further discharge the justice general and his deputes of all proceeding against Henry Wardlaw for the alleged slaughter of Nicoll Magnussoun until the foresaid action of suspension is decided.

SRO, CS.7/228, f.81. See no. 424.

436. Edinburgh, 31 July 1607

Extract special retour in favour of Laurence Sinclair now of Burgh, as heir of the deceased Hew Sinclair of Burgh, his father, in the lands of the barony of Burgh, viz. 36 marks land of Burgh, 33 marks land of Glaitnes, 6 marks land of the great isle of Glaitnes, 4 marks land of the little isle of Glaitnes, 12 marks land of the great isle of Linga, 4 marks land of the little isle of Linga in Quhilsaysound, 4 marks land of Friasetter, 6 marks land of Vassa, 1 mark land of Aswik, 1 mark land of Scelesta, 2½ marks land of Hassabuster, 3 marks land of Kirkabuster, 1½ marks land of Levannep, 1 mark land of Scelbere, 3½ marks land of Newing, 2½ marks land of Grunyefirth, 3 marks land of Clatt in Quhailsay, 6 marks land of Sandwik, with another 3 marks land there, 2½ marks land of Huksetter there, 2 marks land of Levasetter there, 6 ures land of Ska there, 1 mark land of Merrasetter there, ½ mark land of Burght alias Eisthoussis there, 30 marks 2½ ures land of Skerreis, in the parish of Nesting; 4½ marks land of How, with another 2 marks land there, 2 marks land of Hammagarth, 1 mark 6 ures land of Houskour, 4½ marks land of Skarpagarth, 1 mark land of South Kirkgour, 6 marks land in Sound, 2 marks land of Cova, in the parish of Weisdaill; 3 marks land of Nestbuster, 2 marks land of Hammer, 1 mark land of Uphous, 1 mark land called Turneiris in Eastnes, in the parish of Quhitnes; 12 marks land of Unyefirth, 2 marks land of Tuait in Langskaill, 2 marks land of Samlsetter, in the parish of Sandsting and Eisting; 12 marks land of Browaland, 5 marks land of Curcagarth, 9 marks land of Seattar, 4 marks land of Sandasbrught, 6 marks land of Melbie in Sandie, 6 marks land in Grammannatueit, 1½ marks land of Seatter, in the parish of Wallis; 6 marks land of Houlland, 3 marks land of Glusc, in the parish of Northmavene; 12 marks land of [B]ouasetter, 15 marks land of Culbeneisbroch, 8 marks land of Ham and Halversta, 2 marks land, in the parish and island of Bressa; 4 marks land of Burrovo, 3 marks land of Weddersta, 8 marks land of Lingaholme, in the parish of Delting; 4 marks land of Sandweik, 1 mark land of Clett, in the parish of Burra; 9 marks land of (blank) in the isle of Unst; 1 mark land called Unholme, a holm called Langa in Yelscound; and also 18 pennies land of Housbie with the island called Auskerrie, in the island of Stronsay, parish of Sanct Nicolas in Orknay.

SA, GD.144/273/10 (in Latin).

437. Soundburgh, 17 August 1607

Contract between William Bruce of Symbester, on the one part, and James Sinclair of Rapnis, on the other part, whereby James acknowledges receipt of £200 from William, and dispones to William an annualrent of one barrel Yetland butter from his 12 marks land, 6 pennies the mark, of Bw in the town of Exinabu, in the cross parish of Dunrosnes. James binds himself to infeft William in the said annualrent, to be held of James in free blench farm for yearly payment of one penny, if asked; and William binds himself to grant to James a letter of reversion.

Witnesses: Andro Umphray of Berry, John Dune in Lythe, Patrik Paplay, and James Nevin, indweller in Leith, writer hereof.

SRO, RD.1/367, ff.308-10.

438. Scalloway, 31 August 1607

'Disposition by Nicoll Garioche, burgess of Kirkwall, to Thomas Quhyt, indweller in Scalloway, and Geilles Neven, of a tenement in Scalloway. ...

'Witnesses: Jerome Chalmer, George Williamson, Alexander Thomasson, Gilbert Cantlie, and James Jack, NP.'

The original is not known to exist. The above abstract, by Francis Grant, is in OSD, *SN*, 27 January 1894.

439. 24 October 1607

'Umquhill Catrein Androsdochter hir schound.'

The original is not known to exist. One of the writs taken from Ninian Neven's house in Yell, 27 August 1624 (*RPC*, xiv, p.736).

440. Brughe in the isle of South Ronaldsay, 22 January 1608

Contract between Hew Halcro of that Ilk, Edward Ingsetter, Mathow Sinclar of Bruche, Alexander Ingsetter, Ingrahame Mowat, Adam Cromertie of Kirkhous, Magnus Cromertie, John Cromertie in Grimnes, Magnus Cromertie of Caray, (and Robert Birstain), for themselves and taking the burden for the remaining inhabitants of the isle of South Ronaldsay who are fishers at Dunrosnes in Yetland, on the one part, and Patrik, earl of Orknay, lord Yetland, on the other part, whereby the aforenamed persons bind themselves to cause deliver weekly to Patrik or his factors 'thair haill fisches quhilk sall happin to be win in the said parochin of Dunrosnes within the cuntrie of Yetland, baith ling, keilling and saythis, to be delyverit be thame tydlie as they ar gottin, and thair payment to be oulklie everie Setturday at ewin, togidder with thair haill oylie quhilk salhappin to be win be thame in the said parochin; for the quhilk caus the said nobill lord bindis and oblissis him, his airis and assignayis to thankfully content and pay for ilk dussane of sufficient gild keling and ling maid and pay sexteine schillingis money, and for ilk dussane of sufficient gild saithis maid and pay twelff schillingis money, according as is in use to be delyverit to merchandis of befoir; and farder the said nobill lord bindis and oblissis him and his foirsaidis to content and pay to thame for ilk barrell oylie quhilk they salhappin to win in the parochin of Dunrosnes at the ressait thairof, the samin beand sufficient barrellit oylie and merchandabill wair as use is, without watter or dreg, packit in sufficient beir trie bind, the sowme of auchtene pundis money'. Both contracting parties bind themselves to fulfil the terms of the contract, under pain of 500 merks.

Witnesses: Edward Scollay of Strynie, James Levingstoun, William Boswall, Robert Scollay, Thomas Auchinleck younger, writer hereof, and Mr Niniane Halcro, minister at Burray and South Ronaldsay.

SRO, RD.1/180, ff.349-50. See next item and no. 448.

441. Snelsitter in the isle of Wais, 25 January 1608

Contract between Frances Mudie of Breknes, David King, James Sandison, Ronald Setter, Thomas Cromertie, Edwart Mowat, William Donaldsone, John Setter, Magnus Chalmer in Manclet, and Magnus Chalmer in Setter, for themselves and taking the burden for the remaining inhabitants of Hoy and Wais who are fishers at Dunrosnes in Yetland, on the one part, and Patrik, earl of Orknay, lord Yetland, on the other part. (Terms as in no. 440.)

Witnesses: Edward Scollay of Strynie, James Levingstoun, William Boswall, Robert Scollay, Thomas Auchinleck younger, writer hereof, and Robert Stewart, minister.

SRO, RD.1/180, ff.351-2. See previous item.

442. Muness, 7 February 1608, and Cultamalindieis, (blank) 1608

Contract between William Bruce of Simbister, on the one part, and the right honourable Lowrance Bruce of Cultamalindieis, with consent of his eldest son Mr Allexander Bruce, apparent of Cultamalindieis, on the other part, whereby Lowrance acknowledges receipt of 700 merks from William, for which Lowrance dispones to William 20 marks 6 ures land, 9 pennies the mark, in Simbister in Quhailsay, with the island called Onyerholme in Quhailsay Sound, in the parish of Nesting, 'within the mercheis auld and devyssit, beginand on the north syd of the erable landis of Simbister to the sey dyk of Seter, from thair estward to the north dyk of Lewesetter, and from thair eastward to the loche of Hoxsetter, and sua as the loche fallis in the sey; frome thyne sowthwestward to the dyk of Clet and Sandwick, and from Sandwick to the lockeit ness of Simbister, and from thyne to the gairdie callit Hamneseter'. Laurence ratifies the former security of the said lands given to William at Aith in

Esting on 15 September 1586. Lowrance binds himself to grant William two separate infeftments, the one to be held of Lowrance in free blench for payment of one penny, if asked, and the other to be held by resignation or confirmation of the king with Lowrance as immediate superior. If William is evicted from the lands of Simbister, or any part thereof, then William is to have regress to Lowrance's 30 marks land, 6 pennies the mark, in Tresta in Fetlar, in warrandice.

Witnesses: William Bruce, Scippio Bruce, Androw Steill, and Allexander Murquhowsone.

SA, GD.144/254/1. See no. 445.

443. Munes, 18 February 1608

Disposition by Lowrance Bruce of Cultamalindieis, with consent of his eldest son Mr Allexander Bruce, apparent of Cultamalindieis, to his well-beloved friend William Bruce of Simbister, of 20 marks 6 ures land, 9 pennies the mark, in Simbister in Quhailsay, with the island called Onyerholme, in the parish of Nesting, for 700 merks, to be held of Lowrance in free blench for payment of one penny on Whitsunday evening, if required. Precept of sasine.

Witnesses: William Bruce and Scippio Bruce, sons natural of Lowrance, Androw Steill, servant of Lowrance, Allexander Murquhowsone, writer hereof, and Allexander Fordyce.

Sasine given at Symbester at the house and dwelling place of William Bruce of Symbester on 19 March 1608 (at 3 p.m.) by Andro Jansoun, bailie in that part. Witnesses: Allester Murchesoun and Alexander Fordyce, servants of William, Oliver Nicolsoun, wright, and John Fermour, son of William Fermour, notary. William Fermour, notary public.

SA, GD.144/81/4 (disposition) and GD.144/81/3 (sasine).

444. Edinburgh, 11 March 1608

Decreet of court of session in action at instance of Patrik Chene of Essilmonth against Gilbert Assuynisettir, Nicoll Thomassone, Magnus Abirinsla, Magdaleine Thomasdochter, Mr William Hay, Hendrie Kincaid, James Invein, Nicoll Sitter, Magnus Amoussiwell, and Thomas Overbus, for removal from 5 marks land of Swynsitter, 18 marks land of Gott, 15 marks land of Southsitter, 7 marks land of Stewiniswall, 5 marks land of Stromnes, 12 marks land of Kebeista, 6 marks land of Sitter in Koweriwik, 9 marks land of Brindista, and 2 marks land in Eister Croff, in parish of Tingwell. The defenders had been warned to remove at Whitsunday 1607.

The lords of council decern the defenders to remove from their particular lands.

SRO, CS.7/236, f.160.

445. Symbester in Quhalsay, 18 March 1608

Instrument of sasine in favour of William Bruce of Symbester, following on disposition by an honourable man Lawrence Bruce of Cultmalindie, for recompense for service and other gratitudes and good deeds, of Lawrence's lands in the town of Symbester, in the isle of Quhalsay, together with the holm called Ungyerholme, to be held by William of Lawrence in fee and heritage for payment of one penny at Whitsunday in name of blench, if asked. Precept of sasine directed to Andro Johnsoun, 'also contening ane commissioun maid, giffin and grantit be the said Lawrence to the said Williame to be cessionar and assignay in and to the fourth pert of all the saidis Lawrence movabillis guidis and gere efter the said Lawrence deceis, to be intromettit with be the said Williame and disponit be him as his awin proper guidis and geir; as in the said chartour under the said Lawrence signet and subscriptioun, of the dait, at Aith, the fyftene day of September the yeir of god ane thousand fyve hundreth fourscoir and sex yeiris at lenth beris'. Sasine given in the hall and dwelling house of William, at 1 p.m.

Witnesses: Allester Murchesoun and Allexander Fordyce, servants of William, Oliver Nicolsoun, wright, and Johne Fermour, son of William Fermour, notary. William Fermour, notary public.

SA, GD.144/265/11. See no. 442.

446. 8 April 1608

Tack by Laurence Sinclair, vicar of Dunrossness, with consent of James, bishop of Orkney and Yetland, and of the whole chapter of the cathedral church of Orkney, to Malcolm Sinclair of Quendale, and Margaret Sutherland, his spouse, of the teinds, great and small, of the vicarage of Dunrossness, for their lifetimes, and after their decease for the lifetime of two heirs successively, and three nineteen year terms, for yearly payment of £120.

The original is not known to exist. The above abstract is in an 18th century state of process of sale of the Quendale estate (SRO, CS.96/3273, p.60).

447. Skalloway bankis, 1 June 1608

Submission by Mr Gilbert Mowat, minister of Delting, and Andro Giffart of Wedderstay, to Thomas Swyntoun and Mr Andro Dischingtoun, ministers, for the part of Mr Gilbert, and to Arthour Sinclar of Aith and Captain Thomas Knychtsone, for the part of Andro, and in case of variance Edward Scola of Strynie to be 'oversman', for decision of all question and controversy anent the title of the vicarage of Delting.

Witnesses: James Jack, notary public, Mr James Pitcairne, James Mowat, and William Fermour.

Decreet arbitral, dated 4 July 1608 at Skalloway bankis, decerning that the equal half of the teinds of the vicarage of Delting for the crops and years 1604 to 1607 inclusive shall be equally divided between Mr Gilbert and Thomas, and that Mr Gilbert shall pay Andro Giffart the sum of £600 for his right of the vicarage, 'sa that the said Mr Gilbert may the mair peciabillie posses the samen in all tyme cuming, dispensand with the equall half of the teind lambs and woll of sic landis as ar allanerlie in the possessioun and manureing of the said Andro allanerlie, and labourit withe his awin pleuche'. Mr Gilbert's entry to begin the crop and year 1608, according to his presentation.

Witnesses: Mr James Pitcairne, John Cairncors, David King, and David Kincaid.

SRO, RD.1/170, ff.177-8.

448. Soundbrugh, 27 June 1608

Contract between John Neving of Skowsbrugh, Magnus in Gord, Ingraham Sinclare, Ola Sutherland, Robert Ratter, Thomas Sinclair, Laurence Leisk, James Sinclair of Gott, John Scott, Malcome Halcro, Andro Sand, William in Burroland, Malcome in Culbeinsgerth, Hew Halcro, Erasmus in Flottabuster, Laurence Sinclair of Gott, James Sinclair, apparent of Quendaill, for themselves and taking the burden for the remaining inhabitants of Dunrosnes who are fishers in Dunrosnes, on the one part, and Patrik, earl of Orknay, lord Yetland, on the other part, whereby the aforenamed persons bind themselves to cause deliver weekly to Patrik or his factors 'thair haill fisches quhilk sall happin to be win in the said parochin of Dunrosnes within the cuntrie of Yetland, baith ling, keilling and saithis, to be delyverit be thame tydlie as they ar gottin, and thair payment to be oulklie everie Setterday at ewin, togidder with thair haill oylie quhilk salhappin to be win be thame in the said parochin; Resavand sa mekill thairof as may pay my lordis dettis to the Duchmen and Inglismen yeirlie; for the quhilk caus the said nobill lord bindis and oblissis him, his airis and assignayis to thankfully content and pay for ilk dussane of sufficient gild keilling and ling maid and pay sexteine schillingis money, and for ilk dussane of sufficient gild saithis maid and pay twelff schillingis money, according as is in use to be delyverit to merchandis of befoir; And farder the said nobill lord bindis and oblissis him and his foirsaidis to content and pay to thame for ilk barrell oylie quhilk they salhappin to win in the parochin of Dunrosnes at the ressait thairof, the samin beand sufficient barrellit oylie and merchand wair as use is, without watter or dreg, packit in sufficient beir trie bind, the sowme of auchtene pundis money'. The contracting parties bind themselves to fulfil the terms of the contract, under pain of 500 merks.

Witnesses: Edward Scollay of Strynie, Thomas Auchinleck younger, writer hereof, William Fermour, Robert Scollay, and John Fermour.

SRO, RD.1/180, ff.348-9. See nos. 440-1.

449. Sombrochheid, 27 June 1608

Contract between Adam Sinclar of Brow, on the one part, and Patrik, earl of Orknay and Yetland, on the other part, whereby Adam heritably wadsets to Patrik the just equal half of the town and lands of Brow extending to 72 marks land, 6 pennies the mark, with the 'just half of the lynks and fauldis thairof', in the parish of Dunrosnes, with entry for the crop 1608 (including the crop presently on the ground), redeemable on payment by Adam of £1,000. Adam binds himself to deliver to Patrik the four stacks of bere and oats presently standing in the corn yard of Brow. If Adam shall happen to sell or wadset the other half of the lands of Brow then Patrik shall have first offer.

Witnesses: Alexander Stewart of Clatt in Wastry, Frances Sinclar of Uyea, Alexander Bruce, and James Jack, writer hereof.

SRO, CS.7/353, ff.114-6.

450. Skatstay, 12 July 1608

Obligation by Andro Mowat of Howgaland, with consent of Mr Gilbert and James Mowattis, his lawful sons, to his good friend Edward Sinclar of Bulyesetter, for £1,000, payable by 4 July 1609. Andro and his sons bind themselves to make payment 'onlie in wauris and pennyworthis of the pryces underwrittin, betuix the day and dait of thir presentis and the fourt day of Julij nixtocum in the yeir of God Jaj VJc nyne yeiris, but forder delay; provyding alwyis that incaice it salhappin me the said Andro, my saids sones or ony of us ... to content, pay and delyver to the said Eduard ... the soume of ane thowsand merkis money in wairis allanerlie of the pryces and at the times respective undermentionat ... that is to say, ilk barrell butter for four angellis nobillis of gold, the barrell ulie for thrie angellis nobillis of gold foirsaid, all weill packit and fillit up as sufficient merchand wair in barrellis and tries afferis, betuix the day and dait of this present and the feist of midlentroun nixtocum, and the pak of wedmell of the scatt cuttill for four silver dollaris lykwyis betuix the dait of thir presentis and the feist of midsomer nixtocum in the yeir of god Jaj VJc and nyne yeiris, and the place of delyverie thairof to be at the port of Burravo in Yell, of the saidis wairis and not uthairwayis; in that caice to be fried, exonerit and relevit of the foirsaid soume of ane thowsand pundis money abonespecifeit, evin as giff I nor my foirsaidis had nevir beine astrictit thairto, uthairwayis nocht.'

Witnesses: Andro Hawick of Skatstay, Andro Mertene, servant of the earl of Orknay, and James Jack, notary public, writer hereof.

SRO, RD.1/226, ff.89-90.

451. Vosgairth in Unst, 17 July 1608

Disposition by George Wirk, indweller in Quhailsay, to Patrik, earl of Orknay, lord Yetland, of 9 marks uthal land, 12 pennies the mark, in Nesthous in the town of Ysebuster, in the isle of Quhailsay. Precept of sasine directed to William Mansoun, foud in Neip.

Witnesses: Andro Martyne and James Levingstoun, servants of Patrik, Thomas Auchinleck younger, Robert Scollay, Alexander Bruce, notary public, and James Jack, notary public, writer hereof.

Sasine given on 21 July 1608 (at 4 p.m.) to William Sclaitter in Quhalsay, procurator for Patrik, earl of Orkney, lord Yetland. Witnesses: Androw Thomasoun, Robert Huntar, George Suderland, Erasmus Olasoun, Magnus Andersoun, and James Christophersoun, all indwellers in Quhailsay. James Jack and Alexander Bruce, notaries public.

SRO, RH.9/15/84.

452. Uyeasound, 17 July 1608

Precept for summoning forestallers and regraters to compear at the head court at Scalloway bankis.

Eduard Scollay of Strynie, sheref depuit of Orknay and Yetland, and baillie depuit of the regalitie thairof, to my lovittis Magnus Ylesburgh, [*blank*], my officeris in that pairt, conjunct and severallie, specialie constitut, greting; forsameikle as commoun pepill of Northmavin and utheris pairtis of Yetland ar oftymes oppressit, desavit and abusit be ane number of countirfut merchandis, quha undir pretext of ane tred and exchange of wairis pass to and fro among the pepill with prienis, neidillis, preinecodis and utheris improfitabill and innecessar vanities not worthie to be caried throw the cuntrie, and thairwith defameand, the ignorantis ar fed and sustenit upon the vivers quhilkis sould susteine the puir; be quhilk desait and abuse nather can ony honest man have ony necessar furnitour for his money, nor yit the puir native pepill of the cuntrie be sustenit except sum tymeous remeid be put thairto, as is notoriouslie alleged; heirfoir I charge you that ye lauchfullie summond, warne and charge the saidis foirstalleris and regraittaris as sornearis and vagabondis, togidder with [*blank*] and all uthiris byaris and sellaris with thame, as resettaris, fortifearis, assistaris, sustenearis and allowaris of thame; to compeir befoir me and my assessoris at Scalloway bankis the first, secund or thrid dayis of the nixt heid court, callit the lawtyng, in the hour of caus, with continuatioun of dayis, to undirly the law for the said disorder, oppressing, sorneing, assisting and maintenyng of the samen, and heir and sie thameselffis, and ilk ane of thame for thair awin pairtis, decernit to be punished in thair bodies and guidis thairfoir according to the actis of parliament, actis of the cuntrie and lawis of the realme; and that ilk ane of thame compeir for this effect under the pane of xl lib.; that bettir ordour may be estabilished thairanent in tyme cuming; to be observed for the commoun weill according to justice, as ye will answer to me thairupon. The quhilk to do I commit to yow my full power. Be thir presentis, subscryvit with my hand, at Uyeasound the xvij of July 1608.

Eduard Scollay.
A. Martyne.

SA, GD.144/61/12.

453. Still in Fetlar, 19 July 1608

Disposition by Marioun Frissall in Culyevo in North Yell, with consent of James Neill, her spouse, to Patrik, earl of Orknay, lord Yetland, of 5 marks uthal land, 12 pennies the mark, in Nesthous, in the isle of Quhailsay. Precept of sasine directed to William Mansoun, foud of Neip.

Witnesses: Johne Carncorss and James Levingstoun, servants of Patrik, Thomas Auchinlek younger, Robert Scollay, and Alexander Bruce and James Jack, connotaries.

Sasine given on 21 July 1608 (at 4 p.m.) to William Sclaitter, procurator for Patrik, earl of Orknay, lord Yetland. Witnesses: Androw Thomasoun, Robert Huntar, George Suderland, Erasmus Olasoun, Magnus Andersoun, and James Christophersoun, all indwellers in Quhailsay, Alexander Bruce and James Jack, connotaries.

SRO, RH.9/15/85.

454. Still in Fetlar, 19 July 1608

Disposition by Ola Vriounsone in Birroun, brother-son and only heir of Nicoll in Culyeavo, to Patrik, earl of Orknay, lord Yetland, of 5 marks uthal land, 12 pennies the mark, in Nesthous, in the isle of Quhailsay. Precept of sasine directed to William Mansoun.

Witnesses: Johne Carncorss and James Levingstoun, servants of Patrik, Thomas Auchinlek younger, Robert Scollay, Alexander Bruce and James Jack, connotaries.

Sasine given on 21 July 1608 (at 4 p.m.) to William Sclaitter, procurator for Patrik, earl of Orknay, lord Yetland. Witnesses: Androw Thomasoun, Robert Huntar, George Suderland, Erasmus Olasoun, Magnus

Andersoun, and James Christophersoun, all indwellers in Quhailsay, Alexander Bruce and James Jack, connotaries.

SRO, RH.9/15/86.

455. Still in Fetlar, 19 July 1608

Disposition by Marion Erasmusdochter in Fetlar to Patrik, earl of Orknay, lord Yetland, of ½ mark uthal land, 12 pennies the mark, in Nesthous, in the isle of Quhailsay. Precept of sasine directed to William Mansoun, foud in Neip.

Witnesses: Johne Carncorss and James Levingstoun, servants of Patrik, Thomas Auchinlek younger, Robert Scollay, and Alexander Bruce and James Jack, connotaries.

Sasine given on 21 July 1608 (at 4 p.m.) to William Sclaitter, procurator for Patrik, earl of Orknay, lord Yetland. Witnesses: Androw Thomasoun, Robert Huntar, George Suderland, Erasmus Olasoun, Magnus Andersoun, and James Christophersoun, all indwellers in Quhailsay, Alexander Bruce and James Jack, connotaries.

SRO, RH.9/15/87.

456. Skalloway, 25 July 1608

Instructions regarding a tack of kirklands in Yell.

Four mark land in Brekon and six mark land in Toft, all kirkland, vj d. the mark, within the ile of Yell, with houssis, pairtis, pendicilis, fredomes and all richteous pertinentis quhatsumever apertining thairto, usat and wount, set in assidatioun to James Spence, occupear thairof, George Spence, son to umquhill [*sic*], and his airis, for the space of thrie yeiris, beginand his entrie thairto at Whitsounday last wes to cast peittis; And his first crope to be to the yeir of god 1609 yeris, payand thairfore yeirlie iij leispund viij mark meat butter, iij shillings 2 cuttell wodmell, with scatt and the wattill conforme to the rentale, v pultrie foullis, with halk dog and reik hen, dew service as use is, and to uphold the houssis, provyding give the dewitie abovewrittin be not thankfullie payit yeirlie, this present asseddatioun to expyre. Subscryvit with our hand, at Skalloway, the xxv day of July 1608. Payit in girsum to John Aweik, collectour, xij li., and for his entrie thairto vj li.

Registrat Orknay.
R. Scollay.

The original is not known to exist. The above 19th century transcription is in SA, D.16/392/71/100.

457. Kewinsburgh, 29 July 1608 (at 11 a.m.)

Instrument of sasine in favour of Patrik, earl of Orknay, lord Yetland, following on disposition by Nicoll and Mathew Mansonis, brothers, in Vaisgairth in Kewinsburgh, of 10½ marks uthal land in the town of Kewinsburgh, 1½ marks uthal land in Daill, and 1½ marks uthal land in Simlasettir, all 6 pennies the mark, in the parish of Dunrosnes, with precept of sasine directed to Malcolme Symonsoun of Culmisgairth. The disposition, dated 25 July 1608 at Skalloway, was witnessed by Edward Scollay of Strynie, James Levingstoun, Duncan Norrwell and Robert Scollay, servants of Patrik, Patrik Auchinlek, notary public, and James Jack, also notary public, writer hereof. Sasine given to David Leslie, procurator for Patrik, earl of Orknay, lord Yetland.

Witnesses: Magnus Henrysoun in Osewick, James Mansoun in Tow, and Iveir Mansoun in Westano.

SRO, RH.9/15/80.

458. Skalloway bankis, 4 August 1608

Excambion between John Neving of Skousbroch, on the one part, and James Mowat, son of Androw Mowat of Hougoland, on the other part, whereby John dispones to James, 2 marks land, 9 pennies the mark, in Ure called Howssagord, and 1 mark land, 6 pennies the mark, in Liaskoll, with 1 mark land, 6 pennies the mark, in Burroun, all in Northmavin, and James dispones to John, 4 marks land, 6 pennies the mark, in Howasetter, 1½ marks land in North Caldclef, in the parish of Tingual. Precept of sasine.

Witnesses: Mr James Pitcairne, Androw Edmestoun, and Mr Gilbert Mowat.

SA, GD.144/277/9.

459. Dunrosnes, 22 August 1608

Obligation by Malcome Sinclair of Quendaill to Alexander Kincaid, vicar of Waillis: although Alexander has set to Malcome a tack of his vicarage for 7 years, beginning this crop and year 1608, which is the expiry of Malcome's last 19 years' tack thereof, for payment yearly to Alexander of £60, conform to 'auld use and wont', notwithstanding Malcome binds himself during the said tacks (1) to pay yearly to Alexander the vicarage and bishop's umboths of Waillis, amounting to 40 angels or £240, relieving Alexander of 3 barrels butter and 3 barrels oil yearly at 'my lord of Orknayis handis', conform to his letter of tack set to him by the said earl of the umboth, (2) to relieve him of the thirds of the said vicarage, to receive the bishop's visitors when they 'resort to the cuntrie', and (3) to obtain the earl's discharge upon the the said butter and oil during the period of the tack.

Witnesses: James Sinclair, eldest son of Malcome, James Youngar in

Fischerraw, Thomas Blaikberd, and Robert Blak, with sundry others.

SRO, RD.1/206, ff.118-9.

460. Burravo in Yell, 30 August 1608

Contract between James Spens now of Glowpe in Yell, on the one part, and Walter Scott, his brother-in-law, on the other part, whereby James, for ordering, settling and extinguishing all manner of action and debate which might arise anent the heirship lands and moveables underwritten, of his own free will ratifies and confirms the decreets of schound and division made of lands and 'louse gudis' to and in favour of Berita Spens, his sister, and the said Walter, now her spouse, for his interest, after the deceased David Spens of Glowpe and Margaret Frasir, his spouse, as the same is set down in an appointment made between them of the date, at Glowpe, 12 March 1607. James is content with the just two parts of the said lands and moveables, conform to the particular denominations in the foresaid decreets, as the same in particular bears for the said David's part of the date, at Glowpe in Yell, 7 January 1606, and for the said deceased Margaret's part of the date 11 March 1607; and renounces all claims to the just third part of the said lands and moveables, and grants the same since the foresaid division to have appertained to the said Berita, and her spouse for his interest, as their proper heritage. James ratifies and confirms the precept and instrument of sasine given already to Berita and her spouse, as the same under the seal and subscription manual of James Jack, notary public, of the date 24 August 1608 bears. Walter binds himself to be true and faithful to James in all his actions, and that neither he nor his spouse shall dispone or away put any of their lands, heritages or possessions without the advice and consent of James.

Witnesses: Androw Edmestoun, minister of god's word in Yell, James Sutherland in Fetlair, Ninian Nevine, lawful son of John Nevine of Skowisburgh, Robert Scollay, servant of the earl of Orknay, Henrie Stevinsoun, merchant, Walter Ritchie, and James Jack, connotaries.

SRO, RD.11/73 (reg. 24 May 1610).

461. Edinburgh, 14 September 1608

Testament of Margaret Stewart, spouse of William Bruce of Symbester

The testament dative and inventar of the guidis, geir, sowmes of money and dettis pertening to umquile Margaret Stewart, sumtyme spous to William Bruce of Symbester in Yetland, within the parochin of Quhalsay and sherefdome of Yetland, the tyme of hir deceis, quha deceissit upoun the 25 day of November the yeir of god 1607, faythfulie maid and gevin up be the said William Bruce, his spous, as fader and laufull administrator to Johnne, Susanna, Margaret and Rebecka Bruceis, thair laufull bairnis and executoris datives, decernit to thair said umquhile moder be decreit of the commissar of Edinburgh, as the samyn decreit of the dait at Edinburgh the [*blank*] day of September 1608 at lenth proportis, etc.

In the first the said umquhile Margaret Stewart and hir said spous had the guidis, geir, sowmes of money and dettis of the availl and prices eftir following pertening to thame the tyme of hir deceis foirsaid, viz., item, in the barne and barneyaird of Soundburch, 30 bollis of beir, price of the boll with the fodder £3 10s., summa £105; item, mair in the said barne and barneyaird, 30 bollis of aittis, price of the boll with the fodder 50s., summa £75; item, mair thair, 15 mylk ky, price of the pece ourheid £6, summa £90; item, mair thair, 10 oxin, price of the pece ourheid £8, summa £80; item, 16 horssis and meiris, price of the pece ourheid £5, summa £80; item, mair thair, 40 scheipe, price of the pece ourheid £1, summa £40; item, 2 Yetland yollis, price of the pece ourheid £12, summa £24; item, upoun the lands of Symbuster, 8 ky, price of the pece ourheid £7, summa £56; item, 5 oxin thair, price of the pece ourheid £9, summa £45; item, 5 horssis and meiris, price of the pece ourheid, £6, summa £30; item, 40 scheipe, price of the pece ourheid £1, summa £40; item, 2 yollis, price of the pece ourheid £10, summa £20; item, 8 bollis beir, price of the boll ourheid £3 10s., summa £28; item, 5 bollis of aittis, price of the boll £2, summa £10; item, upoun the landis of Uya, in the barne and barneyaird, 30 bollis of beir, price of the boll £4, summa £120; item, mair thair, 40 bollis of aittis, price of the boll with the fodder £2, summa £80; item, 15 ky, price of the pece ourheid £7, summa £105; item, 15 oxin, young and auld, price of the pece ourheid £8, summa £120; item, 160 scheipe, price of the pece ourheid £1, summa £160; item, 10 horssis and meiris, price of the pece ourheid £6, summa £60; item, ane Yetland yoll, price £10; item, 15 swyne, young and auld, price of all £10; item, upoun the ground and landis of Trollis, 10 ky, price of the pece ourheid £8, summa £80; item, 8 oxin, price of the pece ourheid £9, summa £72; item, 7 horssis and meiris, price of the pece ourheid £6, summa £42; item, mair, 10 bollis beir, price of the boll £4, summa £40; item, mair, 10 bollis of aittis, price of the boll £2, summa £20; item, mair on that rowme, certane swyne and geiss, estimat all to £10; item, 2 yollis, price of baith £16; item, of reddy money, the sowme of £100; item, in utencilis and domicilis, with the abuilyementis of hir bodie, with silver wark, estimat to the sowme of £266 13s.4d.

Summa of the inventar: £2,034 13s.4d.

Followis the dettis awin to the deid:

Item, thair was awin to the said umquhill Margaret Stewart and hir said spous, be Andro Wod of Stravethie and [*blank*] his tennentis, 4 chalderis of beir, pryce of the boll 5 merks, summa £213 6s.8d.; item, be John Weymes of Craigtoun, £200; item, be James Weymes, indweller in Leith, conforme to his obligatioun, the soume of 650 merks.

Summa of the dettis awin to the deid: £846 13s.4d.

Summa of the inventar with the dettis: £2,881 6s.8d.

Followis the dettis awin be the deid:

Item, thair was awin be the said umquhill Margaret Stewart and hir said spous, to [*blank*] laird of Coupmalyndie, elder, the sowme of 900 merks; item, to Patrik, erle of Orknay, the sowme of 160 merks; item, to Alexander Murchiesone, hynd, for his boll and bounteth, 100 merks; item, to Thomas Watterstoun, hynd, for his boll and bounteth in anno 1607, 100 merks; item, to Patrik Thomassone, servand and hynd, in anno foirsaid, for his boll and bounteth, 100 merks; item, to Airchbald Strang, hynd and servand, for his boll and bounteth in anno foirsaid, 100 merks; item, to Nicoll Thomsone, servand, of fie and bounteth, 20 merks; item, to Thomas Skartey, servand, of fie and bounteth, 40 merks; item, to James Coustiane, servand, for his fie and bounteth, 40 merks; item, to Williame Corstiane, servand, of fie and bounteth, £20; item, to John Irving, servand, of fie and bounteth, £20; item, to Marioun Flett, servand, for hir fie and bounteth, 20 merks; item, to Margaret Irving, servand, of fie and bounteth, 10 merks; item, to Marioun Irving, servand, of fie and bounteth, 10 merks money.

Summa of the dettis awin be the deid: £1,106 13s.4d.

Restis of frie geir, the dettis deducit: £1,784 13s.4d.

To be devydit in thrie partis, deidis part is £594 17s.9d.

Quhairof the quot is componit for 20 merks.

We, Mr John Arthour, etc., understanding that eftir dew summoning and laufull warning maid be forme of edict oppinlie as effeiris of the executoris and intromettoris, etc., we decernit thairintill as our decreit gevin thairupoun beiris, conforme to the quhilk, etc., quhairupoun Mr Robert Henrysoun of Holland in Stronsay is becum cautioun, etc., as ane act beiris.

SRO, CC.8/8/44, ff.154-5.

462. Skalloway bankis, 27 September 1608

Extract decreet in action at instance of Captain William Sinclair and John Neven of Skousbrugh against William Sinclar in Ustanes.

The quhilk day in presence of me Eduard Scollay of Strynnie, sheref deput of Orknay and Yetland, anent the actioun and caus persewit be Capitane William Sinclar, commissioner for the airis of Brugh, and John Neven of Scousbrugh, contrair and aganes William Sinclar in Ustanes, makand mentioun that quhair the saidis persewers hes undoubtit richt and titill in and to the outfredome of Bransammerland in the parochin of Tingwall, quhilk the said William hes wrangouslie mellit with and [*illegible*] his awin proffeit, and will in no wayis as yit remuif thairfra, nor pay the proffeit thairof to the saidis compleneris pro rato during the space of his intromissiounis and cossing thairof, as the summonds raissit, and now as of befoir producit thairanent in the self beiris. The said John Neven, persewar, compeirand personallie, and the said Capitain William be James Neven, his procurator, and lykwyis the said William, defendar, compeirand personallie, thair reasounis and allegeances hard and considerit, the forsaid judge, efter mature deliberatioun, decernit as is underwrittin, because the said William compeirand as said is absolutlie referrit the richt and titill of the forsaid outfredome to the persewer thair probatioun; adding thairwith that gif they sall happin to pruif the samyn that he sall renunce all richt and possessioun he had, hes, or may have thairto; quhairupon the saidis persewers tuik and offerit presentlie to preif thair said richt in judgment *per testes legittimos et eciam alio modo quo d*[*torn*]. Nochttheless the forsaid judge upon certaine ressonable consideratiounis decernis and ordainis the said parties to compeir upon the ground of the forsaid outfredome the aucht day of November nixtocum; and thair in presence of Arthour Sinclar of Ayth, judge delegat and commissioner to that effect, to heir and sie ane lawfull hagrie or perambulatioun halden thairupon the auld marchis of richt, and his decreit thairintill *secundum visa allegate et probata*; and that the parties compeir to curie, as they will win or tyne in the caus.

Extractum de libro actorum dicte Jacobus Jak eiusdem pro tempore scribam.

SA, SC.12/65/1/57. See next item.

463. Skalloway bankis, 28 September 1608

Commission by Edward Scollay of Strynie, sheriff-depute of Orkney and Shetland, to Arthour Sinclar of Ayth.

Be it kend till all men be thir presentis, me Edward Scollay of Strynnie, sheref and justice deput of Orknay and Yetland, forsamekill as thair is ane actioun depending betuix Capitane William Sinclar, commissioner for the airis of Brugh, John Neven of Skousbrugh, on the ane part, and William Sinclar in Ustanes, on the uther part, anent the richt and titill of the fredome of Branshamberland, in the parochin of Tingwall, quhilk actioun through the seasoun and tyme of yeir can not dewlie be now reasonit and decydit; Thairfoir to have maid, constitut and ordanit, and be the tenour heirof, makis, constitutis and ordainis Arthour Sinclar of Ayth my verrie lawfull and undoubtit commissioner to the effect underwrittin, gevand, grantand and committand to him my full and frie power, express mandatorie and charge to pas upon the day undermentionat to the ground of the landis of Bransammerland; and thair be perambulatioun thairof tak dew tryall and cognitioun how far and to quhilk of the saidis parties of auld is extendit and properlie apperteinis the outfredome of the samyn;

and to that effect persones of inqueist maist famous, the best knawin, he verilie to caus charge and convein with him upon the aucht day of November, presence of his court, then to affix members thairof, to creat and admit persones of inqueist, to caus be sworne witnessis, likwyis to be sworne to examinat the ground as said is, to perambulat the march conforme to tryall, to sett and proper to stand and remain as perpetuall marchis of the said outfredome in tyme cuming; and for effectuatting of the premissis the parties to caus cherge and convein befoir him the said day and place to heir and sie the proces of perambulatioun orderlie deducit, and the [pre]senc of the ane verifiet, lawfullie summond, not to prejudge the uther, decreit to pronunce thairintill permittand to all parties ther just and lawfull defences; and generallie all and sundrie uther thingis to do, use, haunt and exercice, requyrit of the law in the caus and matter of perambulatioun. Subscryvit at Scalloway bankis, the xxviij of September 1608.

SA, SC.12/65/1/57 (on same sheet as no. 462).

464. Skalloway bankis, 5 October 1608

Obligation by Andro Edmestoun, vicar of Yell, to Edward Scollay of Strynie, sheriff-depute and chamberlain of Orknay and Yetland, for £1,351 8s.10d. in respect of Andro's intromissions as collector of the duties of Yell, Fetlar, Unst and Northmavine.

Witnesses: Petir Symsone, minister at Nesting, Walter Richie, servant of Sir John Arnot of Barswik, knight, Robert Scollay, and James Jak, notary public, writer hereof.

SRO, RD.1/152, ff.198-9.

465. Edinburgh, 8 November 1608

Decreet of court of session at instance of William Bruce of Simbister against William Fermour, notary public in Dunrosnes, for delivery of the contract between said William Bruce, on the one part, and Frances Sinclair of Uya, on the other part, dated 8 April 1608, whereby Frances disponed to William the 16 marks land of the Kirkhous of Olnafirth under reversion of 500 merks, together with the charter and sasine following thereon; and also the renunciation made by the said Frances, and James and Margaret Sinclairis, his brother and sister, with consent of William Bruce, spouse of said Margaret (*sic*), in which they renounced in the pursuer's favour all tacks pertaining to them of lands and possessions, and all goods and gear to which they had any right, title or kindness, through the decease of their father and mother. The writs had been left by the pursuer in the hands of William Fermour, maker and former thereof, upon trust and confidence that he would deliver them to him, but now, upon collusion with other parties, William Fermour refuses to deliver them.

The lords of council decern the defender to produce the writs and to have them delivered to the pursuer, or else to allege why they should not be delivered.

SRO, CS.7/235, f.305; CS.7/238, ff.12-3. William Bruce had been married to Margaret Stewart, who died on 25 November 1607 (see no. 461); she was the mother of Frances Sinclair.

466. Innersand, 14 November 1608 (at 10 a.m.)

Instrument of sasine in favour of Jerome Umphray of Sand, and Margaret Murray, his spouse, following on disposition by Magnus Mychaelsoun in Sandsound, with consent of Andro Magnussoun, his eldest son, of 1½ marks uthal land, 12 pennies the mark, in the town of Innersand, in the parish of Sandsting and Aithsting. Sasine given by Magnus to Jerome, and to Walter Thomsoun, burgess of Aberdene, attorney for Margaret.

Witnesses: Johnne Peirsoun in Eister Skeld, Andro Andersoun, chapman in Sand, Robert Linkletter, grieve in Sand, Magnus Mathosoune there, and James Neven, notary public.

SA, GD.144/9/18.

467. Strotholme and Brugh, 26 November 1608

Instrument of sasine in favour of an honourable woman Jeane Bruce, relict of Hew Sinclair of Brugh, and now spouse to Thomas Blak, to the third and terce of the lands of the barony of Brugh and the manor place of Strotholme. Precept was directed by David Brysone, Alexander Douglas, James Chalmers and Mr William Stewart, macers, sheriffs of the sheriffdoms of Orkney and Yetland and bailies of the regality thereof, by commission under testimony of the great seal, to William Fordyce, officer, narrating that 'upone the last day of Julij last bypast Jeane Bruce relict of umquhile Hew Sinclair of Brugh wes befoir us in ane court of the said sherefdome and regaletie respective, than haldin within the tolbuith of the brugh of Edinburgh, laufullie servit and cognoscit to ane ressonabill terce and thrid of all and sindrie the landis and utheris respective eftirmentionat quhairin hir said umquhile spous deit last vestit and sesit as of fie', viz., (1) the lands and barony of Brugh comprehending 36 marks land of Brugh, 33 marks land of Glaitnes, 6 marks land of the 'mekill yle' of Glaitnes, 4 marks land of the little isle of Glaitnes, 12 marks land of the 'mekill yle' of Linga, 4 marks land of the little isle of Linga in Quhailsay Sound, 4 marks land of Firasetter, 6 marks land of Wassa, 1 mark land of Aswik, 1 mark land of Skelsta, 2½ marks land of Husabuster, 3 marks land of Kirkabuster, 1½ marks land of Levanip, 1 mark land of Skenrie, 3½ marks land of Neving, 2½ marks land of Grunyefrith, 3 marks land of Clet in Quhailsey, 6 marks land of

Sandwik, together with another 3 marks land there, 2½ marks land of Huksetter there, 2 marks land of Levasetter there, 6 ures land of Ska there, 1 mark land of Merasetter there, ½ mark land of Brugh alias Eisthouses there, 30 marks 2½ ures land of Skeres, in the parish of Nesting; 4½ marks land of How, together with another 2 marks land there, 2 marks land of Hamagaris, 1 mark land 6 ures land of Houskourie, 4½ marks land of Skarpagarth, 1 mark land of South Kirkgair, 6 marks land in Sound, 2 marks land of Cova, in the parish of Weisdaill; 3 marks land of Nesbuster, 2 marks land of Hammar, 1 mark land of Uphous, 1 mark land called Cairnes in Eistines, in the parish of Quhytnes; 12 marks land of Unyefirth, 2 marks land of Tuait in Langskaill, 2 marks land of Sanilsatter, in the parish of Sandsting and Eisting; 12 marks land of Browalland, 5 marks land of Curcigarth, 9 marks land of Seatter, 4 marks land of Foudebrugh, 6 marks land of Melbie in Sandis, 6 marks land in Gramanatwatt, 1½ marks land of Seatter, in the parish of Wallis; 6 marks land of Howland, 3 marks of Glouff, in the parish of Northmaven; 12 marks land of Levasetter, 15 marks land of Culbeinsbrugh, 8 marks land of Ham and Hoversta, 2 marks land, in the parish and isle of Bressa; 4 marks land of Burrovo, 3 marks land of Weddersta, 8 marks land of Lingaholme, in the parish of Delting; 4 marks land of Sandwik, 1 mark land of Clet, in the parish of Burra; 9 marks land of (blank) in the isle of Unst; 1 mark land called Unholme and holm called Linga in Yelsound, with sasine to be given on the lands of Brugh; (2) the 18 pennyland of Housbie and isle called Auskerrie in the isle of Stronsay, parish of Sanctmichell, in Orkney, with sasine to be given on the land of Auskerrie; and (3) the manor place of Strotholme, being the deceased Hew's second mansion, for Jean's habitation during her lifetime, conform to the laws and practices of this realm: 'the quhilk terce and thrid the said Jean seill at the schadow be cavilles cassin thairupone'.

Sasine given by William Fordyce at the manor place of Strotholme at 9 a.m. in the presence of Mathow Forrester of Hamarsland, Henry Kneland in Stratholmenes, Henry Chalmer in Howgoland, and Arthour Cathanacht in Wydbuster; and at Brugh at 1 p.m. in presence of Captain William Sinclair, David Stewart in Brugh, Hew Tarrell in Beinstay, the saids Mathow Forrester, Henry Kneland, and Henry Chalmer, and Bartill Ewinistoun in Strotholme. James Neven, notary public.

SA, SC.12/65/1/58.

468. Edinburgh, 26 November 1608

Decreet of court of session in action at instance of William Bruce of Symbister against Edward Sinclair of Marresetter, for removal from the 'sey buithis' of Hamsetter, as proper parts and pertinents of the pursuer's lands of Symbister. Edward had been warned to remove at Whitsunday 1608.

The lords of council decern the defender to remove from the land.

SRO, CS.7/238, f.65. Edward Sinclair was put to the horn on 13 July 1611 for not complying with the decreet (SRO, DI.3/40, ff.332-4).

469. Edinburgh, 26 November 1608

Decreet of court of session in action at instance of William Bruce of Symbister against Jerhome Leslie in Breiwick for removal from 2 marks land, 12 pennies the mark, of Brewick, in the parish of Tingwall. Jerhome had been warned to remove at Whitsunday 1607.

The lords of council decern the defender to remove from the land.

SRO, CS.7/238, ff.65-6.

470. Melbie, 3 December 1608 (at 2 p.m.)

Instrument of sasine in favour of Gilbert Gifhert and Katherin Umphray, his spouse, following on disposition, dated 9 September 1604 at Wederstay, by Andro Gifhert of Wederstay, father of Gilbert, of 18 marks uthell land, 8 pennies the mark, of Melbie, 9 marks uthell land, 12 pennies the mark, of Hugsettir, and 2 marks uthell land, 12 pennies the mark, in Estasetter, in the parish of Sandnes; 18 marks uthell land of Isbuster, in the parish of Delting, and 3 lasts king's land, set in feu by my lord of Orknay and his commissioners to Andro, in the said parish, with reservation to Andro and his spouse of the liferent of the lands of Isbuster and the three lasts of king's land, conform to contract of marriage, dated 10 January 1604 at Burweik, between Gilbert, on the one part, and Andro Umphray, father of Katherin, on the other part. Precept of sasine directed to Jherom Umphray of Sand. Witnesses to disposition: Johne Gifhert, son of Andro, Peter Robertsoun, and Mathew Robertsoun, foud at Delting.

Sasine given to Thomas Chein of Valay, procurator for Gilbert, and Katherin. Witnesses: Andro Wischert in Melbie, Andro Bult there, Hieronimus Bult there, Erasmus in (illegible) there, Patrik Bult there, William Red, officer, Andrew Andersoun, merchant, William (illegible)air, servant of Andro Umphray of Berrie, and James Neven, notary public.

SA, D.10/17/4.

471. Wallay, 8 December 1608 (?)

Obligation by Arthour Irving of Ure to Thomas Auchinlek, for payment of 72 angel nobles, if decreet of warrandice is obtained by Thomas against Thomas Cheyne of Walay for payment of said sum. Thomas Cheyne was on 5 August 1588 (*sic*) pursued by Patrik, earl of Orknay, in a sheriff court held at Skalloway bank by David Kennedy, sheriff depute for the time, and Thomas Auchinlek, clerk of court, for payment of 72 angel nobles, due by the deceased Mr Robert Cheyne, father of Thomas

Cheyne; whereupon Thomas obtained decreet absolving him as heir to his father of said sum. Now of new Thomas Auchinlek has intended action in cause of warrandice against Thomas before Edward Scollay, sheriff depute of Orknay and Yetland.

Witnesses: Mr William Hay, archdeacon of Yeitland, Walter Hay and Francis Thanne(?).

SRO, CS.290/32. When the bond was registered, on 3 June 1609, Arthur Irving's procurator became cautioner for Thomas Cheyne that if it was found by the lords of council that Thomas Cheyne ought to warrand Thomas Auchinlek, commissary of Orknay, at the hands of Patrik, earl of Orknay, of 70 angel nobles (owed to the deceased Robert, earl of Orknay), Arthur Irving would cause him do the same.

There is another caution (SRO, CS.290/32, reg. 11 July 1609) where Frances Mudie of Braknes becomes cautioner for Thomas Cheyne to keep scatheless Thomas Auchinlek at the hands of Patrik, earl of Orknay, anent payment of 70 angel nobles owed by the deceased Mr Robert Cheyne and the deceased Mr Jerome Cheyne, his father brother, to the deceased Robert, earl of Orknay.

472. Edinburgh, 17 December 1608

Decreet of court of session in action at instance of Laurence Bruce of Cultmalindies against Patrik, earl of Orknay, lord Yetland, and Thomas Levingstoun of Ballintone, his cautioner, for contravention of act of lawburrows, dated 12 January 1603.

The first alleged instance of contravention occurred on 10 July 1604, when Lawrence Bruce, intending to transport himself, his servants, and goods from his place of Mownes in the isle of Unst to Dunrosnes, and had put in his boat certain of his trunks, butter and fish, to the quantity of three lasts of gear, and directed Schewart Erasmussone and James Davidsone, his servants, to take the boat and goods to the port of Uyeasound, when, on that same day, Captain Allan Lentrone, domestic servitor to the earl, and captain of his ship called the *Dunkirkar*, came in the said ship with the earl's servants, skippers and mariners, and violently took, apprehended and intromitted with the said boat and the goods and gear therein, and compelled the said servants of Laurence, 'being within the foirsaid boit to cum out of the samyn boit and to enter within the said ship, and thaireftir reft and awaytuik the said boit and haill guidis foirsaidis thairintill, and detenit the foirnamit persones as prisonares within the schip foirsaid be the space of fyve or sex dayes, albeit thay war oure fre leiges and servandis to the said Laurence'.

The second instance of contravention occurred on 19 July 1604, when Laurence Bruce, 'being myndit, for eschewing of the monyfold oppressiones done and committit aganes him' by Patrik, earl of Orknay, 'to repair to the boundis of Lawdian, Fyiff and Stratherne for doing of his lawchfull effairis, and to that effect haveing conditionat and aggreit with Andro Adeson, merchant in Sanctandrois, for his transporting and fraught, and being inbarkit and enterit within the said Andro Adesoneis crear at Sounburghheid', after proclamation by the said earl that none should transport Laurence furth of Yetland under the pain of death, Laurence was forced to leave the said crear and come ashore. Immediately after his coming on land, on the same day, he was violently taken and apprehended by William Stewart, James Crawfurd, Alexander Leggat, Robert Mous, and divers others, to the number of twenty persons or thereby, all domestic servants to the earl, who 'forceit and compellit him, haveing his buittis and spurris on, to gang bak with thame on fute throw moss and mure and wildernes be the space of twentie sex myles' to the earl's castle of Skalloway and to Skallowaybank, where Laurence was detained captive for three or four days.

The lords of council decern Patrik, earl of Orknay, to have contravened lawburrows in respect of the second instance, and therefore Thomas Levingstoun of Ballintone, as cautioner, to have incurred the pain of £5,000. The lords decern the said earl and his cautioner, jointly and severally, to make payment of the said sum, half to the king and half to Laurence Bruce, conform to act of parliament.

CS.15/103 (summons, dated 18 December 1605); SRO, CS.7/239, ff.152-3. As regards the first alleged instance of contravention it was claimed by the defence that, on 15 July 1604, as soon as the earl of Orknay learned of the matter, he had put Laurence Bruce's servants to liberty, and restored the boat and all the goods and gear therein. Depositions of witnesses for proving of the points of the second instance of contravention were taken in Edinburgh in February and March 1607 (SRO, CS.15/103), from which additional information is provided as follows:

'William Ramsay in Dysart, servand to the lard of Parbrothe, of the aige 46 yeiris or thairby, mariet, depones that he being send be his maister, the lard of Parbrothe, to Yetland in cumpanie with the lard of Colpmalyndie from Scotland, and salit from Dysart to Yetland, and quhen thai come thair he remanit with Colpmalyndie in his awin hous of Moynes quhill it plesit the lard of Colpmalyndie to reteir him self bak agane towartis Scotland, and the said lard and his deponar being myndit towartis the inland of Scotland, they come to Soundbrughheid, and this deponar finding ane crear of Sanctandrois quhais maister was David Fyiff, he inbarkit within the samin and maid conditioun with the skippar to transport him towartis Lowthiane for hyre, and as he was within the ship or crear, being twa pair of butlandis from the shoir, thair come aff shoir in ane boit to the crear the lard of Colpmalyndie, and quhen he come to the crear the skippar callit David Fyiff and the merchand of the crear, quhais name he rememberis nocht, howsone evir thai saw Colpmalyndie within the crear thay refusit to mak saill with Colpmalyndie, saying that thai war dischargit be the erle of Orknayis proclamatioun to do the samin to transport the said lard of Colpmalyndie out of Yetland. Then the skipper and mariners left the crear and pass in ane boitt to the shoir and left Colpmalindie in the crear behind thame, and quhen thai come to the shoir this deponar hard the foyd of Yetland, quhais name he rememberis nocht, cry with ane loud voice to Colpmalyndie, "Come on shoir to speik with the ladie Orknay, for ye will nocht get leif to mak sail quhill ye come on shoir". Then Colpmalyndie anserit and said "That seing I can nocht get leif in peax to mak sail, and that the skipper and merchant hes left the crear for my caus, necessitur compellis me to mak to schoir agane". Thairfoir he passit in the boit again eftir that he had tariet ane hour in the crear, and come to land on shoir, and this deponar quhen he saw Colpmalindie cum to shoir, he saw the foyd accumpaneit with sundrie personis tak Colpmalyndie with thame aff the shoir. Askit quhair thai tuik him he kennis nocht bot thai tuik him out of the sycht, and howsone Colpmalyndie come to shoir and the foyd had tane him aff shoir, the skipper and merchand come aff shoir in ane boit to the crear, and than thai weyit the crear and come to Sanctandrois the thrid day thaireftir, and kennis na mair in the mater be ressoun he was nocht on shoir eftir that Colpmalyndie come to shoir to sie quhat become of him thaireftir. And that this was all upoun the nynetein day of July 1604.'

'Thomas Rankeine in Dysart, mariner thair, of the aige of 50 yeiris or thairby, mariet, deponis that he saw Colpmalyndie cum within the crear quhairof Andro Adesoun was merchand in Soundbrughheid, and the said merchand and mariner come to shoir howsone Colpmalindie come within the crear and said thai durst nocht transport the said lard of Colpmalyndie towartis the inland of Scotland out of Yetland, and saw the foid accumpaneit with sindrie personis convoy Colpmalyndie up the cuntrey. Addendo, that William Fermour, foyd of Yetland, come to this deponar quha was lyand in raid with his awin crear and desyrit for fraucht to transport him to the country of Buchane, and forbad him to transport ony man and speciallie the lard of Colpmalyndeis to the inland of Scotland under the pane of deid, and the very day libellit, the nynetein day of July, Colpmalyndie come to this deponar and desyrit him for fraucht to transport him to Buchan, quha anserit, "I dar nocht do it for I am commandit be the foyd in my lordis name nocht to do the samin, for I am dischargit to transport ony man furthe of Yetland"; and thairfoir Colpmalyndie tuik ane boit and come in to the crear libellit, and thai refusit also to transport him as he hes deponit, and was compellit to pas to shoir again, and Andro Adesounis crear maid saill without Colpmalyndeis. And sayis that be the voice of the cuntrey the foyd with his complicis tuik him to Skellwabankis, my lord Orknayis hous.'

'Andro Broun in Myresyde, under the duik of Levenax, of the aige of 30 yeiris or thairby, mariet, deponis that he saw William Fermour, baillie and foyd, and John Ecfurd, officar of Yetland, pas within ane boyt with certane his complicis from the shoir syde of Soundbrughheid towartis Andro Adesounis crear, twa pair of butlandis from the shoir, and quhen he come thair he brocht with him furthe of the crear the merchand and skipper and haill cumpanie; but Colpmalyndie wald nocht cum furthe of the crear, and Colpmalyndie seing that he culd nocht mak saill without the skipper and cumpanie, he cryit for the boit and he come to shoir, and quhen he come thair he lugit in John Scottis hous thair; and within twa dayis thaireftir the said William Fermour, accumpaneit with William Stewart, James Craufurd, Alexander Legat, Robert Mous, Mans Lutfut, and syndrie utheris, with swordis and pistolaitis, come to the said John Scottis hous and brocht to him ane lytill neg, and he pat on his buittis and raid sex mylis to Mayvik, and fra Mayvik he was tane perforce be the saidis personis to Skallowy on his fut with his buittis on, be the space of fourtene myllis be ressoun no man mycht ryid of gait; and as he come with the foirsaidis personis, quha war domestill servandis to the erle of Orknay, to Skallowy, and was tane to the castell of Skallowy, and tariet thair half ane hour and spak with the ladie, and within ane half hour thairefter he was desyrit to gang to Lilas Boyd, ane taverner besyd Skellwy bankis, and on the morne dynit with my ladie Orknay, and he tariet still thair thrie or four dayis quhill it plesit my lord of Orknay lat him away, and than salit in ane hering boit to Soundbrughheid, and furth thairof come in the mayne of Scotland. The deponar was present all the tyme with Colpmalyndie, bayth in Soundbrughheid and als convoyit him to Skallowy bankis.'

'James Wishart in Dysart, burgess thair, of the aige of 45 yeiris or thairby, mariet, deponis that he being in Yeitland quhair he arryvit from Dysart thair about the tent day of Junij 1604, and haveing landit at Hildisweik in Yetland quhair he remanit for the space of 20 dayis or thairby, and quhen he was thair Magnus Illisbrughe come to him, being foud of that part of Yetland, and commandit him, being merchand of ane bark thair, that he sald nocht transport na passingeris to na part of the continent land of Scotland, and speciallie nocht to transport the lard of Colpmalyndie, as he wald be anserable to my lord Orknay upoun thair lyvis, and eftir that he had remanit 20 dayis or thairby in Hildisweik he come with his bark to Soundbrughheid and landit thair, and tariet thair ane moneth in Soundbrughheid, and in the menetyme Colpmalyndie inbarkit within ane bark of Sanctandrois pertening to Andro Adesoun, and had aggreit with thame for his transporting to the continent land of Scotland.'

Included in the process papers (SRO, CS.15/103) is a petition to Patrik, earl of Orkney, by Osie Scott in Refirth (unsubscribed), for relief of oppression against him by Laurence Bruce. On the reverse of the petition is a precept, dated 17 June 1604, whereby Laurence Bruce was charged to find caution on 30 June 1604. Also in the papers is a notarial instrument, dated 18 July 1604, recording Laurence Bruce's refusal to find lawburrows and caution. It would appear that the defence produced these documents to justify the apprehension of Laurence Bruce at Sumburghhead on 19 July 1604. The documents are as follows:

1. 'My lord, unto your lordship humlie meneis and schawis I your lordshipis servitor Osie Scott in Refirth, that quhair Laurence Bruce of Culthemalindeis, sumtyme shereff deput of this cuntrie, maid ane pretendit quenquir of mony landis, and be his authoritie and power settillit himself in possessioun of the samin, ejectit the rycht possessouris thairfra quha had na power to compeditat and dowbill out the caus againest him, amangis quhom he hes usit me as ane, and wald masterfullie debar me fra my twelf mark land in Refirth, quhilks ar disponit to me in excambioun be my brother Salamone Scott, notwithstanding that I upone my seising hes obtenit peciabill possessioun thir dyverss yeiris, togidder with ane decret againes my said brother for warrandend of the same [see *CB1*, pp.43-44, 23 August 1602], quhilk seising and decreit I haiff presentlie redie to schaw your lordship; nevertheless the said Laurence Bruce be himself, his servandis and tennentis in his name, trublis me continewalie in the said possessioun of my foirsaid landis, and becaus I will not renunce it and giff it ouir to him, he forgis all the quarrellis that he can againest me, hes raisit letteris fra the lordis of counsell and chargit me to find lawboris; lyk as he hes presentlie brocht hame now letteris to trubill me with sum uthir chairges anent my compeirance befoir the saidis lordis, evin at thai wer na justice to be had within your lordshipis jurisductioun, off set purpois giff he could get me out of the cuntrie to gartak my lyfe, quhilk is aganis all equitie. In respeck we may have justice befoir your lordship in this cuntrie, heirfoir I beseik your lordship for the eternall god his caus to settile sic guid ordour for the suppressing of the said Laurence bangssterie and opressioun, that I amang uthir puir men of the cuntrie may bruik my awin in pece, and haif sum assurance that I sall not be invadit, molestit nor trublit in my bodie and possessioun of my landis in tyme cuming uthirwyse nor be ordour of law, under sic paines as it sall pleis your lordship till apoynt, and your lordshipis anser maist humblie I beseik.'

'At Scalloway bankis the xvij of Junij 1604. Becaus my lord hes sene the seasing and decreit within mentionat, commandis and ordanes the baillie of Yell to help, serve and defend the complenar in peceabill possessioun of his landis of Refirth within mentionat, ay and quhill he be lauchfullie callit and ordorlie put thairfra be the law; and becaus the said complenar hes giffen his bodilie aith that he feiris and dredis Laurence Bruce of Cultemalyndies bodily harme, ordanes and commandis the said baillie and officaris of Yell to pass, command and charge the said Laurence to find sufficient cautioun and souirtie actit in the buikis of this sherefdome that the said complenar sall not be invadit, persewit nor trublitt in his bodie, landis, possessiounis, guidis nor geir at ony tyme heireftir uthirwayis nor be ordor of law, undir the panes contenit in the act of parliament, be the said Laurence nor nane uthir according to that said act of lawsourtie, and that within sex dayis of the said charge undir the same pane.

'Orknay
'A. Martyne

'Upone the last day of Junij 1604, I Jaspert Cullen, officer, past at command of the precept abonewretin and chargit Lawrence Bruce of Cultemalindeis to find lausouertie to Ossie Scott of Refert, conforme to the tenour of the said precept in all pointis, and this I did to the said Laurence, he being personalie apprehendit, yeir, day and moneth foirsaid. Befoir thir witnessis: Magnus Norske, minister at Unst, Walter Makriche, officer thair, and James Ossuald, tailleour.'

2. 'At Johnne Scottis duelling hous the xviij day of July the yeir of god Jaij VIc and four yeiris, in presence of me William Fermour, notar publict and witnes efter following, Lawrence Bruce of Cultmalindie being chergit, personalie apprehendit, be James Levingstoun, servitor to the erle of Orknay, as commissioner for his lordship, and be vertew of his lordshipis ampill commissioun directit to that effect, to find lawburrowis and cautioun to Osie Scot, that he and his, his guidis and geir, sall be harmles and skaithles of the said Lawrence Bruce and all that he may lat or stay, according to his lordshipis precept directit thairupoun, quhairof the coppy is deliverit to the said Laurence,

he hes refusit the said cherge and will nocht obey it, quhairupoun the said James Levingstoun tuik instrument. This done at the shoir of Exanabu, the day and yeir foirsaid, at xij houris forrow nowne or thairabout. Befoir thir witness: Maister James Pitcairne and Thomas Swentoun, ministeris, Johne Swentoun, sone to the said Thomas, James Kintor younger, and Hercules Hay, with uthiris divers.

'Ita est Wilhelmus Fermour, notarius publicus, in
premissis rogatus teste hoc meo chyrographo.'

473. Edinburgh, 4 February 1609

Decreet of court of session in action at instance of William Bruce of Symbister against Patrik, earl of Orknay, lord Yetland, Frances Sinclair of Uya, Robert Sinclair of Ramnego, Adam Sinclair of Brow, John Fermour, son of William Fermour, 'auldfod', John Stevinsoun in Exanabie, and Richard Leisk in Toap, for coming to the town and lands of Sowmburgh on divers days in June and July 1608, and 'ryffing, breking and straiking up of the durris and lockis of the saidis outsettis, houssis, bigginis, barnis and byris, entering of thamselves, thair men, tennentis and servandis thairin, closing and dyking with ane greit heich bred dyke biggit of faill, stane, eard and utheris materallis of ane greit quantitie of the saidis landis of Sowmburgh, lyand upoun grene growand cornis thairon, for the tyme extending in quantitie to thrie akeris of land nixt contigue adjacent to the said Erle his castell in the toun of Sowmburgh callit the New Hall, thinking to appropriat the samyn to himselff and his said castell, eitting and destroying of the grene cornis than growand upoun the said landis of Sowmburgh perteining to the said William Bruce as his awin proper cornis and sawin be him thairon the seasoun nixt immediatelie preceiding', and thereby ejecting the pursuer, and for spulyie of the green growing corns, extending to the sowing of 200 bolls oats, price of the boll with the fodder £5, and 80 bolls bere, price of the boll with the fodder £6; and for spulyie from the said town and lands of Sowmburgh of 30 milk ky, price of the piece £18; 100 milk ewes with their followers, price of the piece £2; 25 work horses, price of the piece £15; 8 mares with their followers, price of the piece £12; 2 'staneit' horses, price of the piece £15; 20 oxen, price of the piece £18; 20 head of stots and stirks, price of the piece £6; and furth of the great barn, 2 chalders of 'threschin and dicht' bere, price of the boll £6; 30 bolls 'threschin and dicht' oats, price of the boll £4; and furth of the barnyard, 2 stacks of bere, at 2 chalders bere, price of the boll with the fodder £7; and furth of the outsets, houses, biggings, barns and tofts, a great chest of oak, well locked and banded, price thereof £10; and furth of the said chest, a silver piece and a silver mazer, the silver piece weighing 18 ounces, price thereof £54, and the silver mazer weighing 24 ounces, price thereof £72; a dozen silver spoons at 18 ounces, price of the ounce £3 10s.; furth of the said chest, 'velvet raissit stuff, stemyng, Holland claith, lynning claith, worset schankis', valued at £300; a locked box, price thereof £3;

furth of the said locked box, of gold and silver, £1,400; a chest of fir, locked and banded, price thereof £8; furth of the same, 20 pairs of linen sheets, price of each pair £5; 20 pairs of white plaids, price of each pair £6; 20 'sewit' bed coverings, price of the piece £12; 2 stands of 'dornick naprie' price of each stand £20; 4 'cop-burde towellis' of Holland claith, price of the piece £3; 4 stands of common napry, price of each stand £8; 2 'burde claiths' of green cloth, price of the piece £20; 6 pairs of 'fyne schone', price of each pair 33s.4d.; another chest of 'walnett trie', price thereof £8; 2 bibles, price of the piece £10; the old chronicles and history of Scotland in English, price thereof £10; the Acts of Parliament, price thereof £10; the Denss chronicle containing the history of Denmark, price £20; a book containing the universal great chart and description of the world, price thereof £20; an account book containing the whole discharges between the said William Bruce, pursuer, and his tenants, the interest and damage of the same, 500 merks; a discharge subscribed by Frances, Robert and James Sinclairis, and William Fermour, notary, to the said William Bruce, of the date at Troill and Boddene the (blank) day of March 1608, discharging him of all things whatsoever that they could lay to his charge before the date thereof, together with the evidents of Norvick and Symbister; 10 feather beds with 'bousteris', price of the piece with a 'cod' £12; 10 stone weight of 'pewder weschell', price of each stone £10; 15 iron pots, price of the piece £3; 6 brass pots, price of the pot £6; an 'aquavitie of pott with flaik and furnitour', price thereof £30; 6 brass pans, price of the piece £3; 2 pairs of 'raxis' and 4 'speittis', price £12; 4 crooks, price of the piece £2; 2 lavers and 2 basins, price of the piece £5; 6 brass chandlers, price of the piece 50s.; 4 hagbuts, price of the piece £10, 12 halberts, price of the piece £2; a 'corslet of pruiff with the heid peice with the ledge and the harnes thairto', price £20; 50 pairs of 'weit ledder schone to servandis', price of the pair £1; 60 stones of cut iron, price of the stone 30s.; 2 lasts of great Rochell salt, price of the last with the 'tries' £60; a last of Scots salt, price of the last with the 'tries', £36; 12 lasts of 'twm barrellis', price of the last £10; 4 barrels of tar, price of the barrel £10; 30 stones of lint, price of the stone £5; 20 stones weight of hemp, price of each stone thereof £3; 20 stones weight of 'takill tow', price of each stone weight thereof £3; 2 great meal girnels, price of the piece £10; of oatmeal furth of the same, 40 bolls, price of the boll £4; 2 great malt girnels, price of the piece £15; furth of the said girnels, 100 bolls malt, price of the boll £6; 4 boats with their furniture, price of the piece £60; 20 double herring nets, price of the piece £12; of herring slain by each of the said pursuer's boats and 'thrie' (*sic*) nets, 3 lasts, price of the last £60, 'of the quhilkis boittis, furnitour and nettis the said William Bruce wes in use of fisheing of hering and uther quhyte fishe on the sea foiranent the coist of the saidis landis of Swonburgh, and bringing of the samin to the coist, peir and schoir of the saidis landis, using and disponing thairupoun at his plesur, and without the quhilkis boittis, furnitour and nettis, he could not use the said fischeing, the samin fischeing and commoditie thairof being ane proper pertinent and commoditie of the saidis landis of Swonburgh, and so thairby wranguslie, violentlie and maisterfullie ejecting of the said William Bruce furth of his said fisheing and commoditie thairof, and spoliation of him of his possessioun of the samin'.

The lords of council decern Patrik, earl of Orknay, Robert Sinclair in Ramnego, Frances Sinclair in Uya, Adam Sinclair of Brow, John Stevinsoun, officer, in Exanabie, and John Fermour, to have done wrong in intruding themselves in the possession of the town and lands of Swonburgh and of the said fishings, and for the spulyie thereof, and decern the said defenders to desist and cease therefrom, and to restore the pursuer again to his possession thereof; and likewise decern the earl of Orknay and foresaid defenders to have done wrong in parking, closing and dyking of the said part of the lands of Swonburgh, and decern them to desist and cease therefrom, and to demolish, cast down and take away the said dyke, and make the same in as good estate in all conditions as it was before the closing and dyking thereof, and to restore the said William Bruce to his possession of the same; and in like manner the lords of council decern the said Patrik, earl of Orknay, and foresaid defenders to have done wrong in the spulyie, eating and destroying of the green corns growing on the lands of Swonburgh, and to pay to William Bruce the value and prices thereof; and to have done wrong in the spulyie of the goods and gear abovewritten, and decern the foresaid defenders to restore the same to the pursuer, or else the values and prices thereof. The lords of council absolve Richard Leisk in Toap from all the points of the summons, and decern him quit and free therefrom in time to come, because the pursuer failed in proving of the same against him. The defenders are decerned to pay the pursuer £20 in expenses, together with £5 to the lords' collector.

SRO, CS.7/238, ff.307-11. A certified extract of this decreet (SA, D.8/10) is printed in *Archaeologica Scotica*, iv, pp.390-8). According to letters of horning raised against Patrik, earl of Orknay, on 2 August 1608, the spulyie of William Bruce's house of Soundburgh took place on 2 July 1608 (SRO, DI.3/33, ff.57-9). When the action first came before the lords of council on 3 November 1608 the following defenders were also cited: James Sinclair of Ropnes, James Sinclair of Gott, Laurence Sinclair of Houss, Laurence Sinclair of Ustaness, William Fermour, 'auldfold', James Kyntor in Wolsness, and Malcolm Kyntor (SRO, CS.7/238, ff.4-5). Adam Sinclair of Brow was put to the horn for not finding lawburrows on 25 November 1608 (SRO, DI.3/32, ff.227-8), and relaxed from the horn on 8 December 1608 (SRO, DI.3/33, ff.191-2).

474. Edinburgh, 9 February 1609

Letters at instance of James Mowat, lawful son of Andro Mowat of Hougaland, against Magnus Mowat in Burrayfirth, charging the said Magnus to fulfil his part of contract of excambion, dated at Urafirth in

Northmaven on 23 January 1605, whereby Magnus disponed to James his 9 marks land, 8 pennies the mark, in Eist Burrayfirth in the parish of Aithsting, in exchange for lands disponed to him by the said James, under pain of rebellion.

SRO, DI.3/41, ff.245-7. Magnus Mowat was put to the horn on 13 November 1610, but the horning was relaxed on 27 December 1610 on the grounds that Magnus never subscribed the contract of excambion. He alleged that Mr James Pitcairn, minister, father-in-law of James Mowat, accompanied with his associates, had come to his dwelling house, and had compelled him to go with them to Urrafirth in Northmaven, where he had been shown the contract and requested to command a notary, because he could not write himself, to subscribe the same for him, which Magnus had refused to do, whereupon the said James Mowat cruelly hurt and wounded Magnus with a drawing sword, and notwithstanding Mr James Pitcairn, who was not even a notary, had subscribed the contract for him (SRO, DI.3/41, ff.347-8).

475. Edinburgh, 2 March 1609

Complaint by Thomas Blak, servitor to the king, to the privy council, against Patrik, earl of Orknay, for divers acts of oppression and seeking his slaughter, narrating that, on 10 July 1608, Captain Allane Lentroun, Thomas Lentroun, his son, Alexander McCulloch, Elias Kneland, Alexander Cogill, the said earl's gunner, Archibald Graven, his fiddler, Robert Mous, Robert Maxwell, his trumpeter, all domestic servitors to the said earl, with other servants, 'and with convocatioun of his majesteis leigeis in armes to the nowmer of xxxvj persounis of the said erllis speciall causing, command, sending, directioun and hounding out', came to the complainer's dwelling house in the isle of Quhailsay in Yetland, 'and thair violentlie brak up the duris ... enterit thairintill with drawin swordis in thair handis, searchit and socht the said complenair throw all pairtis of the samyn, scoggit the beddis thairof, and sua effrayit his spous, being thair for the tyme, that scho than pairtit with bairne, to the extrame hasard of hir lyf, and tuk ane boit and went to ane holme efter the same maner, socht the said complenair and brak up ane skoo quhairin thair wes fische drying, and reft and awaytuk with thame a grite quantitie of the samyn dry fische; and thay missing the said complenair being than suirlie informit that he had fled for just feir of his lyf to the laird of Cultemalindeis his house in the uther end of that cuntrey of Yetland, thay than resolveing to have his lyf, schippit in ane schip or grite weare bark of the said erllis a noumer of grite brasin and yrne peceis for beseigeing of the said complenair in his said house and battering of the samyn, and come thairwithall be sea directlie to the said place, quhair the said complenair wes in sober and quiet maner for the tyme, and at thair arryveing thair had not faillit to have put the samyn munitioun on schore, and beseiget the said complenair within the said house, wer not be the providence of god upoun occasioun of some adverteisment frome this cuntrey to the said erll he causit stay the saidis persounis fra the forder attempting of that wicked purpois'.

PC.1/24, pp.468-70. The complaint also narrates an act of oppression against Thomas Blak committed in Orkney in 1601.

476. Sand, 16 April 1609

Contract between Gilbert Makreyth and Robert Makreyth, his eldest son, on the one part, and Jherome Umphray of Sand, taking the burden on him for Agnes Umphray his eldest daughter, on the other part, whereby Robert binds himself to complete a band of matrimony with Agnes by 28 December 1609, and Jherome binds himself to pay Robert 300 merks by 1 November 1611, in satisfaction of all lands, goods etc. that Robert may claim in name of heritage after the decease of Jherome or Margaret Murray his spouse. Gilbert binds himself at the solemnisation of the marriage to infeft Robert and Agnes in 600 merks lying in the hands of the right honourable Alexander Fraser of Phillorth, and in 400 merks lying in the hands of Patrik Smyth, burgess of Fraserburgh, and on Gilbert's death to infeft them in 500 merks, presently in the hands of Patrik Gibson of Sheriffmylne, indweller in Elgin. Robert binds himself that after his decease Agnes shall get 'equall halffers' of any lands, goods etc. conquest by him. If the contract is broken the party breaker will pay the party keeper £1,000.

Witnesses: Robert Murray of Stainedaill, and James and Robert Makreyths, sons to Gilbert and brothers to Robert.

SRO, RD.1/195, f.133.

477. Edinburgh, 3 June 1609

Decreet of court of session in action at instance of James Sinclair, son lawful of the deceased (*sic*, cf. no. 532) Malcolme Sinclair of Quendall, against John Neving of Skrowisburgh, William Sinclair in Quhome, Gregorius in Lie, Adam Sinclair of Brow, Olay in Quendall, and all feuars and tenants of the prebendary called the 'croce stouk foundit within the colledge kirk of Dunrosnes', for payment of rents and duties of all years bypast which are unpaid. James has a lifetime gift of the said prebendary, granted under the privy seal on 21 June 1590 (no. 171).

The lords of council decern the defenders to make payment of all fruits and rents for all years bygone which are unpaid.

SRO, CS.7/243, ff.216-7.

478. Cannogait, 16 June 1609

Discharge by Patrik, earl of Orknay, to Malcome Sinclair of Quendaill, of the umboth duties of Dunrosnes (4 angels for the price of each barrel of 12 barrels butter, and 3 angels for the price of each barrel of 6 barrels of oil), the duty of Wallis (4 angels for the price of each barrel of 3 barrels butter, and 3 angels for the price of each barrel of 3 barrels oil), the umboths of Sandsting and Aithsting (20 angel nobles), and the duties of St Petiris Stowk in Fair Isle (7 angel nobles), of the crop 1608, conform to the tack by Patrik to Malcolm.

Witnesses: Michaell Balfour of Garth, Mr James King, notary, writer hereof, and James Annand, servant of Patrik.

SRO, RD.1/161, f.135.

479. Gillisbrek, 17 June 1609

Will of Magnus Hamsone in Gillisbrek.

At Gillisbrek in Lunesting the xvij day of Junij the yeir of god Jaj VJc and nyne yeiris. The quhilk day, in presens of William Magnussone of Neip, underfold of Nesting, Lunesting, Quhailsay and the Skerreis, and me, Peter Simsone, minister and witness underwrittin, Magnus Hamsone in Gillisbrek, seik in bodie bot sound in memorie and haill in spreit, willinglie and frelie enteris and possessis Robert Magnussone, his eldest sone, in his awin dwelling place and houssis in Gillisbrek and all and sindrie his utheris houssis, landis, takis, roumes, stedingis and possessiounis quhilkis he in that hour possessit and injoyit; and makis, nominatis and constitutis the said Robert, his sone, his onlie executour and intromittour with his haill guidis and geir and to be comptabill thairof during his lyfetyme; with power to the said Robert to give up inventar thairof efter his deceis and to bruik the samen as his onlie air and executour and nocht to answer nor mak payment to ony clamearis, calleris or persewaris nor to pay ony debtis quhatsumever to ony personis quhill the samen be tryet befoir my lord or his deputtis, and in speciall to Hew Sinclair, his airis or executouris: protesting befoir god and in his presens that all dispositiounis, wodsettis and alienatiounis that he maid to the said Hew wes aganis his will and that he wes compellit thairto, and that he never ressavit payment for the landis of North Neip, Magnelandholme, Skerreis and Gardoun, bot ane angell nobill, and this he tuik upon his conscience as he sould answer at the day of judgement quhen the secreittis of all heartis sall be disclosit. In witnes heirof the said Magnus desyrit the said foud to draw his usit mark thairto and me the said Peter Simsone, minister, to subscryve thir presentis as his latter will and legacie, becaus he could nocht wryt himself, day, yeir and place afoirsaid, befoir thir witnesses: David Strang in Orgill, Nicoll Adamesone in Vidlon, and Robert Achesoun, with utheris divers.

W. M.

P. Simsone, minister of
Nesting, Lunesting,
Quhailsay and Skerreis.

SRO, CC.17/2/2, f.131.

480. Edinburgh, 4 July 1609

Contract between Patrik, earl of Orknay, lord Yetland, as principal, with consent of Sir John Arnot of Berswick, knight, and Patrik, lord Gray, as cautioners, on the one part, and William Bruce of Symbester, on the other part. Forasmuch as William has on 4 February 1609 obtained a decreet of eviction and spulyie before the lords of council against Patrik and others (no. 473), William discharges Patrik of his part thereof, and declares Patrik to be quit and free of the said decreet. For which cause Patrik discharges William of the sum of 160 merks which William was in use to pay yearly to Patrik for the lands called the Provest lands pertaining to the king of Denmark for all years past and in time coming. Patrik also sets in tack to William the 29 marks land presently occupied by William and his tenants, and pertaining to Patrik heritably, in the town of Norwick in Unst, free of all gersums until Patrik pays William the sum of 500 merks in William's house in Symbester, for yearly payment by William to Patrik of the butter, wadmell, scat, victual and teind, 'usit and wont'. Patrik shall deliver to William 10 'ky', 10 oxen and horses, all good and sufficient, 12 barrels bere and 12 barrels oats, sufficient stuff of the growth of the rooms of Quhyttenes and Trondray, by Easter 1610, and failing delivery to pay £20 for each oxen, £10 for each horse, £10 for each barrel of bere, and £6 for each barrel of oats. And further, Patrik for the causes abovewritten, grants to William for life the duties of the 9 marks land in Symbester and 9 marks land in Hamnavo, extending yearly to £30, with power to William to use and dispone upon the said duties. Patrik consents 'that the hous biggit by his lordship on the schoir of Vigmavo besyde the said William his baikhous be ather dimolishit and castin down be the said William or utherwyis bruikit and josit as he pleissis to his awin use and behuife'. Patrik shall concur, fortify and assist William in taking and apprehending of the persons who evicted him and his tenants furth of the lands of Somebrugh, and who are denounced rebels and put to the horn, and shall assist William in the poinding of their goods and gear or apprising of their lands, and in all William's honest and lawfull affairs. Patrik shall also subscribe and deliver to William during all the days of his lifetime a letter of bailiary of the isle of Unst or the parish of Dunrosnes.

Witnesses: Mr John Home of Swansheil, Andro Gray, servant of Patrik, lord Gray. Written by George Sutherland, servant of Anthonie Quhyte, writer in Edinburgh.

SRO, RD.1/176, ff.10-12.

481. 5 July 1609

Precept by Patrik, earl of Orkney, to Edward Scollay.

Eduard Scolay, ye sall caus mett aff and misour to William Halcro sa meikill boundis of breid and lenthe as is contenit within his chartour quhilk was giffin to his mother be us quhen we was master of Orknay; and gif ony pretend rycht to the said boundis ye sall caus put it to ane poynt, and put William Halcro, his mother, to ane eis according to hir rycht; this ye faill not to do. Subscryvit with our hand, v July 1609.

Your master
Orknay

SA, D.10/9/1.

482. Olaberie, 11 July 1609

Contract between Andro Mowat of Howgoland, and John Mowat, apparent thereof, with consent of Cristien Stewart, spouse of said John, on the one part, and Mr James Pitcairne, minister at Northmavine, on the other part, whereby Andro renounces to Mr James 'the richt, use, government and dispositioun of the haill rent, leving and dewties of all ... thair landis within the cuntrie of Yetland, togidder with the lordis of Norowayis landis presentlie in thair possessioun ... the said Mr James his entrie thairto beand and begynnand to this instant crope and yeir of god Jaj VJc and nyne yeris, and thairefter to be upliftit be him and the said Johnne Mowat coniunctlie, alwayis uset, imployit and disponit upone be the said Mr James allanerlie, ay and quhill the full redemptioun, outquytting and recoverie of sic landis thairof as lyis in wodsett or uthir burding and danger quhatsumevir', with reservation to Andro of 'his rowmes of Brevick, Stenhous, Howgaland and Lien, frie of all debt or dewtie to be requyrit thairof, as also the landsetter town of Papa, and the fischingis in Veaskerie'. Mr James binds himself to employ the 'rent, leving and dewteis' as will extend to in money 'according to guid estimatioun', to redeem yearly thereof after first paying and satisfying the lords of Noroway of their debts and duties.

Witnesses: Edward Scollay of Strynie, Thomas Swentoun, minister at Kirkwall, John Swentoun, his son, minister at Holme, Mr Robert Swentoun, minister at Wallis, James Mowat, son of said Andro, and James Jack, notary public, writer hereof.

SRO, RD.1/165, ff.187-8.

483. Cannogait, 13 July 1609

Contract between William Bruce of Simbaster, on the one part, and Adam Sinclair of Brow, as principal, and Malcolm Sinclair of Condaill and Thomas Blak in Strome, as cautioners. Forasmuch as William has obtained a decreet of eviction and spulyie against Adam and others (no. 473), upon which William raised letters in four forms charging Adam to fulfill the said decreet, and for his disobedience Adam was denounced rebel, and was taken and put in ward in the tolbooth of the Cannogait where he presently remains, and because William is unwilling to use any rigour or extremity against Adam, William discharges Adam of all sums of money due by him by reason of the decreet, and consents to Adam's relaxation from the letters of horning, and that he be put to freedom and liberty, for which Adam binds himself to deliver to William at Someburgh, 6 ky (or £20 for each), 5 oxen (or £30 for each), 4 barrels of bere (or £10 for each barrel) and 4 barrels of oats (or £8 for each barrel), and if it is found that Adam has 'mellit' with any other goods or gear of William's he shall make restitution. Likewise, Adam renounces the letter of reversion given by William to Adam for the redemption of the 12 marks land, 8 pennies the mark, of Clumlie, in the parish of Dunrosnes, 'as the samyn lyis within the dykis of Clumlie', so that the foresaid lands may abide and remain with William perpetually for ever. Further, Adam grants 'fredome and full libertie to the said William Bruce, his airis and successoris in the land of Someburgh and Skatnes, and to his tenenttis and possessoris of samyn landis, to caist and win upoun the ground of the land of Browabrek pertening to the said Adam as a part of his landis of Brow, yeirly, the number and quantitie of aucht fadom, ten fute high, ten futt bread, and ten fitt of lenth, ilk fadome, of peattis, and to carie, transport, leid and awaytak the samyn furth of the ground of the said landis of Browabrek, to the said William Bruce his said landis of Someburgh and Skatnes, at libertie of gaittis and passages, frie isch and entrie, to and in fra the samyn, but ony stope, trubill or impediment to be maid thairintill be the said Adam or his foresaids'. In respect that Frances Sinclair of Uya and Robert Sinclair, his brother, were assisters and partakers of the committing of the spulyie and eviction foresaid, Adam binds himself neither to assist, supply or maintain them, directly or indirectly, against William and his tenants, under pain of perjury, infamy and defamation. Adam binds himself to fortify and maintain William in all his honest and lawfull affairs, and if Adam fails to keep the above clauses than William shall take full and free access in the foresaid decreet of eviction and spulyie.

Witnesses: Mr John Sinclair, servant of my Lord Berridaill, Michaell Balfour of Garth, George Conynghame, goldsmith, burgess of the Cannogait, and George Sutherland, servant of Antonie Quhyte, writer in Edinburgh, writer hereof.

SRO, RD.1/189, ff.371-2.

484. Edinburgh, 17 and 19 July 1609

Letters of procuratory by Lawrence Sinclar of Burghe, with consent of Mr Alexander Bruce, fiar of Cultmalindie, Robert Mentethe of Egilsay, and James Prymrois, portioner of Newlandis, his curators, in favour of his well-beloved uncle Captain William Sinclar, as factor and intromitter with his rents and living, for this instant crop and year 1609, and of all years preceding since the death of his father Hew Sinclar of Burghe, with full power to Captain William, providing he makes 'compt, rakning and payment to me and my curatoris forsaidis within the burgh of Edinburgh of his intromissionis'.

Witnesses: Mr Robert Hendirsone, and Edmund Sinclar of Flottay.

SA, SC.12/65/1/59.

485. Edinburgh, Leith and Coupmalindie, 19, 25 and 28 July 1609

Contract between Jean Bruce, relict of Hew Sinclar of Brugh, with consent of Thomas Blak of Strolme, now her spouse, on the one part, and Laurence Sinclar now of Brugh, her son, with consent of Mr Alexander Bruce of Coupmalyndeis younger, Captain William Sinclair, Robert Menteith of Eglischaw and James Prymrois, portioner of Newlands, his curators, on the other part, whereby Jean resigns her right of liferent and conjunct fee or terce of the lands which she might claim of Laurence by decease of his father furth of the lands and living of Brugh, or other lands pertaining to him wherein 'Hew deit last vest and sesit', with the exception of the lands underwritten, in which Laurence binds himself to infeft his mother in liferent, viz. 36 marks land, 6 pennies the mark, of Strolme with the mansion, manor place and pertinents of the same, 5 marks land, 8 pennies the mark of Olyir there, 14½ marks land, 6 pennies the mark, of Underbrek, 6 marks land, 9 pennies the mark, of Heone, 3 marks land, 9 pennies the mark, of Hammer, 1 mark land, 8 pennies the mark, of Uistinnes, ½ mark land, 8 pennies the mark, of Houfe, 1 mark land, 6 pennies the mark, of Unyeberrie, 3 marks land, 6 pennies the mark, of Nesbuster, 3 marks land, 6 pennies the mark, of Hammerisland, 7 marks land, 6 pennies the mark, of Stromnes, 6 marks land, 6 pennies the mark, of Hagristay, (illegible) marks land, 8 pennies the mark, of Cova, (illegible) marks land, 8 pennies the mark, of Helyesetter, (illegible) of Coitesoun, (illegible) marks land, 8 pennies the mark, of Nether (illegible), (illegible) marks land, 8 pennies the mark, of (illegible), (illegible) marks land, (illegible) pennies the mark, of Unyegarth, 6 marks land, 8 pennies the mark, of Skarpagarth, 6½ marks land, 6 pennies the mark, of Hamragarth, 2 marks 6 ures land, 12 pennies the mark, of Housgoir, 7 marks land, 12 pennies the mark, of Howfe in Weisdaill, 1 mark land, 9 pennies the mark, of Moustowe, 3½ marks land, 6 pennies the mark, of Degrand, 2 marks land, 9 pennies the mark, of Kirgoir, 3 marks land, 8 pennies the mark, of Trestrie, 3 marks land, 6 pennies the mark, of Sandsound, 1½ marks land, 12 pennies the mark, of Inner Sand, 11 marks land, 9 pennies the mark, of Eister Skeld, 17 marks land, 9 pennies the mark, of Unyefirth, 1 mark land, 6 pennies the mark, of Efirth, 3 marks land, 6 pennies the mark, of Langaskaill, 2 marks land,

8 pennies the mark, of Brek, 6 marks land, 8 pennies the mark, of Grunyevo, 4 marks land, 8 pennies the mark, of Burroland, 9 marks land, 6 pennies the mark, of Backy, 2 marks land, 12 pennies the mark, of Outhilstoft, 5 marks land, 12 pennies the mark, of Gardone, 13 marks land, 8 pennies the mark, of Swennesetterbrett, 3 marks land, 6 pennies the mark, of Nes there, 2 marks land, 6 pennies the mark, of Nether Holme, 1 mark land, 12 pennies the mark, of Laxvo, 3 marks land, 9 pennies the mark, of Sandfrie, 16 marks land, 9 pennies the mark, of Biggey, 8 marks land, 6 pennies the mark, of the holm of Unyearrie, 1 mark land, 9 pennies the mark, of Majer, 3 marks land of Seitter, 4½ marks land, 12 pennies the mark, of Semblesetter, 12 marks land, 9 pennies the mark, of Browland, 6 marks land, 8 pennies the mark, of Garmonetwat, 4 marks land, 8 pennies the mark, of Footabruch, 6 marks land, 8 pennies the mark, of Curcagar, 9 marks land, 8 pennies the mark, of Setter, 6 marks land, 8 pennies the mark, of Mewie, 1 mark land of Howasetter, 3 marks land, 6 pennies the mark, of Brounatwat, in the parishes of Quhytnes and Weisdaill, Eiststing and Sandsting, Walis, Delting, Tinguald, (illegible) the great holm of Gletnes and holm (illegible). Laurence binds himself to pay Jean, his mother, yearly for her lifetime the sum of 12 angel nobles in fine gold at Lammas, together with 48 meals victual, two parts bere and the third part meal, of the weight and measure of Orkney, all to be weighed on the malt pundlar and delivered to Jeane at Skalloway bankis between Yule and Candlemas, the times 'usit and wont'. It is specially agreed upon between the parties that 'during the lyftyme of Jeane it sall be lesum to hir and hir said spous to have the haill use and possession, propertie and grundricht of sex fisching bottes within the landis and yles of Skerreis togidder with ane licence, propertie and grundricht to thair awin proper fischingis bottes'.

Witnesses: James Stewart of Gramsay, William Bruce of Symbuster, Mr Robert Hendersone of Holland, Edmond Sinclair of Flotta, Johne Thomsone, writer in Edinburgh, and Mr Andro Logane, writer.

SRO, RD.1/163, ff.232-5. See no. 467.

486. Edinburgh, 3 August 1609

Letters at instance of Thomas Blak of Strome against Captain William Sincler, Edward Sincler of Maresetter, Andro Hawick of Scattista, Edward Sincler of Bulyesetter, William Sincler of Radwick, Jerhome Umphra of Sand, Frances Nicolsoun in Hagerstaw, and John of Strolmefurth, who having conceived a hatred and malice against the complainer, not only pursue him for his bodily harm and slaughter, at the instigation of Patrik, earl of Orknay, but also trouble and molest him in the possession of his lands of Strome 'be casting of faill, turf and devot thairupoun, pasturing of thair guidis, and eiting of the grass and hayit medowis thairwith of the samin, be shuitting of his cunyngis in the linkis of the samyn land, selchis and otterfische within the boundis thairof, and fowlling of fowllis with netis and dogis thairin', charging them to find caution and lawburrows that the complainer shall be harmless and scatheless, under pain of £500.

SRO, DI.3/38, ff.352-4. On 10 April 1610 Captain William Sincler, Andro Hawick of Scattista, Edward Sincler of Bulyeasetter, and Frances Nicolsoun were put to the horn for not finding caution. Edward Sincler of Bulyesetter was relaxed from the horn on 19 May 1610 on the grounds that he had not had time to come from Yetland to find caution in such a short space (SRO, DI.3/38, ff.400-1).

487. Dunrosnes, 23 August 1609

Obligation by Malcome Sinclaire of Quendall to his good friend Andro Adesone, citizen in St. Androis, for £500 for 'the rest of the price of ane schip callit the *Johne*', which Andro has sold to Malcome, to be paid by 15 April 1610 at St. Androis.

Witnesses: David Ogstoun, burgess of Montrois, James Merschell, notary public, writer hereof, David Adesoun, son of said Andro, and Thomas Blakbeard.

SRO, RD.1/180, ff.315-6.

488. Culyevo in Yell, 24 August 1609

Obligation by James Crawfurd, fold of Unst, to the honourable Edward Scollay of Strynie, for £208 2s.4d. in respect of his intromissions with the 'unlawis of Unst, and wattill, girsummis, taxatioun, my awin restis of the land maillis and scatt of the landis occupeit be me' for the year 1608 and preceding years.

James Crawfurd subscribes with his hand led touching the pen by Andro Edmestoun, minister at Yell. Witnesses: Magnus Ditken, Dutch merchant at Uyeaso(nd), John Stephanson, Dutch merchant at Culyevo, William Magnusson of Gairdie, Robert Scollay, servant of Patrik, earl of Orknay, lord Yetland, writer hereof, Daniell Nisbeit and James Nisbeit (who writes: 'Jeg Jacb Nispüt for nimo').

SRO, RD.11, box 72.

489. Burravo, 29 August 1609

Obligation by Olaw Sutherland, foud of Fetlair, to Edward Scollay of Strynie, sheriff-depute and chamberlain of Yetland, for £124 19s.10d. 'for the girsumes of the king and kirklandis of Fetlair set be my lord' in 1608, and the arrears of butter and oil of the king and kirkland mails, scat and cornteind of the isle of the crop 1608, whereof Olaw is appointed collector.

Witnesses: Andro Edmestoun, minister of Yell, sometime notary public, Andro Hawik of Scatsta, Patrik Hog, minister at Fetlair, and Robert Scollay, servant of Patrik, earl of Orknay, lord Yetland, writer hereof. P. Symsone also subscribes as a witness.

SRO, RD.1/171, f.117; SRO, RD.11/72 (reg. 8 May 1610).

490. Burravo, 29 August 1609

Obligation by John Aweik, foud of Yell, to Edward Scollay of Strynie, sheriff-depute and chamberlain of Yetland, for £238 9s. in respect of his intromissions with the gersums of the isle of Yell in 1608, the wattle of the said isle of the crop 1607, the taxation owing in the isle in 1609, and the arrears of the king and kirkland mails, scat and cornteind in the said isle of the crops 1607 and 1608, whereof John is appointed collector, and of all other arrears committed to John's collection.

Witnesses: Andro Edmestoun, minister at Yell, Patrik Hog, minister at Fetlair, James Sutherland, indweller there, and Robert Scollay, servant of Patrik, earl of Orknay.

SRO, RD.1/171, f.118.

491. Skalloway bankis, 13 September 1609

Obligation by Andro Edmestoun, minister at Yell, to his good friend Edward Scollay of Strynie, sheriff-depute and chamberlain of Yetland, for £300.

Witnesses: Jerom Umphray of Sand, Andro Gifherd of Woddersta, Alexander Bruce, notary public, and Robert Scollay, writer hereof.

SRO, RD.1/171, ff.116-7.

492. Skalloway bankis, 21 September 1609

Discharge by Edward Scollay of Strynie, sheriff-depute and chamberlain of Yeitland, to William Halcro, of complete payment of the feu mails of the houses, tenement, yard and pertinents presently possessed by him and his mother, in the town of Skalloway bankis, and also for the piece of waste ground which lies at the east end thereof which formerly pertained to Alexander Butter, extending to 14s. yearly for each, and that for this present year 1610 (altered from 1609) and all preceding years.

SA, D.10/9/2.

493. Hous, 25 October 1609

Disposition by Margaret Sinclair and Robert Tulloch, her spouse, and

Laurence Thomassoun, son of the deceased Katherin Sinclair, heirs of the deceased James Sinclair of Norbuster, her father, to an honourable man and their good friend Laurence Sinclair, son and apparent heir of Arthour Sinclair of Aithe, of 4 marks uthel land, 6 pennies the mark, in the isle of Halverey, in the parish of Burray. Precept of sasine.

Witnesses: James Sinclair of (blank), Arthour Barclay, son of the deceased Mr Thomas Barclay of Cuplahillis, Heino Grasmuller, Dutche merchant, and James Neven, burgess of Edinburgh, notary public, writer hereof.

SA, D.10/20/2.

494. Edinburgh, 10 November 1609

Decreet of court of session in action at instance of William Sinclare of Ustines against Patrik, earl of Orknay, lord Yetland, Andro Giffart of Weddersta, and Alexander Bruce, servitor to the said earl, for eviction in April, May and June 1608 from his lands and room of Ustines, and spulyie of livestock, furnishings and writs therefrom, in June, September and October 1608.

The lords of council continue the summons until 18 December 1609, and ordain the pursuer to have letters to summon witnesses and probation, etc.

SRO, CS.7/244, f.261.

495. Scalloway, December 1609

'Sasine ... on precept of sasine by Edward Scollay of Strynie, commissioner for Patrick, earl of Orkney, in favour of William Halcro, upon which precept Arthur Sinclair of Aith gave sasine to Anna Nicoll, relict of Henry Halcro, in liferent, and to William and Jerome Halcro, in fee, of lands in the town of Scalloway bankis.

Witnesses: Malcolm Halcro of Hoswick, Hew Halcro of Aithsetter, Hew Halcro, his eldest son, Nicoll Halcro in Culbensgarth, and Robert Tulloch, servitor to the said Arthur Sinclair. James Marischall, NP.'

The original is not known to exist. The above abstract, by Francis Grant, is in OSD, *SN*, 3 February 1894.

496. Skalloway bankis, 8 December 1609

Disposition by Malcolme Halcro in Linksetter to his loving friend Alexander Bruce, notary public in Yetland, of ½ mark land, 9 pennies the mark, in the town of Bervitsetter, in the parish of Delting. Precept of sasine.

Witnesses: Mr William Hay, archdeacon of Yetland, Johne Kant, Alexander Thomasone, foud of Tingwald, Gilbert Kantlie in Skalloway bankis, and James Marischall, notary public, writer hereof.

SA, GD.144/273/8.

497. Hammer in Northmavin, 11 January 1610

Disposition by Thomas Tulloch of Fiblasetter, with consent of Bessie Laing, his spouse, to his good friend and loving kinsman Mr Gilbert Mowat, minister of Delting, of his ½ mark land, 'paying in yeirly dewtie ane lispund butter', in Nibon, in the parish of Northmavin. Precept of sasine.

Witnesses: Mr James Pitcairne, vicar of Northmavin, Androw Hawick, bailie of Northmavin, James Mowat, Bartil Hawick, and Alexander Bruce, notary public.

GH.

498. Melbie, 5 February 1610

Excambion whereby Andro Wishert in Melbie dispones to his good friend Gilbert Gifhairt of Huiksetter and his spouse Katherine Umphray, 1½ marks land, 12 pennies the mark, in the toun of Huiksetter, in the parish of Sandnes, and Gilbert dispones to Andro, and Marioun Reid, his spouse, 2 marks land, 8 pennies the mark (torn).

Mr Robert Swentoun and John Sutherland subscribe on behalf of Andro Wishert. Witnesses: Thomas Cheyne of Walay, Jherome Umphray of Sand, William Reid, Andro Colt, and Erasmus Blandis.

SA, Nicolson Papers. Mark of Andro Wischert.

499. Edinburgh, 7 February 1610

Will of William Sinclair of Ustanes

The testament and latter will of William Sinclair of Ustanes in Yetland, maid and geven up be himself in Edinburch, the sevinth day of Februar Jaj VJc ten yeiris, befoir thir witnessis, Robert Menteath of Egilsay, John Menteath, his brother germane, James Howtoun, servitor to the laird of Kerss, and Thomas Young, messenger. As to the inventar of his guidis and geir he remittis the samen to the upgeving of his executoris; and also of the inventar of the debtis auchtand to him, debtis auchtand be him, he referis also to the upgeving of his executoris. Legacie, first he levis his saull to god, and his bodie to be buried in the commoun buriell. Item, he nominatis Elizabeth Sinclair, his spous, and Lowrence Sinclair, his eldest sone, his onlie executoris and intromettoris with his guidis and geir. He ordanis his wyf to bruik the equall halfe of his haill landis induring hir lyfetyme, and his eldest sone the uther half, and efter hir deceis the haill landis to returne to hir eldest sone. Item, he levis his haill guidis, his debtis being payit, to his wyf and sone equallie betuix thame. He levis Arthour Sinclair of Aith, his brother, to be oursear that his wyff ressave na wrang at na handis, as he will anser to god. Item, he is adebtit to Thomas Young, servitor to Mr Thomas Barclay, the soume of £40. Item, to Bessie Thomesone £11 8s. Item, to Thomas Knychtsone £6. Item, to Katherene Ker £22, and schoe hes a doublet of velvet in wod thairof. Item, to Jonet Watsone £6. Item, to James Primrois, referris the samen to the said James particular compt baith for wreattis, debursmentis to doctoris and apoticareis, and all uther furneisching, to be payit of the first and reddiest baith upon himself and utherwayis.

In witness quhairof the said William hes subscrivit thir presentis with my hand, day, month and yeir foirsaid. And declaris that in cais ony persone have just caus of forder debtis, he ordanis the samen to be payit.

William Sinclair

R. Menteath, witnes.
John Menteath, witnes.

SRO, CC.17/2/2, f.157.

500. Cloddasetter, 13 March 1610

Obligation by Andro Hawick of Skatistay to Mr James Pitcairn, minister of Northmavin, for (torn). Andro dispones to Mr James and Ursula Sinclair 2 lispunds 16 marks butter and 4 cuttles wadmell as annual rent from 3 marks land, 12 pennies the mark, in Firth, and 1 mark land in Southgardin in Laxo, together with the full gersums thereof, during the period of non-redemption.

Witnesses: James Mowat, Bartill Hawick, and Gilbert Mowat, writer hereof.

SRO, RD.1/188, f.25 (second series of pagination).

501. 18 March 1610

'Instrument of sasine in favor of Laurence Bruce of Cultmalindie, proceeding upon a few charter, dated 5 August 1589, by Mitchell Balfour of Mountquhanie and Arthur Sinclair of Arlye [*rectius* Aith], nominated commissioners for Robert, earl of Orkney and Zetland .. of ... ten merks udal land in Gluss, 12 pennies the merk, and 3 merks land, 9 pennies the merk, called *pro rege*, in the parish of Northmavine.'

The original is not known to exist. The above abstract is in SA, D.6/194/12 (Inventory of titles of the estate of Busta, in Messrs Greigs' possession, 1840).

502. Scalloway bankis, 16 April 1610

Contract between Arthur Cowie, skipper and owner of the ship called the *George*, on the one part, and Androu Umphray of Berry, on the other part, whereby Arthur sells the said bark to Androu and has received 'ane sex pund piece in arllis and part payment thereof'. Arthur binds himself to deliver at the port of Leith within 48 hours 'nixt efter this present leading that is presentlie and salbe put in hir at Scalloway bankis be delyverit aff hir, boddim frie in all walteris, befoir the deat hearof, and furneist as scho is presentlie with floitboit, saillis, ankeris, towis, with rax, kettill, chissell, walter barrell, aill barrell, and finallie with all readschip that scho presentlie possessis'. Androu binds himself to pay Arthur £1,200, of which £800 is payable within 6 hours of delivery and £400 at Candlemas 1611, at Androu's dwelling house in Scalloway. Arthur binds himself to carry for Androu 'tua last of geir presentlie, he bringing it to the afoirsaid schip syde quhair scho presentlie lyis, fraucht free to Leith, togidder with himself and company to resaive and saill the said schip, as he plesis to put in'.

Witnesses: James Cheyne of Pennen in Buchane, Patrik Ross, burgess of Aberdeen, James Thomasone, son of Alexander, foud of Laxfuird, Mr William Hay, archdeacon of Yetland, and John Baxter, notary, writer hereof.

SRO, RD.1/170, ff.218-19; SRO, RD.11/72 (reg. 11 May 1610).

503. Mowanes, 12 May 1610

Disposition by Laurence Bruce of Cultemalyndies to Andro Bruce of Sandweik, his lawful son, and heirs male of the surname and arms of Bruce, of the lands of Mowanes and Scollaytoft and Netherhoull, all lying within the dykes of Mowanes, extending to 72 marks land, 6 pennies the mark, with the castle and other pertinents, presently occupied by Laurence, 2 marks land in Utterskaw, 1 mark land in Underfaill there, 4 marks land in Hammeriskaw, 3 marks land in Norweik, 2 marks land of Westerhous in Clibberveik, 1½ marks land in Houll, 2 marks land in Burrawfirth, ½ mark land in Soitland, 7 marks land in Howland, 2½ marks land of Burgh in Ballyestaw, 3 marks land in Westerhous there, 1½ marks land in Langascoill there, 5½ marks land in Upsuall, 1½ mark land in Baltie, 4 marks land in Clowgon, 4 marks land of Burgh in Colvadaill, another 8 marks land there, 3 marks land in Gairdone there, 10 ures land in Vris, 3 marks land in Guidone, 5 marks land in Seitter, 1½ marks land in Sandweik, 1½ marks land in Hannigarth, 4 marks land in Ramnego, 1½ marks land in Murasetter, 1 mark land in Mainland, 1½ marks land in Still, 6 marks land in Howgaland, 4 marks land in Snarroway, 12 marks land in Vigay, 1 mark land in Hammer, 5 marks land in Lind, 9 marks land in Mewhous, 1 mark land in Colvasetter, another 1 mark land in Howgaland, another 1 mark land in Mainland, and 2 marks land in Cauldbak, all at 6 pennies the mark, in the isle of Unst; 35 marks land of Tresta, 19 marks 6 ures land of Strand in Bigtoun, presently occupied by

Laurence, 3 marks 6 ures land in Funyie, 2 marks 6 ures land in Litlieland, another 1 mark land there, 3 marks 2 ures land in Gruting, 4 marks land of Gibhous in Aithe, 5 marks land in Vailyie, 1 mark land in Seitter, 5½ marks land in Clowdone, 2½ marks land in Northdaill, 10 marks land in Southdaill and Failyie, 1 mark land in Huskasetter, 1 mark land in Foirland, 1 mark 3 ures land in Sand, 4 marks 6 ures land in Hammer, 6 marks land of Favervell, 7 marks 2 ures land in Urie, and 2 marks land in Urasetter, all at 6 pennies the mark, in the isle of Fetler; 6 marks land, 9 pennies the mark, in Lumbustaw, 10 marks 2 ures land, 9 pennies the mark, in Colvasetter, 11 marks land, 9 pennies the mark, in Sellawfirth, 10 marks land, 9 pennies the mark, in Vassesur, 3½ marks land, 9 pennies the mark, in Ottersweik, 5 marks land, 7 pennies the mark, in Gravene, 8½ marks land, 8 pennies the mark, in Guidsir, the isle of Grunyie estimated to 8 marks land, 1½ marks land, 6 pennies the mark, in Staineseitter, 1½ marks land, 8 pennies the mark, in Bowasetter, 7 marks land, 7 pennies the mark, in Seitter, 1 mark land, 9 pennies the mark, in Estregairthe, 4½ marks land, 9 pennies the mark, in Gamistaw, 1 mark land, 9 pennies the mark, in Southladie, 13 marks 6 ures land, 9 pennies the mark, in Kettilsetter, 2 marks land, 8 pennies the mark, in Hamnavo, 3 marks land, 8 pennies the mark, in Orphosaw, 1½ marks land, and 12 pennies the mark, in Fisholme, in the isle of Yell; 6 marks land, 12 pennies the mark, in Firth, 2 marks land, 9 pennies the mark, in Cauldbak, 5 marks land, 6 pennies the mark, of Bacca in Olnafirth, in the parish of Delting; 9 marks land in Gluss and another 13 marks feulands there, 12 pennies the mark, ½ mark land in Burrane there, 44 marks land, 9 pennies the mark, in Hildisweik, 18 marks land, 8 pennies the mark, in Overure there, 2 marks land, 9 pennies the mark, in Ure, 3 marks land, 9 pennies the mark, in Ocratang, in the parish of Northmaving; and in the parishes of Aithsting, Sandsting, Wallis, Tingwall and Dunrosnes, 10 marks land, 8 pennies the mark, in Howaseitter, 19½ marks land, 9 pennies the mark, in Twot, 1½ marks land, 8 pennies the mark, in Kirkhous, 3 marks land, 8 pennies the mark, in Langascoill, 2½ marks land, 9 pennies the mark, in Breck, 49 marks land, 8 pennies the mark, in Aith, 1 mark land, 12 pennies the mark, in Semblasetter, 20 marks feulands, 9 pennies the mark, in Cloustaw, 3 marks land, 9 pennies the mark, in Seitter, 4 marks land, 9 pennies the mark, in Nowisburgh, 4 marks land, 8 pennies the mark, in Selvesetter, 1½ marks land, 9 pennies the mark, in Vasquie, 6½ marks land, 8 pennies the mark, in Burrowland, in the said parish of Wallis, 5 marks land, 8 pennies the mark, in Brebustaw, 6 marks land, 8 pennies the mark, in Grunyevo, ½ mark land, 6 pennies the mark, in Howsetter, in the parish of Tingwall, 3 marks land, 6 pennies the mark, in Strand, in the parish of Tingwall, 20 marks land, 8 pennies the mark, in Grunyestaw, in the isle of Brassay, 1 mark land, 6 pennies the mark, in Ley, 1 mark land, 6 pennies the mark, in Daill, and 1 mark land in Exambie, in the parish of Dunrosness; together with any other lands in the lordship of Yetland which pertain to Laurence; with reservation to Laurence of the liferent of the forenamed lands. Laurence constitutes Andro his assignee in all actions raised, or to be raised, by him before the lords of council and session, with the exception of the action against Osea Scot in Raefirth to which Laurence has made John and Laurence Bruces, his natural sons, assignees. Precept of sasine.

Witnesses: Andro Giffhart of Wedderstaw, Johne Gifhart, his son, William Tyrie of Busbies, Alexander Bruce, notary public, Hew Tarrell, servant to Laurence Sinclar of Burgh, David Pitcarnis of Voisgirth, James Mershell, notary public, writer hereof, and Walter Cant of the West Mylne of Aberdour.

SRO, RD.1/261, ff.389-93; SRO, CS.15/157 (extract deed subscribed by depute clerk register).

504. Edinburgh, 3 July 1610.

Decreet of court of session in action at instance of Laurence Bruce of Cultmalyndies against Ossie Scot for removal from 12½ marks land in Refert in the isle of Yell. Ossie had been warned to remove at Whitsunday 1609.

The lords of council decern the defender to remove from the land.

SRO, CS.7/254, ff.213-4. On 5 September 1611 Osea Scot was put to the horn at the instance of Laurence Bruce for non-removal (SRO, DI.1/1, ff.345-7). Cf. note to no. 472.

505. Edinburgh, 11 July 1610

Decreet of court of session in action at instance of Laurence Bruce of Cultmalyndeis against Daniel Johnestoun for removal from 4 marks land, 9 pennies the mark, in Otterswick, in the parish of Yeale. Daniel had been warned to remove at Whitsunday 1610.

The lords of council decern the defender to remove from the land.

SRO, CS.7/254, ff.254-5.

506. Edinburgh, 11 July 1610

Decreet of court of session in action at instance of Jean Bruce, liferentrix of the lands underwritten, and Thomas Blak, her spouse, for his interest, against Henry Cheyne in Stopnes, tenant of 7 marks 6 ures in Stopnes, in the parish of Waillis, William Sinclair of Raewik, tenant of 3 marks land, 9 pennies the mark, in Eister Skaill, in the parish of Fasling, Thomas Magnesoun in Baka, tenant of 9 marks land in Baka, in the parish of

Delting, (blank) Rendell in South Lady, tenant of 3 marks land in South Lady, in the south parish of Yell, Henry Cleland in Stromnes, tenant of 7 marks land in Stromnes, Frances Nicolsoun in Haggarsta, tenant of 6 marks land in Haggarsta, Jerome Umphra in Inner Sand, tenant of 1½ marks land, 12 pennies the mark, in Inner Sand, in the parish of Sandsting, 1 mark land, 6 pennies the mark, in Asta, in the parish of Tingwall, and 4½ marks land, 12 pennies the mark, in Semnlesetter, in the parish of Esting, Yansie Yanisoun in Howffe, tenant of 9 marks land, 12 pennies the mark, in Howffe, in the parish of Wisdaill, John Stromefuird of Stromefuird, tenant of 12 marks land, 6 pennies the mark, in Stromefuird, in the parish of Wisdaill, Erik Thomassoun in Cote, tenant of 8 marks land, 8 pennies the mark, in Cote, in the parish of Wisdaill, Erasmus Thomassoun in Owirbister, tenant of 4 marks land, 8 pennies the mark, in Owirsetter, and Thomas Owersound in Howle, tenant of 12 marks land, 12 pennies the mark, in Howle, in the parish of Wisdaill, for removal from the aforementioned lands. The defenders had been warned to remove at Whitsunday 1608.

The lords of council decern the defenders to remove from their respective lands.

SRO, CS.7/254, ff.245-6.

507. Edinburgh, 11 July 1610

Decreet of court of session in action at instance of Laurence Bruce of Cultmalindeis, Nicoll McClogan in Fetlar, his tenant, James Strang in Veilyie there, Olaw Gregorsoun there, Cristopher Gregorsoun there, Robert in Crosbekir there, James in Fairwell there, Olaw Sutherland there, James Sutherland there, Edward Sinclare of Bulyeasetter, for themselves and the remaining tenants in the isle of Fetlar, Salomone Scott in Yell, John Obak there, John Avvik there, Osea Scott there, David Tulloch there, Magnus Wischart there, William Spens there, William Nisbit there, John Newbebak there, Thomas Tulloch there, David Tulloch there, Piter in Burgh there, Mairtene in Burgh there, Magnus in Howland there, (blank) in Hamnavo there, (blank) Thomsoun there, Thomas Blak in Biga, for themselves and the remaining tenants of the isle of Yell, against Andro Edmonstoun, minister at the kirk of Yell, on the first part, Patrik Hog, minister at Fetler, on the second part, William Bannatyne of Garesay, tacksman of the vicarages of Yell and Fetler, on the third part, Sir John Arnot of Berswick, knight, assignee to the said William Bannatyne in the aforesaid tack, on the fourth part, and Patrik, earl of Orknay, lord Yetland, on the fifth part, for troubling the complainers for payment of the teinds and duties of the year 1608.

The lords of council decern the complainers to make payment of the duties to Sir John Arnot, as assignee of William Bannatyne to the tack, dated 15 December 1594 and 6 July 1595, by Mr James Lauder, vicar of Yell and Fetlar (no. 229), conform to the contract, dated 16 June 1596, made between John Arnot, burgess of Edinburgh, on the one part, and William Bannatyne of Gairsay, on the other part, whereby William, for certain sums of money paid by the said John to William, and others in his name, disponed to him divers lands, and also for security constituted John, his assignee in divers tacks, and in particular the aforesaid tack. The other parties are discharged of all further charging, poinding, troubling or molesting of the complainers for the vicarage teinds during the said Sir John Arnot's right thereto.

SRO, CS.7/256, ff.2-4.

508. Scalloway bankis, 20 July 1610

Testimonial that Edward Sinclar of Marrasetter is heir to the deceased Oliver Sinclar of Esthouse, his brother.

Till all and sindrie quhome it effeiris, to quhais knawlege thir presentis sall cum, we undersubscryveand dois testifie and beir witnes that in all tymes bygane past memorie of man thair hes bene ane ancient law, custome, and consuetude within the cuntrey of Yetland, be the quhilk it hes bene inviolablie observit that quhan ony landit man, haveand landis within the said cuntrey, depairtit this mortal lyffe, the haill landis and heretage appertening to him in his lyftyme immediatlie efter his deceis war equallie and lawchfullie divydit amangis his haill bairnis, alsweill sones as dochteris, comptand alwayis tua sisteris pairtis for ane brotheris pairt, and being sua divydit the eldest brother had na farder prerogative abone the rest of his brother except the first chois of the pairtis and parcellis of the landis divydit; and that it is trew and of veritie that umquhile Henrie Sinclar of Burgh deceissand at the faith and peace of our umquhile soverane lady Marie, be the grace of god queine of Scottis, left behind him four sones on lyffe, viz., umquhile Hew Sinclar of Burgh, his eldest sone, Capitane Williame Sinclar, his second sone, Eduard Sinclar of Marrasetter, the thrid, and umquhile Oliver Sinclar of Esthous the fourth, thay than being all minors of the aige of four, fyve, or sax yeiris or thairby, and during the tyme of thair minoriteis the rentis of the haill landis and heretage, togidder with the haill moveabill guidis pertening to the said umquhile Henrie the tyme of his deceis, war intromettit with and uptaine be the said umquhile Hew Sinclar, the eldest of the saidis four brether, his tutors and curators for the tyme, and at the perfyte aige of the said umquhile Oliver the said umquhile Hew, conforme to the said ancient law and custome inviolablie observit within the said cuntrey of Yetland, as said is, delyverit and resignit to the said umquhile Oliver his brotheris pairt, being a fourth pairt of the landis and heretage pertening to the said umquhile Henrie the tyme of his said deceis, to wit, auchtene merk land in Esthous in Quhytness, aucht pennyis the merk, sax merk land in Wodbuster in Quhytness, sax pennyis the merk, sax merk land in Hagrasetter, sex pennyis the merk, aucht merk land in Kirkgord in Weisdaill, aucht pennyis the merk, four merk land in Trestay in Aithsting, nyne pennyis the merk, and four merk land in Burgh at Yelsound within the parochin of Delting, nyne pennyis the merk; quhilkis landis as being the fourth pairt of the haill landis pertening to the said umquhile Henrie Sinclar of Burgh, the said umquhile Oliver, his feird sone, bruikit and possest fra the tyme of his entrie thairto (quhilk was in the beginning of his perfyte aige) contenuawlie to the day of his deceis, be the space of tuentie aucht yeiris, togidder as his awin proper land and heretage haldin frielie of the king for payment of scat and wattell and of the teynd therof to the kirk, according to the custome of the said cuntrey and as is payit be utheris heretors of landis within the samyn, but stop, trubill, impediment, contradictioun, or interruptioun maid thairto be ony persone or personis quhatsumever; and that it is lykewayis trew and of veritie that the said umquhile Oliver Sinclar deit in peciabill possessioun of the landis particularlie abonenameit as his awin proper landis and heretage haldin be him as said is for payment of the dewtie foirsaid at the faith and peace of our soverane lord James, be the grace of god king of Grit Britan, Franc, and Ireland, defendar of the faith, and that the said Eduard Sinclar of Marrasetter is neirest and lawchfull air to the said umquhile Oliver Sinclar his brother of all and haill the landis abonewrittin, and that he is of perfyte aige. Quhilkis all and sindrie premissis we undersubscryveand testifie to be trew and of veritie to all and sindrie quhome it effeiris, be thir presentis subscryvit with our handis at Skalloway bankis the tuentie day of July the yeir of god Jaj VJc and ten yeiris.

Eduerd Scollay of Strynie, sheref deput of Orknay and Yetland
Arthur Sinclar of Aythe
Laurence Sinclar
Alexander Thomasone, fould of Thingvell
Andro Umphray of Berrie
Alexander Bruce, notarius
J. Sinclair, fiar off Quandell.

SRO, RH.9/15/78. Printed in *REO*, no. lxxxvi.

509. Edinburgh, 24 July 1610

Decreet of court of session in action at instance of Andro Bruce of Sanwik, tutor dative of Laurence Sinclair of Burgh, against Captain William Sinclair, brother german of the deceased Hew Sinclair of Burgh and one of the curators of the said Laurence, for intrusion in possession of the lands of Burgh, Beinstay, Garth, the lands of Skirreis, the isles of Mekill and Littill Lingay, and Flewgarth, and eviction of Andro in August and September 1608, and also for the spulyie of the goods and gear underwritten. The defender alleged that he should be absolved from the spulyie because the goods were in possession of the deceased Hew Sinclair, father of Laurence Sinclair, at the time of his decease, and that at the decease of Robert Sinclair, eldest son of the said Hew, the said Captain William Sinclair, with consent of the said Laurence, intromitted in the said goods and gear by authority of the sheriff of Orknay. The defender was content to make the same forthcoming to whomsoever had interest thereto as accorded of the law. The pursuer replied that the allegation ought to be repelled because the goods and gear pertained to him, and had been in his possession as properly belonging to him for at least one year before the time of the spulyie. The inventory of the goods and gear is as follows: 'In the first, in the aill seller, thrie barrellis, ane wirt standand tub, ane sey, ane laidgalloun, ane seipbaille (?), tua pair of gantreis; item, in the pantrie, ane towme kist for cauld meit with ane towme almrie; item, in the hall, tua buirdis, thrie furmes, ane auld grein clayth with twentie hoillis thairin, sevintin auld cushingis, tua cheiris, ane pair of tabillis, ane uthir cheker without men, ane hingand chandler of brass with sex flomis, ane pair of taingis, ane boit saill, ane towme kist; item, in ane almrie thair, sextin gilt stoupis, four brasin chandleris, tua auld basingis, ane basin, tua laweris, ane basin for ane barbour, ane Dutche plait for eggis with ane fute, ane dussone of tyn plaittis, four toueris (?), ane dussoun of truncheoris, xxxviij saseris, ane salt falt, ane tyne can, four lame cannis, tua drinking glassis, tua glaissing flakattis; item, in the heichest loft abone the hall, ane drum, tua auld compass, fourscoir glassing flakkattis with heidis, ane balk with ane pair of wiching brodis with ane irone wecht of tua stane or thairby, ane pair of schippis haikis; item, in the loft abone the hall, ane kist with the knok of the yet thairin with sum naillis for the yet, sum uther irne work, ane barrell; item, in the chalmer within the loft, ane litill kist with sum comptis and auld missive letteris, ane litill tyn chandler, ane brasin cok; item, ane uther kist with sum sadill geir, ane pair of trabuschettis, with sum missive letteris and auld comptis; item, ane hagbut without the wark, ane quaver with sum arrowis, ane cais for silver, ane buffet stuill, twa glassin flakattis; item, ane uther kist with sum auld comptis of Burgh, ane barrell with sum canone powder, ane flag for ane ship; item, ane towme harvest barrell; item, ane uther litill towme trunk; item, in the chalmer at the end of the hall, ane firn bed with ane fedder bed and ane boustar, ane buffet stuill; item, in the mid chalmer, tua firne beddis towme with ane buffet stuill; item, in the inner chalmer, ane standand bed with ane fedder bed, thrie boustaris, ane pair of courteingis with ane auld pand, thrie chalmer pottis, ane litell bybell prentit at Dort; item, ane candell kist with sum candell; item, in the chalmer abone the kiching, sex auld sewit coveringis, thrie uther auld wovin coveringis, aucht pair of blancattis, tua pair of lynyng cheittis, tua pair of lyneing cheittis, ane cod, ane boustar, thrie auld lineing burdclaithes, sevin lyneing servittis, ten hardin servittis, thrie hardin towallis, ane pair of sewit courteingis, ane auld grein courtene, ane towme kist, four fixit firn beddis towme; item, in the chalmer abone the brewhous, four fixit firn beddis towme; item, in the eistmaist sellar under the lang loft, tua towme girnallis, tua trochis, ane pykpot, ane towme punscheoun, tua towme barrellis, ane ulie can, four phellis, ane pair of airis, ane pondlair with ane stane, ane guis pane, sex silver sponis; item, in ane uther sellar, fyve towme beiff faittes; item, within the kiching, sex irone poittis, tua pannis, tua pair of raxis, tua spettis, ane grus pane; item, ane rosting yrone, ane pair of tayngis, xvij tyne plaittis, ane dussoun of tyne trunscheoris; item, in the brewhous, ane caldroun set upoun the furnace with ane fatt, ane firn bed; item, in the buith at Hamnanes, sex standis for olie quhairin thair is ane litell barrell half barrell olie or thairby, ane barrell of tare, the great boittis geir: item, at Brugh, nyne milkand ky, aucht drawand oxin, ane buill, four quyakis of thrie yeir auldis, tua uther bullis, fyve stirkis of ane yeir auld, fyve work horss; item, ane uther meikle hors, four meiris for wark, four young meires, ane staig: item, at the buill of Garth, sevin meilkand ky, thrie quyokis of four yeir auld, four quyokis of tua yeir auld, thriescoir geis of ane yeir auld, fyve drawand oxin, tua oxin stirkis, sevin horss and meiris; item, at the buill of Beinstay, sex milkand ky, thrie oxin, thrie meiris, ane hors, ane stirk of ane yeir auld; item, at Catferth, tua meiris; item, at Aswik, tua ky, and ane cruikit hors'.

The lords of council continue the summons for hearing proof, and ordain the pursuer to have letters to summon witnesses and probation, and to produce evidence, and decern that in the event of the pursuer proving the summons the lords will have special regard to the pursuer's oath to be given by him touching the quantity and prices of the particular goods and gear spulyied from him, and if found to be exorbitant they will tax and moderate the same to such conformity as is most agreeable to equity and reason.

SRO, CS.7/243, ff.276-7: CS.7/257, ff.8-10.

510. Edinburgh, 27 July 1610

Decreet of court of session in action at instance of Jean Bruce, relict of Hew Sinclair of Burgh, and Thomas Blak of Stroholme, now her spouse, for his interest, against the undernoted for payment of debts, viz. (1) Thomas Magnesoun in Cote, 24 gulyeouns for the price of a new boat bought by him in 1603 (price of the gulyeoun, 24s.); (2) Olla Williamson in Wester Skaillie, 9 gulyeouns borrowed by him in 1603; (3) Anthone Onirsoune, 4 gulyeouns borrowed by him in 1603; (4) Dandie Ollasoun, 6½ gulyeouns borrowed by him in 1602; (5) Olla Halyebuster in

Halyebuster, 53s.4d. borrowed by him in 1602; (6) Magnus Nicolsoun in Staniswall, 6 gulyeouns 4 shillings borrowed by him in 1603; (7) Turberrie Mertinesoun, £4 borrowed by him in 1603; (8) Olla Nicolsoun in Halyesetter and Marioun Poilisdochter, 24 gulyeouns 11 shillings wares and 6 cans oil (price of the can, 10s.) borrowed by them in 1603; (9) Nicoll Johnsoun in Howffe, 14 gulyeouns borrowed by him in 1603; (10) Margaret Knychtsoun in Stromnes and Henry Cleland, her spouse, 34 gulyeouns being for the price of a new boat bought by them in 1603, and for the arrears of the duties of Stromnes, occupied by them yearly, for 1604, 1605 and 1606; (11) William Fordyce and Jonet Sinclair, his spouse, 6 angels of gold borrowed by them in 1603 (price of the angel, £6); (12) David Sinclair, underfoud of Burray, 24 gulyeouns for the price of a new boat bought in 1604; (13) Nicoll Ollasoun in Hagarsta, 3 lispunds butter promised by him to Jean Bruce for liberty to pasture his goods on a part of her conjunct-fee lands of Stromnes and Hagarstae for the years 1607, 1608 and 1609 (price of the lispund, £3); (14) John Strang in Hamnivo, £15, partly borrowed by him in 1603, and partly for the duties of a part of Jean's conjunct-fee lands of Skelberrie occupied by him in 1603; (15) John Johnsoun in Howffe, £11 12s. borrowed by him in 1604; (16) Alexander Johnsoun alias Laxfuird, £24 borrowed by him in 1603, together with 3 barrels Spanish salt likewise borrowed by him in 1603 (price of the barrel, £5); (17) Robert Mansoun in Gillesbrek, son and heir of the deceased Magnus Mansoun, 120 gulyeouns, viz. 40 lispunds butter, 40 bulls oil, and 40 gulyeouns hard fish (price of the gulyeoun, £2), faithfully promised by the said Robert, as heir to his father, to be paid 'at ane certain day bygane', together with 70 gulyeouns owed by him conform 'to ane futit compt maid thairanent'; and (18) Edward Sinclair of Bulyesetter, 5 barrels butter (price of the barrel, 10 rix dollars), 5 barrels oil (price of the barrel, 8 rix dollars), 5 packs wadmell (price of the pack, 4½ rix dollars), 2 dakers hides (price of the daker, 12 rix dollars), bought by him upon his own peril of spilling in October 1609 (price of each dollar, £3).

The lords of council decern the defenders to pay Jean Bruce, and her said spouse for his interest, the sums of money and debts as specified above.

SRO, CS.7/257, ff.53-5; SRO, CS.290/34 (25 January 1611).

511. Edinburgh, 28 July 1610

Decreet of court of session in action at instance of Jean Bruce, relict of Hew Sinclair of Burgh, and Thomas Blak of Stroholme, now her spouse, for his interest, against Hary Cheyne of Stopnes, for payment of the duties of 7 marks 6 ures land, 9 pennies the mark, of Stopnes, for the years 1604 to 1609, viz., £4 of silver duty, 4 lispunds butter (price of the lispund, £3), and 4 shillings wadmell (price of the shilling, 6s.8d.), yearly. The pursuer alleges she is infefted in the foresaid lands for her lifetime.

The lords of council absolve the defender and decern him free and quit from the points of the summons in time coming, because the defender made faith that he occupied and possessed the foresaid lands for the said years as his own heritage, and that he was never obliged to pay any duties for the said lands, either to the deceased Hew Sinclair of Burgh, or to Jean Bruce, his spouse, and whatever duty he was in use to pay for the said lands he paid the same to the earl of Orknay.

SRO, CS.7/257, ff.66-7.

512. Edinburgh, 31 July 1610

Decreet of court of session in action at instance of Jean Bruce, relict of Hew Sinclair of Burgh, and Thomas Blak of Stroholme, now her spouse, for his interest, against the undernoted for payment of duties, viz. (1) Henrie Cleland in Stromnes, £4 silver, 4 lispunds butter (price of the lispund, £3), 4 shillings wadmell (price of the shilling, 6s.8d.), yearly, for the years 1605 to 1609, for 7 marks land of Stromnes; (2) Yainsie Yainsoun in Howffe, £4 10s. silver, 6 lispunds butter, 6 shillings wadmell, yearly, for the years 1606 to 1609, for 9 marks land of Howffe; (3) John Stromefurde, £4 10s. silver, 4 lispunds butter, 4 shillings wadmell, yearly, for the years 1607 to 1609, for 12 marks land of Stromefuird; (5) Erik Thomassoun in Cote, £3 silver, 4 lispunds butter, 4 shillings wadmell, yearly, for the years 1607 to 1609, for 8 marks land of Cote; (5) Erasmus Thomassoun in Owirbister, £2 silver, 2 lispunds butter, 2 shillings, wadmell, yearly, for the years 1608 and 1609, for 4 marks land of Underbister; (6) Thomas Ouirsoun in Howle, £4 10s. silver, 6 lispunds butter, 6 shillings wadmell, yearly, for the years 1607 to 1609, for 12 marks land of Houll; and (7) Frances Nicolsoun in Haggarsta, 50s. silver, 3 lispunds butter, 3 shillings wadmell, yearly, for the years 1601 to 1609, for 6 marks land, 6 pennies the mark, of the lands of Haggarsta.

The lords of council decern the defenders to pay the pursuer the duties specified above.

SRO, CS.7/257, ff.82-3. The pursuer alleged that she was infefted in the liferent of 3 marks land, 9 pennies the mark, of Eister Skaillie, 7 marks 6 ures land, 9 pennies the mark, in Stopnes, 9 marks land, 8 pennies the mark, of Baka, 7 marks land, 8 pennies the mark, of Stromnes, 1½ marks land, 12 pennies the mark, of Innersand, 4½ marks land, 12 pennies the mark, of Simlesetter, 1 mark land, 6 pennies the mark, of the lands of Asta, 9 marks land, 12 pennies the mark, of the lands of Howffe, 12 marks land, 6 pennies the mark, of Stromefuird, 8 marks land, 8 pennies the mark, of Cote, 4 marks land, 8 pennies the mark, of Ouirbister, and 12 marks land, 12 pennies the mark, of Howle.

513. Scalloway, 3 August 1610

'Sasine ....: compeared John Sinclair, son and apparent heir to William

Sinclair in Scalloway-banks, bearing a charter by Arthur Sinclair of Aith to him, and Marion Halcro, his spouse, of subjects in Scalloway, dated 22nd May 1610. William Fermour, NP.'

The original is not known to exist. The above abstract, by Francis Grant, is in OSD, *SN*, 3 February 1894.

514. Skowisburgh, 4 August 1610

Contract between Johne Neven of Skowisburgh, and with him Ninian Neven, his son, on the one part, and Andro Edmestoun, minister of god's word at Yell, taking the burden for Ussula Edmestoun, his daughter, on the other part, whereby Ninian binds himself to marry Ussula by 1 November 1611. Johne binds himself to infeft Ninian and Ussula in his heritable land in the isle of Unst extending to 30 marks land, 6 pennies the mark, and in his 4 marks land, 9 pennies the mark, in Gremistay, and 2 marks land, 12 pennies the mark, in Burraness, in the parish of Delting, extending in quantity to 40 marks land at 6 pennies the mark, with reservation of the liferent to Johne. If Johne dies before Katherine Mowat, his spouse, then Katherine shall enjoy the said 4 marks land in Gremistay together with 14 marks of the rest of the 40 marks land. Andro binds himself to pay 500 merks in name of tocher immediately after the accomplishment of the marriage.

Witnesses: Mr James Pitcairne, vicar of Northmaving, Mr Gilbert Mowat, minister at Delting, James Kintoir, elder, and Alexander Milne.

SRO, CC.17/5/1, f.53.

515. 11 August 1610

Discharge by Eduard Scollay of Strynie, sheriff-depute and chamberlain of Yeitland, to William Halcro of payment of the feu mails of houses, tenement, yard and pertinents possessed by him and his mother in the town of Skalloway bankis, and also for the piece of waste ground which lies at the east end thereof which previously pertained to Alexander Butter, extending to 14s. yearly 'foir ilk ane of them', for the year 1610.

SA, D.10/9/3.

516. Burravo, 28 August 1610

Discharge by Edward Scollay of Strynie to Lawrence Bruce of Cultmalindeis.

I Edward Scollay of Strynie, chalmerlain of Yeitland, be the tennour heirof grantis me to have ressavit fra the handis of Lawrence Bruce of Cultmalindeis just compt, rakning and compleit payment of the butter and maillis and scatt of the landis of Traistay, and for his pairt of the scat of Toun and Velyie, and for the kirkland maillis of Traistay, Toun, Velyie and Helyesnes, for the crop and yeir of god Jaj VJc and nyne yeiris, quhairof I hald me weill content, satisfieit and payit, exoneris, quietclamis and dischergis him and his airis thairof for evir; Be thir presentis, subscryvit with my hand, at Burravo, the xxviij day of August 1610.

Eduerd Scollay.

GH.

517. Burravo, 30 August 1610

Obligation by Garth Williamson, cooper, skipper, indweller in Crussen(?), to Edward Scollay of Strynie, in name of Johne Ewik, foud of Yell, for £220.

Witnesses: Andro Edmestoun, minister at Yell, Johne Mowat of Olaberrie, Johne Edmestoun, James Sutherland in Odsta, and Robert Scollay, writer hereof.

SRO, CC.17/5/1, f.27. In the deed warrant (OA, SC.11/5/1610/3) Garth Williamson subscribes 'Garryt Wylliamzon van [*?*Courlanyssie]'.

518. Wodderstay, 4 September 1610

Obligation by Andro Hawick of Scatsta to his good friend Edward Scollay of Strynie, sheriff depute and chamberlain of Yetland, for £118 16s. for the arrears of wattle of Delting, and gersums thereof, and for £46 4s. arrears owing to Alexander Bruce for scat and landmails of the crops preceding.

Witnesses: Andro Giffhart of Woddersta, Bartill Hawik in Sand (?), Olaw Magnussone, apparent of Ilisbrugh, and Robert Scollay, writer hereof.

SRO, RD.1/182, f.348.

519. Scalloway, 8 November 1610

'Sasine ... on charter by Alexander Bult to William Halcro of a tenement in Scalloway. James Neven, NP.'

The original is not known to exist. The above abstract, by Francis Grant, is in OSD, *SN*, 3 February 1894.

520. 15 November 1610

'Disposition by Arthur Sinclair of Aith, with consent of Margaret Colville, his spouse, and Laurence Sinclair, his eldest son, to his second son James Sinclair, of 15 merks land with the pertinents lying in the towns of Fluagarth, Sandvo and Burravo, in the parish of Northmaven, which lands he had excambed for lands in Trondra with Patrick, earl of Orkney. ...

'Witnesses: James Kynter, elder, George Williamson, Patrick Ross, and William Fermour, NP, writer hereof.'

The original is not known to exist. The above abstract, by Francis Grant, is in OSD, *SN*, 3 February 1894.

521. Scalloway, 17 November 1610

'Disposition by Arthur Sinclair of Aith, with consent of Margaret Colville, his spouse, and of Laurence Sinclair, his eldest son, to James Sinclair, his second son, of the tacks which he had of the vicarage of Unst, and of 200 dollars which he had upon Andrew Mowat's land, 250 merks upon Jerome Umphray's lands, eleven score pounds upon John Wishart's lands, 28 angel nobles upon umquhile William Sinclair of Ustaness his lands, 300 merks upon the lands of umquhile Henry Halcro, eight score pounds upon Alexander Laxford's lands, 20 angel nobles upon Andrew Hawick's lands, and upon his brother David Sinclair's lands. ...

'Witnesses: James Kyntor, elder, George Williamson, Patrick Ross, and William Fermour, NP.'

The original is not known to exist. The above abstract, by Francis Grant, is in OSD, *SN*, 3 February 1894.

522. Edinburgh, 9 January 1611

Summons at instance of Androw Umphray of Berrie against Nicoll Hendersone in Nos for removal from 2 marks uthell land in the town of Noist in the parish of Dunrosnes. Nicoll had been warned to remove at Whitsunday 1608.

Nicoll is charged to compear before the lords of council and session on 15 May 1611.

SRO, CS.15/117. No decreet has been traced in respect of this summons.

523. Edinburgh, 15 January 1611

Summons at instance of James Johnestoun, lawful son of Alexander Thomasone of Laxfurde, against Alexander Bruce, sometime servitor to Patrik, earl of Orknay, and now indweller in Skelberry in Lunistong, for payment of debts, viz. (1) 63 'auld rex silver dolouris', at £3 the piece, received by Alexander Bruce in custody and keeping from Elizabeth Boyne, spouse of the said Alexander Thomasone, in about April 1606.; (2) £300 owed by Alexander Bruce to Alexander Thomasone and his spouse for his charges, expenses, board and entertainment during his remaining with them in their dwelling house, yearly in 1605, 1606 and 1607; (3) £120 owed by Alexander Bruce for the board, charges, expenses and entertainment of George Blak and John Georgesone, his servants, for the said years; (4) £30 for the price of a pair of pistols received by Alexander Bruce from Alexander Thomasone in about July 1603; (5) 20 old silver dollars received by Alexander Bruce from Yean Brem, Dutchman, in name of Alexander Thomasone in part payment of a greater sum that he was caution for the said Yean; (6) 3 old silver dollars borrowed by Alexander Bruce from Alexander Thomasone in about January 1604. The foresaid debts were assigned by Alexander Thomasone and his spouse to the said James on 15 November 1611.

Alexander Bruce is charged to compear before the lords of council and session on 25 May 1611.

SRO, CS.15/117. No decreet has been traced in respect of this summons.

524. Cullensburgh, 26 January 1611

'Charter by Magnus in Storgagarth, with consent of his spouse and Thomas Manson, his eldest son, to Laurence Sinclair of Aith, of 2 merks in Storgagarth, in the parish of Dunrossness. ...

'Witnesses: Hew Halcro, younger, William Halcro, David Leslie, and others. Sasine annexed, dated 30th March 1611.'

The original is not known to exist. The above abstract, by Francis Grant, is in OSD, *SN*, 3 February 1894.

525. Edinburgh, 26 January 1611

Decreet of court of session in action at instance of Patrik Ross, burgess of Abirdene, against Andro Edmestoun, minister at Yell, and Alexander Bruce in the mainland of Yetland, for loss and damages arising from shortfall in delivery of wadmell of Yetland sold by Patrik, earl of Orknay, to the pursuer, viz. (1) by contract between Sir John Arnot of Berswick, knight, in name of the said earl, and the pursuer, of the date at Edinburgh in 1603, for sale of 200 packs, upon which the said earl directed his precept to Andro Edmestoun, then his chamberlain, for answering of the pursuer of the said wadmell of sufficient stuff and measure; and (2) by contract between the said earl and the pursuer, dated at Kirkwall on 29 March 1604, for sale of 200 packs for delivery by midsummer 1604 at the port of Laxfuirde, upon which the said earl directed a precept to Alexander Bruce, then his chamberlain, commanding him that the said stuff should be sufficient and well measured. Andro Edmestoun had delivered to the pursuer 160 packs wadmell in 1603, and Alexander Bruce had delivered 180 packs wadmell in 1604. The just measure of each pack should have contained 60 cuttles, each cuttle 'estimat to half ane ell and half ane quarter of Scottis measour'. The pursuer received the said wadmell from the said persons upon their word and honesty to be of the sufficiency foresaid, but found that some packs contained only 50 cuttles, some 54, and some 56. The pursuer, by the unjust dealing and insufficiency of the measure, had not only been prejudiced and injured in the sum of 500 merks, but also, by the insufficiency of the measure, of 10 packs from each of the said persons, which at the market price at the time of the selling of the wadmell of £12 for each pack extended to £240. The procurator for the pursuer, however, passed from the summons against Alexander Bruce, and insisted only against Andro Edmestoun for payment of his part of the sums of money abovementioned.

The lords of council decern Andro Edmestoun to pay the pursuer 200 merks incurred by him, wherein he was hurt, prejudiced and injured, and likewise £120 for the insufficiency of 10 packs of wadmell, and ordain Andro Edmestoun to pay the pursuer £10 for expenses, together with £2 to the lords' collector.

SRO, CS.7/252, f.107, and CS.7/256, ff.446-8; SRO, CS.290/34 (13 May 1611).

526. Edinburgh, 26 April 1611

Precept for remission to John Neving in Skowisburgh for the slaughter of Magnus Mowat of Burrafirth in 158(blank), by firing a missile (*subita jaculatione machine*), regarded as negligence following a letter of slains dated 5 February 1581-2.

SRO, PS.1/80, f.1. In Latin.

527. Edinburgh, 28 May 1611

Summons at instance of Patrik Ross, burgess of Aberdeen, against his creditors, for payment of amounts owing, viz. (1) David Keid in Skalloway bankis, £60 for 4 ky, and £60 for 2 oxen, bought by the said Patrik from Patrik, earl of Orknay, conform to his precept directed to the said David; (2) Christane Sinclair, lawful daughter of William Sinclair of Ustanes, £40 for certain merchandise bought by her since 24 December 1610; (3) Gilbert Makreth in (blank), £14 for 'ane barrell salt keilin', and a wedder sheep which he promised to pay the said Patrik in July 1610; (4) Robert Makreth in Futaburghe, son of Gilbert Makreth, £12 for a barrel of 'salt keilin' and a wedder sheep which was promised to the said Patrik in July 1610, and also £12 for a barrel of 'salt keilin', which was promised to Patrik 2 years ago or thereby; (5) Androw Hawik of Skatstay, £28 for an ox, and £4 for a fine ox kid, which he promised to pay the said Patrik in November 1610; (6) Bartell Hawik, lawful son of said Androw, £12 for half a barrel of oil, and 40s. silver received by the said Bartell from Androw in Laxwo on behalf of James Nevin in Leith, 2 years ago or thereby, which he promised often to pay the said James and whereunto the said Patrik is now assignee; and (7) James Inksetter in Buray, £10 for certain merchandise bought from the said Patrik since 25 December 1610.

The defenders are charged to compear before the lords of council and session to answer the summons.

SRO, CS.15/117. No decreet has been traced in respect of this summons.

528. Edinburgh, 28 May 1611.

Acts of the Privy Council of Scotland discharging foreign laws in Orkney and Shetland, and appointing Mr Henry Aitken as commissary.

Forsamekle as the kingis majestie and his predicessouris of famous memorie with the consent and auctoritie of thair esteatis of parliament hes statute and ordanit that all and sindrie the subjectis of this kingdome sould lieve and be governit under the lawis and statutis of this realme allanarlie, and be no law of foreyne countreyis, as in the actis maid thairanent at lenth is contenit, nochtwithstanding it is of treuthe that some personis beiring pouer of magistracie within the boundis of Orknay and Yetland hes thir divers yeiris bigane maist unlauchfullie tane upoun thame for thair awne privat gayne and commoditie to judge the inhabitantis of the saidis cuntreyis be foreyne lawis, making choise sometymes of foreyne lawis and sometymes of the proper lawis of this kingdome, as thay find mater of gayne and commoditie, in heich contempt of our soverane lord, and to the grite hurt and prejudice of his majesteis subjectis. Thairfoir the lordis of secreit counsaill hes dischargeit ... the saidis foreyne lawis, ordaning the same to be no forder usit within the saidis cuntreyis of Orknay and Yetland at ony tyme heirefter; and that letters of publicatioun be direct heirupoun, commanding and inhibiting all and sindrie personis beiring office of magistracie and judicatorie within the same, that nane of thame presome nor tak upoun hand at ony tyme heirefter, to judge or censure the inhabitantis within the saidis boundis be foreyne lawis, nor to proceid in ony actioun or caus criminall or civile according to foreyne lawis, bot to use the proper lawis of this kingdome to his majesties subjectis in all thair actionis and caussis, as thay and ilk ane of thame will answer upoun the contrarie at thair heichest perell.

Forsamekle as the office of commissariat within the boundis of Orknay and Yetland hes beine thir mony yeiris bigane verie far obscurit, pairtlie be the iniquitie of the tyme, and be the usurpatioun whilk utheris judgeis and magistratis within the saidis boundis tooke upoun thame of a grite many of the actionis and caussis proper and competent to the commissariat jurisdictione; and seing the reverend fader in god James bischop of Orknay hes now maid choise of Maister Henrye Aitkin, a famous man of goode credite, judgement, knoulege and experience, to administrat that office, and to gif justice to his majesteis people in all and everiething concerning the same: thairfoir the lordis of secreit counsaill ordanis letteris to be direct to command and charge all and sindrie the inhabitantis within the saidis boundis to reverence, acknouledge and obey the commissair foirsaid nominat and appointit be the said bischop in everie thing concerning the said office. And siclik to command, charge and inhibite all and sindrie uthiris judgeis and magistratis within the saidis boundis, that nane of thame presome nor tak upoun hand to ressave befoir thame the decisioun of ony actioun or caus proper and competent to the said commissair: dischargeing thame thairof and of thair officeris in that parte be thir presentis, and under the pane to be callit, persewit and punist for the same in thair personis and goodis without favour.

PC.1/26, ff.53-4. On the same date the Privy Council charged the keepers of the castles of Kirkwall and Scalloway to give them up within 24 hours, under pain of treason (f.41: see *RPC*, ix, pp.181-2), and proclaimed other acts concerning Orkney and Shetland (*ibid.*, pp.185-7).

529. Edinburgh, 5 June 1611

Decreet of court of session in action at instance of Laurence Sinclair of Burgh, and Captain William Sinclair, Mr Alexander Bruce, fiar of Cultmalyndies, Robert Menteith of Eglischaw, and James Primrois, portioner of Newlandis in Dunfermeling, his curators, against David Hogsitter in Hogsitter, tenant of 4 marks land, 9 pennies the mark, in the town of Hogsitter, Nicoll Wolsitter, tenant of 9 marks land, 8 pennies the mark, in Wolsitter, and Robert Mansoun in Gillesbrek and Magnus of Flamista, tenants of 4 marks land, 12 pennies the mark, in Flamista, for removal from the foresaid lands. The defenders had been warned to remove at Whitsunday 1610. The lands pertain to Laurence as udal lands, 'haldin and bruikit be the said persewar and his predecessouris, as the remanent inhabitantis of the lordship of Yetland haldis and bruikis udall land within the said lordship'.

The lords of council decern the defenders to remove from the said udal lands.

SRO, CS.7/260, ff.313-4.

530. Edinburgh, 5 June 1611

Decreet of court of session in action at instance of Alexander Bruce in Skelberrie, as assignee of Harman Sweman, against Alexander Thomasone, William Hay, minister at Tyngwell, and John Andersone in Staithseter, for payment of 16 auld dollars owing to complainer by Harman Sweman, burgess and merchant of Breim, the price of each dollar £3, together with £100 for the profit and commodity thereof, and that of the first and the readiest of the moneys owing by the defenders to the said Harman.

The lords of council ordain letters to be directed to warn the defenders to compear personally on 20 July 1611 to give their oaths of verity upon the points of the summons, failing which they shall be held *pro confesse* and a decreet given against them.

SRO, CS.7/262, f.137.

531. Skalloway bank, 29 June 1611

Obligation by Laurence Bruce elder of Cultmalindeis to be cautioner and lawburrows for William Bruce of Symbester, and likewise the said Laurence and the said William to be cautioners and lawburrows for Robert Bruce, lawful son of the said William, Walter Cant, his son-in-law, William Bruce, his natural son, and John Martinson, his servant, and for their kin, that Arthour Sinclair of Hous, Laurence and James Sinclairis, his sons, and Henry Sinclair, son of the deceased Oliver Sinclair of Ropnes, and all their other kin, shall be harmless and scatheless, under pain of £10,000 *toties quoties*, and that they shall produce the said Robert and William Bruces, Walter Cant and John Martinson before the privy council on the first Thursday in November next, under the foresaid pain of £10,000.

Witnesses: Thomas Levingstoun of Pantoun, Laurence Sinclair of Burgh, John Arnot younger, Thomas Blak of Strome, Andro Umphra of Berrie, and Mr Harie Aitken, writer hereof.

SRO, PC.6/11 (registered on 28 January 1612). This obligation was obtained by James, bishop of Orknay, when he was in Shetland. According to a complaint to the privy council on 21 January 1612, based on information by William Bruce of Simbister, the bishop, as his majesty's commissioner, on his arrival in Shetland in June 1611, having heard of some trouble likely to fall out between Robert Bruce, son of William Bruce of Simbister, and Laurence Sincler, son of Arthour Sincler of Hous, had summoned both parties before him in the town of Skalloway. While William and his son were attending the bishop at his lodging, Laurence, hearing of their being in the said town, immediately convened James Sincler, his brother, Walter Hay, servitor of Laurence, and others to the number of forty, all armed, and had fiercely assaulted William and wounded him with two-handed swords. All this had happened 'hard by the yet' of the Bishop's lodgings. William's son and son-in-law, coming to William's relief, had also been assaulted and left for dead (*RPC*, ix, p.320). See nos. 532-3.

532. Castle of Skalloway, 29 June 1611

Obligation by Malcolm Sinclair of Quendaill and Mr James Pitcarne, minister at Northmavene, to be cautioners and lawburrows for Arthor Sinclair of Hous, Laurence and James Sinclairis, his sons, and Henry Sinclair, son of the deceased (blank) Sinclair of Rapness, and for their kin, that William Bruce of Symbester, Robert Bruce, his lawful son, William Bruce, his natural son, and Walter Cant, his son-in-law, and all their other kin, shall be harmless and scatheless, under pain of £10,000 *toties qoties*, and also that they shall enter and produce the said Laurence, James and Henry Sinclairis before the privy council on the first Thursday of November next, under the foresaid pain of £10,000.

Witnesses: Thomas Levingstoun of Pantoun, James Sinclair, apparent of

Quendaill, John Arnot younger, Andro Umphra of Berrie, Mr Harie Aitkin, commissary of Orknay, and Robert Mudie, notary public, writer hereof.

SRO, PC.6/11 (registered on 28 January 1612). This obligation was obtained by James, bishop of Orknay, when he was in Shetland. See nos. 531 and 533.

533. Castle of Skalloway, 29 June 1611

Obligation by John Neving of Skoisburgh and Andro Edmonstoun, minister at Yell, to be cautioners and lawburrows for Ninian Neving, son lawful of the said John, and for his kin, that William Bruce of Symbester, Robert Bruce, his lawful son, William Bruce, his natural son, Walter Cant, his son-in-law, and all their other kin, shall be harmless and scatheless, under pain of 5,000 merks *toties quoties*, and also that the said Ninian shall compear before the privy council on the first Thursday of November next, under the foresaid pain of 5,000 merks.

Witnesses: Thomas Levingstoun of Pantone, James Sinclair, apparent of Quendaill, Andro Umphra of Berrie, Mr Harie Aitkin, commissary of Orknay, and Robert Mudie, notary public, writer hereof.

SRO, PC.6/11 (registered on 28 January 1612). This obligation was obtained by James, bishop of Orknay, when he was in Shetland. See nos. 531-2.

534. Edinburgh, 4 July 1611

Letters of horning at instance of William Bruce of Symbister, against Mr Gilbert Mowatt, minister at Delting, for not finding surety and lawburrows in complaint by William against Edward Sinclair of Marrasetter, Anthonie Sympsoun of Ley, William Sympsoun of Howk, James Craufford of Unstinis, Gilbert Mowat, James Kintor, elder and younger, Malcolme Kyntor, Thomas Blakbeard in Skellbery, Sinclairis (*sic*), John Gorthie, Andro and Bartilmo Hawickis of Scatstye.

SRO, DI.1/3, ff.129-9.

535. Edinburgh, 13 July 1611

Letters of horning at instance of William Bruce of Symbister, against James Neving of Skowsbroche, for not finding lawburrows in action by William against Adam Sincler of Brow, James Neving of Scosbruche, Laurence Sincler of Hous, James Sincler of Gott, Laurence Sinclair of Ustaness, William Fermour of Dunrosness, Richard Leisk of Toop, (blank), Laurence Sincler, brother to said Adam, Olla and William Sincleris, brothers to James Sincler of Gott, John Fermour, son to William, and Malcome Kintor, son to James Kintor in Dunrosnes.

SRO, DI.3/40, ff.335-6.

536. Laxfuird, 26 July 1611

Contract between Elizabeth Sinclare, relict of William Sinclare of Ustanes, and Laurence Sinclare of Ustanes, taking the burden for Cristane Sinclare, daughter of the deceased William and Elizabeth, on the one part, and Thomas Sinclare in Thuirsar in Cathnes, on the other part, whereby 'Thomas sall, god willing, marie and have to wyfe the said Cristane, and sall compleit and solemnizat the halie band of matrimony with hir in presens of Chrystis congregatioun' by 20 August 1612. Elizabeth and Laurence bind themselves to pay Thomas in name of 'tocher gude' the sum of 500 merks, and Thomas binds himself 'to mak the said Cristane equall halfer and portioner of all his gudis, wone or to be wone, present and to cum; And gif it sall happin the saidis Thomas and Cristane to by or conqueis ony landis betuix thame during thair lyftymes, the said Thomas sall vest and seas the said Cristane thairin be chartour and seasing to be bruikit be hir during hir lyftyme, and sall also seas the airis lauchfullie to be gottin betuix thame in the samyn as thair awin proper heritage; quhilkis failyeing returning againe efter the said Cristane's deceis the ane half to the said Thomas's airis and the uther half thairof to the said Cristane's airis be equall portiones; and gif na landis happinis to be conqueis be thame in thair lyftymes the said Cristane to have efter the said Thomas's deceis, gif the said Thomas happinis first to depart this lyfe, the equall half of his movabill gudis or ellis the said fyve hundreth merkis quhilk the said Cristane pleissis to chus, and the same to be in hir optioun'.

Witnesses: Andro Haweik of Scatsta, William Sinclare of Raweik, Henry Sinclare of Swenyng, and Patrik Hog, minister at Fetlar, writer hereof.

SRO, RD.1/207, ff.350-1.

537. Edinburgh, 27 July 1611

Decreet of court of session in action at instance of William Bruce of Symbister against James Neving for removal from 5 marks land of Caldcluff in the parish of Tingwall. James had been warned to remove at Whitsunday 1611.

The lords of council decern the defender to remove from the said land.

SRO, CS.7/264, f.267. James Neving was put to the horn on 21 November 1611 for not removing (SRO, DI.1/4, ff.121-3).

538. 14 August 1611

'Charter by Arthur Sinclair of Aith, with consent of Margaret Colville, his spouse, and Laurence Sinclair, his eldest son, to James Sinclair, his second son, of 5 merks land in Burrafirth, pertaining sometime to John Wishart, and 4 merks land in Garderhouse, in the parish of Sandsting, with precept of sasine directed to Mr Gilbert Mouat, minister, and Magnus Ollasone, written by Robert Kaa, servitor to David Heart, sheriff-clerk of Orkney and Zetland.

'Witnesses: David Sinclair of Huntar, Andrew Umphray of Berrie, Patrick Ros, John Robsoune, and others.'

The original is not known to exist. The above abstract, by Francis Grant, is in OSD, *SN*, 10 February 1894.

539. Scalloway, 14 August 1611

'Disposition by Arthur Sinclair of Aith, with consent of Margaret Colville, his spouse, and Laurence Sinclair, his eldest lawful son, to James Sinclair, his second son, of a yearly annual rent of 4 lispunds of butter, 4 shillings of wadmell, together with the yearly sum of nine merks land, and ten pennies usual money of Scotland, upliftable from the nine merks land of Asta, pertaining to Jerom Umphray, called St. Geilles Stouk, until the redemption of the said lands by repayment of 400 merks; also the 24 merks land pertaining to umquhile William Sinclair of Ustaness, in the parish of Whiteness, and, under reversion foresaid, the 8 marks land in Graven, in the parish of Delting, wadset to him by Andrew Hawick of Scatsta; also 12 merks in Sandsound in parish of Sandsting, wadset to him by Magdalen Thomasdochter, Magnus Halcro, her spouse, and Marion, Ingagarth and Barbara Halcro, her children. ...

'Witnesses: Andrew Umphray of Berrie, David Sinclair of Hunto, John Robisoun, messenger, Robert Tulloch, servitor to said Arthur, David Heart, sheriff clerk of Orkney and Zetland, Robert Kaa, his servitor, writer hereof, and Patrick Ross, merchant, burgess of Aberdeen.'

The original is not known to exist. The above abstract, by Francis Grant, is in OSD, *SN*, 10 February 1894.

540. Scalloway, 14 August 1611

'Charter by Alexander Thomassone, sometime in Laxfurd, now indweller in Scalloway, for nine score pounds paid by Arthur Sinclair of Aith, in name and on behalf of James Sinclair, his second lawful son, dispones to the said James 7 merks land in Gott, in the parish of Tingwall. Written by Robert Kaa. ...

'Witnesses: Andrew Umphray of Berrie, David Sinclair of Hunto, Patrick Ross, merchant, burgess of Aberdeen, John Robisoun, messenger, Robert Tulloch, servitor to said Arthur, David Heart, NP.'

'Sasine thereon dated 22nd October 1611. Laurence Sinclair, son to umquhile William Sinclair of Ustaness, attorney; sasine given in presence of Barthol Hawick, son to Andrew Hawick of Scatsta, Nicol Halcro in Ursland, Donald in Scalloway, David Heart, sometime NP in diocese of St Andrews, now of Orkney.'

The originals are not known to exist. The above abstracts, by Francis Grant, are in OSD, *SN*, 10 February 1894. According to another abstract, in a late 17th century Inventory of writs in the custody of Laurence Sinclair of Sandsound (GH), the lands were 6 pennies the merk.

541. 16 August 1611

Will of Mr James Pitcairn, minister of Northmaving.

Imprimus, I commit my saule and my bodie unto my god quha hath creat it, and to his deir sone Jesus quha hes redemit me, and to the halie spreit quha hes feillit the treuth of my salvatioun in my heart. Item, I leave to my wyff Ursula Sinclair all and haill my landis within Northmaving, that is to say Hamnavo, Sandwick, Awsetter, Urafirth, with the haill uthall in Orbuster and Avisgarth. Item, I leave to hir the haill moveablis upone my foirsaid rowmes with cornis, croppis, cattell, kyne, scheip, oxen, horsis, meiris, swyne, with all uther plenisching pertening to the saidis rowmes. Item, I leave to hir the haill silver wark with the haill naiprie and bedding and weschell within my hous at Urafirth. That nane of my bairnis truble nor molest hir induring hir lyfetyme, and efter it sall pleis god to call hir to his mercie, it is my will that Mr Gilbert Mowat redeme my landis from Johne Swentoun, viz., fourtie mark land vj d. mark. Item, it is my will, and I direct this to be done, that the haill moveablis be divydit efter hir deceis betuix Jonet, Martha, Cristiane and Agnes except the silver wark quhilk I leave to Mr Gilbert, and these quha hes gottin least tocher guid to be considerit with a better part of the moveablis, in special James Nyven. Item, I leave to James Mowat seven hundreth merkis in Andro Edmestounis hand; item, ane hundreth dolouris restand to me be his father; item, ane hundreth merks upone Tangsetter; item, fourtie dolouris in Andro Hawickis hand; quhilk foirsaid sowme with the annualrent thairof will mount a thowsand pundis and mair betwix the dait heirof and the therme thairat, quhairat I am adebtit in payment of a thowsand punds in tocher guid to him. This my foirsaid will I leave to my executoris, Arthour Sinclair of Aith, John Mowat of Hugoland, Andro Edmestoun, minister at Yell, and Mr Gilbert Mowat, and failyeing of Arthour Sinclair, his sone Laurence in his name.

Sic subscribitur, J. Pitcairne, with my hand.

SRO, CC.17/2/2, ff.4-5.

542. Skalloway bankis, 16 August 1611

Contract between Andro Umphra of Berrie, owner of the bark called the *Fortoun*, on the one part, and Patrik Ross, burgess of Abirdene, on the other part, whereby Andro sells all the fish in his bark, to wit 2,500 keling ('sex scoir and four reckonit for the hundreth, and eleven hundreth for the thousand ourheid'), 80 ling, and 2,500 coll fish ('rekning sex scoir four for the hundreth'), for which Patrik is to pay Andro £16 sterling for each thousand keling. Andro is to transport the fish to the port of Newcastell in England, freight free, with Patrik only paying the customs thereof. It is further agreed that 'quhatsomever salt fishes or dry the said Patrik hes of his awin, reckoning the thousand salt fishes twa last and ane half, and aucht hundreth dry fishes to ane last, the quhilk fishes being inbarkit within the said Andro his bark, and transportit in lykmanner to the said port of Newcastell', Patrik shall pay in freight for each last of fish the sum of £16 16s. Scots; and whatever other gear Patrik 'sall imbark in the said bark, sic as oylie, hydes or skinnis, the said Patrik oblissis him to put the same ashoir in Scotland, wind and wedder servand, for sic fraucht as ony uther merchand payis betuix Yetland and Scotland for the last of geir'. For this Andro has hired his boat to Patrik to the port of Newcastell 'sufficient watterticht, under and abone, haveing ane sufficient skipper, pylot, marineris, sufficient siefast marineris, with sufficient ankeris, corbillis, towis, mastis, saillis, fyre, freshe water, and sufficient boat for ressaveing and delyvering of marineris, and all uther necessaries belonging to ane ship; and efter the said barkis arryving, godwilling, at Newcastell thair to remaine at the said port the spaice of xv dayes attending on the said merchand for selling of his fishes; quhilk xv dayis being expyrit the said Patrik sall content and pay to the said awner the sumis of monie abonenumeret togidder with his fraucht as said is. Attour the partie breikar is oblist to pay to the partie keper the sume of x li. sterling monie, and in cais of not payment being maid be the said Patrik, the said xv dayis being bypast, he oblissis him to pay to the said awner for ilk day he lyis efter the said xv dayis in his default ane rois nobill for ilk day, the said ten pund sterling and rois nobill to be liquidat and aggreit upoun be baith the parteis respectiveis'.

Witnesses: Alexander Thomassoun, Robert Wilsoun, and Gilbert Cantlie in Skalloway bankis, writer hereof.

SRO, RD.1/189, f.422.

543. Soundbbrucheid, 18 August 1611

Obligation by Andro Umfra of Berrie to David Slewman, merchant, burgess of Edinburgh, by which Andro, for certain sums of money paid to him, sells to David 'sevin barrellis full of gude and sufficient Yetland ulie of the richt gadge, ticht and sufficient merchand wair', and binds himself to deliver the said oil at the port of Soundbrucheheid by 2 March 1612, failing which to pay David £30 for each barrel that is not delivered.

Witnesses: James Brown, skipper, John Greg, James Martine, and Thomas Greiff, servant of David Slewman, writer hereof.

SRO, RD.1/193, f.419.

544. Burravo, 3 September 1611

Tack by Thomas Levingstoun, sheriff depute, to Arthour Frissell, of land in Bakhous in Yell.

Bakhous, ane merk thair, viij d. the merk, with the pertinentis set to Arthour Frissell, occupyer of the samen, and his airis be Thomas Levingstoun of Ballintone, sheref-deput of Orknay and Yetland, haveing full power and commissioun to that effect, for the space of thrie yeiris nixt efter the entrie thairof quhilk was to the casting of peattis at Whitsunday last bypast, and the first croppe to be in to the yeir of god Jaj VJc and twell yeiris; reserveand alwayis libertie to wyn mynis and minerallis, coillis and coilheuchis, gif ony be within the said land, and reserveand also libertie to big saltpannis and to cast peattis thairto upone the samen landis gif neid be; payand thairfoir yeirlie ½ leispund meit butter, iij cuttell wodmell, scat and wattell conforme to the rentall, iij quarteris pultrie, ane halk dog, ane reik hen, dew service, uphalding the houssis, and observeing the contract maid betuix my lord erle of Orknay and the inhabitantis of the yle of Yell concerning the fisching sa far as appertenes to the said Arthures pairt thairof; and gif he or his airis feilye heirintill, this tak to expyre and be null. Subscrivit at Burravo the thrid day of September 1611; Payand in gersum to David Heart at the shereffis directioun xxxvj s.

Thomas Livinstoun

Registrat
D. Heart

SA, D.16/391/1.

545. Edinburgh, 11 September 1611

Bond of caution by Robert Menteith of Egilshaw for William Bruce of Symbester and Robert Bruce, his son, and for Walter Cant, his son-in-law, that they shall compear before the justice or his deputes in the tolbooth of Edinburgh on 25 September 1611 in connection with their alleged participation in the slaughter of Andro Pitcairne, committed within the town of Skalloway on 22 June 1611.

SRO, JC.19/3. The pursuer in the action in the justiciary court was Laurence Sinclair of Hous, as master of the deceased Andro Pitcarne; however, following letters by the king directing that the diet be deserted, no trial took place (SRO, JC.2/5, f.7). See nos. 549-50.

546. 21 September 1611

'Sasine ...; compeared James Pitcairn in Urafirth, procurator for James Sinclair, son lawful to Arthur Sinclair of Aith, holding in his hands a charter granted by the said Arthur, with consent of Margaret Colville, his spouse, and Laurence Sinclair, his eldest son, in favour of the said James Sinclair, of an annual rent of 20 auld silver dollars, sold to them by John

Mowat of Hugoland, and Christian Stewart, his spouse, from the 15 merk 6 ures land of Sullom, 3 merks in Turvaysetter, and 4 in Swenesetter, in the parish of Northmaven. Precept of sasine directed to Barthol Hawick, son of Andrew Hawick of Scatsta, dated at Scalloway, 14th August 1611.

'Witnesses: David Sinclair of Hunto, Andrew Umphray of Berrie, Patrick Ross, merchant, burgess of Aberdeen, John Robisoun, Robert Tulloch, servitor to said Arthur Sinclair, David Heart, sheriff-clerk of Orkney and Zetland, and Robert Kaa, writer hereof.'

The original is not known to exist. The above abstract, by Francis Grant, is in OSD, *SN*, 10 February 1894.

547. Quendell and Skalloway bankis, 24 September 1611

Contract between David Adesone, son of the deceased Andro Adesone, citizen in Sanct Androis, and brother german of the deceased John Adesone, on the one part, and Issobell Sincler, relict of the said Johne, and now spouse of Duncane Scolaw, on the other part, whereby David binds himself to pay Issobell the sum of 400 merks for all manner of right and title that she may claim after the decease of her husband. Issobell binds herself to deliver to David the account book of his deceased brother, and assigns to him all other debts, obligations, goods and gear, pertaining to the deceased John, which sums of money and debts Issobell shall allow to David in part payment of the said sum of 400 merks. In addition Issobell, with consent of Malcolme Sincler and his son James Sincler, renounces in favour of David all right and title which she may claim to the booths, houses and yard at the eastshore of Exinabu which the deceased Andro and John Adesoneis built.

Witnesses: Johnne Burne, captain of the castle of Skalloway, James Beinstoun, servant of Edward Scollay of Strynie, James Jonstoun, servant of Thomas Levingstoun of Ballintoun, and Robert Kae, writer.

SRO, RD.1/196, ff.47-8.

548. Edinburgh, 1 October 1611

Letters charging Robert Stewart, base son of the earl of Orknay, Thomas Afflek, Alexander Leggatt, John Guild, William Kirknes, and (blank) Bankis, soldiers and servants of the said earl, all residing in Orknay, and Laurence Sinclair of Ustines, James Kintor, younger, Andro Hawick of Scattista, James Craufurde, William Fermour, notary, and Adam Sinclair of Brow, servants of the said earl of Yetland (*sic*), to answer for their sins of iniquity and wickedness.

RPC, ix, p.258. On 5 March 1612 Laurence Sinclair of Ustnes, James Kintor, younger, Andro Hawick of Scattistay, James Craufurd, William Fermour, notary, Adam Sinclair of Brow, Donald Fiddes in Skallowaybank, and Frances Sinclair of Uyea, all servants of Patrik, earl of Orknay, were denounced as rebels for committing all kind of iniquity and wickedness in the country of Yetland, disdaining his Majesty's commissioners and overthrowing the poor inhabitants thereof, and disturbing the peace of the said country (*RPC*, ix, p.347).

549. Edinburgh, 10 and 12 October 1611

Submission, dated 10 October 1611, by Laurence Sinclair, apparent of Aithe, James Sinclair, his brother, Niniane Neving, son of Johne Neving of Skowisburgh, Mr Gilbert and James Mowattis, brothers of Johnne Mowat of Hoggoland, and Mr James Pitcarne, minister at Northmaven, for themselves, and taking the burden for their kin, friends and assisters, 'quhom they may sopeorlat, and specially for the four branchis, kyn and frendis of the umquhile Andro Pitcairne, son to the said Mr James', on the one part, and William Bruce of Symbaster, and Walter Cant, his son-in-law, for themselves, and also William taking the burden for Robert and William Bruces, his sons, Allester Fordyce, messenger, and Allester Morchisoun, merchant, and likewise the said William Bruce, elder, and Walter Cant taking the burden on them for their kin, friends and assisters, on the other part, to Henrie Pitcarne of that ilk, Sir John Prestoun of Valafeild, knight, and Archibald Prymrois, portioner of Newlands or any two of them, as judges arbitrators and amicable compositors, chosen for the part of Laurens Sinclair and others foresaid, and to Sir George Bruce of Carnok, knight, Mr Alexander Bruce, fiar of Cultmalindeis, and Johnne Baillie of Braidshaw, or any two of them, as judges arbitrators and amicable compositors, for the part of William Bruce and others foresaid, and in case of variance the decreet arbitral to be given by James, bishop of Orknay and Yetland, as oversman, anent the mutilation, hurting and wounding of William Bruce, his sons and son-in-law and others committed by Laurens Sinclair and his friends, and anent the slaughter of Andro Pitcairn, and also the hurting and wounding of Laurens and his friends at the same time, committed by William Bruce and his friends.

Witnesses: James Law, son of James, bishop of Orknay, David Pitcairnis, fiar of that ilk, Patrik Bruce, brother of (blank) Bruce of Wodsyde, Robert Monteyth of Eglischaw, and John Ker, servant of James Kynneir, writer to the signet.

Decreet arbitral, dated 12 October 1611, decerning that (1) Mr James Pitcairn, for himself, and taking the burden for the bairns of the deceased Andro Pitcarne, and his four branches kin, and Niniane Neving, for himself as brother uterine of the deceased Andro Pitcarne, with express advice and consent of Laurens Sinclair, James Sinclair, Mr Gilbert and James Mowattis, for themselves, and taking the burden on them for their kin, to remit and discharge all rancour, malice, hatred, grudge and feud, and all action of displeasure which they have against William Bruce, Robert and William Bruces, his sons, Walter Cant, his son-in-law, Allester Fordyce and Allester Morchisoun, for the slaughter of Andro Pitcarne, and to grant a letter of slains to the said persons for the slaughter; (2) Mr James Pitcarne to cause the bairns of the deceased Andro Pitcarne ratify and approve this decreet arbitral and letter of slains 'efter thair lawful and perfyt age of xxj yeiris'; (3) both parties renounce, and discharge the other of all feuds, grudges, questions, wrongs, unkindnesses and actions standing between them, and to continue in mutual love, amity and friendship, and not to hurt, trouble or molest the other, under pain of 10,000 merks; (4) the parties shall not receive, supply, fortify, assist, maintain or defend any person denounced or put to the horn at the instance of the other party, under pain of £1,000; (5) William Bruce, for himself, and taking the burden for the others, shall pay to Mr James Pitcarne, on behalf and for the utility of the natural bairns of Andro Pitcairne, the sum of 1,200 merks to be divided equally between them in name of 'kinbuitt and assythment' of the slaughter of Andro; (6) William Bruce shall pay Mr James Pitcairn, in name and behalf foresaid, the sum of £100 in expenses; and (7) William Bruce shall renounce and discharge Mr James Pitcairn for the alleged spoliation from the lands of Olaberrie of two 'ky', and also discharge Laurens Sinclair for the alleged intromitting with and receiving of any goods or gear taken by Frances Sinclair, son-in-law of said William, from William.

Witnesses: Mr Thomas Barclay of Cowplahillis, David Pitcarne, fiar of that ilk, Alexander Bruce, son of Sir George Bruce, James Stewart of Burray, Andro Pitcarne of Innernethie, and John Ker, servant of James Kynneir, writer to the signet.

SRO, RD.1/189, ff.134-7. See following item.

550. Edinburgh, 12 October 1611

Letter of slains by Mr James Pitcairne, minister at Northmaven, for himself, and taking the burden for the bairns natural of Andro Pitcairne, his son, and for his remaining four branches kin and friends, and Ninian Neving, son of John Neving of Skowesburgh, for himself, and as brother uterine of the said deceased Andro, with assent of Laurens Sinclair, apparent of Aith, James Sinclair, his brother, Mr Gilbert and James Mowattis, and also Laurens Sinclair, Mr Gilbert and James Mowattis, for themselves, their 'kin, freindis, all thair assisteris, partie and partakeris quhom we may sopeorlatt', for observing, keeping and fulfilling of the decreet arbitral of this date, whereby they renounce and discharge all rancour, malice, feud, hatred, grudge, evil will, and all actions of displeasure which they have or may have against William Bruce of Symbaster, Robert and William Bruces, his sons, Walter Cant, Allester Fordyce, and Allester Morchisoun, or against John Morchisoun, Laurens Bruce of Copmalindeis, David Bruce, Thomas Blak of Strolme, William Thomassone, Laurens Sinclair of Brugh, and Hutcheoun McPhaill of Dornoch, or any of them, their kin, friends and assisters for the slaughter of Andro Pitcarne committed on 28 June 1611, so that they shall be unhurt, unharmed, unaccused, untroubled and unmolested for the slaughter; and receive William Bruce, his sons, friends and others, and their kin, friends and partakers, in amity, love and friendship, faithfully committing themselves to observe and keep the same in all time coming, under pain of perjury and defamation; and consent that the king grants his remission to the forenamed persons for the slaughter.

Witnesses: Mr Thomas Barclay of Cowplahillis, David Pitcarne, fiar of that ilk, Alexander Bruce, son of Sir George Bruce of Carnok, James Stewart of Burray, Andro Pitcarne of Innernethie, and John Ker, servant of James Kynneir, writer.

SRO, RD.1/189, ff.137-8. See previous item.

551. Skallowaybankis, 23 October 1611

Obligation by Malcolm Sinclair of Quondaill, and James Sinclair, fiar of Quondaill, his eldest son, to Patrik, earl of Orknay, lord Yetland, justice, sheriff, lord and bailie heritable of the regalities of Orknay and Yetland, discharging the summons and decreet of exemption, 'gif ony be raisit and purchest at our instance, eximand us, oure tennentis and servandis fra the judgement and jurisdictioun of the said noble erle, his deputis and substitutes', together with the letters of lawburrows raised and executed against the said earl at their instance, and acts of caution and other actions following thereupon, binding themselves also never to seek such exemption in the future 'without just cause to be maid to us be the said noble erle, quhilk caus salbe laufullie verefiit and provin befoir we do in the contrair heirof', but to submit to his judgment, 'and behave our selffis dewtifullie ... in all respectis as becumes in tyme cuming', under pain of £1,000, the declarator of 'failyie to pas simplie upone sex dayes warning without ony forder proces or citatioun'.

Written by Robert Kaa, servitor to David Heart, sheriff clerk of Orknay and Yetland. Witnesses: Patrik Halcro, son of the deceased William Halcro of Acris, John Burne in Skallowaybankis, Andro Lawson, merchant burgess of Edinburgh, David Heart and Robert Kaa.

SRO, RD.1/190, ff.13-14.

552. Castle of Skalloway, 23 October 1611

Letters of horning at instance of William Halcro in Skalloway against Mertein Duddingstoun in Skalloway banks, for not finding lawburrows in action by William against Andro Umphray of Berrie, Jerome Umphray of Sand, his father's brother, Malcolm Sinclair of Quendell, James Sinclair of Bow, his son, Maichael Balfour in Gairth, James Tulloch in Rowsay in Stronye, Mertein Duddingstoun in Skalloway banks, Jerom Leslie of Brawick, James Nicolsone in Caldcliff, John Adesone, son to Andro

Adesone, citizen of St Androis, and Henry Sinclair, brother's son of Malcolm Sinclair of Quondell.

SRO, DI.85/1, ff.67-8.

553. Skalloway bankis, 24 October 1611

Disposition by David Adesone, citizen of Sanct Androis, for himself and as assignee of the deceased Andro Adesone, his father, and heir of the deceased John Adesone, his brother, to James Sinclair, fiar of Quondell, of all debts owing to him by divers persons in Yetland, with the exception of the debts owing by James Sinclair of Gatt, and of the booth and houses built by his deceased father upon the lands of Exinabu, in return for the said James having become cautioner, at David's request, for payment to Sir John Arnot of Berswik, knight, of the sum of £504.

Witnesses: Jerom Umphray of Sand, George Sinclare, brother german of James, John Sutherland, minister at Sandsting, David Heart, sheriff-clerk of Orknay and Yetland, and Robert Kaie, servant of David Heart, writer hereof.

SRO, RD.1/207, ff.367-9.

554. Edinburgh, 19 December 1611

Decreet of court of session in action at instance of William Bruce of Symbester against Frances Sinclar of Uya for spoliation in April 1608 from the lands of Uya of 16 oxen, price of the piece £15; 17 ky, price of the piece £12; 6 three year old quoys, price of the piece £6; 6 oxen stirks, price of the piece £6; a year old mare, price £5; 2 stud mares, price of the piece 20 merks; 100 ewes, price of the piece 2 merks; 80 yeld sheep, price of the piece £1; 5 swyne, price of the piece £3; 2 furnished beds, price of the piece £20; 3 iron pots, £4; 'ane stane of powder weschell', £8; 2 kists, price of the piece £5; 20 bolls meal, price of the boll £5; 20 bolls malt, price of the boll £6; 40 bolls bere, price of the boll £6; and 2 fish-boats, price of the piece £24; and likewise for withholding from William the profits of the said mares, ky, ewes, sheep and boats from the time of the spoliation until 17 June 1610, being the date of the summons, viz., 26s.8d. yearly for each of the mares, £3 yearly for the work, hire-gang and labour of each of the oxen; £24 yearly for the profit of each boat in fishing; and 8 merks yearly for the milk, stock butter and cheese of each of the ky.

The lords of council decern Frances Sinclar to have done wrong in the spoliation and withholding, and ordain him to restore the said livestock and goods to William Bruce, together with payment of the aforesaid profits thereof. The defender is decerned to pay the pursuer £20 in expenses, together with £5 to the lords' collector.

SRO, CS.7/268, ff.167-8. The lords of council had granted letters on 12 December 1610 to the pursuer for William Cruikshank, indweller in Leith, John Bruce and Scipio Bruce, to be summoned as witnesses (SRO, CS.7/268, ff.112-3). A certified extract of the above decreet, dated 21 December 1610, is in SA, GD.144/86/25.

Glossary

Note. All references are to document numbers.

Abulyement Garments, equipment
Accidentis Casual sums
Ad perpetuam rei memoriam For perpetual memory of the matter
Advocation Process whereby a judgement by an inferior court is brought up for review
Air (509) Oar
Airschipe Inherited, inheritance
Allanerlie Only
Allegeance Allegation
Almrie (509) Cupboard
Angel (noble) (4, 47, 49, 89, 90, 132, 134, 144, 156, 164, 169, 188, 189, 190, 207, 225, 239, 246, 248, 261, 266, 269, 270, 271, 302, 327, 331, 344, 353, 384, 391, 409, 411, 429, 433, 450, 459, 471, 485, 510, 521) English coin = about 10 merks Scots
Apparrelling (18) Equipment
Appordoune Pardon
Aquavitie (473) Whisky
Ark (409) Chest, especially for holding meal
Arllis (502) Money given in confirmation of a bargain
Arrestment Action of seizing by legal authority
Assedation Lease
Assedator One who grants a lease
Assignation (letters of) Instrument whereby a right is assigned
Assignee Person in whose favour an assignation is granted
Assoilyeis Acquits or absolves from charge
Assysor (20a) Juryman (*and see* **Essyss**)
Assythment (549) Satisfaction, especially by way of compensation for injury or loss
Attemptatis (257) Outrages
Attoure Moreover, above
Auldfo(l)d (473) Old foud (*q.v.*)
Ausetter coipe (223) A payment made by a tenant for a lease
Avising Counsel
Ay and quhill Until
Ayng/Enge/Eyng (154, 197, 338) Possession

Backbond Deed attaching a qualification to the terms of another document
Backeoutyeok ? (*see* **Outyok**)
Balk (509) Beam of a balance or pair of scales
Banat (379) Bonnet
Bangssterie (472) Violent or bullying behaviour
Barce (216) Small cannon

Barne and rais of the stok (263) [As] one of the children of the stock/family
Bayrun *see* **Byrun**
Beir treis/Tries (143, 322, 440, 448) ?Beer barrels
Beiting (4) Repairing
Big(g)in(g)s Building(s)
Bind (162) Measure
Blanch/Blenche ferme On the tenure of blancheferme (a nominal quit-rent)
Blank (71) Document with blank spaces
Boden in feir of weir (353) Armed and in warlike array
Boll Measure of grain, etc.
Bond of maintenance (108) Contract anent protection granted by one person to another
Bonnett (228) Additional piece laced to a sail
Boukis of mutton (243) Carcases
Bounteth (461) Bounty, gratuity
Bousteris (473) Bolsters
Bow teind (70) Teind of cattle
Braquells (409) ?
Breks (409) Trousers
Brenner (388) ?Bremen
Brockin men (23) Impoverished and violent men
Brother/Bruther part (217) Part of heritage which passed to a brother
Brouk/Bruik Enjoy
Broustaris (381) Brewers
Bruittit Rumoured
Bruther *see* **Brother/Bruther part**
Buchtis of lynis (431) Lengths of fishing lines
Buffet stuill (509) Stool with sides
Buill (509) Animal shelter
Buithis (156) Booths
Bull (of ulie) (351) Measurement of oil = 1/9 barrel
Burd triestis (427) Trestle table
Burdis (273) Boards
Burnt marks (256) Marks of land (*q.v.*), orginally valued in (burnt) silver
Butlandis (472) Length of a pair of 'butts' (marks for archery practice, at each end of a range)
Byrun dewties/landmails/meillis Duties/rents due for past periods
Calsay (369) Paved part of a street
Can (195, 222, 320, 510) Measurement of/container for oil = 1/36 barrel
Canons'/Channonis landis (102, 103, 178, 194, 282, 293, 350, 377) Lands in Shetland which originally belonged to the canons of Kirkwall Cathedral
Cant, in the (273) Broad
Casualties Incidental items of income or revenue
Cautioner One who becomes security for another
Chalder (344, 461, 473) Measure of capacity for grain, etc.
Chandleiris (409, 509) Candlestick or chandelier
Channonis landis *see* **Canons' lands**
Checker (509) Chess board
Checkes (184) Cheeks
Cheittis (509) Sheets

Clare constat, precept of Sasine granted to an heir by the superior
Clenging (435) Clearing from charge
Cloaster land (427) Land in Shetland pertaining to the Munkeliv monastery in Bergen
Clokis (427) ?Cloaks
Cod (473, 509) Pillow
Coilheuchis (544) Coal-workings
Coipman/Copeman dollars (53, 134) Merchants' dollars
Cok, brasin (509) ?Weathercock; ?tap or spigot
Coll fish (542) Coal fish
Collation Formal admission to a benefice of one presented by a patron
Collis (381) Coal
Commissary Official appointed to exercise consistorial jurisdiction, esp. with regard to inheritance
Compear Appear
Compeditat (472) ?Contested
Compositioun Sum or its equivalent paid in settlement
Condampnatour Condemnatory
Conjunct-fee Joint possession
Connotar Notary acting jointly with another
Conqueist Purchased
Consuetude Custom
Cop-burde (473) Piece of furniture for display or keeping of cups, etc.
Copeman *see* **Coipman/Copeman dollars**
Corbillis (542) Thick wooden beams
Cordel (228) Rope
Corn teind (136, 144, 489) Tithe paid in corn or equivalent
Corslet of pruiff (473) Defensive body-garment.
Cossing (462) Exchanging (of lands)
Cost syd men (381) Men living at the coast
Cote/Quot silver (58, 192, 415, 461) Revenue from deceased person's moveable estate, payable for confirmation of testament
Countirfut (452) Counterfeit
Craig (343) Crag or rock
Crear (472) Small trading vessel
Cruikit (509) Lame
Cuibbil (228) ?Rowing boat; ?tub for rain water
Curie (462) ?Court
Cuttell/Cuttill/Cuttle (32, 99, 114, 147, 197, 269, 401, 411, 450, 456, 500, 525, 544) Shetland ell, c.2 feet in length
Cutter (427) Coulter (of a plough)

Da(i)ker (415, 510) Set of ten
Daill (228, 273) Deal or plank
Dampnefeit (298) Injured by causing loss
Dang (353) Beat, struck
Dead-dome (393) ?Sentence of death
Decreet Decision of court
Decreet arbitral Decision made by arbiters
Defalkit (23) Reduced, subtracted

Deforcement (347) The crime of forcibly preventing an officer of the law from doing his duty
Delydit (269) ?Delineated
Dempt Adjudged
Dettis Debts
Dicht Cleaned
Distreny(i)e Take possession of by seizing or enforcing payment
Ditty Indictment
Dogar ludge (381) Lodge of a fisher from a doggar (*q.v.*)
Doggar (381, 391) Two-masted fishing vessel
Doggers (226) Owners of or sailors on doggers
Dollar/Dol(l)our (14, 84, 97, 207, 221, 228, 248, 269, 290, 293, 327, 335, 336, 342, 344, 346, 368, 382, 388, 409, 450, 521, 523, 530, 541, 546) Dollar (worth £3 Scots in 1622) (*and see* **Coipman dollar, Rex dollar, Thaler, Yopeindaill**)
Domicelis/Domicile Household effects
Doom/Dome Judicial decision/sentence
Dornick naprie (473) Table linen
Doubland (180) Doubling
Doublatt (409) Close-fitting garment
Double poinding (85) *see* **Poinding**
Dowbill out (472) Make a duplicate copy of
Dreg (143, 440) Sediment
Dutch German

Eardreis *see* **Pleuche ...**
Effeiris (20a) Pertains
Eis, put to ane (481) Bring to a settlement
Eme (24) Uncle
Enge *see* **Ayng**
Equippage/Quippage (226, 230) Crew of a ship
Escheat Confiscate, confiscation
Eschewing Avoiding
Eschewit (353) Escaped
Essyss (324) Assize (*and see* **Assysor**)
Evident (124) Document establishing heritable right
Excambion/Excamying Exchange of lands
Excressence (74) Increase
Exhorter (27, 103, 240) One appointed to give religious exhortation under a minister
Eximand (551) Exempting
Expremit Expressed
Eyng *see* **Ayng**

Factory, commision of Commission authorising one to act as factor
Fad(d)om(e) (of peats) (378, 483) Cubic measurement of peats, differing from place to place
Faill/Fuill Turf
Failyie Fail, fault, failure
Faittis (183) Vats

Falt (509) Vat
Faltar (358) Committer of a fault
Fast gear/guidis (234, 409) Immovable property
Fathold wode (230) ?Vat-wood
Fathoms of peats *see* **Fad(d)om(e)**
Fat(t) guid (19, 30) Butter and oil, lit. vat goods
Fauldis (449) Enclosures for animals
Fee, in (111) In feudal or heritable possession
Fence, fencit (174, 294) To open a court's proceedings by uttering a formula forbidding interruption; (of a court) opened in this way
Feriot ... dayis (116) Days when it is unlawful to hold courts, etc. (e.g. at harvest)
Ferme victuallis (23) Rents etc. paid in kind
Feu ferme Tenure of land in feu
Firn (509) Fir
Flaik (473) ?Flagon or frame
Flemis bind (162) Flemish measure
Fleting/flitting (and) furing (99, 349) Conveyance from one place to another, esp. by sea
Floitt boitt, floitboit (228, 502) A ship's boat
Flomis (509) ??Arms of a chandelier.
Foid/Fo(i)ld/Fou(l)d/Fowd(e)/Foyd (24, 68, 109, 112, 134, 176, 183, 196, 259, 294, 296, 298, 300, 304, 332, 342, 346, 348, 356, 359, 366, 372, 373, 378, 389, 395, 399, 400, 403, 420, 427, 451, 453, 455, 470, 472, 479, 488, 489, 490, 496, 502, 508, 517) (i) Governor of Shetland; more usually (ii) =underfold/underfoud, *q.v.*
Foirfolkis People previously mentioned
Foirstalleris (452) Purchasers of merchandise before it is brought to the market
Fold/Foud/Fowd(e)/Foyd *see* **Foid etc.**
Foldrie/Foudrie/Foudry (23, 34, 86, 111, 131, 289, 395) Jurisdiction of a foud/underfoud
Followar (343) Young of an animal going with its parent
Forfaltis (198) Forfeits
Forrow Before
Forsameikill Forasmuch
Fortoun (207) Chance
Foudrie/Foudry *see* **Foldrie etc.**
Foyd *see* **Foid etc.**
Fredome (291, 463) Common land
Frelsay (29) ?Give freedom to.
Fuill *see* **Faill**
Furing *see* **Fleting (and) furing**
Furnitour (452) Equipment

Gadge (543) Standard of measure/quantity
Gairdie (442) Enclosure
Gaitt, of (472) Road
Gantreis (509) Wooden stand for barrels
Gartak (472) ?Cause take
Gersum/Girsum(e)/Grassum Entry payment for a lease

Gild (keling, etc.) (440, 448) Of full value
Gimmers (432) Year-old ewes
Give If
Glaissing flakattis (509) Glass flasks
Goullovin/Gudling/Gulleon/Gullion/Gulyenn/Gulyeon/Gulyeoun/Gulyion (19, 21, 29, 30, 134, 159, 172, 225, 263, 269, 272, 327, 347, 351, 352, 384, 415, 427, 431, 510) Value-unit for wares (sometimes = 24s. Scots); occasionally a weight for fish (where a g. = 2 lispunds (*q.v.*)
Grandsir (295) Grandfather or great-grandfather
Grassum *see* **Gersum etc.**
Grice (243) Young pigs
Grippit (324) Seized
Grus pane (509) ?Guis pane (*q.v.*)
Gudam (127) Grandmother
Gudfather (409) Father-in-law
Gudling *see* **Goullovin etc.**
Guidsir Grandfather
Guis pane (509) Large cooking pan
Gulleon/Gullion/Gulyenn/Gulyeon/Gulyeoun/Gulyion *see* **Goullovin etc.**
Gund (327) Gun

Hagbut (473, 509) Hand-gun
Hagrie (462) Riding of marches
Haidbull/Haid booll/Heid bull (402, 431) Head house of an estate
Haik (509) Frame for drying or catching fish
Halbert (473) Weapon: combination of spear and battle-axe
Halfferis/Halveris (431, 476, 536) Jointly, in partnership
Halk dog (456, 544) Land tax of a dog for feeding royal hawks
Handlene (381) Fishing line managed by the hand
Hant/Haunt (187, 463) Practise
Hard fische (132, 341, 351) Dried fish
Hardin (509) Harden (used of coarse flax cloth)
Heid (200) Behead
Horn, put to the Outlawed
Hynd (461) Farm-servant
Hyregang (218, 554) Hire

Iche(w) Termination (of lease)
Ilk(ane) Each
In perpetuam Perpetually
Incontinent Immediately
Incuntrie (111) Inner part of the country
Indenture (32) Contract
Induirlie (20a) ?Obstinately
Infeftment Act of being invested in heritable property; document specifying that infeftment
Inlaik (141) To become absent (by death)
Inland (472) Interior parts
Inlandismen (257) Local men
Insicht/Insycht (and) plenissing Household furnishings

Instrument of sasine *see* **Sasine**
Instruments, to ask Call for a notarial instrument
Insycht *see* **Insicht etc.**
Interlocutor/Interloquitor Judgment
Intertenement (110) Entertainment, maintenance
Iyo (295) Granddaughter

Jak (409) ?Roasting-jack
Jame (353) Projecting wing of a building
Joiss(it) Possess(ed)
Justice air (349) Circuit court of the sovereign's justice

Kaponis (187) Capons
Keilling handillingis (226) Cod-fish trade
Keling/Keilin (381, 415) Cod-fish
Kendle Kindle
Kinbuitt (549) Compensation for manslaughter
Kindness/Kyndnes (20a, 411) Prescriptive right to occupy a holding or tack
King's land (74, 132, 156, 385, 391, 470) Royal lands
Kistis (427) Chests
Knappald (230) Clapboard
Knok of the yet (509) Knocker on a gate
Kod *see* **Cod**
Kruk (419) Hook on which a gate is suspended
Ky(e), kyne Cows
Kyndlie posessionis (108) Property held in kindness (*q.v.*)
Kyndlie rowmis (108) Possessions belonging to someone as 'kindly' possessor (see previous item)
Kyndnes *see* **Kindness etc.**

Lach (353) Low
Laidgalloun (509) Vessel for ladling and carrying liquids
Laiff Remainder
Laistis *see* **Last**
Lambes Lammas
Lame (509) Earthenware or china
Land sett tirtoun/Landsetter town (223, 482) Payment made by a tenant for a lease
Landlyar (226) Small boat for going ashore from a larger vessel
Landmail(l)s Land rents
Landskyld (42) Land rent
Last/Laist (183, 216, 228, 249, 253, 273, 472, 502, 542) Measurement of weight (= 12 barrels)
Last of land (20a, 30, 89, 90, 94, 97, 98, 114, 126, 129, 132, 156, 172, 223, 240, 258, 274, 296, 300, 307, 353, 378, 391, 404, 411, 470) Block of 16-24 marks of land (*q.v.*)
Lawburrows Surety required from one that he will not harm another
Laweris (509) Vessel to hold water for washing; jug for wine
Lawrightman (32, 88, 263, 278, 332, 362, 363, 399, 409, 426) Parochial officer (see Introduction)

Lawsourtie (472) Surety that one person will not injure another
Lawting/Lawtyng (99, 262, 452) Head court of Shetland
Leanger (114) Tax paid in cloth
Lector (38) Cleric whose duty originally consisted in reading church lessons
Leid (381) ?Cauldron
Leill/Lelelie Loyal(ly)
Lespund/Lispund (4, 14, 32, 99, 114, 147, 151, 164, 195, 197, 222, 236, 246, 269, 342, 351, 401, 411, 418, 431, 510, 511, 512, 539) Measurement of weight (= *circa* 1/12 barrel)
Lesum Lawful
Letter of slains *see* **Slains, letter of**
Letters of assignation *see* **Assignation, letters of**
Letters of marque *see* **Marque, letters of**
Letters of monition *see* **Monition, letters of**
Letters of procuratory *see* **Procuratory, letters of**
Letters of reversion *see* **Reversion, letters of**
Libell Formal statement of grounds on which a prosecution is made
Libellit/Lybellit Alleged
Liferent Enjoyment for life of income from a property
Liquidat sowme Penalty specified in a contract for breach of the contract
Lispund *see* **Lespund/Lispund**
Lokitnes (197, 411, 442) Ness or headland cut off from the mainland, presumably by a dyke
Lords of Norway (20a, 172, 300, 482) Landowners in Norway who had estates in Shetland
Lords' modifiers (282) Commissioners for assessing ministers' stipends
Lous 'Loose' *i.e.* not packed
Lous out (of lands) (64, 66) Free from encumbrance by paying debt
Lugeis (419) Lodges, residences
Lybellit *see* **Libellit**

Madder (183, 241) Root of the plant madder (as commodity)
Maeche (95) Male connexion by marriage
Maillis Rents
Malt pundlar (485) Instrument for weighing malt
Marcheand with (25) Adjacent to
Mark, merchant *see* **Mercheant (usit) mark**
Mark/Merk (of) (land) Unit of valuation of arable land: about an acre (*and see* **Burnt marks**)
Mark/Merk (of butter) Measurement of weight: 1/24 of a lispund (*q.v.*)
Marque, letters of (183, 241) License to take reprisals at sea
Mascope/Moscrope (327) Company of merchants
Masher (409) ?= Mazer (*q.v.*)
Mazer (473) Drinking bowl
Meassis, pairs of (427) ?Straw baskets
Meat/Meit butter (322, 418, 456, 544) Edible butter
Meill (269) Measurement of butter and oil
Meines Declares
Meit buird (427) Dining-table
Meithis (298) Boundary markers

Mell/Mellit with Interfere(d with)
Merch(e)ant (usit) mark (34, 38, 48, 56, 57, 64, 66, 104, 270, 359, 362) Certifying mark used by a merchant or signatory
Merk (of money) 13s.4d. Scots
Mett (481) Measure
Midlentroun (450) Mid-Lent
Missine (228) Mizzen
Modifeit (20a) Assessed (of amount of payment)
Monition, letters of (9) Formal charge by an ecclesiastical judge to someone to carry out an action
Moscrope *see* **mascope**
Movable goods Personal possessions
Multures (23) Duties paid to a mill's proprietor

Nebloomes (409) ?
Neg (472) Nag
Noble *see* **Angel (noble)**
Nolt (226, 243) Cattle
Nonentrie (198) Usually failure to enter into possession of a property or feudal casualty, here apparently desuetude
Nychtbouris (402) Neighbours
Ob. Obula: one half
Odal/Outhell/Owthell/Uthal(l)/Uthel(l) Allodial (property) (*and see* **Owthaill men**)
Oilyie *see* **Ule**
Oncoactit Uncompelled
Onderfold *see* **Underfo(i)ld etc.**
Onlockit (134) Unlocked
Onsettis *see* **Unsettis**
Opgester *see* **Upgester**
Ort (327, 336) The fourth part
Otterfische (486) Otter
Oulklie Weekly
Oursear (499) Person appointed in legal document to see that its terms are carried out
Outbrekis (181, 207) Land newly broken out
Outfredome (463) Common pasture
Outred (402) Pay what is due to
Outset(ti)s (473) Holdings newly broken out
Outyok/Utyoik (oxen) (384, 427) Trained to outer yoke
Oversman (447, 549) One appointed to decide between different judgments of arbiters
Owthaill men (226) Udallers: people holding by allodial tenure
Owthell *see* **Odal etc.**
Oyeisses (22) Normally granddaughters: here presumably grandsons

Pa(c)k/Peck (of wadmell) (97, 114, 129, 238, 269, 380, 391, 415, 450, 510) Measurement of cloth: 60 cuttells (*q.v.*)
Paiking (226) Packing

Pand (509) Pan
Pandsett (154) Placed (used here of land) in another's hands as security for debt
Pan offer (340) Pledge
Parking (473) Enclosing
Paroch(in) Parish
Pendicilis (456) Pieces of land subsidiary to another
Pennies the merk The number or rate of 'pennies' (*q.v.*) of wadmell and butter paid by each mark of land (*q.v.*) in rent
Penny (of butter or wadmell) (32, 147, 323) Of butter = 1/6 of a lispund (*q.v.*); of wadmell = 1/2 cuttell (*q.v.*)
Pennyland (369, 467) Measurement of arable land in Orkney
Pennyworthis (450) What a penny will buy in goods
***Per testes legitimos et eciam alio modo quo d...* (462)** By legitimate witnesses and what other means ...
Pewder/Powder weschell (473, 554) Pewter ware
Phellis (509) Vessels for holding liquids
Pilleit (183) Robbed
Plate sleives (409) ?Sleeve of cloth, with steel plates sewn in
Play (134) Litigation
Plenish(ing), Plenis(sing) *see* **Insicht etc.**
Pleuche at eardreis with sky mischell (427) ? (mischell = handle of plough)
Poind(ing) Seizing or selling under warrant
Powder weschell *see* **Pewder/Powder weschell**
Prebend/Prebendary Ecclesiastical benefice formerly attached to a cathedral; the holder of that benefice
Precept of clare constat *see* **Clare constat, precept of**
Precept of sasine *see* **Sasine, precept of**
Preinecodis (452) Pincushions
Presoun (160) Parish
Prienis (452) Pins
***Pro confesse* (530)** To have confessed
Pro rege Belonging to the crown
Process/Prossus (20a) ?Process of law
Procuratory, letters of Deed constituting a procurator or attorney
***Promittendo de rato* (357)** 'Shorthand way of representing a stereotyped formula in a procuratory, which would have run in full (in translation) "promising to hold firm and stable everything which the procurators perform in my name"' (*CB2*, glossary)
Provestis landis (391, 411, 480) Land in Shetland belonging to the provost of Norway (cf. **197, 238**)
Pund (of butter) (42) = Lespund, *q.v.*
Pundlar *see* **Malt pundlar**
Punscheon (509) Puncheon, large cask for liquids
Pykpot (509) Pitch pot
Pype wode (230) ?Cask wood

Qanever (183) At some indefinite time in the future
Quarter (269) Fourth part of an ell
Quayes/Quoy/Quoyokis/Quyakis (409, 415, 431, 509, 554) Heifer(s)
Quenquir (472) ?Conquest, purchase

Quentiene (400) ?Conscience
Quhill Until
Quhit (183) Wheat
Quippage *see* **Equippage**
Quot silver *see* **Cote silver**
Quoy/Quoyokis/Quyakis *see* **Quayes etc.**
Quyis (151) Enclosures
Quytcleamis Renounces
Quyte Acquit

Raid (472) Road, place where ships ride at anchor
Raissit stuff (473) Embroidered cloth
Raxis (473, 502, 509) Framework to support a spit or other cooking utencil
Readschip (502) Equipment
Rectius More correctly
Reduction (of decreet) Annulment
Reestit (243, 418) Smoked
Reft (472) Plundered
Regraters/Regraittaris (452) Buyers who resell for profit
Reif (99) Plunder
Reik hen (456, 544) Hen paid by householder as part of rent
Reparelling (4) Repairing
Revaris (99) Robbers
Reversion, letters of Deed giving debtor who has borrowed money on security of land right to redeem
Rex/Rix dollar (18, 256, 364, 510, 523) Silver coin
Rig and randell/rander/rendal (197, 352, 391) Runrig: system of agriculture where plots are intermixed
Rip (419) Wisp
Rois nobill/Roisnoble (141, 542) English coin: the rose noble
Roith(e) (104, 240) Right of heir to redeem udal land
Roithismen (66) Udal heirs
Rooms/Roumes Lands, territories
Rosting yrone (509) Gridiron
Rouks (243) Ricks
Run beir tre (344) ? (*cf.* **Beir treis**)
Rung (424) Cudgel
Rychtis man (20a) ?Just possessor; ?= **Roithismen** (*q.v.*)
Ryff(ing) Tear(ing) up, destroy(ing) (of land, property)
Ryplie Thoughtfully

Samaing/Sameying/Samming/Samyne (20a, 104, 240, 391) Joint possession
Samin/Samyn(e) The same
Samyne *see* **Samaing**
Saseris (509) Saucers
Sasine/Se(i)sing Putting in possession of land, originally by handing over of earth and stone, later by registration of an **Instrument of sasine** (*q.v.*)
Sasine, instrument of Document recording sasine
Sasine, precept of Warrant for infeftment (*q.v.*)

Scat(t)/Skait Scat, a tax on land
Schakkis (344) ?Shakes
Schankis *see* **Worset schankis**
Schip pund (183) Measurement of weight
Schone (379, 473) Shoes
Schound/Schownd/Schuind/Sheund/Shownd (bill) (10, 198, 279, 354, 394, 398, 402, 409, 431, 439, 460) Meeting held after death of landowner, etc., to partition inheritance
Scoggit (475) Normally concealed; here apparently searched
Secundum visa allegata et probata **(462)** According to what has been seen, alleged and proven
Seig (183) ?Lay seige to
Seill at the schadow be cavilles cassin thairupone (467) A phrase used in the kenning of a widow to her terce (*q.v.*). The widow received one in three rigs by lot ('be cavilles'), beginning on the 'shadow' side of the property.
Seipbaille (509) ?Ball of soap
Se(i)sing *see* **Sasine etc.**
Selchis (486) Seals
Service (of heir) (408) Procedure whereby heritable property is transferred to an heir
Sex haring bot (431) Six-oared boat (*and see* **Sixairn**)
Sey (i) (200, 442, 468) Sea
Sey (ii) (509) Wooden tub with two handles for carrying
Sheund/Shownd (bill) *see* **Schound etc.**
Shilling (of wadmell) (4, 14, 32, 114, 147, 164, 197, 236, 246, 269, 342, 401, 411, 431, 510, 511, 512, 539) Measurement of cloth = 6 cuttells (*q.v*)
Simplicitur Simply
Sixairn (409) Six-oared boat (*and see* **Sex haring bot**)
Skait *see* **Scat**
Skaithe Damage, hurt
Skaithles Unharmed
Skaitt (226) Skate
Skewhoussis, Skoo (226, 475) Open-built hut for drying food, esp. fish
Slains, letter of (526, 549, 550) Letters subscribed by relatives of a person who had been killed, declaring they had received an assythment (*q.v.*), and concurring in an application to the crown for a pardon for the offender
Slokin(g) (240, 324) Extinguishing
Sopeorlat(t) (549, 550) ?Support, succour
Sornearis (452) Scroungers
Spanging (353) Jerking
Spe(i)ttis (473, 509) Spits
Spulyie Despoil, spoliation
Staig (343, 509) Young horse not broken to work
Staiking (20) Supplying needs
Stallars (102, 103, 178) Vicars who serve in a cathedral
Stand (of clothes) (379) Outfit
Staneit horses (473) Stallions
Steid rowmes (269) Steadings
Stemyng (473) Woollen or worsted cloth
Stofa/Stoiff (4, 88) Prestigious house

Stock/Stok/Stouk/Stowk (17, 110, 113, 135, 171, 229, 282, 477, 478, 539) = Prebend (*q.v.*)
Stoik/Stok (25, 263, 275) Stock (of family)
Stoupis (509) Tankards
Stowth Theft
Straiking up (473) Breaking or bursting open
Stud(e) mares (343, 554) Brood mares
Suit (of court) Obligation by a tenant to attend a lord's court
***Super inserto libello* (20a)** Inserted in the libel above
Sye (427) Scythe

Tack Lease
Tack duty Payment made for a lease
Tacksman Lessee
Taffrowmerall (285) ?Innkeeper
Taingis (509) Tongs
Takill tow (473) Tackle rope
Teind(s)/Teindsheaves Tithes (*and see* **Bow teind, Corn teind**)
Temporaletie As a temporal possession of the church
Terce (269, 467) The liferent of one-third of a husband's heritage given by law to a widow.
Thack/Thak (29, 427) Thatch
Thaler (60, 216) Dollar
Thesaurar Treasurer
Tinsall/Tinsill Loss, forfeiture
Tint Lost, forfeited
Tocher (gude/guid) Property given as a bride's dowry
Tofall (419) Lean-to building
Tofts/Toiftis (151, 332, 473) Sites of homesteads
Toties quoties As often as/each time (something happens)
Toueris (509) ?Tureens (by metathesis)
Towis (502, 542) Ropes (*and see* **Takill tow**)
Towme Empty
Trabuschettis (509) Scales
Trie(s)/Tre/Treis (215, 297, 322, 344, 388, 450, 473) Wood, barrel (*and see* **Beir treis**)
Truncheoris (509) Trenchers
Tryn (183) ?
Tumulis (151) Town fields
Twm Empty
Tydlie (440) ?Timeously; ?In good condition
Tyne Lose

Udach (198) =Udal (probably a misspelling)
Udal *see* **Odal etc.**
Ule/Ulie/Oilyie Oil
Umbot(h)(s) (180, 196, 239, 269, 320, 459, 478) Rents originally paid to the bishop of Orkney
Umbothsman (22, 88) Agent, representative (*cf.* ombudsman)

Umquhill Deceased
Underfo(i)ld/Underfoud/Onderfold Parish bailie
Underfoldrie/Underfoudry (176, 193) Parish bailiary
Unlaid gaittis (411) ?Unmade paths
Unlaws (23, 131, 207, 378, 488) Fines
Unsettis/Onsettis (4, 419) ?Satellite farms
Uour *see* **Ure**
Upgaistry/Upgaistrie/Upgestry (in) (29, 304, 332) Contract or arrangement whereby an elderly person is cared for by younger relatives
Upgestir/Opgester (29, 337) Elderly person cared for by younger relatives
Ure/Ur(is)/Uour (of land) (25, 26, 28, 32, 42, 64, 80, 148, 156, 160, 207, 225, 270, 304, 310, 319, 330, 354, 368, 392, 408, 409, 431, 436, 442, 443, 467, 485, 503, 506, 511, 512, 546) Eighth part of a mark (of land)
Utencill Domestic equipment
Uthal(l)/Uthel(l) *see* **Odal etc.**
Utyoik *see* **Outyok**

Veveris/Vivers (230, 353, 452) Food, provisions
Vyet aitis (431) ?Weighed oats

Wadmell/Wattmell/Wedmell/Wodmell Coarse cloth, mainly used for payment of taxation and rent in Shetland
Wadset/Wedsett Mortgage
Waiff guddis (174) ?'Stray' goods: cf. **Waith**
Waith (wreck and) Flotsam and jetsam
Walter(s) (143, 502) Water
Wanscoitt (230) Wainscot
Warrandice Undertaking by a granter to indemnify a buyer
Wat(t)ill/Wattle (111, 114, 132, 138, 147, 151, 207, 214, 411, 488, 490, 518) Tax originally paid as hospitality to the sheriff or foud, later commuted into money
Wedder/Wodder Wether
Weschell (541) Vessels (*and see* **Pewder weschell**)
Whinger (393) Short stabbing sword
Wiching brodis (509) Scales
Wirt standand tub (509) Tub for brewing
Wod (499) Pledge
Wodder *see* **Wedder**
Worset schankis (473) Woollen stockings
Wot (294) Vote

Ye(i)ld (nolt/kye/scheipe) (243, 269, 415, 431, 554) Barren
Yet/Yett Gate
Yollis (461) Yoals, small rowing boats
Yopeindaill/Yopingdaill (22, 293) Dollar

Index

Note. Many of the native Shetlanders mentioned in the documents did not have fixed surnames, but were distinguished by the addition of a patronymic or place-name to their Christian name (Anna Magnusdochter; Andrew Sand). They therefore appear in the index under their Christian names. When it is difficult to decide if a name is a fixed surname or not (Beae; Yelt) a cross-reference is given.

As explained in the Introduction, many of the names in the documents, especially place-names, are mis-spelled. No attempt has been made to correct these spellings in the index; but where they are grotesque they have been placed in inverted commas.

The following abbreviations have been used for parishes: Ai Aithsting, Br Bressay, Bu Burra, De Delting, Du Dunrossness, Fe Fetlar, Gu Gulberwick, Lu Lunnasting, Ne Nesting, No Northmavine, Sa Sandsting, Ti Tingwall, Un Unst, Wa Walls, We Weisdale, Wha Whalsay, Whi Whiteness, Ye Yell.

All references are to document numbers.

B

C

O